THE CLINIC AND THE COURT

Law and medicine can be caught in a tight embrace. They both play a central role in the politics of harm, making decisions regarding what counts as injury and what might be the most suitable forms of redress or remedy. But where do law and medicine converge and diverge in their responses to, and understandings of, harm and suffering? Using empirical case studies from Europe, the Americas and Africa, *The Clinic and the Court* brings together leading medical and legal anthropologists to explore this question.

IAN HARPER is a trained medical practitioner and social anthropologist, working at the University of Edinburgh.

TOBIAS KELLY teaches social anthropology at the University of Edinburgh, where his research interests include human rights, political and legal anthropology and modern British cultural history.

AKSHAY KHANNA is a research fellow at the Institute of Development Studies, University of Sussex.

CAMBRIDGE STUDIES IN LAW AND SOCIETY

Cambridge Studies in Law and Society aims to publish the best scholarly work on legal discourse and practice in its social and institutional contexts, combining theoretical insights and empirical research.

The fields that it covers are: studies of law in action; the sociology of law; the anthropology of law; cultural studies of law, including the role of legal discourses in social formations; law and economics; law and politics; and studies of governance. The books consider all forms of legal discourse across societies, rather than being limited to lawyers' discourses alone.

The series editors come from a range of disciplines: academic law; socio-legal studies; sociology; and anthropology. All have been actively involved in teaching and writing about law in context.

Series editors

Chris Arup *Monash University, Victoria*

Sally Engle Merry *New York University*

Susan Silbey *Massachusetts Institute of Technology*

A list of books in the series can be found at the back of this book.

THE CLINIC AND THE COURT

Law, Medicine and Anthropology

Ian Harper
University of Edinburgh

Tobias Kelly
University of Edinburgh

Akshay Khanna
Institute of Development Studies

CAMBRIDGE
UNIVERSITY PRESS

CAMBRIDGE
UNIVERSITY PRESS

University Printing House, Cambridge CB2 8BS, United Kingdom

Cambridge University Press is part of the University of Cambridge.

It furthers the University's mission by disseminating knowledge in the pursuit of education, learning and research at the highest international levels of excellence.

www.cambridge.org
Information on this title: www.cambridge.org/9781107076242

First published 2015

A catalogue record for this publication is available from the British Library

Library of Congress Cataloguing in Publication data
The clinic and the court : law, medicine and anthropology / edited by Ian Harper, Tobias Kelly, Akshay Khanna.
    pages   cm. – (Cambridge studies in law and society)
Includes bibliographical references and index.
ISBN 978-1-107-07624-2 (hardback)
1. Medical laws and legislation.   2. Medical jurisprudence.   3. Applied anthropology.
I. Harper, Ian, 1962– editor.   II. Kelly, Tobias, editor.   III. Khanna, Akshay, editor.
K3601.C55   2015
344.04'1 – dc23   2015005494

ISBN 978-1-107-07624-2 Hardback

CONTENTS

CONTENTS

CONTRIBUTING AUTHORS

João Biehl
Princeton University

John Borneman
Princeton University

Estelle d'Halluin
Université de Nantes, CENS

Lydie Fialová
University of Edinburgh

Ian Harper
University of Edinburgh

Tobias Kelly
University of Edinburgh

Akshay Khanna
Institute of Development Studies

Rebecca Marsland
University of Edinburgh

Gethin Rees
University of Southampton

Naomi Richards
University of the West of Scotland

Henrik Ronsbo
Dignity: Danish Institute Against Torture

Miriam Ticktin
New School for Social Research

ACKNOWLEDGEMENTS

We would like to thank the ESRC for their generous assistance in supporting the original workshop upon which this book is based. The workshop benefitted greatly from the participation of Aditya Bharadwaj, Sharon Cowan, Stefan Ecks, Roger Jeffery and Jonathan Spencer. We would especially like to thank Anastassis Panagiotopoulos for ensuring that the workshop ran smoothly. More recently, Lucy Lowe's help has been essential in putting this volume together. We would also like to thank Finola O'Sullivan and Rebecca Roberts at Cambridge University Press for their patience and support. João Biehl's chapter has previously appeared in a slightly modified form as 'The Judicialization of Biopolitics: Claiming the Right to Pharmaceuticals in Brazilian Courts' *American Ethnologist*, 2013, 40(3): 419–436. Chapter 10 is based on accounts in and drawn from John Borneman, 2015. Cruel Intentions: The Ritual Rehab of Child Molesters. Chicago: University of Chicago Press.

INTRODUCTION

Tobias Kelly, Ian Harper and Akshay Khanna

In the spring of 2013, the parents of Robbie Crane, a severely disabled 13 year old boy, won an out of court settlement of over £7 million from the English National Health Service. When Robbie was born he was seriously ill with a congenital heart defect. He underwent an operation when he was just a few days old, which seemed to be a success.[1] However, something went wrong during the ventilation afterwards. Robbie was left with cerebral palsy, limited speech, learning difficulties and behavioural problems. He will require round-the-clock care for the rest of his life. The settlement was designed to reflect compensation for any medical negligence, as well as to cover the cost of Robbie's future care. Such cases are far from rare. According to a report in 2012, the English NHS spent over £15 billion on medical negligence claims a year.[2] That is nearly one seventh of the entire NHS budget.

Ian Brady appeared before a mental health tribunal in Manchester in the summer of 2013. Brady is one of the most notorious serial killers in modern British history. In 1966, he was found guilty of the murder of three children and sentenced to life imprisonment. Nearly twenty years after first being sent to prison, Brady was diagnosed as a paranoid schizophrenic with a severe personality disorder, and sent to a high security psychiatric hospital. In 1999 he went on hunger strike, protesting against his incarceration. As Brady was being detained in a psychiatric hospital, doctors were permitted to continue his treatment and force-feed Brady against his will. Brady was therefore appearing before the tribunal to argue that he was no longer mentally ill and should be

1

transferred to prison, so that he could have control over the time and manner of his own death.[3] His appeal was turned down.

In December 1998 Diane Blood gave birth to a baby boy. The boy's biological father had died more than four years previously.[4] Following a protracted legal battle, Ms Blood had won the right to artificial insemination with her husband's sperm. Ms Blood and her husband had been planning to have children when he was struck down with meningitis. She persuaded the doctors to remove her partner's sperm while he lay on life support. However, because the sperm was not removed with Mr Blood's consent, the hospital was not legally allowed to hand it over to Ms Blood. In February 1998, Ms Blood won the right to take the sperm abroad. The court ruled that although it was illegal to use sperm taken without consent in the UK, there was nothing in the law that prevented the insemination taking place outside the country. Ms Blood would eventually have two sons, Liam and Joel, after visiting a Belgian clinic. It was not until 2002, and a change in the law, that Mr Blood's name could be put on the birth certificate, as prior to this, fathers who were dead at the moment of conception could not be legally recognised as parents.

In 2001 Stephen Kelly was found guilty of recklessly causing injury to another by the High Court of Justiciary in Glasgow after infecting a woman to whom he had not declared his HIV status. Sentenced to five years in prison, this was the first successful case of the criminalisation of HIV transmission in Scotland (Chalmers 2002). Beyond the UK, in many parts of the world HIV transmission has been criminalised. Despite limited evidence that this has any public health benefit, a number of other countries have now added this measure as an aspect of the attempts to control the HIV epidemic.

Between 400 and 1200 patients died 'as a result of poor care' at Stafford Hospital between January 2005 and March 2009.[5] These deaths were revealed through statistical analysis, which enabled comparisons of death rates to be produced between hospitals, raising alarms should these lie outside of a deemed acceptable range. In a damning indictment of audit practices, Robert Francis, QC, the barrister chairing the public enquiry that followed, suggested that the 'NHS culture' was to blame, and that this focused 'on doing the system's business – not that of the patients'.[6] This stimulated an ongoing debate into the question of legal sanctions, and whether senior managers at the NHS could face criminal prosecution if they were deemed to be not open about mistakes that had been made, or whether already available provision of manslaughter law that can be levelled against doctors, or a corporate version of this, could force greater accountability.

As the above five examples attest, law and medicine can be caught in a tight embrace. Although these examples are all taken from the UK, similar processes are at work around the world, from the USA to India, from the Czech Republic to South Africa, from France to Germany, Guatemala, Brazil and beyond. Clinicians may try to heal pain and suffering, but what counts as necessary or unnecessary suffering, suffering that should be prevented or allowed to continue, can be decided by the law. Furthermore, when medicine is unable to heal, the law can be called upon to provide redress. Litigation is often seen as the answer to medical needs and public health claims when doctors and public health physicians come up against their limits. Medical negligence cases, such as that of Robbie Crane's, involve lawyers deciding what clinicians can and should have done when confronted by a sick patient, as well as providing financial remedy for clinically inflicted distress. In the Brady mental health tribunal, it was the judges who had to decide which clinical diagnosis was most appropriate, and therefore implicitly whether the suffering caused by force-feeding was worse than the suffering caused by lack of treatment and potential suicide. It was not doctors who would decide how Brady would end his life, but a judge. In 2001 it was a judge who made the decision that Stephen Kelly was guilty of recklessly injuring his girlfriend when he failed to tell her he had HIV and subsequently infected her. Following the Mid Staffordshire Hospital deaths, it was suggested that criminal negligence charges might also be levelled at senior managers in the NHS. As such, and at multiple levels, medicine can be said to operate in the shadow of the law, as clinical, public health and institutional decisions are shaped by their potential legal outcomes.

Yet the movement is not all one way. Legal processes, for example, can rely on clinical evidence in order to make decisions. It is clinicians who tell the court what particular symptoms might mean and what forms of treatment are possible. The mental health tribunal relied on psychiatric evidence to decide whether Brady was clinically sane or not. The Robbie Crane litigation similarly needed clinical evidence in order to determine whether the staff at the hospital where he was born had exercised the required level of care. Law also has to respond to medical advances and new forms of diagnosis. Paranoid schizophrenia has been a diagnosis with shifting parameters and definitions reflected in the evolving Diagnostic and Statistical Manual (DSM) revisions, but the law is dependent on these shifting terrains of knowledge at particular moments in time. It was not proposed as a distinct clinical diagnosis when Ian Brady was originally sent to prison in the late 1960s, yet subsequent diagnoses were dependent on new categorisations of the condition. The development of IVF as a therapeutic treatment has also created new and challenging legal problems. Issues of parenthood, such as in the Diane Blood case, would simply not be legal problems if it was not for clinical developments. In another register, it has been the development of the capacity to collate and analyse complex statistical data sets that has allowed the emergence of thinking of larger institutional complexes as legal entities in relation to health outcomes.

The ways in which we acknowledge, and attach importance to pain and suffering, can be understood as a constitutive feature of modern political and social life (Brown 1995). Pain and suffering are deeply implicated in what it means to be human in contemporary societies. Alongside, or even instead of, a concern with equality, exploitation and fairness, claims about the nature, distribution and adequacy of the response to pain and suffering play an important part in the formation of collective identities and the distribution of resources. Pain and suffering, however, are never self-evident. Neither are the responses to pain and suffering. What counts as necessary and unnecessary, preventable and unpreventable distress, and what counts as adequate and suitable responses are profoundly political and cultural processes. Law and medicine are key to this wider politics of harm, deciding on what counts as injury, and what are the most suitable forms of redress. But both law and medicine also claim to lay out spaces for redemption, for cure, for healing and redress.

As law and medicine respond to harm and suffering, they become entwined. Let's take the concept of injury, for example, to illustrate the close relationship. Injury is a legal term par excellence. It derives from the Latin words 'in' and 'jus', meaning 'against justice' (Jain 2006: 4). Legally speaking, injury involves a violation of rights. Yet although injury can imply financial loss or damage to reputation, the archetypical modern image of injury is a body (or mind) in pain. Injury is therefore widely seen as a problem that can be addressed through medical intervention. However, the very fact that we refer to physical or mental damage by a term that implies justice or its absence, despite us not being necessarily conscious of this metaphorical inheritance, speaks to the powerful place of law in our imaginations of harm.

Death too, to give another example, is simultaneously a medical and a legal category rather than the self-evident end of life. As Margaret

Lock has famously shown, the category of brain death requires both clinical and legal interventions (Lock 2002). Developments in medical technology have forced a re-evaluation of the very distinction between life and death. In order for organs to be harvested for donation, bodies have to be legally dead – or a clinician could be charged with homicide – but clinically alive, as otherwise the organs would be medically useless. Anglo-American law has decided that this event takes place in the brain, rather than the heart. Medicine had to respond by providing ways in which the exact time of brain death could be identified.

The relationship between law and medicine can, equally, be symbiotic or collaborative. In a sense, both law and medicine may be understood as practices in the management of uncertainty. In the context of law, this is not just in relation to 'subjective' elements such as 'intention' and mens rea,[7] but in the very processes through which 'facts' are assessed, produced and appreciated in a court of law. This is most obvious in adversarial systems of law, where litigating parties are typically engaged in making objects and chronologies intelligible. The production of 'facts' is thus contingent upon such things as the resources available to contesting parties, the diversity of principles in laws relating to procedure and evidence, the political milieu and most significantly, the very ability of the court to sense, recognise and name objects. The legal process is in this sense the identification of 'true' facts in the face of ambiguity. Also, as several chapters in this volume suggest, the practice of medicine is about the production of facts in the face of disparate possibilities. The process of diagnosis, for instance, is an inherently intersubjective process where physicians and patients are entangled in a negotiation of their realities, and the languages and metaphors through which bodily or psychological experiences gain intelligibility. The diagnosis of a syndrome such as AIDS, i.e. the enumeration and identification of 'symptoms' and the recognition of patterns is an obvious case in point. Here again we see the socially, economically, politically, procedurally and epistemologically contingent process of producing certainty in the face of ambiguity. What is interesting is the ways in which, often, both law and medicine project the responsibility of this management of uncertainty onto each other, thus mutually reaffirming their positivist claims, their authority in speaking objective truths.

Yet the relationship between law and medicine can also be deeply uneasy. The ways in which lawyers and clinicians try to understand the world, as well as the responses they put in place, can be very different. Lawyers may understand harm through legal languages and definitions of injury, victim and perpetrator. Medical practitioners might think about harm in terms of categories of disease and pathology translated from the subjective illnesses of patients. The law courts allocate compensation and redress. Medical practitioners try to alter the course of disease processes, and thus heal and alleviate suffering, albeit within narrow medically defined parameters. As two high status forms of expert knowledge, it is not always clear which, or how, either should predominate in particular contexts. The law can marshal far greater resources, it can decide what can and should be done, and can invoke legal sovereignty to do so. However, it is this political dominance of the law that medicine counters through access to levels of intimate knowledge that is simply unavailable to the law. A legal decision might provide formal redress – which in certain circumstances might assist with healing as broadly socially defined – but clinicians can, and frequently do, improve the subjective feelings of being unwell through their clinical interventions.

ANTHROPOLOGY, THE LAW AND MEDICINE

Historically, legal and medical anthropology have often talked past each other. We publish in different journals and go to different conference panels. Yet over the past ten years at least there has been an increasing convergence of analytical and ethnographic interests. Issues such as biological citizenship and its wider family of terms (Petryna 2003; Rose 2007; Nguyen 2010) have brought the importance of rights and the sovereign power of the state over bodies, life and death to the heart of medical anthropology (Das and Poole 2004; Inda 2005). Similarly, a concern with the provision of pharmaceuticals and their place within particular economies of ownership and need, has meant that legal property regimes have been a key object of analysis (Petryna et al. 2006; Hayden 2007; Petryna 2009). Many medical anthropologists have become interested in exploring the implications of institutional and expert responses to suffering, turning to issues historically more associated with legal anthropology, such as human rights, citizenship and bureaucracy (Farmer 2001, 2004; Fassin and Rechtman 2009; Biehl and Petryna 2013; Redfield 2013).

In this volume we acknowledge these intellectual shifts and explore the intersections of, and relationship between, law and medicine. The book asks: How do those working in law and medicine seek to understand harm and suffering, and allocate remedies? What are the points of convergence and contradiction between law, medicine and their own sub-disciplines, as they seek to understand and respond to harm and suffering? Are new spaces for political and moral action created by the intersection of law and medicine? Crucially, we do not take the central role of law and medicine in responses to harm and suffering as self-evident. As law and medicine define and categorise, options are closed down, just as new ones are opened up. What happens, for example, to a sense of mutual obligation for the sick and unwell when they are framed in terms of legal rights? What issues arise when medical care is determined and overshadowed by the potential for criminal redress? Such questions allow us to explore the relationship between a politics of suffering, expert claims to privilege insight, and the potential for remedy and redress. Rather than reify law and medicine as two separate ways of interacting with the world abstracted from each other and their conditions of entanglement, we argue that responses to harm and suffering have to be understood in terms of their enactment and engagement within specific local contexts. Hence, the issues are ones that are fundamentally and necessarily open to ethnographic investigation.

The volume is organised into two sections. The first section deals with the different ways in which legal and medical processes understand, confront and conceptualise harm and suffering, in short, an epistemological exploration. The second section deals with the ways in which law and medicine understand and allocate remedies to harms, that is the more practical side of how interventions are managed. The distinction between understanding harm and providing remedy is of course not hard and fast. Remedy is only possible once harms have been identified, and harms are seldom categorised for abstract reasons, but often with the aim of providing some form of alleviation. While there may be a case for some of the chapters appearing in either section, we have made the division as a way of pulling out and emphasising important analytical themes and as a heuristic undertaking. Before addressing issues of pain and suffering, remedy and redress in more detail, it will be useful to examine what types of expert knowledge are represented by both law and medicine.

EXPERT KNOWLEDGE

Law and medicine are both highly technical forms of expert knowledge. They seek to define, categorise and regulate. Indeed, they may be the archetypal form of modern expertise (Carr 2010). Law and medicine are both backed by powerful institutions and bureaucracies, such as hospitals and courts, not to mention universities. Law and medicine are high status, highly paid professions, represented by powerful lobbying bodies. They are also both learned at university, and contain languages and forms that are only available to the initiated (Sinclair 1997; Mertz 2007). Law and medicine both fundamentally involve a claim to superior positivist knowledge by those who speak in their name. Finally, in all their technical specialisms, law and medicine can also both be seen as highly pragmatic forms of knowledge, concerned with getting things done, rather than philosophical hair-splitting or political negotiation. Doctors want to make their patients better. Lawyers want to come to a final legal decision.

However, even though law and medicine may both be pragmatic disciplines, they can produce very different relationships between means and ends. Legal processes aim to seek finality, as they look to end the debate and come to a legal decision. In doing so, they frequently turn in on themselves, referring to little else than the law. As Bruno Latour has famously argued, writing about the French Conseil D'Etat, legal decision-making is a process of trying to move beyond questions of fact as fast as possible, in order to arrive at legal debates (Latour 2004). Legal processes then become concerned fundamentally with reaching a decision that is legally justifiable, rather than making a profound statement. The law is what matters, not the outside world (Riles 2006). Law, ideologically at least, claims a self-referentiality, that gestures to other laws, and other cases. While new objects and issues are constantly entering the legal realm, especially following developments in medicine and clinical practice, legal regimes always try to articulate these new arrivals within self-referential terms, as though they already always existed in the legal realm, and are merely finding articulation through new interpretation.[8] As far as legal actors are concerned, there is no need to look elsewhere, as in the end, it is the judge who decides what happens and the outcome of a legal case. As such, once a decision is reached, it is final. In the common law system it can be appealed, but only on matters of law, not on fact. The facts of the case are frozen in time when a judge comes to a decision. Law decides on both the means and the ends.

Medical decisions, in contrast, are often provisional and open to being revised in the light of clinical advances or as a patient's health fails or improves. As Foucault has argued, modern medicine is marked by a concern with observation and the clinical gaze (Foucault 2003). Clinical categories may shape what is seen, and the clinician may cultivate a sense of detachment from the body being observed, but the clinician always returns to that same body. Medicine has no luxury of near total self-referentiality. It must always look beyond itself to the sick patient, whose responses it can never totally control. Although medicine too is a field with a strong sense of its own traditions, canons and principles, however diverse, any attempt to transform the world into its own terms can reach its limits when it confronts a mind or body in pain which seems to resist medical intervention. A diagnosis is only useful and clinically correct if it helps the patient's condition improve. There is relatively less space to switch off the outside world, to say 'clinically speaking the decision was right'. Biographical narrative, individual history and life intervene (Bowker and Starr 1999). It is no coincidence that many general practitioners and community health workers rapidly come up against the limits of the purer forms of disease abstraction in the everydayness of their patients' lives, and turn to other modalities of intervention to help them in their struggles with being subjectively unwell. Medical means and ends, when compared to the law at least, are relatively more open and contingent.

A contrast between a 'distanced' law and an 'engaged' medicine can be overplayed of course. Lawyers are not always unconcerned with the outside world. Doctors too can also be relatively satisfied with a clinical outcome, irrespective of how the patient feels about it. An asthma sufferer, for example, may have a decrease in the constriction of their bronchioles – the medical outcome of an intervention – but still not feel that well in themselves. A surgical intervention might be a technical success, even in the absence of subjective improvement in well-being. Furthermore, to talk about law and medicine, the clinic and the court, doctors and lawyers, as unified entities, and coherent bodies of knowledge is untenable. While both law and medicine may have relative coherence as professional identities, both also have a tendency to fracture and contradict, breaking down into sub-fields. Criminal law, civil law and administrative law can have very different assumptions and goals, as can surgery, psychiatry, public health and palliative care, to give but a few examples. In such situations, law and medicine have been known to submit to one another, the ability to resolve internal contradictions. The recent case where the Supreme Court of India reinstated Section 377, the colonial anti-sodomy law, provides us with an instance of this. Parties on both sides of the litigation introduced medical evidence to support their cases – those that sought to get rid of the antiquated law filed evidence that homosexuality was no longer considered a 'disease', that the protection of human rights of same-sex desiring people was a central tenet of public health policy, and that the continuation of the law in force had mental health implications for gay, lesbian, bisexual and transgender citizens. The parties in support of the law similarly introduced medical opinion to the contrary, claiming that homosexuality was indeed a curable affliction, one responsible for the spread of the HIV epidemic and which must thus remain criminalised. The court, in this case, was called upon to act as an arbiter of what constituted 'good' science, and to resolve the apparent conflict within the realm of medicine. Conversely, in the making of HIV/AIDS policy, the government's National AIDS Control Organisation was essentially tasked with the responsibility of identifying 'good' law, having to decide between the fact that homosexuality was, in effect, criminalised under Indian law, and the constitutionally guaranteed Right to Life, which included the Right to Health. What we see here is a circularity, where the practices of law and medicine draw upon each other for the resolution of their own internal conflicts, and always in the context of pragmatic questions. As inherently pragmatic disciplines and sub-disciplines, law and medicine are always context specific, trying to answer very particular questions at very particular moments, and for particular ends.

There is an obvious danger in presenting law and medicine as self-enclosed, all-powerful forms of knowledge, despite the sovereign forms of power invested in them. It is also important to recognise their limits, hesitations and inconsistencies. Neither law, nor medicine, even in their own eyes, is all knowing and all seeing. There are limits to their expertise. People will die for reasons that are beyond medical knowledge; indeed, death itself brings medicine abruptly up against the limits of its domain (even if defining the moment of its coming can be complicated). The law can become confused. Clinical categories can contradict one another – as different bundles of signs and symptoms from the reading of the contours of the body are placed in different diagnostic categories – as can the law. Judges are as fallible as doctors. It is in these spaces of uncertainty that innovation can take place. It is here that the space for ethnographic investigation is most needed. Law and medicine, in all their various and contradictory forms, interact and contradict, producing new potentials and closing down old.

RECOGNISING HARM AND SUFFERING

The pictures from Abu-Ghraib seemed to shock most of the world. Images of Iraqi men being humiliated and punished by their smiling American captors sent out a chilling message. For many people, such photographs seemed to encapsulate all that was wrong with the Anglo-American invasion. Even those who supported the war professed to be shocked and sickened by what they were shown. The photographs of bodies in pain appeared to provide self-evident and easily recognisable evidence of wrongdoing that transcended political, cultural and religious boundaries. Complex arguments about international law or military strategy paled into insignificance alongside pictures of a naked man with electrodes attached to his fingers. While we might differ on issues of international politics, it was as if we could all come together to agree that the treatment of prisoners in this way was wrong.

Suffering and pain seem universal. As Miriam Ticktin has argued, there is a widespread assumption that we recognise suffering as self-evident because it seems to be universal human experience (Ticktin 2011: 11; see also Fassin and Rechtman 2009). But suffering and pain must be made legible, categorised and distinguished, in order to be given moral and social meaning. While being widely thought of as universal, pain and suffering can appear inscrutable. Elaine Scarry has claimed that physical pain leads to the unmaking of the world, and can stand beyond language (Scarry 1984). It is the ability of the torture, for example, to destroy our capacity for language and communication that, for Scarry, makes it so morally problematic. Yet, as Veena Das has persuasively written, pain is never simply a private experience, but has fundamentally social dimensions (Das 1997). The statement, 'I am in pain' does not simply describe an interior state, but also voices a complaint, a call for help and assistance. The issue is both one of the person in pain communicating their experiences, and crucially of the audience to see, hear and recognise what is in front of them.

Law and medicine are two privileged sites for the recognition of pain and suffering and involve very particular ways of seeing and knowing. The reading of the mind or body for signs of pain is a historically located process, and is as much aesthetic and technical, as emotional. The result is that some forms of pain and suffering are discursively brought into view, whereas others are left illegible. Harm must be made legible in order to be politically and socially salient. Rebecca Marsland examines, in this volume, how public health bylaws allow the Tanzanian state to make forms of harm visible, those derived from witchcraft, mourning and inheritance – forms that are deemed traditional and superstitious. In 2002, new bylaws legislating against traditions of the Nyakyusa deemed to be detrimental to public health were announced throughout Kyela District (Tanzania). In this chapter, she shows how particular articulations of 'tradition' in public health and law produce particular visions of harm. Once identified and made visible, they can become the focus of state sanctioned reform.

The clinical gaze has a very particular way of reading the body for signs of suffering, illness and disease. As Michel Foucault has argued, there was a shift in the late eighteenth century towards inferential interpretation of outward signs (Foucault 2003; Crossland 2009). Diseases came to be thought to be knowable through their observable symptoms. Otherwise hidden and unobservable processes could now be seen and heard. In her contribution to this volume, Ticktin explores how an inferential logic that attempts to read signs of suffering for hidden causes, can be applied to ever new contexts. For Ticktin, the 'innocent victim' is deemed the most morally legitimate recipient of humanitarian interventions. However, as more and more is revealed about victims and survivors, more and more innocence is compromised. The attempt to reveal and make this legible runs the risk of undermining the humanitarian project. In this context, after children, non-human animals can become the locus of this search for innocence. Meaningful signs of suffering previously observed in humans can be read from the bodies of non-human animals. Humanitarian psychiatry, for example, is applied to non-human animals. Elephants are diagnosed with post traumatic stress disorder (PTSD). Veterinary forensic medicine also becomes a diagnostic tool for revealing animal suffering, as well as, importantly, human cruelty. While a concern with animal suffering is far from new, in the early twenty-first century it is increasingly perceived through technical forms, which were previously linked to human beings. In doing so, Ticktin shows how humanitarian techniques can be spread to novel areas, revealing ever wider forms of suffering as morally urgent.

Law and medicine do not simply bring particular forms of pain and suffering into view. They also attribute moral and political meanings to that pain and suffering. Not all pain and suffering is thought to be problematic. Pain and suffering on its own has no inherent social or political implication, it engenders no 'natural' response (Laqueur 1989). Above all, attributing a cause to suffering can make it seem relatively legitimate or illegitimate, acceptable or unacceptable, a source of moral scandal or a source of moral reassurance. Pain and suffering without an apparent cause, can create particular disquiet. But, as Clifford Geertz wrote, if pain and suffering can be attributed with a cause, people can 'morosely or joyfully, grimly or cavalierly . . . endure it' (Geertz 1977: 104). Objectifying back pain, for example, through X-rays that reveal lesions can bring great relief: a cause has been found and it is not 'all in the mind', a judgement that can be hugely stigmatising (Jackson 1994). If suffering is seen to have different causes it can engender very different moral responses. For example, the pain from falling out of a tree, or drinking too much alcohol, produces different social and political reactions to the pain caused by child abuse, or cancer. The attribution of causes can make pain and suffering morally meaningful, and socially acceptable.

Law and medicine are two of the central devices used for distinguishing between different types of cause. Yet, as Tobias Kelly shows in this volume, both forms of expert knowledge can have very different understandings of causation. His chapter focuses on medico legal reports written about torture survivors in the UK immigration and asylum process. Legally speaking, torture is not just pain and suffering, but pain and suffering deliberately inflicted by public agents for specific purposes. Medico legal reports are therefore asked to attest to the apparent causes of scars and marks left on people's bodies. Yet medical and legal understandings of causation can come into conflict. Legal processes try to strip away all other possible causes, only to be left with those that are deemed legally relevant. They also rely on a positive and mechanistic notion of change. Medical notions of causation can be, in contrast, much more open ended, and subject to revision, depending on how a patient responds. Medical notions of causation can also operate at several levels simultaneously, with causal agents including insects, bacteria or even lifestyles. It is the difference between these two very different ways of conceptualising pain and suffering that opens up space to deny that torture has taken place.

In her contribution to this volume, Lydie Fialová shows how psychiatric medicine and criminal law can understand harm in very different ways. Her chapter focuses on a Czech psychiatric hospital, and the particular case of a man who she calls 'Josef K'. Josef killed his own mother, but was found not guilty on the grounds of insanity. In this process Josef's act was reclassified from crime to illness. His family, however, interpreted the murder as an unforgiveable wrong, while Josef was himself unsure how to interpret the act – refusing to identify with it in any way. A diagnosis of schizophrenia was particularly significant, as schizophrenia was more likely to be perceived as external to the person, treatable but not curable – in contrast to psychopathy (redefined in the DSM as 'antisocial personality disorder'), which might be seen as an inherent trait of the person. This distinction between causes that were seen to be external and those thought to be internal to Josef had implications for the extent to which he was thought to be culpable for the death of his mother. We see another example here of the ways in which law and medicine seek to delineate different types of causation. Ultimately, though, Fialová suggests that it is impossible to draw a neat line between insanity and crime, which is reflected in the very structure of secure psychiatric hospitals.

Anthropology has often criticised institutionalised forms of knowledge for abstracting, reifying and distorting the experience of suffering. Adriana Petryna, for example, has shown how, in the aftermath of the Chernobyl nuclear disaster, suffering was rationalised into a bureaucratic object (Petryna 2003). Definitions of radiation injury were elaborated through particular technical categories (2003: 35). Legitimate and recognised injury was limited to that which was biomedically measurable and calculable. Suffering had to be clinically legible and knowable for it to count, even though scientific knowledge in the area was provisional at best. For Veena Das, writing in the context of the Union Carbide chemical plant disaster in Bhopal, such bureaucratic forms of knowledge result in a constant stripping away from the experience of the survivor (Das 1997). Suffering is appropriated through technical forms of knowledge. The suffering survivor becomes an object for the exercise of power, and the moral implications of their own suffering are effectively extinguished. Such criticism of bureaucratisation effectively builds on Lyotard's notion of the *differend* (Lyotard 1989). For Lyotard, there are situations where wrongdoing or harm cannot adequately be represented. The result is an effective silencing of the victim. It is not that they cannot speak, but rather that they cannot express their experiences fully in the languages that are demanded by those who might respond. Law and medicine, for example, demand that harms be understood and expressed in very specific ways. Whether the anthropologist can reclaim these representational spaces, and better represent the experience of suffering is a moot point, and one we reflect upon below.

At one level the critique of bureaucratic forms of knowledge for failing to represent the suffering of survivors and victims is very powerful, as it reintroduces an ethnographic thickness to the experiences of survivors and the sick. At another level, though, there is a danger of failing to treat technical forms of expertise as ethnographically interesting in their own right. The suffering of the 'victim' is presented as the most authentic ground, and potentially flattens suffering itself into this particular form of ethnographic truth. It is, after all, another discursive translating away. Yet, when clinicians and lawyers attempt to understand the nature and implications of very specific forms of suffering, they do so with very particular ends. As fundamentally pragmatic forms of expertise, lawyers and clinicians are not in principle concerned with reproducing suffering in its full phenomenological complexity (Williams 2007). It would be perverse to reproduce an assault in a criminal trial, or for a doctor to deliberately infect themself with the TB bacillus (as witnessed by the response to scientist and HIV denialist Peter Deusberg injecting himself with HIV infected blood). Instead, the attempt is to understand assault, in order to get a criminal conviction, to diagnose TB in order to provide treatment. Profound philosophical and political questions about the nature of harm can be suspended in the name of getting something done. When clinicians and lawyers attempt to understand the nature and implications of very specific forms of suffering they can do so with very particular ends, such as allocating legal entitlements or providing relief from pain.

Lawyers can often seem somewhat distanced from suffering. This is not to say that there are not many profoundly empathetic lawyers, for whom the nature of suffering is of great importance. It is to say though, that legally speaking, for lawyers what is important is not suffering in and of itself, but a breach of a legal norm. Indeed, some forms of suffering may be deemed legal, such as that caused by the death penalty or incarceration, and therefore legally irrelevant in and of themselves. Courts do not object, necessarily, to the pain of state execution, as this is seen, in many jurisdictions, as being legally justified. Harm must also take on a particular structure to be legally recognised. To be a legal violation, there must be a victim and a perpetrator. Structural harms, and those that are not the product of some sort of intentional action or negligence, are hard to legally recognise. Evidential barriers must also be met. Legally persuasive proof must be provided that a harm has taken place, and that a particular person is culpable.

Distance from suffering is not so straightforward for all clinicians. Again this is not to say that clinicians do not comprehend suffering through distinct clinical categories. It is to point out again though, that a clinician can be forced to confront the body in front of them, in ways that lawyers are not. There are of course many forms of medicine that, in practice, abstract away from the body. Laboratory technicians, who deal with blood samples, viruses and bacilli, are an obvious example. However, there are other forms of medicine, such as general pracitioners, for example, who constantly have to deal with and respond to the person in front of them. The result is that the ethical tensions faced by such clinicians in the face of perceived suffering can be particularly acute. In her chapter in this volume, Estelle d'Halluin shows the tensions between pragmatic, technical and ethical forms of action. Her chapter examines how French doctors decide whether or not to produce medico legal reports for immigrants and asylum seekers. These reports can play a central role in persuading the French immigration authorities whether or not to allow the migrant to stay in France. Some doctors follow mechanical procedures, where they simply document every clinical fact, irrespective of the potential impact of doing so for the client's asylum case. Some doctors will decide whether to produce certificates, not on the basis of clinical signs but on whether they believed the client's story. Others will refuse if they think the certificate will be harmful to the client's asylum case. For d'Halluin, clinicians can be torn between the empathetic desire to be close to their clients and the demand to produce a formal technical document. The result is a fine-grained and context-specific negotiation of what might count as justice.

Forensic medicine produced a very specific manner of making the body legible, and of bringing harm into view for particular ends. Neither entirely legal, nor entirely clinical, forensic practice can sit awkwardly at the juncture between legal and medical means and ends. In his chapter in this volume, Gethin Rees examines the tensions between the production of legal evidence and the need to provide therapeutic care when forensic nurses are confronted with rape survivors. Forensic medical examiners in Canada and the UK have clinical obligations to survivors of rape, yet they must also collect evidence from the body of the person before them, and maintain a critical distance from the account that the complainant is providing. However, any dichotomy of objective evidence and subjective care is partially collapsed, as a more or less compassionate approach to patient care can change the ways in which evidence is collected. Sympathetic care can produce more legally persuasive evidence. Rees's chapter also ultimately reminds us that the line between the recognition of harm and the allocation of remedy is far from absolute. Recognition can in itself be a form of remedy, and remedy cannot begin before recognition takes place. Post-rape interventions therefore combine elements of the legal and the medical, creating a new space of action, a point that will be taken up in the final section of this introduction.

UNDERSTANDING AND ALLOCATING REMEDY

The second section of this collection deals with the ways in which law and medicine understand and allocate remedies to harm. Medicine can aim to heal and alleviate. The medical definition of remedy is a specific treatment for an injury or a disease condition. But legal processes can also produce relief and repair. More generally, remedy means to redress a moral wrong, or specifically legal redress when used in law. In this process, both law and medicine can both come up against the limits of their knowledge and their capacity to shape the world, deferring to one another. The finality of law can provide 'closure' to clinical uncertainty, and, vice versa, clinical practice can provide an attempt to intervene directly in minds and bodies that more distanced forms of legality find difficult.

Human rights legislation as applied to health has been central to the changing boundaries between medicine and the law in relation to the application of remedy. João Biehl's chapter in this volume explores this development, and examines how the Brazilian courts are intervening in deciding who gets medical treatment and in what ways. In the wake of the rise of rights-based activism into access to HIV/AIDS treatment right-to-health litigation has become the key mechanism through which Brazilians are able to access healthcare. This richly ethnographic chapter reveals how the boundaries of the medical and legal are frequently blurred, where we see 'the judiciary as a sort of pharmacy, the public defender as a physician, the physician as an activist, the patient association as a legal council...' Anthropology here has to struggle with these boundaries, and the complexity and with the contradictions in our taken-for-granted understanding of the roles, functions and norms of these institutional forms. In a biopolitical context where public health has become increasingly both privatised and more and more dependent on the consumption of pharmaceuticals (or pharmaceuticalisation), the right of access to pharmaceuticals has come to predominate. Access to medical remedies here, in this fast-changing public system, particularly for the poor and marginalised, is mediated through the increasing use of the courts. The judges overseeing these cases nearly always grant access to the medicines requested, seeing this as being entirely consistent with the constitution and the right to health. The law here has come to be seen as a mechanism for access where treatment protocols and cost-effectiveness discourses limit their availability. Seen by Biehl as a 'minimal political belonging', it is a field of temporal imminence, a legal relief to the increasingly market driven field of health and access to services.

As Biehl points to the potential of human rights legislation in leveraging access to remedy in the context of Brazil, Ian Harper's chapter also points to the limits of the legal domain in the realm of public health. The rise of multidrug-resistant tuberculosis (MDRTB) across the globe has stimulated differing responses, in varied national contexts. He compares the situation of the USA with South Africa, and their responses to the rise of MDRTB. In the USA attempts to regulate and limit the travel of one individual diagnosed with MDRTB – Andrew Speaker – as he travelled across Europe and to Canada allowed the application of old laws, and called on the idioms of post-9/11 security concerns. The ensuing legal tussle over Andrew Speaker's own rights to privacy, as he sued and was in turn countersued should be read as the oscillating limits of the law applied to individual and the public's right not to be exposed to infection. Remedy here moves beyond that of the individual to that of the broader public. When Harper presented this paper to a public health audience in South Africa, their reaction to the idea that we can respond to the epidemic by controlling the movement of individuals was met with disbelief. This made little sense given the scale of the MDR epidemic they are currently facing. The limits of legislation are realised in this context – where attempts to deal with the problem in fortressed hospitals has been met with resistance and even riots – and where the current capacity to deal with the epidemic is overwhelmed by the scale of the problem. Here the social, political, economic and structural complexities become paramount, and point to the need to deal with issues more broadly than just through translation into legal and juridical debates, or as a problem of regulating the movement of individuals. Here, as with Biehl's chapter, the limits of remedy at the interface of medicine and the law are starkly highlighted.

A potentially more optimistic perspective on the ability of law to provide remedies is presented in Naomi Richards' contribution to this volume. In her chapter she describes how the terminally ill can turn to the law in order to try and bring closure to what would otherwise be ambiguous end-of-life decisions. She draws on the UK case of Debbie

Purdy, who was living with multiple sclerosis, and who mounted a legal challenge against the potential criminal legal repercussions for her partner, Omar Puente, should he assist her in travelling abroad to a jurisdiction where she could lawfully be helped to die. The Suicide Act in the UK states that it is illegal to assist others in the act of suicide. Medically she cannot be cured of this degenerative condition, but she turned to the law to provide a remedy that would make her final days more bearable – an assisted death. Rather than a dispassionate and abstract ruling, the comfort provided by the High Court's ruling in the couple's favour, provided the emotional and moral relief that they sought. Even if the terms of the ruling have since been challenged and questioned following their case, it was the law that provided a remedy, in the absence of medicine's capacity to sustain a dignified life.

The three chapters in this section attest to the ways in which the law is being appropriated in order to assist in anticipating future harm. John Borneman, in his contribution to this volume, also demonstrates how the vagaries of the future are managed, in this case in relation to the clinical rehabilitation for child sex offenders. Drawing on fieldwork with sex offenders in Germany, the chapter shows how it is the potential risk of repetition that is important for both law and medicine here. While the law requires that there is an assurance for the public that there will be no repetition of the act, the therapist attempts to gain access to the unconscious workings of the individual, and to articulate transformation at this deepest of psychic levels.

Henrik Ronsbo, in turn, explores how remedy is being provided for, in situations of extreme pain and grief, in a context of genocide and conflict. Guatemala emerged from decades of violent conflict, and with this, up to 200 000 individuals were killed or disappeared. A network of organisations drew on psychosocial interventions to focus on the survivors and assist in the alleviation of their suffering. These 'platforms of recognition' are the result of a field of interaction involving donors and NGOs (thus within the field of development), and therapists and their clientele in this particular political context. This approach to the idea of remedy as trauma, moves beyond the conceptualisation of trauma as a tool of 'empire' (Fassin and Rechtman 2009) to the inherently relational emergence, where traditional relationships of patronage are reformed by newer claims based on a rights based framework. A new space is thus carved out where new hopes and fears are expressible in the emergent Guatemalan democracy.

THE POLITICAL SPACE BETWEEN LAW
AND MEDICINE

We see through these chapters how, as law and medicine interact, potentially new forms of political action, understandings of harm and forms of redress are produced. The spaces between the clinic and the court create the possibility for new claims based on the sick or vulnerable body or the traumatised mind.

Crucially, these claims cannot simply be reduced to the claims of legal subjects. This is a much fuller notion of legal personhood that cannot be reduced to formal citizenship or its absence. The people making them are seen to bleed, to haemorrhage and to cry in pain. Nor, though, can these claims be reduced to the biological substrate upon which medicine ekes out its interventions. They do not simply involve biological forms of living, and cannot be reduced to 'bare life'. Rather, they involve active and often disruptive claims and counter-claims that do not fit neatly into legal categories, based as they are on the lived experience of pain, suffering and its potential alleviation. At stake here are forms of subject-making that cannot simply be reduced to subjectification. If they are biological citizens, or therapeutic citizens, or pharmaceutical citizens (Rose 2007; Petryna 2003; Nguyen 2010; Ecks 2005), they are citizens in the sense of being active, entitled and often unruly, embedded into institutions of rule, but never wholly subsumed by them. They are, in this sense, subjects gaining intelligibility, simultaneously, in at least the two registers of law and medicine, but inscribed in the space between them.

The above insight has significant implications for the ways in which we understand the forms and possibilities of the subject of political action. Foucault's undeniable influence on both legal and medical anthropology has often implied an underlying concern with the question of the constitutive effects of the law and medicine respectively. The assumption here is that these discourses somehow produce subjects. In the context of law, the question is how engagement with law constitutes us as subjects. Structurally similar is the question in the context of medicine – how engagement with medical discourse and apparatus, in requiring us to occupy the 'patient role' for instance, generates the conditions for the relationship with the self. But as the chapters in this volume suggest, innovations in and of the subject lie between these registers, in the tensions and resolutions within and between them. The political subject, then, cannot be considered through a focus on the constitutive potential of these discourses, but rather on their failure to do so.

The theoretical implication of this argument is that the subject can no more be considered an internal conversation instigated by, or circumscribed by, the limits of the language of law, or of medicine. Rather, we might consider the subject as the effects generated in engagements with these registers, as a series of vehicles that we occupy in political contestation. The political subject might then usefully be considered as neither 'internal' (as in a relationship to the self instigated or required by an authoritative discourse), nor 'external' (as a performance of a form intelligible in the authoritative discourse), but rather, in-between. It is in this sense that the failure of law and medicine to constitute the subject generates the space for the political subject, and the potential for new, transformative forms of political action.

It is as crucial to recognise that as law and medicine interact, and as the space between them generates political action, their categories and forms are transformed. Crucially, as Ian Hacking has pointed out, clinical categories are not simply abstract disembodied forms of regulation. Instead, they have a social life of their own (Hacking 1995). Clinical categories are taken up and used by the people they are applied to. A 'looping effect' can take place, where clinical categories are given flesh and bones, shot through with emotional content as lived realities. People come to live their diagnosis as victims of trauma, as autistic, or bipolar, for example, and in this process the very meanings and implications of the applied categories are transformed. Exactly the same thing could be said about law. Legal categories are not simply cold, artificial and distant. They can also be thick and full of meaning, being lived out in everyday life. Thus both medical and legal labelling goes to the heart of their experience of what it means to be a citizen and even a human being. Law and medicine can be, to paraphrase Hacking, 'engines for making up people' (Hacking 1995), but once these engines are started, they can have a life of their own. In the spaces between the clinic and the court, there are forms of political and social action that cannot be reduced simply to biopower, bare life or neoliberalism. Whether this space is seen as restricting and regulatory, or liberatory, the juridical languages of rights, law and punishment, create the possibility for new claims based on the sick or vulnerable body and the traumatised mind. As the chapters in this book attest, the analysis of these news spaces is an inherently anthropological project, as the entanglement of law and medicine point to the crucial dimension of what it means to be human today.

NOTES

1 '£7.3m payout for brain-damaged boy from Hertfordshire', BBC News, 13 March 2013, available at: www.bbc.co.uk/news/uk-england-beds-bucks-herts-21861568
2 'NHS facing £15.7bn for rising number of clinical negligence claims', Daily Telegraph, 7 February 2012, available at: www.telegraph.co.uk/news/politics/9065534/NHS-facing-15.7bn-for-rising-number-of-clinical-negligence-claims.html
3 'Moors Murderer Ian Brady banned from carrying pens', BBC News, 18 June 2013, available at: www.bbc.co.uk/news/uk-22953626
4 'A baby boy for Diane Blood', The Independent, 12 December 1998, available at: www.independent.co.uk/news/a-baby-boy-for-diane-blood-1190812.html
5 'Mid Staffs report calls for sweeping changes to improve patient safety', The Guardian, 6 February 2013, available at: www.theguardian.com/society/2013/feb/06/mid-staffordshire-report-sweeing-changes?guni=Article:in%20body%20link
6 'NHS culture at Mid Staffs that tolerated low standards and sold patients short', The Guardian, 6 February 2013, available at: www.theguardian.com/society/2013/feb/06/nhs-mid-staffs
7 In jurisprudence criminal responsibility is, broadly, based on the assessment of two elements – the actus reus ('guilty act') relating to whether a given act has been done by a person or not (did X pull the trigger, for instance?), and mens rea ('guilty mind') or the 'mental state' that makes the act meaningful (did X 'intend' to kill Y by pulling the trigger? Did s/he intend to simply injure Y? Did s/he know that pulling the trigger might cause the death of Y? Ought X to have known that this act might lead to the death of Y? etc.). Except where there is an explicit admission of intention, mens rea is typically 'inferred' – it cannot, strictly speaking, be 'known', but rather be assumed.
8 The enrichment of the meaning of the 'Right to Life' to cover such issues as issues of livelihood, bonded labour, child labour, housing, health, privacy, education, sexual harassment at the workplace, domestic violence, marriage, clean environment and dignity, is seen not as an introduction of new objects into the law, but merely the act of a more full interpretation of already existing provisions.

REFERENCES

Biehl, J. and Petryna, A. 2013. 'Critical Global Health', in Biehl, J. and Petryna, A. (eds.), When People Come First: Critical Studies in Global Health. Princeton and Oxford: Princeton University Press

Bowker, G. C. and Starr, S. L. 1999. *Sorting Things Out: Classification and Its Consequences*. Cambridge, MA, and London: The MIT Press

Brown, W. 1995. *States of Injury*. Princeton: Princeton University Press

Carr, E. Summerson. 2010. 'Enactments of Expertise', *Annual Review of Anthropology* 39: 17–32

Chalmers, J. 2002. 'The Criminalisation of HIV transmission', *Sexually Transmitted Infections* 78(6): 448–451

Crossland, Z. 2009. 'Of Clues and Signs: The Dead Body and Its Evidential Traces', *American Anthropologist* 111(1):69–80

Das, V. 1997. *Critical Events: An Anthropological Perspective on Contemporary India*. Delhi: Oxford University Press

Das, V. and Poole, D. 2004. 'State and Its Margins: Comparative Ethnographies', in Das, V. and Poole, D. (eds.), *Anthropology in the Margins of the State*. Oxford and New York: Oxford University Press

Ecks, S. 2005. 'Pharmaceutical Citizenship: Antidepressant Marketing and the Promise of Demarginalization in India', *Anthropology & Medicine* 12(3): 239–254

Fassin, D. and Rechtman, R. 2009. *The Empire of Trauma: An Inquiry into the Condition of Victimhood*. Princeton: Princeton University Press

Farmer, P. 2001. *Infections and Inequalities: The Modern Plagues*. Berkeley: University of California Press

2004. *Pathologies of Power: Health, Human Rights, and the New War on the Poor*. Berkeley, Los Angeles and London: University of California Press

Foucault, M. 2003. *The Birth of the Clinic*. London: Routledge

Geertz, C. 1977. *The Interpretation of Cultures*. New York: Basic Books

Hacking, I. 1995. *Rewriting the Soul: Multiple Personality and the Science of Memory*. Princeton: Princeton University Press

Hayden, C. 2007. 'A Generic Solution? Pharmaceuticals and the Politics of the Similar in Mexico', *Current Anthropology* 48(4): 475–495

Inda, J. 2005. 'Analytics of the Modern: An Introduction', in Inda, J. (ed.), *Anthropologies of Modernity: Foucault, Governmentality, and Life Politics*. Malden, Oxford and Carlton: Blackwell Publishing

Jackson, J. 1994. 'Chronic Pain and the Tension between Body as Subject and Object', in Csordas, T. (ed.), *Embodiment and Experience: The Existential Ground of Culture and Health*. Cambridge: Cambridge University Press

Jain, S. L. 2006. *Injury: The Politics of Product Design and Safety Law in the United States*. Princeton: Princeton University Press

Laqueur, T. 1989. 'Bodies, Details and the Humanitarian Narrative', in Hunt, L. (ed.), *The New Cultural History*. Berkeley: University of California Press

Latour, B. 2004. *The Making of Law: An Ethnography of the Conseil D'Etat*. Cambridge: Polity

Lock, M. 2002. *Twice Dead: Organ Transplants and the Reinvention of Death*. Berkeley: California University Press

Lyotard, J.-F. 1989. *Differend: Phrases in Dispute*. Minneapolis: University of Minnesota Press

Mertz, E. 2007. *The Language of Law School. Learning to 'Think Like a Lawyer'*. New York: Oxford University Press

Nguyen, V.-K. 2010. *Republic of Therapy: Triage and Sovereignty in West Africa's Time of AIDS*. Durham: Duke University Press

Petryna, A. 2003. *Life Exposed: Biological Citizens After Chernobyl*. Princeton: Princeton University Press

2009. *When Experiments Travel: Clinical Trials and the Global Search for Human Subjects*. Princeton and Oxford: Princeton University Press

Petryna, A., Lakoff, A. and Kleinman, A. (eds.) 2006. *Global Pharmaceuticals: Ethics, Markets, Practices*. Durham: Duke University Press

Redfield, P. 2013. *Life in Crisis: The Ethical Journey of Doctors Without Borders*. Berkeley, Los Angeles and London: University of California Press

Riles, A. 2006. 'Anthropology, Human Rights and Legal Knowledge: Culture in an Iron Cage', *American Anthropologist* 108(1): 52–65

Rose, N. 2007. *The Power of Life Itself: Biomedicine, Power and Subjectivity in the Twenty-First Century*. Princeton: Princeton University Press

Scarry, E. 1984. *The Body in Pain: The Making and Unmaking of the World*. Oxford: Oxford University Press. Introduction

Sinclair, S. 1997. *Making Doctors: An Institutional Apprenticeship*. Oxford: Berg

Ticktin, M. 2011. *Casualties of Care: Immigration and the Politics of Humanitarianism in France*. Berkeley: University of California Press

Williams, A. 2007. 'Human Rights and Law: Between Sufferance and Insufferability', *Law Quarterly Review* 123: 133–158

PART ONE

RECOGNISING HARM AND SUFFERING

CHAPTER ONE

KEEPING MAGICAL HARM INVISIBLE: PUBLIC HEALTH, WITCHCRAFT AND THE LAW IN KYELA, TANZANIA

Rebecca Marsland

As Kelly, Harper and Khanna argue in the introduction to this book, an important function of both medicine and the law is that they make harm visible, although they do so in different ways.[1] One of the corollaries of this process of making harm visible, and 'legible', is that it enables the associated suffering to be given moral and social meaning, frequently through the attribution of causality. However, when it comes to the harm caused by witchcraft in African countries, both the law and (bio)medicine have struggled because for them the causal link between witchcraft and harm that is put forward by its victims does not exist, indeed practices of magical harm do not exist. For both the law and medicine, it is those who believe in witchcraft who cause harm, and this is where an impasse has developed – between those who consider themselves to be the victims of magical harm, and the state authorities who have a mandate to protect them from harm.

As far as the law is concerned, those who believe themselves to be the victims of witchcraft can cause harm, because they at best slander those who they believe to be witches through practices of accusation and divination, and at worst cause accused witches physical harm or even kill them. The law seems to protect those who are accused of witchcraft instead of the victims of witchcraft. In East Africa the responsibility to protect people from the potentially fatal sickness and misfortune caused by witchcraft has fallen to an indigenous public health (Feierman 1985, 1999, 2010; Last 1999; Marsland 2014; Waite 1992). Practitioners of biomedicine in Africa are generally unsympathetic to belief in witchcraft, arguing that the belief is a threat to public health. From this perspective, people who think they are victims of witchcraft are a threat to themselves because they visit traditional healers whose medicines may cause harm, or who may delay patients from seeking help at a hospital or local health centre. Some nurses and doctors, however, recognize the problem and may believe in witchcraft themselves or refer patients who they cannot treat to traditional healers (Langwick 2011, 2008).

In this chapter, an attempt to solve this problem will be examined. In Kyela District in the south-west of Tanzania, some local bylaws were proposed against what were described as the 'misleading traditions of the Nyakyusa'. These bylaws appear to solve a problem of indigenous public health – a form of witchcraft, that is in itself part of a system of indigenous law – by drawing on the official law of the state, and on the formal public health system. By officially dealing with the spread of infectious disease at Nyakyusa funerals, the bylaws conceal their widely perceived purpose of preventing witchcraft. Their efficacy lies in their ability to keep magical harm invisible within a state statute, while simultaneously being open to an alternative reading by the local population as being explicitly concerned with a local form of witchcraft and solve a matter that is of concern to both indigenous and official forms of public health.

WITCHCRAFT AND THE LAW

Colonial and postcolonial legal regimes have a restricted ability to make magical harm visible. This is an ontological matter because it is concerned with the nature of reality. The law rarely accepts that witchcraft might be real, but when it does, as we will see below, matters become messy and complicated. In Tanzania, where many people are troubled by what is for them a very real risk of magical harm, members of the population wish that the law could protect them from witches. In their view, the law does the very opposite. Since the implementation of the witchcraft ordinances during the colonial period, those who accuse people of witchcraft are liable to be prosecuted, while suspected witches are left alone. It is well documented in the study of witchcraft in Africa that the law will persecute those who are victims of witchcraft, but not witches themselves.

State officials are essentially faced with an ontological problem when deciding how to deal with witchcraft accusations (Langwick 2011). To generalize, many citizens regard witchcraft as real, whereas a modern state cannot. There is a contradiction – a modern state apparatus cannot recognize witchcraft without either undermining its claim to rationality or appearing to be publicly taking part in the nefarious world of witchcraft. However, it must also protect its citizens, who see witchcraft as real, and it faces criticism, or worse, when citizens take matters into their own hands through forms of vigilantism. It is important to distinguish what activities can be seen in public from those that cannot: a state cannot publicly recognize witchcraft. Yet, at the same time, it must publicly be seen to be doing something about it.

The ethnographic record tells of a wide variety of ways in which people try to control or prevent witchcraft in African countries. In the precolonial period, poison oracles were widely used to identify witches (Evans-Pritchard 1976; Langwick 2011: 43). However, colonial and postcolonial legal regimes have widely cracked down on such practices. Poison oracles were banned during the colonial period when the witchcraft ordinances were introduced, which in turn led to changes in the nature of anti-witchcraft activity. Likewise, traditional healers were no longer permitted to practise divination in order to identify and accuse witches. In response, anti-witchcraft activities have taken new forms: mass movements, such as witch cleansing in Kenya and Tanzania (Abrahams 1994; Green 1994, 1997; Green and Mesaki 2005; Smith 2005, 2008), witch-finding in Zambia (Auslander 1993) and violent witch hunts in South Africa (Niehaus 2001) and Tanzania (Abrahams 1987; Mesaki 1994). Traditional healers sell protective medicines, which often work by turning back magical harm onto the perpetrator (West 2005). Pentecostal Churches (Meyer 1999) and the Independent African Churches (Ashforth 2005: 182–92) are also major players in the fight against witchcraft.

The main documentary source for information on anti-witchcraft procedures during the colonial and precolonial period in Bunyakyusa[2] is based on the fieldwork of Monica and Godfrey Wilson published in four monographs (1951a, 1957, 1959, 1977) and the Wilson archives at the University of Capetown. Monica described three important kinds of magical harm, all of which are relevant in modified form to the contemporary situation. *Ubulosi* referred to an innate power to cause harm, enabled by the presence of a python in the stomach, and *ubutege* was the use of medicines to trap and hurt a victim (Wilson 1951b). *Ubulosi* and *ubtege* roughly correspond to the classic distinctions drawn between witchcraft and sorcery by Evans-Pritchard (1976). Monica also wrote of another kind of magical harm called *imbepo sya bandu* – which she translated as the 'breath of men'. The angry words of members of the community produced this breath when they 'muttered' or 'murmured' about a person who had committed an offence against them (1951a: 91–108).

'The defenders', or *abamanga*, were responsible for protecting the local population at night and would watch for witches in their dreams (ibid: 96–108). The *abamanga* were often village headmen (*amafumu*). As with witches, the source of their power came from pythons in their stomachs. The day after they identified witches in their dreams, they would make their accusations in public. Once a witch had been accused, he or she would be expected to confess and expel any anger by blowing water from their mouth (ibid: 99). Alternatively, they could take the *umwafi* poison ordeal – if they vomited they were innocent, if they did not they were guilty (ibid: 115–6). When a suspected witch died, a doctor would be called to carry out an autopsy and search for a python in their stomach (ibid: 116–7).

A witch who was identified but did not confess was most often banished from their home to another chiefdom. The banished witch's property was often confiscated by the chief. These measures were considered to be mild – as Chief Mwakilema told Godfrey Wilson in 1935, punishment for witchcraft was much less severe than for sorcery:

> In the old days... If we caught a man as a sorcerer we used to dig a hole and bury his head downwards in it with his buttocks on top, alive, and then take a stake and drive it through him from the anus – so we did also with thieves – not with those caught as *abalosi* [witches], no, then we used sometimes to kill but only with a spear; normally we just took all their goods and cows and burnt their houses and drove them to another country.
>
> (Godfrey and Monica Wilson Archives (BC0880), University of Capetown. D.1.1 Notebook no. 33, p. 29, September 1935, Selya Lubaga)

Under the colonial anti-witchcraft ordinances it was made illegal to divine for or accuse someone of witchcraft, and heavy fines and prison sentences could be used to enforce this, especially if a victim of witchcraft resorted to violence (Fields 1982). In Tanganyika, the 1922 ordinance allowed fines of up to £200 and imprisonment for up to 5 years (Niehaus 2001: 221, note 2). At the time some British commentators were critical. Roberts (1935) and Orde Browne (1935) both presented papers at the International Congress of Anthropological and Ethnological Sciences in London and complained that the laws did not distinguish between 'witchdoctors', who were supposed to protect people against witchcraft, and actual witches and sorcerers who intended to do harm. Some colonial administrators such as Frank Melland and Cullen Young thought it would be preferable to work with 'witchdoctors' (Rutherford 1999: 99) so that the colonial judge would not be seen as the 'ally of the witch' (Fisiy 1998: 149). One of the difficulties with these ordinances is that they did not (could not) recognize the reality of witchcraft, and so punished the 'witchdoctors' who the local population believed could protect them, and protected the 'witches' from accusations.[3]

The witchcraft ordinances meant that people could not accuse an individual of witchcraft. As one man complained to the Wilsons 'The defenders see the witches but cannot name them to anyone.' (Wilson 1951a: 132). The *umwafi* ordeal was illegal, and while the Wilsons thought it might sometimes have been administered in secret, as far as they were aware, the very last time it was used was in 1932 (ibid: 116). They wrote that witchcraft accusations were still frequently heard in the Native Courts, but they were not documented, and that autopsies were also becoming rare.

These changes meant that people had to adapt the ways that they protected themselves against witchcraft. It was now illegal to identify a witch through divination, and so healers developed a new form of intervention – the community witchcraft eradication campaigns, most notably those of the itinerate healer and witch-finder *Mchapi*, who claimed to protect whole communities (Marwick 1950; Richards 1935; Willis 1968, 1970). Other healers turned to providing medicines that protected individuals against witchcraft, or turned magical harm back on a witch. In Bunyakyusa, instead of directly accusing someone of witchcraft people would anonymously place thorns around the door of their house as a strong hint that they should move on (Wilson 1951a: 114, 132). Alternatively, a suspected witch would be socially ostracized, and their life made a misery until they fled (ibid: 132). The British administration no longer permitted chiefs to seize the property of an accused witch (ibid: 119). Increasingly, it was the victims of witchcraft who feared for their lives and had to leave for another village, and so Europeans were widely 'condemned for protecting witches' (ibid: 132). In practice, the British colonial administration appeared to be punishing the belief in witchcraft. The result was that people widely felt abandoned by the state, which was unwilling and unable to protect them from witchcraft.

31

After independence in 1961, the new socialist government main-tained the anti-witchcraft ordinances, which were in line with their modernist views on belief and superstition (Niehaus 2001: 190). This meant that courts continued to prosecute anyone who accused witches. In Sukumaland it caused the local population to resent the state for abandoning them, and in many cases led to violent acts of retribution.[4] Between 1970 and 1988, 3072 Sukuma who were suspected of being witches were killed by vigilante (*sungusungu*) groups. Only seven peo-ple were prosecuted for these killings, indicating the extent to which local state representatives were compromised by their position (Abra-hams 1987; Bukurura 1994; Mesaki 1994).

Across postcolonial Africa, states have faced similar difficulties: they are unwilling to recognize the reality of witches in people's lives, and yet are under considerable pressure to take the issue seriously (Ciekway and Geschiere 1998; Geschiere 2006, Niehaus 2001). Some countries have succumbed to the pressure to prosecute witchcraft, either due to fears over public order, or because state officials themselves felt persecuted by witchcraft. Peter Geschiere and Cyprian Fisiy have written exten-sively about the witchcraft trials in 1980s Cameroon, where state offi-cials were themselves afraid of witches, who either appeared to under-mine rural development projects or who directly threatened the officials themselves. In this context, witches were tried in court and were sub-ject to sentences of up to ten years, on the basis of evidence brought by traditional healers (Fisiy 1998, 1990; Fisiy and Geschiere 1990; Fisiy and Rowlands 1989; Geschiere 2006, 1997; Geschiere and Fisiy 1994). In South Africa, the extensive and extreme violence by young ANC activists against suspected witches in the 1990s endangered stability in post-apartheid townships. In response to this the Ralushai Commis-sion of Inquiry into Witchcraft of 1996 proposed to simultaneously pun-ish those who practise witchcraft, as well as those who accuse another person of being a witch, and attempted to resolve this contradiction by recommending new authorities to regulate the traditional healers and their expertise in identifying witches (Ashforth 2005; Geschiere 2006; Niehaus 2001). Sometimes witchcraft prosecutions have been for narrow political goals. Diane Ciekway (1997, 1998, 1998, 2006), for example, has described how the Kenyan state used the anti-witchcraft ordinance, which in 1966 made the practice of witchcraft a crime against the state, to discipline political dissidents.

Speaking more broadly, any law that attempts to deal directly with witchcraft faces an intractable problem. If a legal framework is to operate within the frame of reference of a 'reasonable man', reasonableness is usually defined within modernist terms, which cannot acknowledge witchcraft as a reality. If the state cannot see something then it does not exist, and therefore it cannot be dealt with in courts. Anyone who believes in witchcraft risks being seen by the state as holding an erroneous view of the world (West 2007: 38), or worse – as insane (Comaroff and Comaroff 2004: 194). This slur on their grasp of reality makes them liable to legal discipline if their beliefs lead them to harm a suspected witch in any way. As a result, witchcraft is visible only as an incorrect belief, and in the eyes of the law it is the victim of the belief – the so-called witch – who suffers harm.

If the state acts as if witchcraft is real, and makes visible in the courts the harm caused by actual witches, a new problem emerges. The courts become implicated in the reputations of suspicious characters – the 'healers' who can supply the proof that someone is a witch. These same healers, however, depend on the very knowledge that makes them suspicious – if they know enough about witchcraft to identify a witch, they could be witches themselves. Peter Geschiere (2006) has argued that this has the effect of associating the courts with nefarious occult activities. In addition to this, he adds, the very fact that the courts take the reality of witchcraft so seriously exaggerates the scale of the problem in the eyes of the local population.[5] Geschiere then adds the final blow to the advisability of state recognition of the reality of witchcraft – it is doomed to failure: by recognizing witchcraft it must act against it, by acting against it the public perception of the scale of the problem is increased, ultimately weakening the state when it fails to contain witchcraft.

Acknowledging the existence of witchcraft – making it visible in the eyes of the law thus seems to be inadvisable. Likewise, failure to act also leads to discontent on the part of populations who feel that governments should be doing something to protect them against magical harm. I will argue that something different is being tried out in Kyela. In the rest of this chapter I want to make the case that in Kyela, public health, which can be 'seen' with considerably less controversy, acts as a proxy for witchcraft. A set of bylaws which were officially proposed in the name of public hygiene, but that are widely regarded to be an anti-witchcraft measure, make use of a kind of doubling that the Comaroffs (2006: 34) have argued is characteristic of the layers of state-like processes and organizations that produce and enact law in the postcolonial context. They describe a 'palimpsest of images' through which the operation of legal processes can only be opaque. These bylaws in Kyela work in this way: through the surface layer of public health can be seen another set of concerns to do with a very particular kind of magical harm which has its origins in a form of indigenous law.

THE BYLAWS AND PUBLIC HEALTH

In 1998 some key leaders of Kyela District government held a consultation to identify what they described as 'misleading traditions' (*mila potovu*) of the Nyakyusa. Figures such as the Chairman of the District Committee (*Halmashauri wa Wilaya*) and the District Medical Officer (DMO) called a meeting to discuss traditions that were felt to be a danger to public health and community development. A meeting of each Ward Development Committee, brought together the Village Chairs, Ward Councillors and other officers to debate local tradition, and the matter was then cascaded down to village level – to canvas opinion of the local community. Once their reports had been returned to the District Offices, they were analysed, and the recommendations were collated into a proposal for some new District Bylaws, legislating against these 'misleading traditions of the Nyakyusa'. The DMO then left to study for his Masters in Public Health in the UK, where he wrote his dissertation on the funeral practices of the Nyakyusa and their relation to the spread of disease. He returned in 2002 when I was in the field.

The bylaws set out to ban a range of practices – mostly relating to funerals and mourning, focusing on the provision of various feasts at different stages of the mourning process, hygiene associated with crowds, matters of inheritance, particularly concerning the welfare of widows, but also onerous responsibilities that can be placed on a son who must inherit from his father. They also stipulated that a man should be able to build himself a brick house, without having to build one first for his father. Anyone found to be breaking these new bylaws could be fined 10 000 Tanzanian shillings or given a prison sentence of between six months and a year.

The bylaws themselves offer no explanation of why these traditions were 'misleading', other than that they had fallen 'out of date', and had 'caused the community to lose their way'. However, a document produced by the National Malaria Control Programme (1999), commended them as a community initiative intended to stem the transmission of malaria. When I asked employees of Kyela District Hospital, and later the DMO himself about them, I was told that the traditions identified were associated with the spread of infectious diseases at funerals, including malaria, diarrhoeal diseases (including cholera), meningitis and sexually transmitted infections including HIV.

Across Africa, funerals are major events (Jindra and Noret 2011) and Nyakyusa funerals are especially renowned in Tanzania for their scale and extravagance. Funerals take place in people's homes, and people are buried in family plots around the side of the house. They can be attended by hundreds of people, require considerable expense on food and beer, and can last for weeks (in the past they would last for months). When I asked about funerals, people would often tell me in disgust about the recent past when women and other key mourners were required to neglect bodily hygiene and wear dirty clothes, walk barefoot, not wash and leave their hair to grow uncombed (leading to infestations with head lice). The home is also neglected – mourners do not sweep the usually meticulously kept ground around a house until the mourning period is over.

Obviously such an event that can take place over a period of weeks or even months, cannot require the attendance of hundreds *every* day – but there are key dates at which 'everybody' (the village, family, friends) must attend – most importantly the burial, which takes place as soon as the corpse and the key mourners have arrived; the side shoot 'funerals' which develop when a set of mourners 'carry' the mourning 'home', thus attracting their own friends and neighbours; the day on which an heir is appointed and matters of inheritance are discussed, and finally the day of the 'sweeping of the ground', which is accompanied by a ritual washing and shaving of the hair of the key women mourners. On these occasions, more people must come to offer comfort and 'help' with grieving. The rest of the time, the 'mourning' is maintained by a key group of the bereaved, their relatives, close friends and neighbours, particularly centring around a group of women, some of whom will sleep over at the funeral ground.

It was these crowds of (mainly) women and children that the DMO told me in an interview in 2002 were such a danger to public health. The very proximity of so many unwashed bodies, defecating in the surrounding bushes, sleeping together – often outside and not under a mosquito net, coughing and breathing on each other, and taking the opportunity to meet their lovers at night, was in his view a hazard. This was the ideal situation for the transmission of infectious diseases, and to make matters worse, he told me, mothers often delayed taking sick infants to the hospital or village clinic, because they were both enjoying themselves and were obligated to stay there and mourn. For him, the rationale behind the bylaws was quite simple. By curtailing the scale of funerals – cutting them down to a three-day event, reducing crowds by stipulating who is entitled to be present, and insisting that basic hygiene measures be followed – washing, wearing shoes and clean clothes, and sleeping under mosquito nets, then the less of a public health risk these events would be (Marsland 2014).

Public health professionals are familiar with the use of the law as a tool to promote health and prevent disease. There are sanitation regulations, reportable diseases and health and safety laws. These are not always only about public health. During the colonial period public health regulations were used to justify racial segregation. In Dar es Salaam, the mile-long road *Nazi Mmoja* that separates off the African-inhabited Kariakoo from the downtown business area inhabited by East African Asians, and the wealthy suburbs which were the domain of the white colonial officers and settlers, was originally intended as a *cordon sanitaire* to stop the African population from infecting the white population with diseases such as malaria, and by a criminalized 'underclass' of young African men (Burton 2005).[6]

In postcolonial Tanzania, there are the annual health inspections known as *Operation Safi* (*safi* means 'clean' in Kiswahili). Villages are toured by health officers, and infringements are met with fines. The inspection is countered by small acts which signify the irrelevance of such exercises – such as boiling water and putting it in a bottle solely to serve the inspector just on that one day of the year. The bylaws dealing with the 'misleading' traditions of the Nyakyusa could easily be seen as falling into the category of a disciplining postcolonial public health law.

I was not, however, convinced that the bylaws were a straightforward instance of public health law, or would even be very effective as a tool to prevent the spread of infectious disease. There seemed to be more efficient ways of achieving that goal. For example, while the stipulation that everyone should sleep under a mosquito net at funerals certainly engaged with a key message that was being promoted vigorously by the National Malaria Control Programme from the late 1990s onwards, it was no more than a partial measure. Most nights of the year, people do not sleep at funerals, and yet, the bylaws failed to consider everyday use of mosquito nets. Often in households that own just one net, the male head of the household would sleep in the only bed with a mosquito net, and his wife and children – the members of the family most vulnerable to severe malaria – would usually sleep without a net together on a mat on the floor. Surely, if the DMO was serious about controlling malaria, he would consider how the most vulnerable members of the population slept at home, not only how they sleep on special occasions? This did not seem to be the case: instead the focus was clearly on the 'irrational' and traditional behaviour of the local population at funerals.

Blaming the spread of disease on tradition and superstition is a common phenomenon in public health, and conveniently obscures structural reasons for the spread of disease (Yoder 1997). Examples include the absence of clean water in many parts of Kyela District, and the high water table which made it difficult for people to build latrines that do not collapse, or the apathy in giving out public health messages, perhaps best exemplified by the boxes of booklets about HIV that languished for months in an office at the District Hospital in seeming disregard of the fact that the District faced one of the highest rates of HIV in the country. A focus on superstition also serves to distinguish differences in social status and expertise (Pigg 1996). Many medical professionals in Kyela District saw the crowds at funerals as 'unsanitary subjects', and blamed them for the diseases from which they suffered (Briggs and Briggs 2003). On the face of it, the rationale behind the bylaws has much in common with colonial public health in that it gains its authority from its own representation of an African population as 'backward'.

However, to understand these bylaws as some kind of postcolonial control which seeks to draw colonial-style distinctions between the 'civilized' and the 'backward' or between the government and the governed is too simplistic. The 'experts' and 'leaders' pushing forward the bylaws were also Nyakyusa – and while their status might have led them to wish to distance and differentiate themselves from the majority of the population of peasant farmers in Kyela District, to some extent they would also be expected to participate in the very practices that they criticized. It was not only the more elite members of the community who wished to see these traditions disappear. The DMO made it clear to me that the consultation exercise had revealed strong opinions about tradition in the District. He told me that people did not wish to stop at supporting bylaws that were concerned with the spread of infectious diseases – in fact, he said that the Ward Development Committees were 'very aggressive' in their desire to add to the list of undesirable traditions. His observation can be backed up by my own numerous interviews and conversations between 2000 and 2009 which almost reproduced word for word strong objections against 'traditions' that were 'bad for development'. It is worth noting at this point that magical harm is associated with an anti-development stance.

The Ward Development Committees added bylaws that were less clearly related to infectious disease control. They banned certain 'feasts' that punctuate the life cycle: *ukupanja ubufyele* – the food cooked for a mother after her first baby is born; *ipijilo* and *kande* – food cooked on the day of a burial and on the days of mourning thereafter; *nendengepo* and *twangalepo* – feasts prepared at inheritance, when a woman returns from 'resting' with her parents to her husband's home, after either a conflict, or his death; and *ukujola imindu* – the food given to the wives of a dead man's brothers after they have swept the burial ground. The only feasts that are not included in the bylaws are those that are concerned with marriage and weddings. All of these meals involved obligatory gift exchanges between classes of relatives, neighbours and friends, and it is argued that they place an unnecessary burden of expectation on the poor. It was also stipulated that young men should be able to build themselves brick houses, before building one for their fathers; and corrections were made to traditions that acted to exclude and dispossess widows of their own and their husband's property. These additions seemed at first to have more to do with economy or what is commonly referred to as 'development' (*maendeleo*) in Tanzania, than they had anything to do with public health.

Just to confuse matters, it seemed that higher up the political ladder, legislating *against* tradition, was indeed unpopular. I had expected this from the majority of people in Kyela – not from the Regional Office and Ministries. Higher-level officials seemed instead to share my initial romanticizing of the sharing of feasts and exchange of gifts as somehow 'community building' – developing a sense of '*umoja*' (unity) as the District Law Officer suggested in an interview in 2009. In 2002, I heard that the Regional Commissioner (RC) had not approved the bylaws, and that they had stalled somewhere in the parliament in Dodoma, but I was assured by local leaders at the time that they had eventually been signed, and were now fully in operation. The DMO had then explained to me the RC's objection in terms of the difference between physicians and politicians – he told me that 'you would have to be a doctor to understand that these traditions are bad, and they are good for politicians – when they go to funerals it is a venue – a good venue – they can talk about many issues when they go there to sympathise – it is very political there.' So, I was not completely surprised to learn when I returned in 2009 and discussed the bylaws with the District law officer (*bwana sheria*) that the bylaws had *never been passed*. They had been 'sent back' because, as she told me, 'it is an African tradition for people to gather and offer comfort and support at a funeral, and to ban this is a very bad thing to do'. She told me that the District Court was powerless to implement the bylaws, and they were not able to impose fines – if someone 'broke' the bylaws, nothing could be done. And yet there seemed to be very little awareness of this 'fact' that there really were *no* bylaws at all against the 'misleading traditions of the Nyakyusa'. Indeed, the vast majority of people who I knew were operating on the understanding that the bylaws were official and firmly established. Perhaps the only hint was that although there was a lot of talk about how necessary the bylaws were, and although their 'existence' had brought about certain changes to funerals, I never succeeded in tracking down an actual case where a person had been fined for infringing them. I heard of cases like this, but once I followed them, inevitably they disappeared into nothing.

To summarize, these bylaws – designed to stop certain traditions – were initially designed as a public health measure to prevent the spread of infectious disease. However, they did not seem to be fit for purpose – there are more effective ways of controlling disease than changing the shape of funerals. One could take from this that the bylaws are about more than controlling disease – perhaps they are about controlling and regulating a population, or an exercise in victim-blaming. But all of these explanations and analyses imply a top-down intervention, and it is clear that those at the very top did not wish to have anything to do with changing or destroying Nyakyusa tradition. Instead, as we will see, the agenda was being set 'lower down' by community leaders, economically ambitious young men and traditional healers. What was it that they wanted to change that was not immediately visible to myself, or to the national government?

INDIGENOUS LAW AND WITCHCRAFT

The first clue to the popularity of the bylaws came from members of the Society for Traditional Healers, who to my surprise were strongly in favour of the bylaws. They told me the traditions of the Nyakyusa were 'very bad indeed'. Somehow I had expected traditional healers to be in favour of tradition (Marsland 2007). They slowly persuaded me however, that feasting and the exchange of gifts was not always the source of unity, reciprocity and mutual support that I had imagined.

It took me a long time to appreciate the potentially negative side of all the feasts and reciprocal relationships based on giving. Conventionally, reciprocity is considered to be a positive thing. Mauss classically demonstrated in 1923 (Mauss 1970 [1923]) how contracts and relationships are made by gifts that are given and returned, and this is echoed by Monica Wilson who described 'the enjoyment of good company' and the 'mutual aid and sympathy' that come from 'eating and drinking together' in Nyakyusa villages. She argued that the giving of feasts 'tends to enhance the solidarity of kin groups and villages' (1951a: 71). Giving 'makes' and repairs relationships. Initially it seemed odd to me that this kind of giving should be so strongly discouraged.

I encountered two main criticisms of these feasts. The first is that they are expensive and a waste of money, if not an opportunity for parasitism of the greedy who wish to freeload resources that could better be used for a household's 'development' (school fees, building a brick house, investment in small business or agricultural inputs). The second resonates with less idealistic views of the gift in the anthropological literature (Mauss 1970 [1924], Bourdieu 1997, Derrida 1992, Schrift 1997), which see a darker side to gift relations – a poison, a violence, an obligation that cannot be met, a relation based on inequality, an impossibility. In this view of gift exchange, reciprocity can be dangerous.

What drives many people in Kyela to take part in practices that they themselves view as 'excessive' consumption? Perhaps here, in the context of the theme of this book, we can remind ourselves that for anthropologists reciprocity (contract and exchange) can be included under the rubric of law (Malinowski 1926 cited in Nader 2002: 85 and Merry 2006: 101). Furthermore, if reciprocity can be understood as within the domain of law, then a failure to respect its rule can presumably be punished. And indeed, according to popular opinion in Kyela it is. Marcel Mauss drew our attention to the double meaning of the gift as both gift and poison. The bond that it creates,

> ...between master and servant, creditor and debtor is a magical and ambiguous thing. It is at the same time good and dangerous; it is thrown at the feet of the contracting party in a gesture that is at the same time one of confidence and one of prudence, of distrust and defiance.
>
> (Mauss 1997 [1924]: 30)

The gifts given and received at funerals are presented in this spirit (even if the embodied practice of giving and receiving is carried out with grace). If the amount of food given towards a feast does not translate into a satisfying meal for those who receive it, guests may complain among themselves, and for the Nyakyusa this is a very dangerous moment indeed. The danger is increased by the intimacy of the kinship group. Marshall Sahlins (2013) has written of the 'mutuality of being' that brings family members together. The conditions of 'intimacy and trust' (Geschiere 2013) set up the conditions of vulnerability that witchcraft requires. In Kyela, the complaints of kin, supported by neighbours, 'murmuring' as Monica Wilson described it, about an inadequate return for a funeral gift – can constitute a form of witchcraft known as *imbepo sya bandu* – the 'breath of men' (Wilson 1951a), or the 'words of the people' as one of my informants put it.[7] Such displeasure and murmuring can make a person ill, and if they do not recognize that its source is an insult to certain members of the community and take steps to remedy their error, then the illness will eventually lead to death. As Mauss put it, a gift 'is always liable to turn against one of them if he would fail to honour the law' (1997 [1924]: 30).

Almost all of the 'misleading traditions' listed in the bylaws are those that, if not observed, can lead to anger, and potentially *imbepo sya bandu*. These words of magical harm can be construed as a form of indigenous law, which could be viewed as a kind of unofficial 'community court' (*makama ya jamii*),[8] in which antisocial behaviour is 'discussed' and *imbepo sya bandu* are used to 'bring legitimate punishment on evil doers' (Wilson 1951a: 102). As one old man confided in me, 'if someone has done something bad that's it. He will go. He will leave'.

These days this indigenous law exists in an uneasy parallel with state law. It operates in a space where the state cannot easily enter – in the realm of sociability and obligation, and the punishment that it metes out: magical harm is one that the state can neither tolerate, nor even recognize as real. While the *mafumu* (headmen), *abamanga* (defenders) and other influential men with 'ability' would have once managed this system on behalf of a chief, since independence the traditional roles of chief and headmen have been abolished, and all that is left are the descendants of headmen and defenders who are rumoured to still hold this power. Their status is ambiguous. On the one hand, they are feared and respected for upholding customary values, while on the other they are hated for going too far in an unregulated and unofficial magical sphere of indigenous law. One can no longer say, as Monica Wilson once wrote, that a 'clear distinction is made by the Nyakyusa between the legal and illegal use of power derived from pythons' (1951a). These days many people say that *imbepo sya bandu* has gone too far. To these critics this indigenous law has become twisted – it allows greedy witches, hungry for food and beer, to use their strength to force others to feed them at times when they are at their most vulnerable (when they are bereaved). In 2002, the general opinion seemed to be that there had been a veritable explosion of deaths related to unsatisfied and unsated witches after funeral feasts. 'Too many people are dying' one informant after another told me – and there were even cases of mini-epidemics of deaths caused by *imbepo sya bandu* in some villages. *Imbepo sya bandu* and funeral feasts had become a public health problem.

The reason why the bylaws are so popular in Kyela is because people hope that they will reduce the extent and power of *imbepo sya bandu*. By making antisocial acts of sociability, such as bringing gifts and taking part in feasts at funerals, illegal they create an environment in which complaints and murmurings are no longer sanctioned, and thus limit the remit of this particular form of indigenous law which is seen to have gone too far. Indeed, by the time of my return to the field in 2009, people were saying that witchcraft – or *imbepo* – was not as prevalent as it had once been.

The bylaws against the 'misleading traditions of the Nyakyusa' then, seem to be an ingenious kind of anti-witchcraft measure. The 'official' legal stance in the Witchcraft Ordinance inherited from the colonial period is that witchcraft is non-existent. The bylaws themselves do not reference witchcraft or *imbepo sya bandu* at all. Instead they allude to 'misleading tradition'. It seems fitting then, that the bylaws do not officially exist. And just like witchcraft – which is invisible or transparent – the bylaws do not make their purpose visible in their written form, and yet 'everyone' knows that combating this particular form of witchcraft is part of their purpose.

CONCLUSION

To conclude, the bylaws against the 'misleading traditions of the Nyakyusa' solve a problem for both the state and the victims of witchcraft. The state is damned if it makes use of the law to intervene against witchcraft, and it is damned if it does not. If it chooses to make visible the harm caused when people accuse individuals of witchcraft then it fails to protect the victims of witchcraft. If it makes the harm caused by witches to their victims visible, by attempting to prosecute witches, the inevitable failure to reduce witchcraft will undermine the public's perception of its strength. If it ignores the problem, then its citizens will perceive that the state does not care for their wellbeing. The difficulty here is that two incompatible visions of reality are being brought to bear on a problem. At the risk of oversimplifying, we can say that, for the state, witchcraft cannot exist, while for the citizen it does.

The bylaws solve this problem because they operate at different onto-logical levels. On the surface they are a tool of public health. They are a straightforward intervention in the unhygienic practices that take place at funerals. At this level the magical harm caused by witchcraft is not visible. From the point of view of the local population, however, they are more than that. The reference to the 'misleading traditions' that take place at funerals and other feasts makes very visible the fact that they are an intervention against a particular form of magical harm – *imbepo sya bandu*. The bylaws do not prosecute those who speak these words of harm, and they do not prosecute those who accuse others of *imbepo sya bandu*. Instead they target practices carried out by the whole community – and by doing so they make it almost impossible for this particular form of magical harm to take place.

NOTES

1 The fieldwork for this research was funded by the ESRC (Award no. R00429934295) between 2000 and 2002, the Hayter Fund and the Munro Fund in 2007 and 2009, and the Carnegie Trust in 2009. Many thanks to Toby Kelly and Ian Harper for their comments on early drafts, and to Yuda Maninga and Coseman Busi Nnwafu for research assistance. Timothy Mwakasekele has provided essential support for this research throughout.

2 Bunyakyusa – the 'country of the Nyakyusa' was known as Rungwe District during the colonial period. It was divided into Rungwe and Kyela Districts some time after independence.

3 Stacey Langwick (2011) has written extensively on how the anti-witchcraft ordinances worked primarily to discipline healers in colonial Tanganyika. During the *maji-maji* rebellion (1905–1907) healers gave medicines which reputedly turned bullets into water to rebels who were fighting the German colonial authorities. The first 1922 Antiwitchcraft Ordinance was intro-duced by the British as a direct reaction to this. Healers were suspect dis-sidents whose practices were to be shaped by law into the innocuous dis-pensing of herbal, non-magical medicines.

4 Sukumaland is a region in the north-west of Tanzania near Lake Victoria, and is named after the main ethnic group who live there – the Sukuma.
5 See also Maia Green's (2005) argument that state tolerance of witch cleansing in southern Tanzania 'entrenches' beliefs in witchcraft.
6 For more on public health and colonial segregation see Curtin 1992, Frenkel and Western 1988 and Goerg 1998.
7 Favret-Saada 1980, Tambiah 1968 and West 2007 have all written about the power of words to cause magical harm.
8 Conversation with Yuda Maninga and Nico, 15 June 2009.

REFERENCES

Abrahams, R. 1994. *Witchcraft in contemporary Tanzania.* Cambridge: African Studies Centre
   1987. 'Sungusungu: village vigilante groups in Tanzania', *African Affairs* 86: 179–96
Ashforth, A. 2005. *Witchcraft, Violence and Democracy in South Africa.* Chicago: University of Chicago Press
Auslander, M. 1993. '"Open the Wombs!": The Symbolic Politics of Modern Ngoni Witchfinding', in Comaroff, J. and Comaroff, J. L. (eds.), *Modernity and Its Malcontents: Ritual and Power in Postcolonial Africa.* Chicago: University of Chicago Press
Bourdieu, P. 1997. 'Marginalia – some additional notes on the gift', in Schrift, D. (ed.), *The Logic of the Gift.* London: Routledge
Briggs, C. and Briggs, C. M. 2003. *Stories in the Time of Cholera: Racial Profiling During a Medical Nightmare.* Berkeley: University of California Press
Bukurura, S. 1994. 'Sungusungu and banishment of suspected witches in Kahama', in R. Abrahams (ed.), *Witchcraft in contemporary Tanzania.* Cambridge: African Studies Centre
Burton, A. 2005. *African Underclass: Urbanisation, Crime and Colonial Order in Dar es Salaam.* Oxford: James Currey
Ciekawy, D. 2006. 'Politicians, party politics and the control of harmful magic', in Kiernan, J. (ed.), *The Power of the Occult in Africa.* Berlin, Hamburg, Munster: LIT Verlag
   1998. 'Witchcraft in Statecraft: Five Technologies of Power in Colonial and Postcolonial Coastal Kenya', *African Studies Review* 41: 119–141
   1997. 'Policing Religious Practice in Contemporary Coastal Kenya', *Political and Legal Anthropology Review* 20: 62–72
Ciekawy, D. and Geschiere, P. 1998. 'Containing Witchcraft: Conflicting Scenarios in Postcolonial Africa', *African Studies Review* 41: 1–14
Comaroff, J. L. and Comaroff, J. 2006. 'Law and disorder in the postcolony: an introduction', in Comaroff, J. and Comaroff, J. L. (eds.), *Law and Disorder in the Postcolony.* Chicago: Chicago University Press

Comaroff, J. and Comaroff, J. L. 2004. 'Criminal Justice, Cultural Justice: the Limits of Liberalism and the Pragmatics of Difference in the New South Africa', *American Ethnologist* 31: 188–204

Curtin, P. 1992. 'Medical Knowledge and Urban Planning in Colonial Tropical Africa', in Feierman, S. and Janzen, J. (eds.), *The Social Basis of Health and Healing in Africa*. Berkeley, Los Angeles, Oxford: University of California Press

Derrida, J. 1992. *Given time: 1. Counterfeit money*. Chicago and London: University of Chicago Press

Evans-Pritchard, E. E. 1976 (1937). *Witchcraft, oracles and magic among the Azande*. Oxford: Oxford University Press

Favret-Saada, J. 1980. *Deadly Words: Witchcraft in the Bocage*. Cambridge: Cambridge University Press

Feierman, S. 2010. 'Healing as social criticism in the time of colonial conquest', *African Studies* 54: 73–88

1999. 'Colonizers, Scholars, and the Creation of Invisible Histories', in Bonell, V. E. and Hunt, L. (eds.), *Beyond the Cultural Turn: New Directions in the Study of Society and Culture*. Berkeley, Los Angeles, London: University of California Press

1985. 'Struggles for control: the social roots of health and healing in modern Africa', *African Studies Review* 28: 73–147

Fields, K. E. 1982. 'Political Contingencies of Witchcraft in Colonial Central Africa: Culture and State in Marxist Theory', *Canadian Journal of African Studies* 16: 567–93

Fisiy, C. F. 1998. 'Containing Occult Practices: Witchcraft Trials in Cameroon', *African Studies Review* 41: 143–163

1990. *Palm Tree Justice in the Bertoua Court of Appeal: the Witchcraft Cases*. Leiden, Netherlands: African Studies Centre

Fisiy, C. F. and Rowlands, M. 1989. 'Sorcery and the Law in Modern Cameroon', *Culture and History* 6: 63–84

Fisiy, C. F. and Geschiere, P. 1990. 'Judges and Witches, or How is the State to Deal with Witchcraft? Examples from Southeast Cameroon', *Cahiers d'Etudes Africaines* 118: 135–156

Frenkel, S. and Western, J. 1988. 'Pretext or Prophylaxis? Racial Segregation and Malarial Mosquitoes in a British Tropical Colony: Sierra Leone', *Annals of the Association of American Geographers* 78: 211–228

Geschiere, P. 2013. *Witchcraft, Intimacy and Trust: Africa in Comparison*. Chicago: University of Chicago Press

2006. 'Witchcraft and the limits of the law', in Comaroff, J. and Comaroff, J. L. (eds.), *Law and Disorder in the Postcolony*. Chicago: University of Chicago Press

1997. *The Modernity of Witchcraft, Politics and the Occult in Postcolonial Africa*. Charlottesville: University of Virginia Press

Geschiere, P. and Fisiy, C. 1994. 'Domesticating Personal Violence – Witch-Craft, Courts and Confessions in Cameroon', *Africa* 3: 323–41

Goerg, O. 1998. 'From Hill Station (Freetown) to Downtown Conakry (First Ward): Comparing French and British Approaches to Segregation in Colonial Cities at the Beginning of the Twentieth Century', *Canadian Journal of African Studies* 32: 1–21

Green, M. 2005. 'Discourses on Inequality. Poverty, Public Bads and Entrenching Witchcraft in Post-adjustment Tanzania', *Anthropological Theory* 5: 247–266

1997. 'Witchcraft Suppression Practices and Movements: Public Politics and the Logic of Purification', *Comparative Studies in Society and History* 39: 319–345

1994. 'Shaving witchcraft in Ulanga. Kunyolewa and the Catholic church', in Abrahams, R. (ed.), *Witchcraft in contemporary Tanzania*. Cambridge: African Studies Centre

Green, M. and Mesaki, S. 2005. 'The Birth of the 'Salon': Poverty, 'Modernization', and Dealing with Witchcraft in Southern Tanzania', *American Ethnologist* 32: 371–388

Jindra, M. and Noret, J. 2011. 'Funerals in Africa. An Introduction', in Jindra, M. and Noret, J. (eds.), *Funerals in Africa. Explorations of a Social Phenomenon*. New York and Oxford: Berghahn Books

Langwick, S. A. 2011. *Bodies, politics and African Healing*. Bloomington and Indianapolis: Indiana University Press

2008. 'Articulate(d) Bodies: Traditional Medicine in a Tanzanian Hospital', *American Ethnologist* 35, 428–439

Last, M. 1999. 'Understanding health', in Allen, T. and Skelton, T. (eds.), *Culture and Global Change*. London: Routledge

Marsland, R. 2014. 'Who are the 'Public' in Public Health? Debating Crowds, Populations and Publics in Tanzania', in Prince, R. and Marsland, R. (eds.), *Making and Unmaking Public Health In Africa: Ethnographic Perspectives*. Athens: Ohio University Press

2007. 'The Modern Traditional Healer: Locating 'Hybridity' in Modern Traditional Medicine, Southern Tanzania', *Journal of Southern African Studies* 33: 751–765

Marwick, M. 1950. 'Another Modern Anti-witchcraft Movement in East Central Africa', *Africa* 20: 100–113

Mauss, M. 1970 [1923]. *The Gift: Forms and Functions of Exchange in Archaic Societies*. London, Cohen and West

1997 [1924]. 'Gift, Gift', in A. D. Schrift (ed.), *The Logic of the Gift. Toward an Ethic of Generosity*. New York, London, Routledge

Merry, S. E. 2006. 'Anthropology and International Law', *Annual Review of Anthropology* 35: 99–116

Mesaki, S. 1994. 'Witch-killing in Sukumaland', in R. Abrahams (ed.), *Witchcraft in Contemporary Tanzania*. Cambridge: Cambridge University Press

Meyer, B. 1999. *Translating the Devil: Religion and Modernity among the Ewe in Ghana*. Edinburgh: Edinburgh University Press (for International African Institute)

Nader, L. 2002. *The life of the Law: Anthropological Projects*. Berkeley, Los Angeles, London, University of California Press

National Malaria Control Programme 1999. *Plan of Action for Accelerated Implementation of Malaria Control in Tanzania*. Dar es Salaam, Ministry of Health, United Republic of Tanzania/World Health Organization

Niehaus, I. A. 2001. *Witchcraft, Power and Politics: Exploring the Occult in the South African Lowveld*. London: Pluto Press

Orde Browne, G. S. J. 1935. 'Witchcraft and British Colonial Rule', *Africa* viii: 481–487

Pigg, S. L. 1996. 'The Credible and the Credulous: the Question of 'Villagers' Beliefs' in Nepal', *Cultural Anthropology* 11: 160–201

Richards, A. I. 1935. 'A Modern Movement of Witch-finders', *Africa* 8: 448–461

Roberts, C. C. 1935. 'Witchcraft and Colonial Legislation', *Africa*, 8: 488–494

Rutherford, B. 1999. 'To Find an African Witch: Anthropology, Modernity and Witch-finding in North-west Zimbabwe', *Critique of Anthropology* 19: 89–109

Sahlins, M. 2013. *What Kinship is . . . And Is Not*. Chicago: University of Chicago Press

Schrift, A. D. 1997. *The Logic of the Gift: Toward an Ethic of Generosity*. New York, London, Routledge

Smith, J. H. 2008. *Bewitching Development. Witchcraft and the Reinvention of Development in Neoliberal Kenya*. Chicago and London: University of Chicago Press

2005. 'Buying a Better Witch Doctor: Witch-finding, Neoliberalism, and the Development Imagination in the Taita Hills, Kenya', *American Ethnologist* 32: 141–158

Tambiah, S. J. 1968. 'The Magical Power of Words', *Man* N. S. 3: 175–208

Waite, G. 1992. 'Public Health in Precolonial East-Central Africa', in Feierman, S. and Janzen, J. (eds.), *The Social Basis of Health and Healing in Africa*. Berkeley, Los Angeles, London: University of California Press

West, H. G. 2007. *Ethnographic Sorcery*. Chicago: Chicago University Press

2005. *Kupilikula: Governance and the Invisible Realm in Mozambique*. Chicago and London: University of Chicago Press

Willis, R. G., 1970. 'Instant Millennium. The Sociology of African Witch Cleansing Cults', in Douglas, M. (ed.), *Witchcraft, Confessions and Accusations*. London: Tavistock

1968. 'Kamcape: an Anti-sorcery Movement in South-west Tanzania' *Africa* 38: 1–15

Wilson, M. 1977. *For Men and Elders: Change in the Relations of Generations and of Men and Women among the Nyakyusa-Ngonde People 1875–1971*. London: International African Institute

1959. *Communal Rituals of the Nyakyusa*. Oxford: Oxford University Press

1957. *Rituals of Kinship among the Nyakyusa*. Oxford: Oxford University Press

1951a. *Good Company: A Study of Nyakyusa Age Villages*. London, New York, Toronto, Oxford University Press for the International African Institute

1951b. 'Witch Beliefs and Social Structure', *American Journal of Sociology* 56: 307–13

Yoder, P. S. 1997. 'Negotiating Relevance, Belief, Knowledge and Practice in International Health Projects', *Medical Anthropology Quarterly* 11: 131–4

CHAPTER TWO

NON-HUMAN SUFFERING: A HUMANITARIAN PROJECT

Miriam Ticktin

In May 2013, New York City mayoral candidates engaged in a debate about their support for animals and animal rights, each trying to outdo the other in showing how much they cared (Taylor 2013). A few days earlier, the New York Attorney General's office had announced a new initiative that focused on animal protection, with two goals: reducing abuses in 'puppy-mills' and shutting down dog-fighting rings in the state (Kaplan and Pilon 2013). And a few months before that, when Hurricane Sandy hit New York and New Jersey, a new set of NGOs came out in full force specifically to rescue animals hurt by the wind and water.

A focus on animal suffering is increasingly present in American life. That said, not all forms of suffering are given the same visibility or moral weight: while the New York City mayoral candidates showed their opposition to the horse carriage industry, calling it 'inhumane' – a word used perhaps surprisingly often in relation to animals – state-makers across the country simultaneously introduced laws making it harder to investigate cruelty in slaughterhouses by making it illegal to take photographs, and making it a crime for animal welfare advocates to cover their affiliations in job applications at plants. These laws enforce the need to turn over evidence of abuse within 24–48 hours, making it impossible to really document illegal activity. So how, why and to what end are certain kinds of animal suffering being rendered visible?

While the concern with animal suffering is far from new, this chapter will suggest that just as human suffering today is largely rendered visible and responded to by the techniques and technologies of humanitarianism, so too, increasingly, is the suffering of animals. That is, there is a simultaneous expansion of the subject of humanity protected by humanitarianism, and its concomitant technologies. While previously, animal suffering might have been the domain of animal welfare experts, biologists or ethologists, today we see animal suffering increasingly represented through the expert discourses that accompany humanitarian forms – in particular, expertise that exists at the intersection of law and medicine. What does non-human suffering look like at this intersection? And what is the relationship between human and non-human forms of suffering if they are rendered visible and knowable by the same technologies?

I will begin by discussing the expansion of humanitarianism to include non-humans, and then think about how medical and legal epistemologies and institutions shape non-human suffering, rendering it visible and treatable in certain forms. My argument is that the visibility of suffering is related to its perceived causes, but what we understand as the causes are themselves shaped by the humanitarian logics and technologies, even as these humanitarian technologies are shifting and changing.

THE EXPANDING POLITICS OF HUMANITARIANISM

In January 2010, newspapers carried a series of stories about homeless Chihuahuas in California being rescued and flown to new homes around North America – from New York City to Houston to Edmonton. In one case, Virgin Airlines donated $12 000 in travel costs for the dogs and their human companions. These flights – termed 'Chihuahua airlifts' – were organised by philanthropists along with the American Society for Prevention of Cruelty to Animals (ASPCA). In one case, the New York Times wrote that '15 homeless dogs from the Bay Area were flown to Kennedy by the airline so they could be adopted by New Yorkers' (Fernandez 2010). Another article stated, 'animal lovers are determined to rescue those that they can from a sad and lonely life in a shelter in California' (Bustamante 2011). Upon arrival, they were given behavioural and medical assessments, to make sure they had adjusted and were fit for adoption. There were people lined up, waiting for the arrival of these dogs, because as one of them said, many 'may come from puppy mills or brokers where they often live in horrible conditions' (Bustamante 2011).

Another story was carried in May 2010, about a two year old female pit bull who was doused in gasoline and set on fire in Baltimore, MD. A young policewoman happened to notice the smoke, and put out the flames with her sweater, but the dog, subsequently named Phoenix, survived for only four days, having received burns on over 95% of her body. The story was picked up in a matter of hours and disseminated nationwide in newspapers, on radio and TV and on websites. The intensity of the response was striking: people responded by offering a $26 000 reward for the culprits; others held a candlelight vigil (Siebert 2010).

Such stories foregrounding the suffering and rescue of animals are becoming increasingly common in American media, and indeed, the story line is familiar. The victims being rescued here resemble those at the heart of humanitarian narratives: poor starving children, innocent women. These stories are powerful; as many scholars have shown, humanitarian narratives helped shape the subject of humanity that we now understand as 'human', joining humanity with its cognate, humane. That is, as Thomas Laqueur has argued, in the late eighteenth century, the human began to be conceived not as a physiological fact but as an 'ethical subject – the protagonist – of humanitarian narrative' (Laqueur 2009: 38). 'Humanity' referred to this shared sentiment of sympathy or benevolence – it did not necessarily mean shared species or biological fact. As Lynn Festa writes in her discussion of humanitarian sensibility, also in the eighteenth century, 'sentimentality is a literary form: a rhetorical structure designed both to incite feelings in readers and to direct those feelings towards their "proper" objects' (Festa 2010: 7). And yet, with the humanitarian narrative, this sentimental form rests on an unstable definition of humanity – it relies on its malleability. On the one hand, the lack of rigorous definition of the human allows for an expansion of the types of life it includes; on the other hand, because of the instability at the heart of the sentimental literary form, it can work on a case-by-case basis, providing a poor or inconsistent basis for ethics (Festa 2010: 5).

If the content of this sentimental form is flexible, what precisely evokes this compassion today – what makes one type of content more compelling than another? The more recent histories and anthropologies of humanitarianism suggest that while humanitarianism is premised on the moral imperative to relieve suffering, whatever its cause, form or context (at least in the form perhaps best embodied by Médecins Sans Frontières or MSF), the innocent victim is often the most morally legitimate sufferer (Ticktin 2011a). Children are perhaps the most exemplary humanitarian subjects today; they are the archetypal innocent victims. It is no accident that children are the face of humanitarianism in fundraising or publicity campaigns; they serve as generic human subjects, outside time and place. Women, too, can more easily inhabit this position of innocent victim, although this gendered subject is also clearly a racialised one, where (certain) women of the global south or 'Third World' are perceived as the most innocent (read 'passive') victims in need of rescue from their (barbaric) men or 'cultures'.[1]

The politics of humanitarianism has entailed both the search for and production of innocent victims, since the 'pure' victim is a placeholder, always just out of reach. There are child soldiers, for instance, as Liisa Malkki points out, which troubles the image of the child as innocent. Indeed, child soldiers are seen as an abomination, a category mistake that leads to them being labelled 'youth' or 'teens' as opposed to 'children' whenever possible, to set aside and protect a time of innocence, when they are still unworldly and untainted (Malkki 2010: 63–4).

Insofar as humanitarianism is dependent on the figure of the innocent victim as the highest moral good – the goal driving humanitarian action, in an attempt to steer clear of explicit political solutions or goals[2] – I want to suggest that it works through a logic of *expansion*, in which new territories of innocence must be discovered and incorporated. The innocent sufferer can never be isolated for long enough to keep it uncorrupted by history or context. In this sense, humanitarianism is constantly displacing politics to the limit of innocence, a border which must be drawn and redrawn.

While animals are selectively incorporated into this politics of humanity in these new ways – and of course the flipside and larger context for this is the overwhelming nature of institutions and practices like factory farming and animal experimentation, which touch billions of animals, leaving just a few to be saved – I do not mean to suggest that they represent a novel terrain of innocence; they have been variously included in and excluded from this category of universal solidarity over time. In the eighteenth century, the sentimental mode that eventually turned into abolitionism was 'notoriously indiscriminate in its choice of objects, embracing not only human beings but lapdogs, dying birds, and (as one eighteenth-century critic grumbled), "efts, toads, bats, every thing that hath life"' (Festa 2010: 5). Indeed, Joanna Bourke (2011) writes how in 1872, a woman known as 'the Earnest

Englishwoman' asked to let women 'become animal' – that is, to be treated as animals – in order to reap the benefits they were denied because they were not part of 'mankind'. So what is new here; how has this politics changed?

In his discussion of the relationship between terrorists and humanity, Faisal Devji (2008), following Hannah Arendt, suggests that 'global humanity' was produced by the very technology that enabled its destruction – i.e. the atom bomb. This technology helped 'humanity' emerge as a global historical actor for the first time. In this sense, global humanity cannot be understood outside the technologies that helped to produce it. Today, humanitarianism relies heavily on the technologies and logics associated with medicine and law. In particular, the 'new humanitarianism', which began with Médecins Sans Frontières (or Doctors Without Borders) in 1971 and is the dominant contemporary form of humanitarianism, focuses primarily on health, suffering and bodily integrity. Their goal has not been to improve the human condition broadly conceived, but to alleviate suffering wherever it occurs, in the form of emergency medical care. They go to crisis zones – wars and natural disasters – and in the name of humanity, they intervene to save lives. They have developed infrastructures, kits and techniques to help in this quest, drawing heavily on those developed for emergency medicine. Even if the new humanitarianism is most closely associated with medicine and health, it also engages in legal support and legislative reform (although much less so than human rights regimes). For instance, in the 1990s in France, MSF worked to provide legal support to people without access to healthcare, helping to draw up the law on universal healthcare coverage (Neuman 2011). Newer work by humanitarians on access to medication has required an engagement with trade law, and legal matters of property.[3]

Insofar as humanitarianism is expanding to include non-human animals, animal suffering is increasingly recognised and governed by technologies that exist at the interface of law and medicine. Yet these technologies are themselves changing, developing in the face of this expansion – how are they helping to shape both humanity and humanitarianism? Humanitarianism often works by inductive reasoning – that is, humanitarians read certain indicators as signs of suffering.[4] If new technologies help us see differently – if we require different indicators of suffering – how might our sensibilities in turn shift? What does suffering look like at this intersection? First, we will turn to the realm of medicine and health.

MEDICINE AND HEALTH

Humanitarianism has helped to structure the forms in which suffering is rendered visible, and the sites and ways in which health practitioners address it. Many of these forms carry over now to non-humans.

Emergencies and disasters

Humanitarians find one of their clearest callings in the arena of natural disasters, where they work to provide aid after earthquakes, tsunamis, hurricanes and so on. As MSF reported, after the Indian Ocean earthquake and tsunami in 2004, they received more money than they could distribute, and asked donors to either keep their money or donate to a different crisis. Indeed, some put the total amount of humanitarian aid donated at $14 billion. This is largely because the victims of natural disasters are seen as innocent sufferers, the victims of natural forces; there is no moral distinction to make about who is guilty and who is innocent, so people feel good about giving. Of course, the humanitarian industry has intervened and provided aid in many places since that tsunami, including in Haiti after the earthquake in 2010, and in Japan, following the earthquake and tsunami in 2011. But in these latter cases, the humanitarian field has been slightly reconfigured. There is a new group of actors engaged in humanitarian response, and a new group of victims being rescued. Most notably, these actors include veterinary forensic scientists and a new breed of NGOs with whom they work; and the victims include not simply humans, but also animals.

Let me turn for a moment to veterinary forensic science; it is a new field of scientific expertise started in 2008, at the University of Florida, with the support of the ASPCA. The goal in applying forensic sciences to veterinary medicine is to aid in the understanding, prevention and prosecution of animal cruelty (Cooper and Cooper 2007). This set of experts is mobilised around identifying, measuring and alleviating animal suffering, and helping to promote animal and human health and welfare. They work in new, 'humanitarian' teams: they join with disaster response teams and emergency animal services and animal relief. For instance, veterinary forensic scientists work with the American Humane Association (AHA) who has a disaster response team; one of AHA's latest projects was a large-scale animal rescue operation in Japan, in response to the tsunami and earthquake. Interestingly, the AHA is an organisation that protects both animals and children, focusing on promoting their interconnected wellbeing; the focus on innocence here is amplified by dealing with both. Veterinary forensic scientists also work with the National Animal Rescue and Response Team, formed in 2006, when disasters like Hurricane Katrina 'impacted more people and their companion animals than in the history of the United States'. These groups and experts engage with the same emergency medical techniques and technologies as other (human) emergency response teams, often working on a model of crisis. They help to identify victims of disasters; they also help to identify whether an animal might have suffered.

So, while the AHA has been involved in animal relief since World War I, when the American War Department asked them to help animals used in war, the nature of how and where they address animal suffering has changed; now, they run a special animal emergency services programme, called 'Red Star Rescue' which goes to disaster scenes with experts, volunteers and mobile resources such as their 82-foot mobile truck/veterinary clinic, carrying rescue boats, emergency equipment, generators, food and medicine. They were active in rescuing animals during Hurricane Sandy, and recently they helped to shelter animals seized in a large-scale animal cruelty case. They respond all over the United States in cases of flood, wildfire, tornado and hurricanes. Their work in Japan and Haiti constitutes a first step into the international realm, aided by new communications technologies and networks.

The development of emergency medicine alongside humanitarian intervention has informed how animal suffering is now recognised and addressed. Without the technical skills and logic of emergency medicine, humanitarian intervention would not have been possible; progress in emergency medicine allowed doctors to treat patients at the site of the injury, rather than bringing the injured to the site of the doctors (i.e. the hospital). Following this logic, animals are now looked for at the site of natural disasters, caught in debris, and they are subject to medical intervention on site, and given shelter and food. Comparable techniques and tools are used for both humans and non-humans. With this focus on emergency, suffering is now identified in the exceptional moment of natural disasters; and here it is recognised in individual bodies – the cat lost in the hurricane, the dog injured by debris. This focus on emergency shapes what we see as the cause of suffering; we focus on the exceptional, often violent event, an aberration to a seemingly otherwise peaceful life (Calhoun 2008). This makes normal, 'everyday' types of suffering – and the structures of power that inform them – more difficult to see; in this sense, industrial farm animal production, which raises and kills over 10 billion animals per year yet does so precisely without event, becomes more difficult to see as animal 'suffering' or as harm.

Psychiatry and trauma

After witnessing the battle of Solferino in 1859, Henry Dunant helped to create the International Committee of the Red Cross (ICRC). That is, the humanitarianism from which our current humanitarian industry is most clearly descended was born to address casualties on the battle-field, in times of war and conflict, not simply in times of natural disaster. Initially, humanitarianism was to keep both soldiers and civilian casualties alive in the most basic ways during wartime, providing emergency medical care, food and shelter. But humanitarianism has expanded its reach in zones of conflict, now including the treatment for trauma or PTSD, and demonstrating that protecting humanity requires protecting a certain kind of mental as well as bodily integrity. The field of humanitarian psychiatry is a relatively new one, dating from the Armenian earthquake of 1988. According to Fassin and Rechtman (2009), it provides a way to name and diagnose suffering, from wars, exile and massacres to forced displacement, and to ask new questions about these old problems. I want to suggest that the new field of animal psychiatry contributes to an evolving humanitarian field.

Animal psychiatry – also called animal psychopathology – is also a relatively new field of expertise. From dogs on Prozac to relieve depression to cats with 'territorial disorders' and parrots treated for their jealousy, animal psychiatry is closely linked to the pharmaceutical industry. While the psychopathologies include depression, anxiety, obsessive compulsive disorder (OCD) and stress, I am most interested here in the expansion of PTSD to animals, as this is a medical diagnosis that can help to authenticate the suffering of (human) victims, working (among other things) to legitimise claims for asylum or requests for humanitarian aid.

Here, suffering is recognised beyond the breach of bodily integrity; there are new technologies that allow us to 'see' into the mind, to recognise emotional disturbance, and these ways of seeing carry over to animal lives. Suffering is recognised through forms of behaviour considered abnormal, but perhaps more significantly, it is increasingly identified through the physiology of psychology such as neuroscience, and its technologies like brain scans, which show impaired brain development (Carter et al. 2009). Scientists attribute such impaired development to traumatic experiences (Bradshaw et al. 2005). That is, suffering is now visible in both brain and behaviour.

The expansion of this medical diagnosis into the lives of animals carries over not only the symptoms but the same purported causes and contexts that produce these symptoms in humans: the diagnosis comes with an attendant cause. As with humans, events such as war, conflict and disaster set the stage for PTSD in animals. There are stories of military dogs in the Iraq war suffering from PTSD.[5] There are also stories of elephants with PTSD. The elephants who suffer from trauma, like humans, come out of conflict zones; they have watched their parents and elders being killed by poachers, and they have been displaced by the destruction (by humans) of their habitats. Scientists say that they have lost their 'social fabric'. They exhibit similar symptoms to humans, such as abnormal startle response, unpredictable asocial behaviour and hyperaggression – this includes young males who supposedly 'rape' and kill rhinoceroses, as well as killing humans – none of which is considered 'normal' elephant behaviour (Siebert 2006). Their brains confirm the trauma, showing impaired development. This has been diagnosed as a 'species-wide trauma' (Bradshaw et al. 2005; Bradshaw and Schore 2007) – a whole new category of suffering.

The causes, again, are related to the technologies that imagine and address suffering. Brain scans and behavioural cues trace certain kinds of events, particularly violent acts, which are also the causes of PTSD in humans. This leaves little space for longer-term histories as causes of suffering, which might include centuries-long projects of resource extraction or depletion. Does one ever get PTSD from a childhood of poverty?

Epidemics

Epidemics are another classic humanitarian problem. We need only think of MSF's role in the cholera epidemic in Haiti, which started in 2010. Yet with epidemics, increasingly, humanitarianism acts alongside biosecurity regimes in what Andrew Lakoff (2010) has called 'global health governance'. Humanitarian interventions work to save individuals during or in the immediate aftermath of an event – whether it be conflict, epidemic or disaster – often in the poorer areas of the world; biosecurity regimes try to predict and protect populations (usually of the wealthier nations) against certain forms of disaster such as terrorist threat or epidemic whose health consequences could be catastrophic, through the new field of 'preparedness'. They work together, explicitly or not, each responsible for a part of the world and for a certain logic. That said, here the field of global health governance has expanded to include a new ecological field, and to produce new notions of what might constitute 'health'.

Yet again, we have new actors and subjects. Veterinary forensic science comes to play, but this side of veterinary forensics is concerned with public health scares. It is concerned with biosecurity and bioterrorism which targets animals or agriculture, and with emerging diseases, and in particular, zoonoses, which are diseases and infections that are naturally transmitted between vertebrate animals and humans. Forensic veterinarians investigate zoonoses that impact humans and animals, and most recently they have been concerned with emerging infections, from BSE (mad cow disease) to Ebola and Marburg disease. They work collaboratively with institutes like 'Med-Vet-Net' which is the European Union's network for zoonose research, where food safety is perhaps the biggest concern.[6]

These various technologies and forms of expertise, such as veterinary forensic science, that address epidemics and expand the terrain of humanitarianism, meet in the emergent form of 'One Health' which is an initiative that incorporates the health of humans, animals and plants, and treats them in relationship to one another. Still relatively amorphous, One Health is a concept that began with the WildLife Conservation Fund, and is now being developed at the level of international multilateral organisations, governments, NGOs, private organisations and individuals as well as educational institutions.[7] Its official goal is to improve the lives of all species – human, animal and plant – through the integration of human medicine, veterinary medicine and environmental science.[8] Ultimately, One Health focuses on health 'at the individual, population and ecosystem levels', moving both humanitarianism and health from the level of the population to the level of the planet.

One Health came into being primarily to counter zoonotic threats, which are on the rise – supposedly three-quarters of emerging infections originated in animals. Ebola, SARS, avian flu and West Nile virus are four examples. Yet now, organisations involved in animal rescue like the AHA have also joined in, seeing the benefits of a joint effort by veterinarians, physicians and ecologists. In particular, they are interested in bringing human and animal medicine into dialogue to benefit both, since their mission is already a joint one to help animals and children. They have organised conferences to examine these links, and promote research on new drugs and technologies. So while bioterrorism and concerns over preparedness for humans are a driving force for this new collaboration (Research Media Ltd 2011), the sentimental humanitarian projects are increasingly merging with those based on fear and security, and forging new ways to envision suffering, and to provide care.

How does animal suffering come into view here? While focused largely on the level of population or species, we see the familiar sentiment of sympathy, coupled with that of fear. On the one hand, animal suffering is seen in terms of its status as a sentinel or indicator of future human pandemics, and of impending ecological disasters; for instance, birds suffering from infection with the H5N1 influenza virus came into view primarily as a potential threat to humans. This was despite the fact that 5000 birds died and only eight humans. As such, it was addressed through the logic of sacrifice rather than rescue. Birds were a threat. The Hong Kong government decided to kill (or 'cull') all live poultry due to the threat of H5N1 (Keck 2013). On the other hand, One Health approaches blur the line between human and animal; there is a focus on sameness in biology, disease and treatment. For instance, the book *Zoobiquity* (Natterson-Horowitz and Bowers 2013) – one version of a One Health approach – spends time discussing shared mental illness among human and non-human animals, such as OCD, depression, eating disorders and self-mutilation (like cutting). It promises better understanding of suffering for both animals and people – for instance, it suggests such an approach can help with the cancer one's dog might have. In both these cases, however, familiar humanitarian emotions are at play, albeit in tension with one another: there is sympathy for the dog with cancer, and fear of the sick monkey that might transmit a virus.

That said, One Health's multifaceted approach – epidemiology is joined with human and social sciences – renders visible new forms of non-human suffering which are addressed through a form of care other than either sacrifice or rescue, and which therefore pushes the boundaries of humanitarianism. For instance, as French epidemiologist François Roger states, due to the One Health approach, foot and mouth disease is now taken on in a different way: previously, farmers may not have paid attention to it in their herds, since few animals die from it, despite many falling sick. Farmers did not recognise the disease as a problem, nor did they realise that their herds were gradually producing less and less (La Cirad 2011). When one includes the social and human aspects of disease, along with epidemiology and ecology, animal suffering due to foot and mouth disease comes into view in new ways, and questions are being asked about how to address their illness: vaccination? For which animals? Should the farming of different animals be kept separate (La Cirad 2011)? Addressing the disease may help improve farmers' livelihoods, but it also helps to alleviate non-human suffering.

Looking at non-human suffering from the angle of 'the clinic' (medicine and health), the individual animal comes into special focus – emergency rescue or intervention and humanitarian psychiatry both work to protect individual integrity, whether it is bodily or mental integrity; some One Health approaches promise this too. Other One Health approaches, however, promote a focus on species or population, focusing on suffering on a broader level, more akin to public health initiatives where the goal is to manage the health of populations, except with a combined human/non-human population. What seems to be true of all of these medical approaches is that they bring the larger environment into view as the cause of suffering: natural disasters, changed or destroyed habitats or 'ecological health'. These constitute the larger context – perhaps even the larger agent or 'actant' (Latour 1988) – and we understand suffering in light of this. We can locate this as part of a shift among humanitarians to increasingly take on the environmental fallout of natural disasters and of conflicts – expanding their temporal reach beyond the immediate present to deal with illnesses or suffering caused by the destruction of the environment. As part of this, forensic vets play a role in merging environmental and humanitarian responses: for instance, they conduct research on oil spills and associated environmental changes that affect wildlife.

With the environment as the key cause of suffering, other forms of suffering – and their causes – fall into the background. For instance, the everyday grinding poverty of Haitians is not emphasised in this framing – and it is not clear what the relationships might be between the earthquake, the Haitian political economy, animal suffering and human suffering. Indeed, despite the use of humanitarian technologies, the human is no longer at the centre of these interventions – the animal and the environment take centre stage.

LAW

While the expansion of humanitarianism to non-humans has enabled animal suffering to become visible in new medical frames, and treatable with new diagnoses and techniques, humanitarianism also renders suffering visible and knowable in other ways. For instance, veterinary forensic scientists collect medical evidence not just to document or help relieve suffering, but to be used in legal cases. When we look from the angle of the courtroom, then, we see a different impact of this expertise, and a different interaction with humans and humanity.

Shared suffering

While medical responses make animal suffering legible in the context of larger environmental changes, legal responses make animal suffering visible primarily in relation to the human, first by expanding the category of humanity itself, and then by using non-human animals as a way to diagnose human criminality. There is little space for non-human difference here; instead, the focus is on the difference between humans, and on ways to make and enforce this difference, via non-humans.

For instance, veterinary forensic science both relies upon and creates an expanded category of shared (human/non-human) suffering. Let me return to my earlier story, where the pit bull, Phoenix, was set on fire. Seventeen year old twin brothers were arrested for setting him on fire. It was decided that they should be tried as adults for the burning of Phoenix, which is in itself significant; one of the factors taken into account when deciding if teenagers should be tried as adults is the type of harm suffered by the victim. One of the forensic veterinarians testifying at the pre-trial hearing said that he selected a photo of Phoenix bundled up in bandages from the burns to use as evidence, rather than the other more gruesome photos. He said, 'It's easy to empathise with burns because we've all been burned, and even if it's only minor, you realise how painful that is' (Siebert 2010: 50). In other words, the idea of shared pain and suffering was critical here; the veterinarian felt the need to foreground a narrative that could evoke human experiences of suffering, and make the court understand the legal subjects in the same frame. Here, shared pain is a mimetic form of sharing, although, as Haraway has argued, relations between human and animal pain may be shared in non-mimetic ways that do not assume one can put oneself in the place of a non-human animal (Haraway 2008: 75).

Indeed, the idea of a shared subjectivity between certain humans and animals grounded in suffering was evoked by forensic veterinarian Melinda Merck, the head of ASPCA's veterinary forensics unit and head of the new Veterinary Forensics Sciences programme at the University of Florida, when she stated that, 'things like sexual assault of children and animals are linked. They are similar victims' (Siebert 2010: 50). The New York Times article on 'the animal-cruelty syndrome' in which the story of Phoenix is recounted is interspersed with portraits of dogs, photographed alone on their blankets, looking into the distance, forlorn; they often reveal evidence of abuse such as scars or gashes. These photos mimic a certain genre of humanitarian photography. For example, a book of photographs of Rwandan children born of rape (by Jonathan Torgovnik 2009) is jarringly similar; the portraits are of women and their children of rape, photographed either alone or in pairs, looking directly at the camera or off into the distance, often scarred physically, and with a deep look of despondency. This comparison is by no means to make light of these experiences of violence or suffering, but simply to note the attempted equivalence in sentimental form.

Indicators of criminality

Just as veterinary forensic science helps to create a victim whose suffering is recognisable and with whom one can sympathise, in other contexts, it works to define and condemn the cruelty that caused the suffering. While its techniques may help expand the human subject to include non-humans, these same technologies may be used to expel subjects from the category of humanity, by categorising them as 'inhumane'.

Veterinary forensic scientists visit crime scenes, sometimes to help with cases of animal cruelty, and sometimes to help investigate human deaths – they work with comparative forensic scientists, such as forensic entomologists, who look for clues in the life cycles of insects (such as maggots) to find out information about decomposing bodies. These veterinarians have played a role in the changing focus on animal cruelty. In the USA, before 1990, only six states had felony provisions in their animal-cruelty laws; now 46 states do. There are several reasons for this, including changing perceptions of animals as part of larger kinship structures, as innocent victims, and as rights-bearing subjects (most recently, dolphins were voted to have the right to legal personhood by the American Association for the Advancement of Science; and great apes actually have *human* rights in Spain), but one key reason that stands out is the belief that acts of animal cruelty are linked to other crimes more narrowly related to humans, such as illegal firearms possession, drug trafficking, gambling, rape, homicide and child and spousal abuse (Siebert 2010).

The link between animal abuse and interpersonal violence has received a lot of recent attention,[9] and the links have been reportedly substantiated such that many US communities now cross-train social service and animal control agencies in how to recognise animal abuse as possible indicators of other abusive behaviours. A 1997 study of 48 of the largest domestic violence and child abuse shelters in the USA found that 85% of women who came also reported incidents of animal abuse (Siebert 2010); and a quarter of battered women delayed going into shelters for fear of the wellbeing of family pets. Some shelters have adapted, offering refuge to abused pets as well as to people. As with paediatricians who must notify the police if they suspect child abuse, veterinarians must notify the police if they suspect abuse in the animals they treat. In fact, *animal*-control officers are now on the list of those bound by law to report suspected *child* abuse; not only that, but several districts and states in the USA have now created online registries that resemble those for sex offenders, tracking animal abusers across county and state lines, with the idea that this would be an early warning system for other crimes.[10]

We can see how this type of veterinary forensic expertise actually works as a new diagnostic of human cruelty or criminality. While the laws are in place to protect against animal cruelty or to protect endangered species, in many ways this allows for the patrolling and disciplining of humans and their relationships with one another, and it allows for new ways to configure who is exemplary of humanity, and who falls on its outer edges – who newly 'becomes animal'. For instance, veterinary forensic science was instrumental in achieving the conviction of American NFL football star Michael Vick for running a dog-fighting ring. A forensic veterinarian found evidence in 'mass graves' on his property where eight pit bulls were buried, corroborating statements by witnesses that the dogs had been killed by processes of hanging, shooting, drowning or slamming them to the ground. He was sentenced to 23 months in jail on a felony charge for his role in the ring, with the judge remarking that Vick had not accepted full responsibility for 'promoting, funding and facilitating this cruel and inhumane sporting activity'. While going into depth on this topic is beyond the purview of this essay, race clearly plays an important role here. His punishment, as many have noted, exceeded that given to other for charges of rape.

Similarly, there are those like former French actress Brigitte Bardot, who also draws on veterinary expertise to make her point, and who has used the treatment of animals to mark and exclude Muslims in France.

Suggesting that the ritualistic sacrifice of sheep for Eid is 'unspeakable' and 'undignified', her discourse contributes to an already anti-immigrant discourse that uses terms such as inhumane, uncivilized and barbaric to describe Muslims. Muslims, in this discourse, exemplify new forms of animality. In the presidential elections in France in the spring of 2012, far-right candidate Marine Le Pen used halal meat and the killing of animals as a cornerstone of her campaign, which helped garner her the biggest vote that a far-right candidate has ever had in recent history: 18% of the vote in the first round.

Legal personhood is modelled on a particular notion of the human individual, and it seems that to hail legal remedies for injury, one must hew close to this subject. Looking from the angle of the courtroom then, animal suffering is rendered visible in human frames, in the ways that suffering is relevant to humans – it is seen as an expanded form of human suffering, nearly identical to it; as such, it allows for those humans who are responsible to be condemned. It functions as an indicator of human criminality, of people who become animal, and redraws the boundary of humanity – allowing in certain companion animals but expelling certain humans. While medical frames push beyond national frameworks to the scale of the ecological, legal frames stay close to national contexts, working with familiar strategies of blame, inclusion and exclusion.

MISSING FRAMES

If law and medicine frame non-human suffering in particular ways, what is outside the frame, or in between the frames? How is this related to the perceived causes of suffering? I want to end with a few brief glimpses.

Non-innocence

Much work has shown that an innocent other is required to enact humanitarian politics – that is, an innocent other provides the subject of sympathy or pity, and the moral imperative to act. The expanding of humanitarian sentiments, practices and technologies to certain non-human animals has indeed carried over the focus on innocence. That is, we see that the fields of both medicine and law have worked to create new innocent subjects; these may be individuals or populations. And they have also worked to create the opposite of innocent, a practice which regularly accompanies humanitarian logics: those who are not innocent are often seen as criminal or as having failed in some important moral way (Ticktin 2011a). In the case of non-human animals, this failure of innocence may take the form of threat – for instance, the threat of those who might be carrying zoonoses. There seems to be little in between: can we see the suffering or injury of the non-innocent, non-threatening animal? Where are those who fall out of such ethical and political designations altogether?

The social and the political

With the expansion of humanitarianism, the fields of law and medicine have worked to both scale up and scale down our visions of suffering. They have created categories and infrastructures that bring individualised animal suffering into focus; and they have also created the backdrop of environmental disaster and ecological health as the cause of this suffering. We either scale down to focus on individuals, or we scale up to look at the environment. But there is little in between. Where are the middle-level scales of the political and the social?

A focus on the human–animal–environment relationship, or some balance of these, renders not only certain kinds of suffering indiscernible, but also certain kinds of social and political formations. Yet, as much scholarship has shown, the boundaries drawn between human and animal have long worked to shape political identities (Hardin 2010). For instance, when animal cruelty is used as a diagnostic of individual human criminality, we may lose sight of other formations that are nevertheless critical parts of this diagnostic, such as race and racism; how do these come to play in the methods of detection and identification used by veterinary forensic scientists? Michael Vick was convicted of animal cruelty (and inhumanity), but he was charged by the same American courtrooms that – according to the United States Bureau of Justice Statistics – send one in three black men to prison. Looking at the human–animal relation outside of its role in maintaining racial orders misunderstands the ways in which we are permitted to care about animal suffering. Here, condemning Vick could never simply be about saving or protecting dogs; looking beyond the frame suggests that it is impossible to separate his conviction from the process of disciplining and teaching 'humanity' to those who are still seen as less civilised.[11]

Similarly, the role of political economy is not allowed to come into focus. Individual animals are saved by medical or legal intervention. However, the medical and legal framing of suffering or injury does not leave room for us to see the workings of capitalism or the drive for profit as causes of suffering, even as they are inseparable from medical and legal practice.[12] We do not see animals in industrial slaughterhouses, because these are not animals suffering or dying as individuals, or even as populations, but as commodities, part of larger supply chains and lifestyles. The laws I mentioned in the opening of this chapter, that stop monitoring in slaughterhouses, ensure this: they stop images that might make us see non-human animals as suffering beings. Yet even such images cannot capture the scale of the slaughter; they focus on particular, suffering beings – not the processes that make it acceptable and even normal. There is no place to see these logics or assemblages, no space in what would be an overcrowded frame to see the ways in which different types of injustice and suffering are related – from exploitation and poverty, to labour conditions and animal cruelty.

Colonial histories or contemporary imperial regimes are also missing or excluded, as are the related inequalities in resource distribution. When PTSD is diagnosed in elephants, we may understand that poaching or habitat destruction by humans are primary causes, yet we do not see these in any detail; rather, our attention is drawn to biological similarities between human and non-human brains. While important, this renders less relevant the effects of diagnosing elephants with species-wide trauma. Who gets blamed for the poaching? For the destruction of elephant habitats? For the PTSD? It is not the elite who may buy concessions for trophy hunting, but the locals who kill elephants to make a few dollars, to subsist or gain status. We do not see how the wars and conflicts that affect elephant territory are shaped by colonial histories of resource extraction; we cannot see with any clarity the many ways that such destruction is driven by the massive inequalities in wealth between the global north and south.

Sovereignty

Humanitarianism, driven by the moral imperative to save lives, has at various times pushed forward the idea of 'le droit d'ingérence' or the 'right to intervene' in sovereign nations in the name of a suffering humanity. While controversial from the moment it was proposed by Bernard Kouchner in the 1980s, it has nevertheless led to the contemporary concept of the 'responsibility to protect' or R2P doctrine, which asserts that the international community has the duty to assume the protection of a state's citizens if the state is unable or unwilling to protect its own citizens. As such, it merges the responsibility to intervene in times of suffering with a right to employ force in the protection of global citizens, merging humanitarianism and militarism in the name of humanity (Pandolfi 2008). When our new non-human humanitarian subjects are perceived in the frame of emergency, the same question of the right to intervene – or the responsibility to protect – raises its head. Which nation-states will be forced to make way for intervention? Which populations? This is particularly relevant in the case of One Health projects, which claim the right to intervene in the name of pandemics. Not surprisingly, the focus for One Health programmes is the global south. Many of these programmes build on the extant infrastructures of development or public health; for instance, la CIRAD – a French state-sponsored research institution for Research on Agronomy and Development – is a key player in the One Health movement in France, and its projects are largely based in Africa and Asia, admittedly because of its history as part of France's colonial apparatus.

Similarly, the right to intervene on a global stage is matched by the right to intervene in the 'private' realm. If certain forms of animal cruelty are indicators of human criminality, whose homes will be invaded and surveilled for these potential forms of criminality? How do such indicators overlap with and get shaped by the history of surveillance of populations of colour in the United States, who have been seen as unable to care for their own children, their own 'innocents'? Welfare has worked as an indicator of the lack of fitness for parenthood. How do such racial histories map onto indicators related to animal suffering?

While I certainly do not want to condemn efforts to alleviate any kind of suffering – human or non-human – we are left to ask whether the ways in which animal suffering is coming into view, at the humanitarian intersection of law and medicine, may elide the political and social differences, inequalities and relationships that are part of the very causes of that suffering, and that get reinforced or reshaped by such new visibilities. Indeed, humanitarianism has a history of complicity in structural inequality. The question is whether new formations of humanitarianism that include non-humans might not only expand humanitarianism, but change its logics, and the forms of care it engages in.

NOTES

1 Much feminist postcolonial theory has demonstrated this; see for example Mohanty (1988); Spivak (1988); Razack (1995); Kapur (2002).

2 Again, I'm referring to humanitarian action largely as a response to emergency in terms of basic human health, exemplified by MSF.

3 Similarly, humanitarianism intersects with the law in other ways: humanitarian exceptions may allow for legal claims, through medical affidavits or other humanitarian clauses. See for instance Fassin and d'Halluin 2005; Kelly 2011; Ticktin 2011a and 2011b.

4 Thank you to Toby Kelly for pointing this out.

5 'Military dog recovers from PTSD after Iraq war', BBC News, 5 August 2010, available at: www.bbc.co.uk/news/world-us-canada-10873444

6 See for instance Frédéric Keck 2008.

7 Among many others, the following promote the One Health concept: the World Bank, the World Organization for Animal Health, the World Health Organization (WHO), the Food and Agricultural Organization (FAO), the US Center for Disease Control, the European Commission, the American Veterinary Association and the One Health Center at University of California's Global Health Institute. Most recently, the Gates Foundation has become involved. www.onehealthinitiative.com/about.php.

8 From One Health mission statement: www.onehealthinitiative.com/mission.php. The AHA is also now pushing the collaboration of research on human and animal health.

9 See for instance Kurst-Swanger 2007 and Rock et al. 2009. There are also many newspaper articles about this.

10 Suffolk County on Long Island in New York was the first to create a registry, but the state of California was the first to put forward such a bill to the State Legislature in February 2010. The most recent is Arizona's House Bill 2310, which again would create a registry of 'convicted animal abusers similar to the state's current sex offender one'. www.abc15.com/dpp/news/region_phoenix_metro/central_phoenix/az-bill-would-treat-animal-abusers-like-sex-offenders#ixzz23NDq5Zy9. See also the New York Times 21 February 2010 'Lawmakers Consider an Animal Abuse Registry' www.nytimes.com/2010/02/22/us/22abuse.html?_r=1&pagewanted=print as well as Siebert 2010.

11 See Asad (2003) on pain as a necessary way to civilise and cultivate humanity. In such cases, pain is not understood either as torture or as suffering.

12 See for instance Bourdieu (1977) on the force of law and how it is shaped profoundly by other political and social practices and realms of power, even while maintaining that it is autonomous.

REFERENCES

Asad, T. 2003. *Formations of the Secular*. Stanford: Stanford University Press

Bourdieu, P. 1977. 'The Force of Law: Toward a Sociology of the Juridical Field', *Hastings Law Journal* 38: 805–853

Bourke, J. 2011. *What it Means to Be Human: Historical Reflections from the 1800s to the Present*. London: Virago

Bradshaw, G. A., Schore, A. N., Poole, J. M., Moss, C. J and Brown, J. L. 2005. 'Elephant Breakdown', *Nature* 433: 807

Bradshaw, G. A. and Schore, A. N. 2007. 'How Elephants are Opening Doors: Developmental Neuroethology, Attachment and Social Context', *Ethology* 113: 426–436

Bustamante, P. 2011. 'Airlift Rescues Abandoned LA Chihuahuas' *Agence France Presse*, 12 February

Calhoun, C. 2008. 'The Imperative to Reduce Suffering: Charity, Progress and Emergencies in the Field of Humanitarian Action', in Barnett, M. and Weiss, T. (eds.), *Humanitarianism in Question: Politics, Power, Ethics.* Ithaca: Cornell University Press

Carter, C. S., Harris, J. and Porges, S. W. 2009. 'Neural and Evolutionary Perspectives on Empathy', in Decety, J. and Ickes, W. (eds.) *The Social Neuroscience of Empathy.* Cambridge, MA: MIT Press

Cooper, J. E. and Cooper, M. E. 2007. *Introduction to Veterinary and Comparative Forensic Medicine.* Oxford: Blackwell Publishing

Devji, F. 2008. *The Terrorist in Search of Humanity: Militant Islam and Global Politics.* New York: Columbia University Press

Fassin, D. and d'Halluin, E. 2005. 'The Truth from the Body: Medical Certificates as Ultimate Evidence for Asylum Seekers', *American Anthropologist* 107(4): 597–608

Fassin, D. and Rechtman, R. 2009. *The Empire of Trauma: An Inquiry into the Condition of Victimhood.* Princeton: Princeton University Press

Fernandez, M. 2010. 'Homeless in California, but Top Dogs in New York', *The New York Times*, 8 January

Festa, L. 2010. 'Humanity Without Feathers', *Humanity: An International Journal of Human Rights, Humanitarianism and Development* 1(1):3–28

Haraway, D. 2008. *When Species Meet.* Minneapolis: University of Minnesota Press

Hardin, R. 2010. 'Narrative, Humanity, and Patrimony in an Equatorial African Forest', in Feldman, I. and Ticktin, M. (eds.), *In the Name of Humanity: the Government of Threat and Care.* Durham: Duke University Press

Kaplan, T. and Pilon, M. 2013. 'With Initiative, Attorney General Focuses on New York's Pets', *The New York Times*, 1 May

Kapur, R. 2002. 'The Tragedy of Victimization Rhetoric: Resurrecting the "Native" Subject in International/Post-Colonial Feminist Legal Politics', *Harvard Human Rights Journal* 15: 1–38

Keck, F. 2013. 'Hong Kong as Sentinel Post' *Limn* 3: 38–40

2008. 'From Mad Cow Disease to Bird Flu: Transformations of Food Safety in France', in A. Lakoff and S. J. Collier (eds.), *Biosecurity Interventions: Global Health and Security in Question.* New York: Columbia University Press

Kelly, T. 2011. *This Side of Silence: Human Rights, Torture, and the Recognition of Cruelty*. Philadelphia: University of Pennsylvania Press

Kurst-Swanger, K. 2007. 'Animal Abuse: The Link to Family Violence', in Jackson, N. A. (ed.), *Encyclopedia of Domestic Violence*. New York: Routledge

La Cirad 2011. 'François Roger: It is Vital to Include Human Sciences in the Fight Against Foot-and-mouth in the South': la CIRAD

Lakoff, A. 2010. 'Two Regimes of Global Health', *Humanity: An International Journal of Human Rights, Humanitarianism and Development* 1(1): 59–80

Laqueur, T. 2009. 'Mourning, Pity and the Work of Narrative in the Making of "Humanity"', in Wilson, R. A. and Brown, R. D. (eds.), *Humanitarianism and Suffering: the Mobilization of Empathy*. Cambridge: Cambridge University Press

Latour, B. 1988. *Science in Action: How to Follow Scientists and Engineers Through Society*. Cambridge: Harvard University Press

Malkki, L. 2010. 'Children, Humanity and the Infantilization of Peace', in Feldman, I. and Ticktin, M. (eds.), *In The Name of Humanity: the Government of Threat and Care*. Durham: Duke University Press

Mohanty, C. 1988. 'Under Western Eyes: Feminist Scholarship and Colonial Discourses' *Feminist Review* 30: 61–88

Natterson-Horowitz, B. and Bowers, K. 2013. *Zoobiquity: The Astonishing Connection Between Human and Animal Health*. New York: Vintage

Neuman, M. 2011. 'France: Managing the Undesirables', in Magone, C., Neuman, M. and Weissman, F. (eds.), *Humanitarian Negotiations Revealed: The MSF Experience*. London: Hurst & Company

Pandolfi, M. 2008. 'Laboratory of Intervention: The Humanitarian Governance of the Postcommunist Balkan Territories', in Good, M.-J. D., Hyde, S., Pinto, S. and Good, B. (eds.), *Postcolonial Disorders*. Berkeley: University of California Press

Razack, S. 1995. 'Domestic Violence as Gender Persecution: Policing the Borders of Nation, Race and Gender', *Canadian Journal of Women and the Law, Revue Femmes et Droit* 8(1): 45–88

Research Media Ltd 2011. *Dr Laura Kahn, on the One Health Initiative: International Innovation*

Rock, M., Buntain, B., Hatfield, J. and Hallfrimsson, B. 2009. 'Animal–human connections, "one health" and the syndemic approach to prevention', *Social Science and Medicine* 68: 991–995

Siebert, C. 2010. 'The Animal-Cruelty Syndrome', in *The New York Times*. pp. 42–51. New York

2006. 'An Elephant Crackup?', in *The New York Times Magazine*. New York

Spivak, G. C. 1988. 'Can the Subaltern Speak?', in Nelson, C. and Grossberg, L. (eds.), *Marxism and the Interpretation of Culture*. Urbana: University of Illinois Press

Taylor, K. 2013. 'Mayoral Hopefuls Express Support for Animal Rights', in *The New York Times*, 6 May

Ticktin, M. 2011a. *Casualties of Care: Immigration and the Politics of Humanitarianism in France*. Berkeley: University of California Press

2011b. 'How Biology Travels: A Humanitarian Trip', *Body & Society* 17(2&3): 139–158

Torgovnik, J. 2009. *Intended Consequences: Rwandan Children Born of Rape*. New York: Aperture

THE CAUSES OF TORTURE: LAW, MEDICINE AND THE ASSESSMENT OF SUFFERING IN BRITISH ASYLUM CLAIMS

Tobias Kelly

Since the late 1960s torture has increasingly been understood as involving a distinct form of suffering.[1] In 1976, for example, the European Court of Human Rights ruled that the use of forced standing, hooding, subjection to noise, deprivation of sleep and deprivation of food and drink by British security forces on Republican prisoners in Northern Ireland did not amount to torture because they did not 'occasion suffering of the peculiar intensity and cruelty implied by the word *torture*.'[2] Similarly, the 1984 UN Convention Against Torture, for example, defines torture as involving 'severe pain or suffering, whether physical or mental'.[3] Even more recently, when the George W. Bush administration was trying to provide legal cover for its treatment of prisoners in Guantanamo Bay, Abu Ghraib and Bagram, one of its lawyers infamously defined torture as an act that caused pain equivalent to major organ failure.[4] In Britain, UK Border Agency Guidance states that in order to count as an Article 3 violation, the incident must 'involve actual bodily injury or intense physical or mental suffering' (UKBA no date, 3). As such, torture is widely seen as being distinguished from other types of ill-treatment by the amount of pain and suffering it causes.

As a specific category of harm, the precise meanings and implications of the word 'torture' stand at the uneasy interface of law and clinical medicine. It is lawyers who have led the way, since the last third of the twentieth century, in defining what does and does not count as torture (Kelly 2012). Legal conventions, decisions and definitions have proliferated. However, given the focus on pain and suffering, clinicians –

especially medical doctors but also psychologists and psychoanalysts – have increasingly become central to attempts to understand torture and its implications. In the early 1970s, there were no specialised centres that provided medical or psychotherapeutic care to torture survivors. By 2010, the umbrella organisation known as the International Rehabilitation Council for Torture Victims (IRCT) had more than 140 members in over 70 countries. In the early 1970s, there was just a trickle of research papers in medical journals that focused on the implications of torture. By the turn of the century, the number of peer-reviewed articles had become a flood. Doctors and other clinicians had, of course, previously worked with torture survivors, but it was only toward the end of the twentieth century that torture came to be seen as a possible distinct field of clinical knowledge. In this context, torture, as a specific category, emerges out of the relationship between legal and medical ways of trying to understand the world.

Crucially, the notion of torture found in human rights claims is not just about pain or suffering but about pain or suffering *caused* in very particular ways. It must involve the complicity or acquiescence of a public official and it must be carried out with specific intentions.[5] It is not the quality or nature of the pain that singles out torture survivors, but the specific cause of their pain. In a broader sense, such notions of causation play an important role in many contemporary methods for distinguishing between different types of suffering. It is causal claims that help us separate out those harms that are thought to be necessary from those that can be prevented (Haskell 2000: 280–306). An injury caused by falling down the stairs, a brawl or domestic violence, to give but a few examples, has very different moral and social implications. Not all suffering is treated as ethically equivalent, and it is only by making causal claims that notions such as guilt and innocence, for example, can be allocated. Indeed, suffering without an identifiable cause can produce particular forms of anxiety (Jackson 2012). There is therefore a reliance on what might be called technologies of causal attribution in order to make causal connections visible, and distinguish between different forms of harm.

This chapter explores one such technology of causal attribution, in the shape of medicolegal reports produced in order to document allegations of torture. The particular focus is on medicolegal reports written as part of claims for asylum in the UK. The writing of such medicolegal reports has to be understood against the background of two processes, which appear to be moving in different directions. The first is the longstanding campaign by human rights organisations to have torture recognised as a specific harm, codified in international and domestic law. By and large, these campaigns have been successful; not only is the absolute prohibition of torture to be found in law, but also torture survivors are, formally at least, singled out for specific entitlements. The second process is the growing apparent scepticism toward asylum seekers. Although the formal standard of proof is relatively low, at reasonable likelihood, the UK Border Agency and immigration tribunals have, in practice, increased the evidential burden required to substantiate a claim of torture. Medicolegal reports are therefore written in a context where torture is legally recognised as an absolute prohibition, but when it comes to individual cases, there is a great deal of scepticism.

The central argument of this chapter is that the space for denying individual acts of torture is built into the ways in which torture is legally defined. In particular, the gap between provisional clinical claims about the causes of pain and suffering, and the legal demand for specific causal certainty creates the space for doubt to grow. Medicolegal reports can be understood as a technology of visibility, designed to bring into view past acts of violence and cruelty. Perhaps uniquely among legal categories, suffering and pain are put at the heart of the legal definition of torture, and lawyers therefore turn to clinicians for evidence about that pain and suffering. Yet open-ended clinical understandings of the causes of suffering and pain come up against the demand for narrow legal certainty. As such, the legal prohibition of torture gives with one hand, promising to protect and prosecute, and takes away with another, by setting conditions of recognition that are very hard to meet. We are close to what William James called the 'sentimentalist fallacy', the tendency 'to shed tears over abstract justice...and never to know these qualities when you meet them in the street' (James 1987: 586–87). It is as if torture is brought into view, only for claimants to be told that the picture lacks enough focus. This is not to say that cynicism and discrimination towards those seeking protection are not important. Rather, it is to say that we need to go one step further back, and examine how the processes through which attempts are made to recognise torture create the spaces through which such scepticism and prejudice are themselves possible. It is the tension between legal and clinical ways of understanding causation that produces the space for denial to take place.

This chapter begins with a description of the writing of one particular medicolegal report, in order to give a sense of the issues at stake. In the second half of the chapter, I examine the general problems and concerns experienced by clinicians involved in writing reports. The description of the particular report is produced following interviews with the doctor, as well as an examination of the case notes, legal documents, and the final medicolegal report. The chapter is based on fieldwork over a period of two years with a leading torture-rehabilitation organisation. This research involved access to the case files of the organisation's clients, as well as interviews with clinicians. In addition, I followed cases through the asylum process and interviewed immigration lawyers and judges.

WRITING A MEDICOLEGAL REPORT

Mehdi Rostami arrived at Heathrow Airport in early 2007 on a forged Bulgarian passport and claimed asylum immediately.[6] He was a 45 year old teacher of English who had left Iran four months previously by boat and arrived in London via India. After being detained briefly, Rostami was released while his asylum claim was processed. The UK Border Agency agreed to delay any decision as his lawyer sought medical evidence to corroborate his claim of torture in Iran. Rostami's lawyer turned to the Medical Foundation for the Care of Victims of Torture.[7] Rostami was already a client of the Medical Foundation, where he was receiving therapy. After an initial delay, Rostami was sent to see Dr Miriam Douglas. Douglas was a local general practitioner who worked for the Medical Foundation on a voluntary basis for a few days a month. Over the course of a few weeks, the doctor and the client met several times for a series of lengthy interviews, lasting a total of nearly six hours, during which time Rostami recounted his story and showed Douglas his injuries.

During these sessions, Rostami told the doctor that he was an activist in the Communist Party, had written several leaflets criticising the Iranian regime, and had led a number of discussion groups for young people in which they could air their grievances. He explained to Douglas that several years prior to coming to the UK, some plainclothes police officers had come to his door in the middle of the night and demanded that he accompany them to the police station. He was handcuffed, blindfolded and taken to a dark cell from which he could hear a recording, played at high volume, of someone reciting the Quran. Within a few hours, the police took him to another cell where they accused him of being responsible for organising some pro-Kurdish demonstrations the previous week.

Rostami went on to tell Douglas that on being returned to his cell, he was pushed down some stairs and, unable to break his fall, landed awkwardly on his right ankle. He heard a cracking noise, which he assumed were his bones breaking and then he lay in his cell, screaming with excruciating pain. Rostami explained that he was imprisoned for a total of 22 days. He was taken upstairs to the interrogation room seven or eight times during his incarceration. During these interrogations he would be beaten all over his body for 30–45 minutes at a time.

In his account to the doctor, Rostami described how on one occasion he was sitting on the chair and his torturers hit both of his big toes repeatedly with a hammer until they started to bleed. Several years later, the toenails were still black and continued to fall out. Rostami also claimed that on another occasion he was sitting on the bench with his hands cuffed behind his back. The men hit his back and he felt a searing pain throughout his body. He said that he thought that this was caused by an electric baton, but he could not be sure. Rostami went on to tell the doctor that on three or four occasions water was slowly dripped onto his head from above for more than an hour. He also told the doctor that he was in constant pain all over his body for the duration of his detention. He had bruises and cuts on his body, face, knuckles and head. Prior to his detention, he had had problems with his stomach once or twice a year, but during his detention this worsened significantly, and he had constant abdominal pain and daily vomiting.

Rostami was released after agreeing to a statement saying that he would never demonstrate publicly again. However, the effects of his detention stayed with him. To this day, Rostami told Douglas, he has a hot, burning pain in the ankle when walking. He described to the doctor how his neck and shoulders are very tense and stiff 'as if there is always someone standing on my back'. He also described how, every morning, after rising from bed, he has terrible pain and stiffness in his chest and back. However, Rostami complained to the doctor that the worst thing is the emotional impact of his treatment. His relationship with his family changed for the worse after his detention. He told the doctor that he became very nervous in crowded places and started to have vivid memories of his time in detention. All sorts of things would trigger these recollections – his wife shouting at their children, the sight of wooden benches and cement floors, and men in military uniform.

The interviews between Rostami and the doctor took longer than normal, as Rostami became increasingly distressed throughout the meetings. During the physical examination, Douglas also noted several scars across Rostami's body. Some of these looked to her like scars from vaccinations or an appendectomy. Rostami also said that some of his scars were from childhood injuries. However, there were three scars, of various lengths, that Rostami claimed were a result of his treatment in detention. Douglas measured the scars and recorded them carefully in a number of diagrams.

A SHORT HISTORY OF THE TORTURE REHABILITATION MOVEMENT

Before examining the report that Douglas wrote following her meetings with Rostami, and what she felt able to say about the effects of torture, it will be useful to put the writing of medicolegal reports within the context of the broader history of the torture rehabilitation movement. The movement should above all be thought of as growing out of human rights concerns. As such, most centres refer to human rights documents in the description of the aims and objectives. However, within this the emphasis of much of the rehabilitation movement was on the care of individual victims, rather than on structural change to prevent torture. More specifically, in the final quarter of the twentieth century, the torture rehabilitation movement grew as a direct response to the arrival of refugee populations in Europe and North America. In the UK, the Medical Foundation for the Care of Victims of Torture grew out of the local Amnesty International medical group. The stress has also always been on what is called the 'holistic approach', with clinicians attending to a client's protection needs – writing reports for asylum applications and tackling issues around housing, health, education or safety, as well as rehabilitation – instead of what was seen as the narrow medicalisation of torture survivors.

There is an ongoing debate among some of those involved in the torture rehabilitation movement as to whether torture survivors should be singled out, both clinically and politically. In 2006, in an editorial in the *British Medical Journal*, Metin criticised some of the psychiatrists at the Medical Foundation for their 'ideological position, which is not supported by any evidence,' for implicitly arguing that torture was a unique form of trauma (Basoglu 2006). Basoglu is a psychiatrist with a behaviourist approach to the treatment of mental health problems and has experience with earthquake and torture survivors in Turkey. In his editorial, he argues that 'our studies show that natural disasters, for example, lead to just as complex traumatic stress problems ... as traumas of human design, such as war and torture' (Basoglu 2006: 1230). Doctors from the Medical Foundation responded by arguing, 'We are not convinced that it is valid to generalise from work with other populations, such as earthquake survivors or war veterans, to torture survivors' (Seltzer et al. 2006).

Many of the clinicians who write medicolegal reports argue for marking out torture as a distinct form of pain and suffering. Yoav Landau-Pope, the former director of clinical services at the Medical Foundation, told me that he thought 'deliberately inflicted trauma is always very different from arbitrary trauma, and individual cruelty is different from collective violence, as it goes to the heart of the self'.[8] From this perspective, torture survivors should be seen as distinct from other people who have lived through violence or trauma (see also Quiroga and Jaranson 2005: 23). Crucially, as we shall see, the issue of whether torture causes distinct forms of suffering needs to be distinguished from whether the aftereffects of torture can be documented to the standards demanded by legal proof.

Research into the sequelae of torture, only really began in the late 1970s, largely on refugees in northern Europe (Eitinger and Weisaeth 1998). Since then, many research articles have been published in medical journals, peaking in the mid 1990s. In the 1970s, led mainly by research in Denmark, there was much talk about the identification of a distinct 'torture syndrome' (see, for example, Amnesty International 1977). Against the background of a wider demand for 'evidence based medicine', clinical evidence that torture survivors have a discrete and an identifiable set of sequelae has proved elusive (Allodi 1991; Jaranson 1998; Mollica and Caspi-Yavin 1992; Turner and Gorst-Unsworth 1990).

There has been relative success in identifying the sequelae of specific forms of torture. X-ray studies have been used to investigate head injuries attributable to torture, skin biopsies to differentiate scars caused by electrical shocks from those caused by other types of burns, and myoglobin levels as an indicator of traumatic muscle destruction, among others (Allodi 1991; Jaranson 1998). However, the tests developed from such research tend to produce a large number of false negatives. They may help identify 15 people who have been electrocuted or had the soles of their feet beaten, but they will also give negative results on another 15 people who have had identical experiences. As such, there is also a real fear that the development of too rigorous tests could raise the standard of proof well above that which is actually required for asylum claims or even legal prosecutions. Perhaps most importantly, such tests are very expensive and well beyond the budgets of most documentation centres.

In general, research into the consequences of torture faces several major problems. It is clearly not possible to carry out the kind of double-blind trials often associated with medical research. In an attempt to get around this problem, in the 1970s, a group of Danish doctors carried out experiments on themselves and on anaesthetised pigs, using electric batons. However, the doctors were met with demonstrations by animal rights protesters and the trials soon stopped (Genefke 2008). Stuart Turner, a psychiatrist who worked with the Medical Foundation in the 1980s and now heads one of the leading general psychological trauma centres in the UK, has written that 'there is no adequate controlled research on the assessment, treatment and clinical outcome of torture survivors' (McIvor and Turner 1995: 709). Research on torture has therefore necessarily often been exploratory.

READING PAIN AND SCARS

Clinicians report that the most common sequelae they encounter with torture survivors are non-specific forms of chronic pain (C. de C. Williams and Amris 2007: 7). Rostami's major complaints to Douglas were about pains in his stomach and back, which incapacitated him for long periods. Douglas wrote in her report that the pain experienced by Rostami could well be 'somatic pain – that is a manifestation of his extreme psychological distress rather than of any underlying physical pathology caused by his mistreatment'. She went on to argue that the pain he reported was frequently found in depressed patients. However, although chronic pain might be the most commonly observed aftereffect of torture, it continues to resist attempts at measurement and therefore offers limited space for specific documentation (IRCT 2009: 15).

The largest part of Douglas's report was taken up in documenting the various scars and lesions that Rostami showed her during their interviews. This is common in many medicolegal reports. To help her interpret the scars, Douglas turned to the Istanbul Protocol. In the context of highly politicised disputes over the implications of medical findings, the Istanbul Protocol was an attempt to set out a clear methodological route through which torture could be documented and injuries linked to specific causes.

The Istanbul Protocol sets out five levels, originally developed by the Medical Foundation in the UK, through which wounds and scars are to be assessed in relation to claims of torture. These are *not consistent, consistent, highly consistent, typical* and *diagnostic*, going from the weakest probable fit between claimed cause and scar to the strongest (OHCHR 2004: 34–35). The precise definition of each of these words is some way from their everyday usage. *Not consistent* is specified as meaning that 'the lesion could not have been caused by the trauma described'. *Consistent* is defined as 'the lesion could have been caused by the trauma described, but it is non-specific and there are many other possible causes'. By describing a lesion as *consistent*, a physician is saying he or she cannot rule out that it was caused in the way claimed, but can say little more. *Highly consistent* is described as meaning that a 'lesion could have been caused by the trauma described, and there are few other possible causes'. The level of probability here is still quite low, however; saying 'there are few other possible causes' does not even necessarily imply that the attributed cause is even the most likely. *Typical* is defined as meaning 'an appearance that is usually found with this type of trauma, but there are other possible causes'. This category is based on a slightly different logic from the previous two, as it is making a direct causal claim, saying that a particular type of torture usually results in these types of scars, without ruling out other possibilities, or even saying torture is the most likely cause. The last category, *diagnostic*, is defined as implying that a scar 'could not have been caused in any way other than that described'. This is by far the strongest claim and, in effect, rules out any other possible causes.

British judges now require that doctors use the Istanbul Protocol in writing reports. An extra gloss was put on the Istanbul Protocol in a 2008 judgement of the Asylum and Immigration Tribunal.[9] In that case, the judge rejected the claim that the submitted medicolegal report was corroborative of the claim of torture and ruled that when claiming a scar was *highly consistent*, report writers had to assess 'other possible causes (whether many, few or unusually few), specifically examining those to gauge how likely they are, bearing in mind what is known about the individual's life history and experiences'.[10] This, in effect, means that the doctor has to weigh the claim of torture alongside other possible causes.

Many doctors say that only certain types of scars or lesions really shout out their causes, with cigarette burns and bullet wounds paramount. To give but a few examples, the Istanbul Protocol states, 'Burning is the form of torture that most frequently leaves permanent changes in the skin. Sometimes, these changes may be of diagnostic value' (OHCHR 2004: 37). Some types of whipping also leave distinct marks. As the Istanbul Protocol puts it, 'These scars are depigmented and often hypertrophic, surrounded by narrow, hyperpigmented stripes' (OHCHR 2004: 37). Such scars can be distinguished from self-flagellation or dermatitis by their length, angle and location.

However, some forms of torture can result in injuries that leave a non-specific appearance. Blunt force trauma, such as being kicked by heavy boots, 'often leaves no or uncharacteristic scars' (IRCT 2009: 7). The Istanbul Protocol further states, 'Anal fissures may persist for many years, but it is normally impossible to differentiate between those caused by torture and those caused by other mechanisms' (OHCHR 2004: 33–24). Furthermore, many forms of torture are expressly designed to leave no marks. Water-boarding is famously almost undetectable after the event. In addition, even forms of torture that do cause more obvious wounds, do not necessarily result in permanent scars (OHCHR 2004: 34). There is not space here to list all the various forms of torture and the claims that have been made about the scars and lesions with which they are associated. The key point is to illustrate the range of causal certainty in claims about the relationship between specific forms of torture and particular sequelae.

In many medicolegal reports, the clinician can go no higher than *consistent*. As part of this research, I examined 35 medicolegal reports in detail. Although it is by no means a fully representative survey, it does give some indication of general patterns. In the examined reports, 345 individual or groups of scars or lesions were classified according to the Istanbul Protocol scale. Of these, 129 were classified as *consistent*, 51 as *highly consistent*, 59 as *typical* and 5 as *diagnostic*. In a further five individual incidents, the clinician said that the scars were *not consistent* with their attribution.

Douglas was able to go as high as *highly consistent* in the classification of Rostami's injuries but no further. In her report, Douglas described the two 2 cm irregular scars on Rostami's kneecaps as being *highly consistent*: 'The scars are most irregular as would be expected when skin is dragged across a stone surface. Another possible cause might be an injury sustained while working outdoors and kneeling on the ground. However,

Mr Rostami's occupation had been sedentary and he has lived in an urban area most of his life so I think this explanation less likely.' It is worth noting that Douglas went higher than the Istanbul Protocol definition of *highly consistent* in stating that the attributed causes were the most likely. The other scar on Rostami's shin was described as *consistent* with either falling down the stairs or a beating, meaning that it could have been caused in the way described, but there were also lots of other possible, and equally persuasive, explanations. Hard purple scars such as this, technically known as keloid scars, are nearly always non-specific in origin, as there is so much swelling. Douglas was keen to stress that the relative absence of obvious physical signs should not be taken as evidence that Rostami's ill-treatment did not happen. She noted in her report: 'At first it might seem implausible that he bears so few scars after describing such significant beating… However, a skilled torturer can inflict a great number of blows and leave no scar. Additionally, the scars often fade with time.' Of the 35 reports I examined, in six cases, the clinician remarked that the absence of scars should not be taken as indicating torture had not taken place.

It is crucial to note here that although it may be hard to give firm causal attributions to particular scars or lesions, individual sequelae do not stand alone. The Istanbul Protocol says that individual scars and injuries have to be assessed in the context of the overall evaluation by the clinician. This means that broader patterns of scars should be taken into consideration. As the Istanbul Protocol states: 'Ultimately, it is the overall evaluation of all lesions and not the consistency of each lesion with a particular form of torture that is important in assessing the torture story' (OHCHR 2004: 37). In seven of the 35 reports I examined, the clinician wrote that the overall pattern of scars was compatible with the account.

UNCOVERING THE UNSEEN

How does the writing of medicolegal reports differ from other clinical practices aimed at uncovering the causes of symptoms or sequelae? The word *diagnosis* is often used by clinicians when talking about torture (see, for example, Danielsen et al. 1997; Goldfeld et al. 1988; Juhler and Vesti 1989; Mollica and Caspi-Yavin 1992; Van Velsen et al. 1996). However, the language of diagnosis is at best an awkward fit to the work of interpreting injuries for medicolegal reports. Medicolegal reports are not about diagnosing a discrete disease or illness but about coming to an opinion about the relative consistency of an account of torture with the scars, lesions and other indicators presented by the claimant.

Many doctors feel that the writing of medicolegal reports shares common features with other types of medical practice, particularly primary care. Doctors commonly have to certify particular conditions as part of bureaucratic processes – such as writing 'sick notes' for employers – which they are aware may be misinterpreted. More importantly, in both primary care and medicolegal reports, clinicians are confronted by people who may be precise and clear but who can equally be inarticulate in describing their symptoms. The clinician then has to piece together a host of sometimes disparate bits of information, filter statements that could lead in the wrong direction and finally try to work out what is wrong. It is a process that one doctor described as 'peering through the glass darkly' and trying to fit together a series of half-glimpsed symptoms to get a sense of what is going on underneath.[11]

However, the ways in which symptoms and causes are linked are very different in primary care and in medicolegal reports. As Richard Jones has shown in his study of the training of forensic clinicians more broadly, there is a need for a shift in language to make the jump from general medicine to forensics (Jones 2003). In general medical practice, clinicians may try to investigate the causes of an illness or injury. However, they might eventually be left without a firm opinion on the cause of a problem. Indeed, a diagnosis may not need a causal attribution, as it is about recognizing a pattern of symptoms that can be treated. The main concern is for the patient to get better. For this reason, an investigation into causation can broadly be thought of as a means to an end, rather than an end in itself. In contrast, in writing medicolegal reports, an opinion about causation is an end in itself, in that a clinician cannot simply write a report about scars without coming to some sort of conclusion about causes. However, in writing medicolegal reports, there is little external space for practical confirmation of an opinion about causation. In general clinical practice, an opinion about causation can be confirmed either by tests or by the patient getting better. In a medicolegal report, the only confirmation of an opinion is how it is treated by the judge, and that explains more about the vagaries of the legal process than the experiences of the client.

In this context, many doctors say they have great difficulty in applying the different levels of probability found in the Istanbul Protocol's categories of *consistent*, *highly consistent* and *diagnostic*. The distinction between an indication of *consistent* and *highly consistent* is that there are 'many other possible causes' in the former and 'few other possible causes' in the latter. Yet, there is no precise guidance on the difference between 'few' and 'many'. Different clinicians can therefore have the same clinical opinion about a scar but classify it differently under the Istanbul Protocol.

The requirement to write about other possible causes can also create concerns.[12] On the one hand, there is no specification as to the level of causal explanation at which the clinician must provide alternatives. Do clinicians have to write about alternatives to blunt objects or military boots? On the other, the requirement to write about alternative explanations means that many clinicians feel they are being asked to push their imaginations to absurd lengths. As one doctor pointed out to me, 'How can I, sitting in a surgery in leafy North London, imagine what it might be like to be a fisherman in Sri Lanka and all the other possible causes of a scar?'[13] A common joke is made about whether doctors should speculate about alien abduction as a possible cause. Douglas felt able to suggest that as Rostami was a teacher he was unlikely to have sustained his injuries to his feet and knees through the normal course of events.

Although the Istanbul Protocol was designed to give stability to the often-ambiguous process of linking scars to claims of torture, given how it is being used in the legal processes it can also add another layer of uncertainty and obfuscation.

PTSD AND BEYOND

In addition to showing the clinician his scars, Rostami told Douglas that he was constantly anxious. He also reported that he had great difficulty sleeping and had frequent panic attacks. The dominant popular image of the torture survivor is not solely of physical suffering but also of psychological trauma. The Istanbul Protocol also notes that common psychological responses among torture survivors include avoidance and emotional numbing, hyperarousal, depression, somatic complaints, sexual dysfunction and psychosis (OHCHR 2004: 46–47). Crucially though, the Istanbul Protocol warns that it 'is important to recognize that not everyone who has been tortured develops a diagnosable mental illness. However, many victims experience profound emotional reactions and psychological symptoms' (OHCHR 2004: 45).

Many clinicians are of the opinion that there is not a determinate causal relationship between any particular method of torture and specific psychological symptoms (OHCHR 2004: 45). Similar symptoms can have different causes, and similar causes can result in different symptoms. Indeed, linear or mechanistic forms of causation are anathema to many forms of psychotherapeutic practice used in the torture rehabilitation movement. Some therapists go so far as to say that the specific cause of trauma is not necessarily the focus of the work. Their clients may be more concerned with housing, family breakdown or their trip to the UK than they are with the initial event of torture that led them to flee, and therefore it is these events that they focus on. Even the therapists who do place torture at the centre of their understanding of trauma do not necessarily focus on it directly. One therapist told me that in the therapy 'you deal with the here and now – torture is still always present – even if not in the form of a history. The way is not to go back and focus on the trauma, as trauma is always emergent – but who knows when it will emerge.'[14] Such an approach seeks to understand how people make sense of their past experience, how this impacts their internal processes and their interpersonal relationships, but it does not seek to uncover what 'really happened' outside the client's own experience of it.

Within the context of the UK torture rehabilitation movement, the overall dominant approach to mental health issues can broadly be described as psychotherapeutic. Within this area is a great variation in approaches, with no one school dominating. Psychiatrists are also far from being in the majority. Broadly speaking, such psychotherapeutic approaches to mental health have historically paid little attention to particular diagnoses in the course of treatment. The assumption has been that the specific nature of symptoms will vary from person to person and will depend on their own biographical experiences.

Along with the broad psychotherapeutic approach to mental health issues is an alternative approach, increasingly so since the 1970s, which I shall gloss here as medical-diagnostic (Horowitz 2002). The publication of the *Diagnostic and Statistical Manual of Mental Disorders–III* (DSM-III) in 1980 by the American Psychiatric Association marked the mainstream victory of the medical-diagnostic model, in the USA at least. However, in a bid to stop professional disputes, the DSM-III by and large leaves out issues of causation to focus on symptoms. Mental health problems are therefore organised by observable symptoms, with little attempt to analyse the relations between disorders and their underlying causes.[15]

One of the few exceptions to the general absence of theories of causation in the DSM-IV is the entry on PTSD, which is defined in the DSM as an anxiety disorder that can develop following exposure to traumatic events. Sources of trauma can include sexual assault, earthquakes, armed conflict, bereavement or torture. However, the experience of some form of trauma is central to any diagnosis of PTSD. Furthermore, the causal event is also often embedded in its symptoms, in the shape of flashbacks or nightmares.

In the absence of a Torture Syndrome, PTSD remains the most widely diagnosed mental health disorder in medicolegal reports, along with depression. The Istanbul Protocol recommends caution in an overly simplistic assumption about the connection between PTSD and torture, saying that there is a 'mistaken and simplistic impression that PTSD is the main psychological consequence of torture' (OHCHR 2004: 48). In Rostami's case, Douglas had said that his symptoms were diagnostic of PTSD, as he experienced flashbacks, sleeping difficulties, avoidance and poor concentration. However, Douglas also added that 'Mr Rostami has severe symptoms of depression and anxiety. In my opinion these are diagnostic of Post Traumatic Stress Disorder.' In writing her report on Rostami, Douglas pointed out that Rostami had many reasons for being depressed, such as his flight from Iran, his separation from his family, and his relative isolation in Glasgow. However, she concluded, 'It is clear that he has been profoundly psychologically disturbed by his torture and detention', drawing a direct line between his treatment in an Iranian police cell and his current psychological issues.

The diagnosis of PTSD has been highly controversial, especially in the context of legal claims (Marsella et al. 1992; Summerfield 1999; Young 1995). In particular, questions have also been raised about the use of PTSD as an evidential tool for uncovering past torture. The Home Office and immigration judges have argued that PTSD is overdiagnosed and easy to fake.[16] In 2002, the Home Office commissioned a report from Dr Leigh Neal, a psychiatrist working with the British military.[17] In the report, Neal claimed that 'vague comments about stress in general and having a poor recollection of anything are almost invariably associated with malingering'. The report was criticized by Dr Stuart Turner, claiming that Neal had problematically generalized from the distinct case of combat veterans, and had failed to take into account the particularities of asylum seekers and refugees, with whom Neal seemed to have very little experience.[18]

A diagnosis of PTSD might initially seem especially useful in medi-colegal reports, as a key criterion for a diagnosis includes the fact that the patient has been exposed to a traumatic event. However, crucially, for the writing of medicolegal reports about torture, a diagnosis of PTSD is not confined to survivors of torture but includes people who have experienced trauma more broadly. As such, a diagnosis of PTSD does not, on its own, indicate whether someone has been tortured and there-fore cannot be used to make specific claims about causation.

CREDIBILITY IN MEDICOLEGAL REPORTS

On what grounds do clinicians make claims about the causes of injuries? What role does believing the person's claims have in relation to the detached assessment of sequelae and symptoms? The courts are very firm in arguing that clinicians are supposed to match reported causes with symptoms and assess the extent to which they do or do not match up. Whether the claimant is telling the truth is simply not an issue for the clinician, and should be left to the judge.[19] However, in practice very few doctors say they can write a medicolegal report without assess-ing whether the person before them is being truthful. Clinicians broadly share the assumption that writing a medicolegal report is a product of the personal encounter between the clinician and the client, with all the intimacies, detachments and ambiguities that the encounter can produce. The credibility of a verbal account is therefore central to the clinical opinion. Among clinicians though, there is a widespread objec-tion to the claim often made by the Home Office and immigration judges that doctors are simply hoodwinked by claimants. Judges often say, for example, that psychiatric reports are based on the account of the claimant and therefore offer little corroborative weight.[20] Some judges even go so far as to argue, to the frustration of many clinicians, that doctors have a professional duty to believe what a patient tells them.[21] Many clinicians argue, in contrast, that although trust between a patient and a clinician is crucial, there is also always a sense that there is more going on than appearances suggest.[22] Clinicians are trained, through analysing what is said and what is unsaid, what people do and what people do not do, to uncover the layers of truth and half-truth that often even the patient will not be fully aware of. As Douglas put it,

'We are not all dewy-eyed optimists and we know that you have to be careful because it is easy to be carried away by a persuasive witness.'[23]

Nearly all clinicians working in the field want to distance themselves from the 'culture of disbelief' that is widely seen as facing refugees in Europe and North America (Fassin and d'Halluin 2007). Yet there is still a widespread sense that people requesting asylum can fabricate or embellish some of their claims.[24] In a context where accounts are subjected to minute scrutiny by immigration officials, and the stakes, should a claimant be sent back, are very high, many clinicians acknowledge that it is perhaps inevitable that some people will misrepresent parts of their account. For those dedicated to the principles of asylum, such half-truths are not thought to undermine the moral basis of the claim, but rather they are treated as an outcome of necessity. The question then is to separate those parts of an account that are true from those parts that are not entirely true and from those parts that are complete fabrications. Perhaps most importantly, some types of inconsistency, which could be taken as evidence of fabrication, can themselves be seen by clinicians as a sign of the authenticity of the account. Indeed, Juliet Cohen, the head doctor of the medicolegal report team at the Medical Foundation has argued that sleep disorder, depression, weight loss and malnutrition, chronic pain and brain injury, all of which are associated with torture survivors, can all lead to difficulties in recall (Cohen 2001).

Given the importance of credibility assessments in writing medicolegal reports, scars, taken in isolation, do not tell the clinician a great deal. Writing in the context of modern French immigration policies, Fassin and d'Halluin have argued that medical reports have meant that the suffering body has become the main legal resource for undocumented migrants (2005). Bodies which can be seen are placed above words that are spoken. If the rest of their story is not believed, at least the pain written on their bodies cannot be denied. It is assumed that physical representations of suffering, in the shape of wounded bodies, have a transparent immediacy. However, in the context of British medicolegal reports at least, torture does not leave marks on bodies that can be easily read.

In assessing Rostami's scars, Dr Douglas had to match the claimed cause with the appearance of the scar or lesion and assess their relative consistency with what Rostami had told her.[25] In her report, Douglas noted that, although Rostami gave a fluent account of his experiences, at several points he had difficulty breathing, paused, shook his head and became tearful. She also noted that Rostami had not tried to claim that all his scars were caused by his mistreatment. In doing so, words, demeanour and physical scars were all compared to one another to produce a clinical opinion. These observations are then checked against the various protocols and diagnostic criteria to make sure that their conclusions would be recognised by other clinicians. A psychological assessment is similarly not simply the taking in of a client's own self-reported symptoms; rather, it involves an assessment of the client's appearance, behaviour, speech and subjective mood. The reading of such signs can be difficult for clinicians, aware as they are of cultural differences in physical and emotional presentations. However, in this process neither bodies nor words are taken at face value but are weighed against one another. Language is interwoven with the corporeal and the visual (cf. Buch 2010; Cavell 1987).

CASUAL CERTAINTY

If clinical notions of causation are provisional and work at multiple levels, they potentially run up against legal demands for the narrowing of claims about the causes of particular injuries and symptoms. As Veena Das has argued, bureaucratic and legal forms of decision-making require that causation be described in mechanistic terms (Das 1995: 142). The law is concerned with stripping away all possible causes, only to leave the legally relevant (Fumerton and Kress 2001; Wright 1987). Although the legal process may allow for uncertainty in the shape of differing standards of proof, once a decision has been made, it is final. Clinical knowledge about causation is much less definitive. This is not to say that causation is not extremely important to clinical practice. The development of laboratory-based tests, for example, has meant that clinicians can increasingly investigate the causes of illnesses and disorders in individual patients. An investigation of causation is also important in order to localise the source of a problem, as well as to plan for future prevention. However, as Sandra Mitchell has argued, notions of causation in medicine can be context specific, and 'fraught with exceptions and contingency' (Mitchell 2010: 65). Historically, there has been a tension in medical diagnosis between a focus on symptoms (nosology) and an emphasis on causes (etiology). Furthermore, objects and processes working at levels as distinct as poverty, insects, sexual behaviour and viruses can all be said to cause medical problems. Finally, clinical theories of causation are inherently provisional and always depend on how a patient responds to treatment. Put bluntly, one key difference between legal and clinical perspectives on causation is that clinicians assume that what is known now may be incomplete and subject to revision, whereas lawyers seek more absolute and definitive views in order to come to a final decision. In writing medicolegal reports, clinical uncertainty about causation therefore has to be held against the forms of certainty demanded by lawyers and judges.

The key issue in writing medicolegal reports is how much, and exactly what, a psychological or scarring report can tell you about the likely causes of past events. Even if documentable traces are left, there is often no linear or necessary causal relation between a particular incident and subsequent symptoms. Scars can have several possible causes, and individual scars need to be assessed within the context of a broader claim. The psychological impacts of torture can also be indirect, ranging from psychosis to a few sleepless nights. In this context, clinicians are rarely, if ever, asked by lawyers to say whether any particular event amounts to torture. Rather, they are requested to express their opinion on the possible causes of specific injuries. The decision of whether a particular injury amounts to torture is one that judges, not clinicians, make at least in the context of medicolegal reports. Indeed, many British clinicians are reluctant to make statements about torture. Douglas did not refer directly to torture in her opinion in the report, but she used the word when referring to Rostami's own account. The Medical Foundation widely advises clinicians against using the word *torture*, taking the position that clinicians should comment on individual injuries and signs of distress, as this is more precise. Furthermore, as torture is a matter of legal definition and not a clinical syndrome, doctors are advised not to stray into areas of legal sensitivity. Medicolegal reports therefore try to link particular physical or psychological wounds to specific events. Torture, as an abstract noun, is much less amenable to clinical documentation than are more specific causes of injury.

CONCLUSIONS

For humanitarian principles, such as the prohibition of torture, to have a purchase on the world they must find techniques for making the distinction between the genuine and the duplicitous, the deserving and the undeserving. Exploring the ways in which this is done helps us understand how we find it possible to turn a blind eye to some forms of suffering or be stirred into action. Talal Asad has provocatively argued that one of the reasons that the category of torture has become an issue of such moral concern is that it appears to be a form of suffering whose levels are calculable (Asad 2003). This chapter suggests exactly the opposite. Whereas the idea that someone should not be tortured may appear firm in principle, in practice producing legally persuasive evidence that a particular person has been tortured is much more difficult. Despite the use of technical forms of knowledge such as medicine and law, stable legally admissible knowledge about the causes of pain and suffering is still hard to produce.

The issue here though is not the ability of medicine and law to grasp and represent the full experience of torture in its entirety – for what would be the point of that? To grasp pain in its fullness would only be to reproduce it (Perrin 2004; contrast Das 1995: 143; Lyotard 1988). The legal recognition of torture is not about sharing intimate experiences, making deep claims about the nature of being or acknowledging the other with all their differences and similarities (e.g. Honneth 1996; Povinelli 2002). Legal recognition is instead instrumental, concerned with the distribution of rights and the acceptance of obligations, and the meeting of the conditions necessary to make those decisions. However, even on its own terms, the legal category of torture resists stable recognition. When the law defines torture, it picks out suffering and its specific causes as important, but then complains that clinical evidence on those issues is too vague. Legal processes demand that people speak the language of law, but then claim that what is being said is not clear.

NOTES

1 The research for this chapter was made possible by an ESRC Research Fellowship.
2 *Ireland v. United Kingdom*, App no 5310/71 (ECtHR, 18 Jan 1978), para 167.
3 Article 1.
4 Memorandum for Alberto R. Gonzales, counsel to the president Re Standards of Conduct for Interrogation under 18 U.S.C. §§ 2340–2340A, pp. 6–7.
5 The full definition in the UN Convention Against Torture 1984 (Article 1) reads: '…"torture" means any act by which severe pain or suffering, whether physical or mental, is intentionally inflicted on a person for such purposes as obtaining from him or a third person information or a confession, punishing him for an act he or a third person has committed or is

suspected of having committed, or intimidating or coercing him or a third person, or for any reason based on discrimination of any kind, when such pain or suffering is inflicted by or at the instigation of or with the consent or acquiescence of a public official or other person acting in an official capacity. It does not include pain or suffering arising only from, inherent in or incidental to lawful sanctions.'

6 Names and details of both the client and the doctor have been changed to protect anonymity.

7 After the research for this article was carried out, the Medical Foundation changed its name to Freedom from Torture.

8 Interview with Yoav Landau-Pope, 28 November 2008.

9 RT (Medical Reports – Causation of Scarring) Sri Lanka [2008] UKAIT 00009.

10 RT (Medical Reports – Causation of Scarring) Sri Lanka [2008] 00009 [42].

11 Interview with doctor, 4 October 2008.

12 RT (Medical Reports – Causation of Scarring) Sri Lanka [2008] UKAIT 00009.

13 Interview with doctor, 10 Nov 2008.

14 Interview with therapist, 1 June 2010.

15 British clinicians, as those elsewhere in Europe, normally use the International Classification of Diseases (ICD), which is produced by the World Health Organization (WHO), rather than the DSM. However, in practice, the ICD broadly mirrors the DSM and has increasingly been brought into line.

16 The Home Office and many judges have argued that only psychiatrists can diagnose PTSD, a claim disputed by many other doctors and psychologists.

17 Leigh Neal, Notes for Assessing Psychiatric Injury in Asylum Seekers, no date, on file with the author.

18 Stuart Turner, A General Response to a Report by Dr Leigh Anthony Neal, 2002, on file with the author.

19 HY (Medical Evidence) Turkey [2004] UKIAT 00048.

20 HE (DRC – Credibility and Psychiatric Reports) DRC [2004] UKIAT 00321, [17].

21 HE (DRC – Credibility and Psychiatric Reports) DRC [2004] UKIAT 00321, [20].

22 As Elizabeth Davis has argued, a concern with the implications of lying has been particularly important in the history of psychiatry (Davis 2010).

23 Interview with doctor, 12 March 2009.

24 For examination of the sense of duplicitousness felt by UNHCR workers, see Sandvik (2009).

25 One result of this is that if a client does not know how a particular injury was sustained, it can be difficult to give an opinion on causation. There is a reliance on survivors being able to pinpoint particular blows and their resulting injuries – for example, when scars that can be examined were not necessarily the result of the blows felt to be most significant at the point of their infliction.

REFERENCES

Allodi, F. 1991. 'Assessment and Treatment of Torture Victims: A Critical Review', *Journal of Nervous and Mental Disease* 179: 4–11

Amnesty International 1977. *Evidence of Torture: Studies by Amnesty International Danish Medical Group.* London: Amnesty International

Asad, T. 2003. *Formations of the Secular: Christianity, Islam, Modernity.* Stanford, Calif.: Stanford University Press

Basoglu, M. 2006. 'Rehabilitation of Traumatised Refugees and Survivors of Torture', *British Medical Journal* 333: 1230–31

Buch, L. 2010. *Uncanny Affect Relations, Enduring Absence and the Ordinary in Families of Detainees in the Occupied Palestinian Territory.* PhD diss., Institute of Anthropology, University of Copenhagen

C. de C. Williams, A. and Amris, K. 2007. 'Pain from Torture', *Pain* 133: 5–8

Cavell, S. 1987. *Disowning Knowledge in Six Plays of Shakespeare.* Cambridge: Cambridge University Press

Cohen, J. 2001. 'Errors of Recall and Credibility: Can Omissions and Discrepancies in Successive Statements Reasonably Be Said to Undermine Credibility of Testimony?', *Medico-Legal Journal* 69: 25–34

Danielsen, L., Karlsmark, T. and Thomsen, H. K. 1997. 'Diagnosis of Skin Lesions Following Electrical Torture', *Romanian Journal of Legal Medicine* 5: 15–20

Das, V. 1995. *Critical Events: An Anthropological Perspective on Contemporary India.* New Delhi: Oxford University Press

Davis, E. 2010. 'The Anti-Social Profile: Deception and Intimacy in Greek Psychiatry', *Cultural Anthropology* 25: 130–64

Eitinger, L. and Weisaeth, L. 1998. 'Torture: History, Treatment and Medical Complicity', in Jaranson, J. and Popkin, M. (eds.), *Caring for Victims of Torture.* Washington, D.C.: American Psychiatric Press, pp. 3–14

Fassin, D. and d'Halluin, E. 2007. 'Critical Evidence: The Politics of Trauma in French Asylum Policies', *Ethos* 35: 300–329

2005. 'The Truth from the Body: Medical Certificates as Ultimate Evidence for Asylum Seekers', *American Anthropologist* 107: 597–608

Fumerton, R. and Kress, K. 2001. 'Causation and the Law: Preemption, Lawful Sufficiency, and Causal Sufficiency', *Law and Contemporary Problems* 64: 101–22

Genefke, I. 2008. 'Action Against Torture', *New Letters* 74: 69–82

Goldfeld, A., Mollica, R., Pesavento, B. and Faraone, S. 1988. 'The Physical and Psychological Sequelae of Torture: Symptomatology and Diagnosis', *Journal of the American Medical Association* 259: 2725–29

Haskell, T. 2000. *Objectivity Is Not Neutrality: Explanatory Schemes in History.* Baltimore: Johns Hopkins University Press

Honneth, A. 1996. *The Struggle for Recognition: The Moral Grammar of Social Conflicts*. Cambridge: Polity

Horowitz, A. V. 2002. *Creating Mental Illness*. Chicago: Chicago University Press

IRCT 2009. *Medical Physical Examination of Alleged Torture Victims: A Practical Guide to the Istanbul Protocol – For Medical Doctors*. Copenhagen: International Rehabilitation Council for Torture Victims

Jaranson, J. 1998. 'The Science and Politics of Rehabilitating Torture Survivors: An Overview', in Jaranson, James and Popkin, Michael (eds.), *Caring for Victims of Torture*. Washington, D.C.: American Psychiatric Press, pp. 14–40

James, J. 1987. *Pragmatism*, in Bruce Kuklick (ed.), *William James: Writings, 1902–1910*(New York: Library of America, 1987).

Jones, R. 2003. 'Wound and Injury Awareness Amongst Students and Doctors', *Journal of Clinical Forensic Medicine* 10: 231–34

Juhler, M. and Vesti, P. 1989. 'Torture: Diagnosis and Rehabilitation', *Medicine and War* 5: 69–79

Kelly, T. 2011. *This Side of Silence: Human Rights, Torture, and the Recognition of Cruelty*. Philadelphia: University of Pennsylvania Press

Lyotard, J.-F. 1988. *The Differend: Phrases in Dispute*. Minneapolis: University of Minnesota Press

Marsella, A., Friedman, M. and Spain, E. H. 1992. 'A Selective Review of the Literature on Ethnocultural Aspects of PTSD', *PTSD Research Quarterly* 2: 1–7

McIvor, R. J. and Turner, S. W. 1995. 'Assessment and Treatment Approaches for Survivors of Torture', *British Journal of Psychiatry* 166: 705–11

Mitchell, S. 2010. *Unsimple Truths: Science, Complexity and Policy*. Chicago: University of Chicago Press

Mollica, R. and Caspi-Yavin, Y. 1992. 'Overview: The Assessment and Diagnosis of Torture Events and Symptoms', in Basoglu, Metin (ed.), *Torture and Its Consequences: Current Treatment Approaches*. Cambridge: Cambridge University Press. pp. 38–55

OHCHR 2004. *Istanbul Protocol: Manual on the Effective Investigation and Documentation of Torture and Other Cruel, Inhuman or Degrading Treatment or Punishment*. Geneva: OHCHR

Perrin, C. 2004. 'Breath from Nowhere: The Silent "Foundation" of Human Rights', *Social and Legal Studies* 13: 133–151

Povinelli, E. 2002. *The Cunning of Recognition: Indigenous Alterities and the Making of Australian Multiculturalism*. Durham, N.C.: Duke University Press

Quiroga, J. and Jaranson, J. 2005. *Politically-Motivated Torture and Its Survivors: A Desk Study Review of the Literature*. Copenhagen: Rehabilitation and Research Centre for Torture Victims

Sandvik, Kristin Bergtora. 2009. 'The Physicality of Legal Consciousness: Suffering and the Production of Credibility in Refugee Resettlement.' In *Humani tarianism and Suffering: The Mobilization of Empathy*, edited by Richard Ashby Wilson and Richard Brown, 233–44. New York: Cambridge University Press

Seltzer, A., Sklan, A. and Patel, N.2006. 'Treating Torture Survivors – There Is No 'Quick Fix' – Response to Metin Basoglu, 2006: Rehabilitation of Traumatised Refugees and Survivors of Torture', *British Medical Journal* 333: 1230–31

Summerfield, D. 1999. 'A Critique of Seven Assumptions Behind Psychological Trauma Programmes in War-Affected Areas', *Social Science and Medicine* 48: 1449–62

Turner, S. and Gorst-Unsworth, C. 1990. 'Psychological Sequelae of Torture. A Descriptive Model', *Journal of Psychiatry* 157: 475–80

UKBA. No date. "Guidance on 'Considering Human Right Claims." http://www.ukba.homeoffice.gov.uk/sitecontent/documents/policyandlaw/asylumprocessguidance/consideringanddecidingtheclaim/guidance/consideringhrclaims.pdf? (accessed 1 November 2009)

Van Velsen, C., Gorst-Unsworth, C. and Turner, S. 1996. 'Survivors of Torture and Organized Violence: Demography and Diagnosis', *Journal of Traumatic Stress* 9: 1981–193

Wright, R. 1987. 'Causation, Responsibility, Risk, Probability, Naked Statistics and Proof: Pruning the Bramble Bush by Clarifying the Concepts', *Iowa Law Review* 73: 1001–77

Young, A. 1995. *Harmony of Illusions: Inventing Posttraumatic Stress Disorder.* Princeton, N.J.: Princeton University Press

CHAPTER FOUR

TRESPASS, CRIME AND INSANITY: THE SOCIAL LIFE OF CATEGORIES

Lydie Fialová

> *Then I went to the school for librarians and publishers in B, and I was as far as in the third year when this fatal episode with my mother happened, when I actually knifed her to death, and then I spend five month in the prison, and afterwards I was transferred – after the prosecution was suspended on the grounds of insanity – I was transferred here to this institution and here I am for a year and a quarter and I am waiting for what is to come.*
>
> *Josef K 2008*

Although it might seem that anyone addressing the notions of crime and insanity, treatment and punishment inevitably finds themselves on Foucaultian territory, my aim in this chapter is not a dialogue with the work of Michel Foucault (1965, 1977), whom I consider a historian of a specific culture of classical France. His studies on the logic and technologies of power certainly have wide resonance and have influenced the ways in which we conceptualise and understand the historicity of contemporary practices, in the areas of both medicine and jurisprudence. However, in this contribution I intend to complement his perspective 'from above' with the perspective 'from within' and my interest is twofold: first, to understand what it means to interpret specific transgressive acts within specific frameworks – in this case moral, medical, legal and religious; second, to examine assumptions about the nature of such seemingly transgressive acts that allow people to place them in such general categories. As Hans Georg Gadamer demonstrated, meaning is not a quality of a thing as such, but is always derived from its context (Gadamer 1994). In this sense, the interpretative context is constitutive of meaning. I am therefore interested in the law and medicine as a resource for the interpretation of human action and behaviour, and in their normative role in human affairs. These interpretations presuppose as well as constitute the moral dimensions of reality.

This chapter will be structured around a case study of a young man whom I shall call Josef K. I encountered him while he was a patient in the forensic ward of a psychiatric hospital. After being found guilty of killing his mother and sentenced to prison, he was later exempted from criminal culpability on the grounds of insanity and transferred to a psychiatric hospital. His act was therefore reclassified – although with a fair amount of uncertainty – from crime to insanity. His family, nevertheless, interpreted the event as an unforgivable trespass, as a guilt from which he could never be absolved. He himself was rather unsure about the nature of his act, claiming a lack of clear memory of the actual event, and refused to identify with the act itself. He was rather confused by the multiple possible interpretations and even the very possibility of 'acting as someone else', as he retrospectively described the event. These shifts in interpretation left him caught in an abyss of in-between categories, living in a psychiatric institution for an indeterminate time with very little hope of resolution and a lack of definite answers.

Drawing on the work of historian Daniela Tinková, namely her book *Crime, Sin, Madness in the Era of Disenchantment of the World* (2004), I will address specific variations on the distinctive categorical registers – moral, medical, legal and religious – that have been used as alternative explanations for the death of the young man's mother. Addressing the notions of intentionality, responsibility and culpability, I will explore the assumptions of these categorical frames with regard to agency, temporality and possibility of resolution. I will also present the current legal and institutional framework for forensic psychiatry and address the ambiguities created by uncertainty that expose the limits of medical and legal expertise with regard to subjectivity of experience. The chapter examines Josef's account of his movement between different registers of expertise and institutional forms – mainly medical and legal – and the ways in which these result in his own sense of alienation from his own acts. It also explores the processes through which criminal law and psychiatry draw on one another in order to make the causes of transgression visible – through expert notions of capacity and culpability. Ultimately though, law and medicine fail to come together in a neat and clean embrace, while Josef's own family continues to maintain moral interpretations of his act that exceed the clinical or the legal. Josef is thus left in a space in-between, a no-man's land, where both law and medicine are ultimately implicitly forced to admit the inadequacy of their claims to either cure or punish.

JOSEF K

Josef was 24 when I met him. He was one of the younger patients on the forensic ward in the Psychiatric Hospital in Kosmonosy. This hospital is located in a small village in North Bohemia and was founded in 1867 on the premises of a former monastery. As the 'Royal Bohemian Provincial Asylum for Insane' the hospital offered a refuge for patients with 'incurable conditions' who were transferred here from the neuropsychiatric clinic in Prague. By 2013, it took care of 650 in-patients and offers treatment for patients from a substantial region of North Bohemia. In addition to acute psychiatric care, the hospital also provides long-term care for patients suffering from chronic forms of psychiatric conditions – patients with dementia, severe forms of mental disability presented alongside mental illness, patients with sexual deviance, and also patients with forensic history. As a researcher (and, officially, a psychiatry trainee) I was working closely with a young psychologist whose primary responsibility was on the forensic ward. It was here that I encountered Josef regularly on the morning ward meetings, as well as at art therapy, hippotherapy and group therapy sessions. Josef also always greeted me eagerly when I was passing the hospital laundry where he worked during the day. He was respected by other patients since he was quite outspoken, rather friendly and a good natured man. 'You should not be misled by his behaviour', said the psychologist one day. 'He is a very clever man indeed. Do you know why he is here? He killed his mother. Supposedly schizophrenia – have you ever seen such a well-compensated schizophrenia? I would think he is more of a psychopath than a schizophrenic.' This doubt about the nature of his condition, presented as a diagnostic dilemma with wide-reaching consequences, was a first reminder that diagnostic categories as written on paper are never self-evident, and can always be otherwise.

One day I asked Josef whether he would be willing to talk with me for about an hour, since I was conducting interviews with people suffering from schizophrenia to learn more about their experiences of illness and its treatment. He agreed. The psychologist allowed me to use her room, which was simply but welcomingly decorated, despite being full of old and partially broken furniture, with piles of books and patient documentation on the floor. I was trying to remember the guidance we received as medical students on the spatial order in the room when conducting interview with potentially 'dangerous' patients – you always have to be closer to the door than the patient is, and have your phone ready close by. However, although I was well aware that I was quite close to a strong and well-built man whose past might cause anxiety, Josef's manners did not directly indicate the need for such precautions. As before, he was friendly and well-mannered, and we soon became immersed in a rather unusual conversation. Although in the beginning I roughly followed the open-ended style of medical interview on the experience of illness, I was much more interested in what it was actually like to experience all these things, to have such a history. I was well aware that his account has been edited by being told over and over again to people of various roles – physicians, friends, police, judges, psychologists, other patients. Josef told me about his childhood in a small spa town, early years in school, playing truant and smoking marijuana, of his military service and adventurous trip to London and disappointing return to the grey, small town of Prague, and his subsequent training in technical and librarian school. As he continued his narrative I asked him at which point did the illness appear? I quote his answer below at length.

Well, officially according to the expert evidence – and that is what I forgot to add before – that in year of 2005 after the symptoms of schizophrenia or psychosis appeared, I was hospitalised in this institution on the A12 ward. I spend there about six or eight weeks and was discharged, with the diagnosis of diminished social adaptability. They did not recognise then that it actually was a schizophrenia, and because of that reassurance I was convinced that I am all right. I ceased to attend to my doctor, and that is why the recurrent relapse came about and that what has happened later in that year of 2006. Then again I heard the voices. It was something like that the neighbours were slandering over me that I only stay in my bed and am not even able to cook my own meals, and more of such flagellant comments on all of my behaviour. And so I went out for a jog and in the park I again heard the voices from the darkness, and here it was a quite cruel persecution already. Then I came back to my family and few days afterwards this happened, I knifed this mum of mine, and ... That day, or the evening before that, I went to play football with my friends. They were all my friends that I knew for long, ever since a primary school days or so, but still I had the feeling that they are all plotting against me, and by means of telepathy soak the energy from me and prevent me from moving and so on. And from the protocol that was brought to me by my lawyer I learned that I behaved strangely and did not respond to their questions and ...I behaved in a non-standard way ... When I came back home and heard the voices that were attacking me constantly, I realised that ...that ...simply that I am against all ... Additionally, I had a delusion that my father is my teacher together with another man, and I just could not fall asleep in the midst of all this, and as a shield against their attacks I took the book by J. R. R. Tolkien Hobbit and when I was reading the words I did not hear the voices but I could not concentrate. I refused to eat the dinner, and finally fell asleep and in the morning I woke up and have heard the voices of all of them, threatening that they tear my brain into pieces, that they steal my memories and lower my intellect, and...well...that was all very intense and...well...I decided to commit suicide and...First I telepathically asked my father to lend me his revolver so that I could shoot myself and my father replied that he no longer trusts me, that I am already too much on their side and he can no longer protect me, that I take over their appearance and behaviour and so I decided to commit suicide with the knife that I took from the kitchen and run out of the house and cut myself four times in my throat in the garden of a café that is very close to us...Because I considered the owner of the café to be against me so this would be kind of my reward to shame him by bleeding out on his garden, so I cut myself four times in my throat but I did not manage to cut strongly enough...Then I tried to spear it in my heart but I also did not succeed, so I returned back home and I did fling at my mother and eventually I knifed her to death. And then my father came and wriggled the knife out of my hands, thrust me down on the floor, fisted on my face and trampled me to the room next door and called the ambulance – I am not sure anymore whether he called the ambulance from there or from the kitchen, and when the ambulance came that informed the police as well so that the police was there too, and after that he simply told me that actually I killed my mother and I said something like that she is strong and would survive it...Then eventually they embarked me into the car and took some urine samples, and took the blood, and then I found myself in the prison cell.[1]

What was striking in this account was the apparent neutrality of the whole narrative, as if Josef was actually absent from the events he recounts. Most of the time, he was using passive rather than active verbs, and at times it almost seemed like he was telling a story of some-one else entirely – rather a matter of fact account, not coloured by any emotional or personal involvement. He would quote the accounts of others, as well as what the experts thought was going on, and referred to the 'expert's' opinion as evidence of what actually happened – as if there were no 'inside' of the experience. He gave an account of being persecuted by the voices, under which influence he first tried to kill himself and when that did not work, he killed his mother who happened to be in the way. He mentions also the mythical world of the Hobbit into which he was trying to immerse himself to escape the 'reality' of being attacked by others, although this 'reality' almost absorbed some of the mythical qualities of the novel and possibly transformed his interpretation of the events. The 'absence' or passivity in the face of psychotic experience was a rather common narrative pattern among the patients I interviewed, but they also often felt deeply touched by what they actually lived through. This did not seem to be the case with Josef and therefore I asked him about that.

> Well, it is kind of . . . It is that if someone is under the influence of the acute episode of the attack of the illness then he behaves like someone else, he experience like someone else. It is rather that a state in which I am now and that in which I was when I was ill – or actually I am still ill because it is untreatable illness or treatable but not curable – it is like I realise it was me who has done that all, or who experienced it all, but I do not identify with that. . . . In my perspective it is all pure madness . . . Something happened that is impossible to de-happen . . . I am sorry for that . . . On the other hand, well, I did not intend to do it, and it just . . . It is not – it was not my intention . . . I loved my mother a lot, and that happened what happened is simply a consequence of the illness that I suffer from . . . And that is also the reason why I am here and not in the prison.

In this part of the narrative we can follow his depiction of illness as a foreign entity that exerts influence over one's behaviour, something that resists any rational explanation and yet takes over and transforms its subject into someone else. The illness is the source of his action in this account. Josef did not identify with his actions, which he considered external to him. He stressed that the act was not intended, which was crucial for the evaluation of his condition – crime or insanity – and mentions two institutions that correspond accordingly with the nature of his act: the prison and the hospital. I therefore asked him about how it came about that he was in the hospital, and whether the fact that he was in the hospital to undergo a treatment (rather than in prison to serve his sentence) had any impact on his perspective on the whole situation.

> I remember it was from the stage when I was brought to the prison and the illness was still strong then I . . . actually . . . I was rather overwhelmed by the illness so I was not really aware of the consequences

of my behaviour. Later when it slowly faded away so first I was full of optimism that in the prison you could actually even study for a degree and that some ten or fifteen years – as various people told me which I incidentally met in the corridor when we went for a walk or so – so they told me that I would be given twelve years possibly, as I am sentenced for the first time. Then I told myself: twelve years, I would be some thirty-five by then, well, it is still possible to start all over again, and I might even go for two thirds, so after eight years I could get out, and so I was still rather full of optimism, but later on I started thinking, you know, eight years, that is still a rather long time, or I might be given fifteen, or they might reappraise it to second degree, because it was effected in especially cruel way, and by then I begun to feel rather nervous, and then ... Actually when I was still in B I read in a newspaper that 'jab-bing medical student was redeemed by insanity' and actually I begun to hope that I might be also given this 'insanity', that it is just impossible that I knifed my mother that I loved her and I did not want to do it, and actually I told this what I experienced to my fellow prisoners that were there with me, and they said to me you are just mad, you are crazy, it could not simply be true, yes, and so I told to myself that there must really be something more to that all than that I would just go and kill my mother.

As in the previous account, the illness was the active force behind his experience, overwhelming him and clouding any 'reasonable' thoughts and consideration. Then, almost as if waking up from a dream and find-ing himself in the prison and finally able to realistically assess his situ-ation, he considered the options he might have in this situation. The idea that the whole experience was an experience of madness is brought to him by reading a newspaper, and it is not Josef but someone else who suggests that his act – that remained incomprehensible for him – might be a sign of insanity. This possible explanation would have a decisive implication for his future. He seemed to be struggling to make sense of the whole situation, almost like trying to solve a puzzle, where there seemed to be something more in the equation than what you might gather from a mere external observation of events. However, this is the most problematic point of the whole case: at one level the analyst might claim that Josef is the only one who has access to his subjective expe-rience, who can tell the truth or lie about the voices and delusions, and who can make judgement about his intentions. Nevertheless, Josef still seemed to be rather confused about the whole thing and claimed he could not actually remember the situation. His own access to the experience, or at least the memory of that experience, was indirect and uncertain:

> Well, the problem is, I do not remember this at all, I have black-out on the situation when I jugged the knife to my mother, and when I caused what I caused, so I just can not recall it. I know I thought my mum is a witch and she sips energy from me and that even the evening before that because she was sleeping there already before that as she did not want to disturb the father in bedroom because she had a cold, so ... Well ... I might have heard something like she is a witch, you must kill at least her, or something like that, and so I did fling at my mother and actually I knifed her to death. ... I first wanted to kill myself because the voices were telling me I must murder for them, sell drugs, well, prostitute, and such things, so I thought I would be their puppet and they would influence me telepathically from distance this community of the people that were all against me.

At this point he offered a rather plausible explanation: acting under command of the voices. He was referring to voices of the illness that caused him to act in this way, as an external source for his act – as though through the acknowledgement of this other explanation the whole event seems much more intelligible and even 'rational'. The motive of a witch escaped the imaginary world and fused with the real one, although it is possibly a retrospective explanation through which he was trying to illuminate his confusion and make his act seem a natural response to the peril he experienced. Nevertheless, this explanation still remained a 'guess', as he claimed to be unable to access his actual experience and capture it in words, since he did not have a clear memory of the events. And although throughout most of his narrative he was aware that the voices were 'outside of himself', external to him, at a certain point this distinction collapsed, where the world of possible delusion and that of the reality merged into one:

> Well, I just was so scared of my own life that ... in the expert's report it is stated that I attempted to eliminate imaginary peril in my surroundings, so because I was so scared by what was happening well how I tried to cut my throat and pierce my heart, that I came to the kitchen where my mum was lying on the floor, and well she is a witch ... And then I recalled the whole conglomerate of people that were against me, and she was a special instance of that peril and so I did fling at my mother and actually I knifed her to death ...

The switch in perspectives allows the killing of Josef's mother to become an intelligible response to the reality of being exposed to horrifying danger. Recognising and acknowledging the possibility of this other reality, however delusional, has far-reaching consequences for evaluation of his act. Here again Josef refers to the expert opinion as a resource for possible interpretation of this event. He presents their explanation as valid, as it confirms the internal logic of his act as a response to his actual experience of danger. It is impossible to tell whether this confusion was a genuine uncertainty on his part, or whether it was an intentional strategy to adopt the narrative of psychotic experience in order to justify the inevitability of his act, as the psychologist suggested. The externalisation of the illness and the attribution of the agency to schizophrenia is significant, as it stands for the distinction between what could be classified as pure psychosis and what constitutes psychopathy. Unlike the experience of psychosis, when someone is genuinely overwhelmed by their delusional experience, in the case of psychopathic personality disorder the cause is essentially the person as such, which remains the agent of the action.

This distinction between psychosis and psychopathy is of utmost importance for the legal assessment of Josef's act. It is in this crucial dilemma of how to classify this act that the questions about the nature and limits of freedom, the tension between reason and passions and the extent of human responsibility and culpability resonate. To understand this multiplicity of interpretations and their validity we need to examine the referential frameworks from which they derive their meaning and the assumptions on which they are based.

TRESPASS, CRIME AND INSANITY

Where they treat of Original Sin, they declare that free will, though impaired in its powers and biased, is not however extinguished. I will not dispute about a name, but since they contend that liberty has by no means been extinguished, they certainly understand that the human will has still some power left to choose good. For where death is not, there is at least some portion of life. They themselves remove all ambiguity when they call it impaired and biased. Therefore, if we believe them, Original Sin has weakened us, so that the defect of our will is not pravity but weakness. For if the will were wholly depraved, its health would not only be impaired but lost until it were renewed. The latter, however, is uniformly the doctrine of Scripture. To omit innumerable passages where

Paul discourses on the nature of the human race, he does not charge free-will with weakness, but declares all men to be useless, alienated from God, and enslaved to the tyranny of sin; so much so, that he says they are unfit to think a good thought. (Romans 3:12; 2 Corinthians 3:5.) We do not however deny, that a will, though bad, remains in man. For the fall of Adam did not take away the will, but made it a slave where it was free. It is not only prone to sin, but is made subject to sin. Of this subject we shall again speak by and by.

This is an excerpt from John Calvin's Antidote to the Sixth Session of the Council of Trent on the Doctrine of Justification (1547). Calvin was responding to the Catholic Church's reaffirmation of the doctrine of free will in response to the Protestant challenge that emphasised God's grace to be the source of Salvation, and rejected their teaching on predestination. Since the sixteenth century, the dispute between determinism and free will that resonated in this debate has moved from theology to philosophy, and later psychology, and most recently, biology. The transition of this debate between various scholarly disciplines reflects shifts in authoritative 'truth discourses', moving from theological through metaphysical to the scientific. We might also follow these shifts in the categories through which transgressive behaviour is conceptualised. The influential Christian notion of sin has long served as a source for the legal categories of transgression, and while the image of criminal was fused with that of sinner, the notion of responsibility provided a link between moral and penal transgression. Throughout the Middle Ages the sovereign monarch represented a divine deputy responsible for earthly justice and therefore provided the appropriate space in which to deal with acts considered as sinful/criminal. The Christian interiorisation of sin, relegated to the individual 'tribunal of conscience' has arguably led to the disappearance of the transcendent category of sin and to a formulation of crime as a trespass of written and clearly formulated earthly law.

In the early modern period, crime ceased to be a private issue between the perpetrator and victim as a transgression of divine law, and became an issue of public interest as an expression of the relationship between the subject and authority. As Daniela Tinková argues in her book *Crime, Sin, Madness in the Era of Disenchantment of the World* (Tinková 2004), the substitution of the Sovereign God and his earthly deputy as a lawgiver by a sovereign state founded through a social contract resulted in the transformation of the concept of trespass of moral code into that of a crime against the society. This gradual shift in transgressive categories also resulted in the conceptual abstraction and generalisation of these categories. In the case of homicide, the legal formulation until late sixteenth century was an 'article against those who slaughter', whereas later it was listed as 'a murder'. The crime came to be defined legally and devoid of any interpersonal relations and without reference to transcendental values – crime is a civil or social harm rather than a sin. This also greatly transformed what was considered an appropriate response: where sin allows for the possibility of atonement and forgiveness, guilt can be redeemed by expiatory rituals; in the case of crime the appropriate response is punishment or, later, a rehabilitation. There is no such thing as forgiveness in the law.

Tinková's claim is that the superiority of God in the hierarchy of protected values was in early modern times substituted by the superiority of the state. The protection of societal – rather than divine – values and principles was to be guaranteed by the public authority. This process, sometimes understood as modernisation and secularisation, shifted the boundaries between religion, the rule of state law and medicine – some acts were reclassified from the realm of the sacred to that of the secular, some decriminalised, and some medicalised. This is not to say that the concept of sin was eradicated, but rather that it had to compete with other potentially more powerful ways of understanding transgression. In the shift from sin to crime there was a redrawing of the territory of what activities properly belong to the sphere of religion or private morality, what are regulated by law, and what are interpreted through the lens of medical discourse. This movement has also changed the concepts of crime, insanity and sin – and freedom – as their context of interpretation was transformed. Crime is now an act committed in full awareness and with an ill intention, and the newly constituted category of madness represents an exemption from this general premise. The pathologisation of criminal behaviour has been a slow process surrounded by scientific debates on the influence of reason and passions on human conduct. It has been popularly assumed that strong instincts can sometimes overrule the moral conscience and force the affected individual to commit offense. In this perspective, the perpetrator becomes the victim of their illness. The crucial concept in this regard is the notion of mental capacity, or competence, and it is on this ground that the exemption of madness from crime – known as insanity defence – has been recognised by a significant number of legal systems.

Criminal law attributes different levels of significance to specific mental disorders. According to the criminal law of the Czech Republic, the criminal act is defined as an act dangerous for the society. The criminal act can be committed only by a person older than 15 years of age who is mentally competent. In the case of the criminal act being committed by a person who is incompetent, criminal responsibility cannot be established: incapacity is defined as a lack or loss of the ability to recognise and understand the nature of the act which is dangerous to the society, or the loss of control over behaviour as a consequence of mental disorder present at the time of the offense. Authority to speak on the issue of free will has often been entrusted to the medical profession, especially to psychiatry. In practice, in order to make a judgement about the significance of a mental disorder, the court is assisted by the experts in psychiatry and clinical psychology. The suspect is examined by two experts in psychiatry (or sexology) who might be assisted by a consultant in clinical psychology. The experts seek to establish relative abilities to recognise and control behaviour with respect to a mental disorder and the specific act. Clinicians are also asked for their opinion on the social dangerousness of the offender with respect to the potential protective measures. The final decision then lies with the court.

Currently, in the Czech Republic, as in many other places, the definition of mental disorder that results either in the loss of capacity of recognition, or in the loss of self-control, or both, is part of both legal and medical categories. However, it is medical categories that are primarily constitutive of the concept of incapacity. The classificatory categories used in forensic psychiatry make a distinction between permanent mental disorders, temporary mental disorders, and invalid (pathological) mental states. The distinction between partial and full incapacity is defined in forensic psychiatry with reference to the ICD-10 categories: full incapacity is related to severe forms of mental illness – schizophrenia, permanent delusional disorders, acute psychotic disorders, schizoaffective disorders, bipolar affective disorder, dementia; post-injury mental states, severe intoxications; severe mental retardation.[2] Partial incapacity is not defined by law, but in practice is understood as a significant diminishment of the recognition or control that occur in less severe forms of mental illness – bipolar disorders, initial stages of dementia, epileptic personality changes; mental states caused by extreme exhaustion and significantly, lighter forms of mental retardation and, significantly, personality disorders. The assumption behind the notion of personality disorder (a category suggested by the psychologist in the case of Josef K as more appropriate than schizophrenia, based on the clinical psychological examination), where the behaviour of the patient is at least partially ego-syntonic, also has implications for the legal attribution of culpability. The legal concept of capacity and responsibility thus relies on medical expert categories. Psychiatric classification is therefore essential for the distinction between partial and full incapacity, which has significant consequences for the measures taken to respond to the act – punishment, treatment or both.

There are three main medical and legal concepts in play in understanding Josef's act: capacity, culpability and dangerousness. Whereas the concept of capacity relates to the ability to understand the nature and consequences of the act and make a judgement based on this understanding – the evaluation of which is within the authority of medicine – the concept of culpability is related to the intentionality of the act and therefore lies within the domain of law. Incapacity can therefore be established on the medical grounds of insanity, while the intentionality of the act corresponds to the legal notions of responsibility and culpability and therefore makes the subject criminally liable. In this way, the legal and the medical are both constitutive for the concept of dangerousness. However, the definition of dangerousness is rather precarious because of the interdisciplinary tension between law and psychiatry as to what the dangerousness refers to – in law this refers to the dangerousness of the act whereas psychiatry is supposed to make a judgement on the dangerousness of the person. These distinctions presuppose different forms of assessment, and additionally result in very different social responses: treatment, punishment, protective treatment, rehabilitation or social isolation – or their various combinations.

In addition to law and medicine, there is yet another dimension to the evaluation of specific behaviour. There still remains the interpersonal dimension, the potential harm to those who are affected by the act, and their response. In the case of Josef it was not just his mother who suffered the harm; the whole family was affected by the loss of his mother. I asked him about how this event affected their relationship.

> Presently, I do not have any contact with my family. About a year ago around this time my father sent me three boxes with my clothes, and the shaving razor, and actually, even before that when I was still in prison he sent me a letter to the life insurance company requesting the cancellation of my contract, and in few simple sentences asked me to sign the letter, and ever since I have no contact with him, nor with my brother and sister, or my grandmother, uncle, cousin, or actually with anyone

from my family....I sent them letters, and attempted to call them – my father indicated the phone numbers of my brother and sister in the protocol, so I have their numbers in my mobile phone, and tried to called them once, and the sister told me I will not talk to you, she was hysterical when she said that, and my brother just cancelled the call. And then my sister sent me a text last year, actually on 2 July, when my mum had a birthday because she always remembered her birthday and has always reminded me because she knew I never remembered, well...she simply wrote me that I have caused her so much pain and suffering that she would never accept me again, and that the death of mum is still very painful and that my mum would have had birthday today.

Josef's family therefore did not accept the expert interpretation of his act; for them it remained a deed for which there is no excuse and no atonement. For them, an irreversible harm had been done, and it was irrelevant what the relevant authorities, acting on behalf of the state, made out of that – it was ultimately an act that effaced and erased Josef from their family. We can see here that there are alternative ways to interpret the situation, each interpretation has its own framework of reference and logic of validity. Insanity is an 'invisible' condition and it takes medical expertise to make it visible and valid. Subsequently, it also requires a willingness on behalf of those around the diagnosed patient to believe and accept this expert interpretation. The medical diagnosis did not seem a credible explanation for Josef's family. Josef himself was rather confused about the whole situation and about the nature of illness that might have caused him to act in this way:

I did not know it is actually the illness, I have never heard of such an illness, none told me the symptoms of the illness, you know, I never had that, that awareness the voices are in my head only, so now when I hear the voice, and it happened on a few occasions here that I have heard voices, I was able to discern that these are indeed voices. So in the case that the voices would come over certain acceptable threshold, it means I would hear them more than thirty seconds once a week, I would report on that, and they would alter the medication, and the therapy, and something would be done about that ... I would inform the doctors that I hear voices or that something strange is happening, that I do not sleep or eat or something like that, that something unusual is going on, because it is never just a change from one moment to the other, it always comes as a complex of curious and strange phenomena that all converge to the final breakout.

Josef here has recourse to the medical explanation of the nature of ill-ness and its symptoms – the voices – that are external to him and should be properly managed by medical means of treatment therapy.

Crucially, the doubts about the nature of Josef's condition held by the psychologist are important: they draw a distinction even within the category of mental illness. Schizophrenia is more likely to be perceived as something external to the person, treatable if not curable, whereas psychopathy as an inherent trait or almost an essence of a person – not treatable by the standard means of biological psychiatry, but also not something entirely punishable, more appropriately subject to isola-tion and attempts to rehabilitation and re-education. This distinction between the external and internal cause is then reflected in the assess-ment of partial or full incompetence and the level of legal culpability.

The authorities that were to decide on Josef's fate had the assistance of various forms of clinical and legal expertise. However, these experts provided multiple and sometimes contradictory, evaluations and inter-pretations: the legal framework first established the act as a crime, and later the psychiatric framework made illness visible as a cause of his behaviour. Psychiatrists evaluated the situation as an act committed under the influence of mental condition – a mental illness that was external to Josef K rather than a deliberate act and intention. However, this judgement was made on the basis of external appearances, while acknowledging the inaccessible interiority of the person. When I asked Josef about his prospects for the future, he acknowledged the complex-ity of making a judgement, and his answer expressed his consignation to the expert opinion:

> It all depends on the expert's reports, how they will judge on my health status, and the danger to society and so on, it is not an easy task, what I did is a great trespass, actually the greatest one can do, that even if I caused it, even if my illness caused it, so it would not be an easy judge-ment to make you know and it all depends on how the situation would evolve...

ONE BAD APPLE CAN SPOIL THE WHOLE BARREL: PUNISHMENT, TREATMENT AND THE PROTECTION OF SOCIETY

The uncertainty about the validity of either criminal or clinical inter-pretations of Josef's act finds its expression in the variety of institutions and institutional regimes aimed at treating and caring for persons who find themselves having committed a transgression. The impossibility of drawing a clear line that separates insanity and crime, and the grey zone that occurs where these two intersect, is reflected also in the structure of institutions. It is not a coincidence that prisons and psychiatric hospitals have historically been part of similar projects of control. Inmates of both of these institutions share similar state of liminality and social seclusion. However, the concurrent fusion of incapacity and dangerousness does not allow some patients/criminals to fit entirely into either of these institutional categories. In the case of Josef, there were multiple transfers between various prisons and a hospital:

> They brought me to R [prison] and there I brawled with another man because I borrowed the book that was on his table and so I throttled him and in that moment the warder was there and he told me that simply I am transferred to B and I told him I don't care, I was there for two days and I did not eat nor drink or I drank but just a little as I thought I am a vampire and suck out the energy telepathically. Eventually, we then went to B [prison hospital], we went by ambulance, with additional police or rather warder escort, and then we arrived to B where I was alone in a kind of admission room where there was only stoneware table, bench, and a bed with iron construction adjusted for restrains, and there I spend eventually a week or maybe ten days in hallucinations and delusions, and then finally they believed me and put me on medication and there I spoke to the doctor and told her my mum was an ill honeycomb that had to be removed and such things, or when she asked me what I am thinking about I told her I plan terrorist attack in Prague underground and so, and then after maybe ten or fourteen days they transferred me to a room where there was a toilet not an Ottoman but a normal one, and where there were these small bedside tables and even the classical hospital bed, and there I was another two or three weeks alone, but in this time I actually read quite a lot and the voices were eventually disappearing, and then actually they put me on a cell with other condemned or accused – no – I must have been with the accused by then. And there in B I was for three month, from November to February, and in February I was transferred again by the escort to P [prison], there I waited for three weeks or maybe a month for the expert verdict and they … they actually decided on the suspension of prosecution and concluded that actually I was insane. And then I was transferred back to R, there I spend three weeks, and then I was transferred here [psychiatric hospital].

The above account, however confused, gives a sense of the uncertainty about how to judge Josef's state and condition. It is interesting to follow the differences in the material world of the institutions – in his account of the prison and of the hospital, Josef would often mention details of the interior of the institution – stoneware table, bench and bed with iron construction adjusted for restrains in the prison; the bedside table and hospital bed, and later the 'home-like feeling' of the hospital. The minimalistic interior of both of these quite nicely and accurately reflects the reduction of life in the space of institutional order. Similarly, his experience of time was also significantly transformed: the suspension of time in between waiting oriented towards the future and his recollection and meditation over the past that were like a key to one of the possible doors – prison, hospital or yet something else. I asked Josef about what it was like to live in this suspended state and location outside of the world, and his response vividly contrasts these two spaces outside the one that he inhabited before the fatal event.

> Well…when I was brought here [the psychiatric hospital], I was just like a rapture, this incredible freedom, because I still had a fresh alive memories of the suffering in the prison, where a man was once daily launched to the courtyard to the concrete corridor, where he could spend this one hour, and then he was strike back to the cell, which was about the same size as this room, where he would spend the rest of twenty-three hours, but even in the prison thanks to that I had a good fellow prisoners – with one exception, he was just an idiot with whom I just could not get around so that they even had to transfer us to different cells – so with the people there I could share what I experienced and we speculated what is going to happen next, what the resolution might be like, and in a way they even helped me materially, they brought me tobacco and such things, because I had no resources, and no contact with the outer world, which helped me to bear even the prison where the lack of freedom was quite extreme relatively well. And then afterward when I was transferred here I thought it is just as on the castle, the cultural room is such a homey room, so I was rather excited about this place, and with the time this euphoria is leaving me and I think that still in comparison to the life I lived before this happened so the lack of freedom, the restriction in rights and freedoms…Well…My perspective on this is that I have done something that you should not do, and even though I was ill the society needs to protect itself, so I would have to spend some time here, so that there is a certainty that the illness is under control, that I am in the remission, that the treatment responds to the symptoms of the illness and endure it here somehow…And so that I have to flog myself to keep in some kind of mental condition, and it is not very easy

you see, because the environment here is rather frustrating, when you think about it, because here are cases more serious than I am, maybe not in the consequences, but in the expressions, they are going through what I went through and sometimes the medication does not work and so on, and every morning you look out on the landscape around through the bars in the window, so it affects you, but still it is better than to spend fifteen years somewhere in the prison, or eighteen, so ... I manage to bear it so far.

In his narrative, the impressions of the environment was infused by a reflection of what the different institutional regimes disclose about the nature of the act, be it a crime or illness. He talked about his fellow inmates with whom he shared his fate for now, and about the time perspective that colours his perception of both his future and his past. A criminal sentence is usually given for a specific time period, whereas treatment – especially in conditions deemed untreatable or incurable – lacks the definitiveness of time and becomes waiting for healing that might never come.

However, neither of the two institutions – prison or psychiatric hospital – are currently considered appropriate for people with both a psychiatric and a criminal history. In 2005 the Czech government approved a plan to establish specially secured detention institutions for patients who cannot be convicted because of their incapacity, and for offenders with severe personality disorder. These detention institutions represent, in some way, a combination of both psychiatric hospitals and prison. The director of the largest psychiatric hospital currently taking care of 1200 patients explained:

Detention institution is an institution where those people should be placed who nowadays are being solved by protective psychiatric or sexological treatment and is aimed for those in whom the treatment cannot fulfil its purpose because their disorder is incurable or they refuse the treatment while remaining socially very dangerous. These patients currently cause a lot of trouble to the psychiatric hospitals since they often interfere with therapeutic regime. They often refuse treatment and convey these attitudes on other patients, they create an atmosphere that not only lacks being therapeutic, but can be extremely hostile towards all therapeutic attempts, and therefore they prevent treatment of others whose therapy might otherwise be successful. On the other hand, these patients cannot be guaranteed adequate therapy in the prisons.[3]

The emphasis on the therapy of even 'incurable' conditions is what makes the regime in such institutions hospital-like. The prison is not considered appropriate for them since it lacks this emphasis on therapy or treatment. Many professionals saw this as a benefit and welcomed the establishment of the detention institution, which would combine psychiatric hospital and prison. The representative of the Ministry of Justice explains the rationale of this decision:

> The judges very often complain that institutions for the execution of punishment are not sufficient for offenders of serious crimes, violent crimes, who were lacking capacity in the moment of their crime. They are given so called institutional corrective education and this institutional corrective education does not fulfil and does not guarantee the basic condition that the offender cannot come into contact with society, in other words, that they can escape from these institution and continue with their criminal activities.[4]

The emphasis here is on re-education, as an addition or substitution of mere punishment imposed on those who commit serious crimes. In 2009 a new law that allowed for secluding inmates in a detention institution came into force. The director of the first detention institution in Brno, who is also a consultant in the psychiatric ward of the nearby prison hospital, described this first institution and the rules that dictate the life there:

> Detention is aimed for dangerous offenders who committed especially severe offenses, and who committed them under the influence of disorder and protective treatment is not effective or cannot provide sufficient protection of the society. In respect to the law they are inmates – neither convicts, nor patients. They are provided health services similar to those in psychiatric hospital, and the building and interiors are more like a prison, we have here warders, cells and security. The security makes it more like a prison, so the risk of escape is minimal. Internal regime however involves treatment and therapy and is therefore more like a healthcare institution. The inmates do not have to wear prison clothes, they can wear their civil clothes – if they have someone who will do the laundry for them – or they can wear institutional clothes from our hospital, i.e. pyjamas. We plan to have community sessions, therapeutic consultations, occupational therapy and workshops, psychotherapeutic group sessions and psychiatric care if required. In comparison to convicts the regime is less strict, the rules regulating the visits, correspondence, packages and walks in the prison space. Detention is aimed for the most

dangerous patients, who in addition often boycott the treatment, and therefore the change of their attitude is necessary so that they cooperate, and then their transfer to psychiatric hospital might be considered where they will have less strict regime.[5]

We can see that this varied and complex mix of punishment and education, care and treatment, isolation and rehabilitation is symptomatic of all these spaces – psychiatric hospital, prison and detention institution. Each of these institutions shares these characteristics to different degrees. With the emergence of detention institutions (where, nevertheless, only people committing a new crime can be transferred from hospitals) this space 'in-between' finds its very expression.

How can we understand this space in-between? In-between in terms of medical and legal categories, in-between in terms of institutional order and in-between in terms of suspended time? Is this third category of 'detention' institution a material affirmation of the ambiguity with regard to the status of these people, an expression of uncertainty about the nature of their act, the confusing mixture of all these possible facets of their behaviour, character and fate? Does this creation of a third category represent a space where uncertainty and ambiguity might more comfortably coexist and inhabit the same space, or where these uncertainties can be hidden away? Either way, such spaces are representative of a doubt over the possibility of cure or re-education, and the pitiful inadequacy of punishment.

NOTES

1 The interviews were conducted in Czech. I have endeavoured to translate them in such a way as to maintain a sense of the tone of the original dialogue, including some ungrammatical utterances.
2 The World Health Organisation's International Classification of Diseases.
3 Czech Radio programme 21 January 2005 following the government's decision to establish detention institutions, www.radio.cz/cz/rubrika/udalosti/v-cesku-vznikne-detencni-ustav.
4 Czech Radio programme 21 January 2005 following the government's decision to establish detention institutions, www.radio.cz/cz/rubrika/udalosti/v-cesku-vznikne-detencni-ustav.
5 Interview for iDNES, 18 March 2009, http://brno.idnes.cz/detence-lecebna-ani-vezeni-rika-sef-ustavu-fii-/brno-zpravy.aspx?c=A090317 200656 brno krc.

REFERENCES

Foucault, M. 1965. *Madness and Civilization. A History of Insanity in the Age of Reason*. New York: Random House

Gadamer, H. G. 1994[1975]. *Truth and Method*. London and New York: Continuum

Tinková, D. 2004. *Hřích, zločin, šílenství v čase odkouzlování světa*. [*Sin, Crime, Insanity in the Age of Disenchantment of the World*]. Prague: Argo

LOCAL JUSTICE IN THE ALLOCATION OF MEDICAL CERTIFICATES DURING FRENCH ASYLUM PROCEDURES: FROM PROTOCOLS TO FACE-TO-FACE INTERACTIONS

Estelle d'Halluin

At the end of World War II, the search for peace was associated with the prevention of genocide and the atrocities that had occurred during the war. Governments were also concerned with solving the problem of Europeans displaced by the conflict. In this context, a consensus was reached on 28 July 1951 over an international refugee protection regime: the United Nations Convention relating to the Status of Refugees was adopted. In France, since borders were closed to labour immigration during the 1970s, asylum seekers have been increasingly suspected by the state of claiming refugee status illegitimately in order to stay in France. Although, during the 1970s, up to 95% of all asylum seekers were granted refugee status, this rate has rapidly declined since the 1980s – dropping to less than 12% at first application in 2013 (25% when taking account the appeals). The procedures to identify eligible candidates have become exacting, and claimants struggle to convince institutions of the veracity of their claims. In this context, a medical certificate, written by a third person – a doctor or a psychologist – which attests to the compatibility between the patient's history and his physical or psychic wounds, has become a fundamental 'piece of evidence'. Thus, during the 1980s, several French medical NGOs, which were originally founded to care for refugees, responded to this increasing need for proof, thereby combining the expert and healing roles (Fassin and d'Halluin 2005).

Originally committed to relieving the suffering of refugees – often exacerbated by the harsh conditions of flight and reception – clinicians were swiftly called upon to give expert medical evidence on individual cases. The original motivation of these doctors in becoming involved in refugee care was overwhelmingly humanitarian and compassionate. It was nonetheless in the name of objective scrutiny that doctors were invited by the state to describe and assess the damage that had been inflicted on asylum seekers in their native country. Doctors were therefore asked to participate in the process of bureaucratic, rather than compassionate recognition. It is therefore important to explore the forms of local justice that emerge when medicine and law meet in the asylum field, and how clinicians try to balance their claims of objectivity with those of ethical commitment.

'Local justice', as coined by Jon Elster (Elster 1992, see also Fox and Swazey 1974), concerns distributive practices ('who gets what, when and how') and principles. The word 'local' refers to the fact that relatively autonomous institutions apply their own variants of a general scheme of distribution. The practices within a given arena in a given country are not as uniform as they could appear at first glance and, thus, ethnography is useful in order to understand the 'conception of justice held by actors who are in a position to influence the selection of specific procedures or criteria to allocate scarce resources' on a local level (Elster 1992: 5). As an analytical concept, 'local justice' was first applied to the medical field (Fox and Swazey 1974; Calabresi and Bobbitt 1978; Elster 1992). During the 1970s, several researchers questioned the way public institutions were allocating rare resources. The research paid special attention to the social procedures that were established and followed by institutions in order to allocate scarce resources on which the survival of each individual might depend. These were essentially 'tragic choices' – as people's lives were at stake. However, the notions of 'tragic choices' and 'local justice' can be applied in other areas. In France, such studies have been recently developed to understand how financial support is granted to poor populations at a local level (Ogien 1999; Fassin 2001a).

In regard to asylum seekers, the *Office Français de Protection des Réfugiés et des Apatrides* (OFPRA) and the *Cour National du Droit d'Asile* (CNDA) are the principal sites where such 'tragic choices' take place. Those applicants whose application for refugee status has been denied can be deported. Most of the time, they are effectively forced to live in an irregular manner, trying to escape deportation. Most research (Good 2006; Rousseau et al. 2002; Kälin 1986; Fassin and Kobelinsky 2012) has been conducted in northern democracies in order to explore the dilemmas faced by judges in deciding to grant or deny refugee status. However, to understand the asylum process, it is also important to understand the various stages before the final interaction between asylum seekers and judges. In this process, the services of legal and medical NGOs play an important role, providing a scarce resource. With limited financial and human resources, they are unable to provide legal advice or deliver a medical certificate to all claimants. As a result, these institutions have established rules to decide who, and under which conditions, will benefit from their services.

These 'local justice' procedures were observed during research that I conducted between 2001 and 2006 with Professor Didier Fassin. We completed interviews with 20 medical doctors, psychiatrists and psychologists in the four principal NGOs working in this domain in the early 2000s: the Françoise Minkowska Center, the Comede or Medical Committee for the Exiled (Comede), the Avre or Association for the Victims of Repression in Exile and the Primo Levi Center. We also consulted the websites of these organisations, the journals they publish and the annual reports they produce. Finally, in order to account for the everyday management of asylum, long-term participant observation was conducted for two years within two organisations: one specialised in medical care (Comede) and the other in juridical assistance (Cimede). In Comede, I attended staff meetings and consultations. They also granted me access to their archives. Interviews were also conducted with the bureaucrats and judges in charge of granting refugee status. Although our research was limited to France, the exchanges and discussions we had with members of other NGOs within the European Network of Treatment and Rehabilitation Centers for Victims of Torture indicate that the problems and dilemmas we analyse in France are part of a much wider European context, with similar legal and institutional constraints, but with somewhat diverse political and moral debates and responses.

This chapter will focus on the way medical certificates are allocated by physicians to asylum seekers in France, a process that cannot be reduced to a straightforward medical act. The chapter will explore how NGOs attempted to produce various forms of justice, how their criteria were legitimised and how members of this NGO moved away from the norms established during regular face-to-face interactions. On one level, the chapter will provide a fine-grained understanding of the production of social inequality in the asylum process, through highlighting the role of the clinicians as gatekeepers, prior to the evaluative process conducted by administrative officers and judges. On another level, the chapter will demonstrate how clinicians can be torn between attempting to get close to the refugee's experience, often with compassion and empathy, and having to produce a formal, technical and objective report, emotionless and detached. First, though, the chapter will explain how and why medical certificates have become so important for a range of actors involved in the asylum process. Second, the chapter will examine various protocols established in the NGO sector to allocate medical certificates. Finally, the chapter will show how face-to-face interactions challenge formally established rules.

NEGOTIATING THE ALLOCATION OF A MEDICAL CERTIFICATE

In February 2004, in a suburb of Paris, inside a room of Comede, a medical NGO, I attended consultations, sitting next to a GP, Dr Laurence (Dr). A Sri Lankan patient (P) entered the room with a translator (T). Dr Laurence introduced me, and the patient authorised my observing of the consultation. The GP asked the patient the reason why he had come to the medical centre. It was to have a medical certificate that he could send to the OFPRA. But it appeared that the patient had missed, without notice, an appointment to be examined and have his medical certificate established. He rummaged in his pockets and brought out a medical certificate justifying his absence.

P: ...
T: He was sick
Dr (having a sullen face, with an irritated tone of voice): I don't need proof ... I'm not happy, I'm not happy, I'm not happy because he didn't come. It meant that someone else who needed such a certificate could not have it that day. I won't give him another appointment. Anyway, he can have a certificate written by another GP downtown.
T: Can any GP provide it?
Dr: Yes, any ... you know, if I had known it was him, I would have never let him in my office. Last time, he insisted on having a certificate. Realising that I was weary of fighting, I agreed to see him ..., gave him "the orange form" and he didn't come! I'm going to write a reference letter for a colleague so that he will have his foot examined.
      The patient keeps a low profile, having round shoulders ...
      ... You know, he just has one scar on his thigh and he doesn't want to understand that such a certificate would harm his case. [She emphasised the word "one"]
P: ...

T: The OFPRA has just summoned him for interview.
Dr: Well. He will tell his story, this is the most important thing. He has a tiny scar. He should have the foot examined. I did not find anything, neither concerning his foot, nor concerning his knee. . . .
(Dr Laurence moved towards the patient.)
. . . He should have come the day of his appointment. I'm not pleased. . . .
(The other day) he was exasperating me so much.
She imitates the patient during the previous consultation:
"Please, Please", he went almost down on his knees . . . So, he doesn't care . . . I'm so displeased.

The talking continued, full of reproaches, until the translator was called upon by another GP in the medical centre. The conversation ended with some explanation in English about how to go to the medical X-ray centre. One more time, Dr Laurence insisted on the high importance of talking to OFPRA rather than presenting a 'risky' medical attestation. The patient went out and Dr Laurence turned back to me: 'I have nothing to say. He was beaten in the street; he was beaten with a stick. From the OFPRA's point of view, it is a bad claim . . . a tiny scar for someone beaten up . . . even if I would not have measured it (the scar).'

During my fieldwork in this NGO, I never saw such a scene recur. Everything during that consultation was unusual: Dr Laurence's irritated tone of voice, her flood of reproaches addressed to the patient for missing his appointment, regrets about her previous decision to grant a certificate to attest to a tiny scar. Usually, in this medical centre, medical expertise follows a two-step procedure. If a patient asks for medical certification about marks of violence during a medical consultation, the GP examines the patient's body to determine whether there is 'material or not' for such a certificate. If so, a document is issued – the 'orange form' – on which the agreement of the GP, the date of the appointment and also the date when the typed out certification will be available are mentioned. During a second consultation, entirely devoted to medical expertise, the GP undertakes an in depth examination, listens to the patient's story of violence, and writes the report.

This is the consultation that the Sri Lankan patient missed, causing Dr Laurence to lose her temper. Perhaps even more than the consultations during which GPs decide whether or not to grant a medical certificate, this scene shows the emotional strain associated with daily allocation decisions. Dr Laurence reminds the patient of his insistent request, how he begged her to provide him with a medical certificate.

The patient's insistence, an expression of worry about the outcome of his asylum case, invites us to ask how medical certificates have become so important in a context of increasing selectivity of asylum grants. The medical certificate is considered a precious good, a rare resource, hence this reproach addressed by Dr Laurence: 'I'm not happy because he didn't come. It meant that someone else who needed such a certificate could not have it that day'. Dr Laurence imitated angrily the attitude of the patient during the previous consultation. In doing so, she expressed the exasperation I observed at that time among medical staff at Comede. Most of the time, GPs expressed their annoyance around a cup of coffee, in the corridor or during staff meetings, seldom in front of the patient. Discontent with the growing demand for medical expertise can be explained through ethical, political and practical issues analysed elsewhere (Fassin and d'Halluin 2005)[1] and by the decrease in therapeutic work it implies. Finally, the scene observed puts into question principles, which had been established in the medical centre, since Dr Laurence reconsidered her previous decision, feeling she departed from Comede's principles of allocation and was 'screwed' by the patient. After recalling the increasing, but shifting, value of medical certificates in the asylum process, we need to ask: what are the principles established by medical centres in deciding whether and how to grant medical certificates to asylum seekers? How were they established? Are they based exclusively on clinical principles or does the political culture of the NGO sector influence them? And how can we explain that once these principles are established, GPs seem to be moving away from them during face-to-face interactions?

THE SHIFTING VALUE OF MEDICAL CERTIFICATES IN THE ASYLUM PROCESS

In the past decades, the body has become a legal resource for asylum seekers, and more broadly for undocumented migrants. As Liisa Malkki noted in East African refugee camps, sometimes, scars that can be seen are placed above words that are spoken by refugees (Malkki, 1996: 384). When there is suspicion about an applicant's story, the pain marked on their bodies, certified by a member of the medical profession, seems more difficult to deny. How though has the value of medical certificates been defined in the French asylum process? First, the increasing value granted to medical certificates in the French asylum process is linked to the broader global immigration policy. Second, the value of medical certificates is not uniform across those people who decide on whether or not to grant refugee status. Finally, considering the high value placed in certain types of medical certificates produced by medical NGOs specialised in medical care for exiled people, there are important questions about how asylum seekers gain access to these organisations.

The enforcing of asylum rights in France depends on the specific political, economic and social contexts, even if international refugee law (such as the Geneva Convention and recent European legislation) is formally binding and universal. During the interwar period, when nation-state building and authoritarianism forced numerous refugees to flee, if one wanted to benefit from refugee status, it was sufficient to belong to a community that was recognised as persecuted (Armenians from Turkey, etc.). After World War II, the 1951 Geneva Conventions established universal protection. But these did not challenge state sovereignty, which left nation-states the power to organise the recognition and protection of specific refugees. Most European states created individualised procedures, which became more demanding after the economic crises of the late twentieth century made foreigners more 'undesirable'. Widely ratified by western European countries, these conventions were applied liberally until the 1980s. Factors such as post-war reconstruction and economic growth, as well as the logic of the Cold War, favoured the reception of refugees, as their number was steadily decreasing. Yet asylum gradually lost its legitimacy in Europe, as economic and social conditions deteriorated. The rise in unemployment and xenophobia led the French government to restrict the immigration of a labour force. Paradoxically, at that time, NGO mobilisation facilitated access to certain basic social rights for immigrants. Since 1975, the French state has delegated and given funds to a network of NGOs that shelter asylum seekers (Massé 1996). At the same time, the number of demands for asylum in Europe has grown, and a discourse that criminalises them has developed. Thus, starting in the late 1980s, the reception of refugees was gradually subordinated to a logic of controlling migratory flows, and policies designed to limit the flow of those requesting asylum were put in place at the national and European levels: surveillance at borders in detention centres, limitation of the expansion and access to shelters, removal of work permits, removal of French language courses and a fast-track procedure. In this process, the French government has been increasingly selective in granting refugee status (Legoux 1995).

If governmental policy thus shapes refugee law enforcement, lower-level decision-makers' activity should also be considered (Anker 1990). Through their daily evaluation practices, what standards do civil agents and judges elaborate and apply? By all accounts, asylum seekers' case histories and interviews remain the major element on which the decision, 'the final verdict', is based. However, a thicker description should be made of rules not created by formal regulation (Gilboy 1991). Anthropologists have carried out interviews with bureaucrats and observed court hearings (Good 2006; Rousseau et al. 2002; Blériot 2003; Kälin 1986; Fassin and Kobelinsky 2012). However, there are relatively few studies based on long-term fieldwork in the bureaucracy, enabling one to observe the whole process, including the training, informal discussions, investigation, deliberation and the interventions of bureaucratic hierarchies. Without such access during the fieldwork upon which this chapter is based, we interviewed members of the French institutions in charge of granting refugee status. In relation to medical evaluation, certificates were viewed differently from one judge to another. They could be 'one clue among others' or, for certain judges, 'what attracts attention' or 'overcomes all remaining doubt'. For others, it was absolutely convincing. Such attitudes explain why, over the past 20 years, the demand for certification has increased, not only in France, but also in most European (Berlin Institut for Comparative Social Research 2006) and North American countries. In a legal and administrative framework in which institutions call into question the truth of the words that asylum seekers produce, the body becomes the site where the subject's truth is tested – or, rather, the site where it is tested by a third party, the doctor, who is supposed to be neutral and knowledgeable (Fassin and d'Halluin 2005).

The writing of medical certificates does not follow a formal, written legal procedure in France. This is why practices are so heterogeneous: some healthcare providers decide that they have to deliver what they are asked for, others decide that they do not have to answer an informal demand, and, if so, can do so on their own terms. Some doctors are trained to produce medical certificates, others are not. Some doctors have a broad knowledge of refugee populations and their experiences, others do not. GPs can indifferently produce an evaluation of physical and psychic wounds, precisely because there is a certain degree of informality; there are no court-appointed experts, even if CNDA is entitled to do it. And yet, this does not mean that each evaluation has the same credibility with decision-makers. To understand the practices of medical evaluation, we need to focus on the medical NGO sector.

Legal anthropology has taught us precisely how to examine how legal cases and discourses can be reproduced outside formal legal institutions (Felstiner and Sarat 1991). In relation to the asylum process in France, medical and legal NGOs constitute two kinds of sites where legal evidence is 'produced' and where asylum seekers are socialised into the formal and informal standards applied by bureaucrats. Multisite observation is important not only because legal institutions are mobilising various kinds of expertise, but also because social movements defending asylum seekers turn to this expertise in order to support their claims as well. In Foucauldian terms, if knowledge can be used as a technology for disciplining or governing a population (Ewijk and Grifhorst 1998), it can also be subverted by subjects to contest the ways they are governed. Legal strategies of subversion are probably the most studied (Coutin 1998; Harvey 2000; Marek 2001; Israel 2001). Nonetheless, medical expertise, anthropological expertise (Good 2006) or 'asylum-seeker narrative expertise' (d'Halluin 2008; Franguiadakis et al. 2004; Barsky 2000) are important elements of refugee law enforcement, partly shaping inequalities in access to refugee protection. As a result, refugee claimants turn 'freely' – influenced by their social network – to the medical associations for help. These medical NGOs have rapidly acquired credibility in the eyes of OFPRA and CNDA – as a result, their services are increasingly in high demand. In turn, their members have had to redefine the division of labour in the institution, and to formulate ethical and practical principles with respect to their role (Hughes 1956) and humanitarian convictions.

BASED ON FAITH OR ON MEDICAL GAZE? THE DIFFERENT PROCEDURES FOR ALLOCATING CERTIFICATES

Do we have to write a certificate when asked for it (to adopt an activist stand or a merely medical one)? Has a GP, at Comede or any other institution, the right to decline the patient's request for medical expertise? What standards should we set to define who is entitled to a medical certificate and who is not? How should we answer lawyers who have increasingly appealed to us because they are under pressure due to the acceleration of the asylum procedure?[2]

These four questions were raised in a Comede staff meeting report in the late 1990s. At that time, asylum requests had increased in France (from 34 352 in 1988 to 54 813 in 1990) and the French government took measures to reduce delay when preparing an asylum case for judgement. In this context, GPs faced an increasing demand for medical certification and decided to organise several staff meetings to discuss the ethical, political and practical stands they should adopt. First, they had to decide whether or not they had the right to decline a patient's request for a medical certification. Article 76 in the Code of medical ethics of France specifies the obligation to deliver a medical certificate prescribed by laws or regulations. Thirteen years later, Comede made a clear-cut answer to this question in its guidebook: 'A doctor can always refuse to deliver a certificate which has not been prescribed by regulation'. Although some regulations enable the National Asylum Appeal Court to ask for formal medical expertise, these have never been implemented. As a result, Comede's medical practitioners consider that they do not have to answer unconditionally an informal request. But in doing so, they have to answer precisely the third question: 'What standards should we set to define who is entitled to a medical certificate and who is not?' Even if during an interview in 2002 the director of the medical centre stated that 'medical certification is based on a special relationship between a doctor and his patient, a matter of personal ethic', there are few rules which guide their allocation in the centre.

The principles followed by GPs for granting medical certificates in medical centres are sometimes described in guidelines. At other times, guidelines are more informal and can be only be understood by interviewing medical practitioners about their actual practices. Different kinds of procedures seem to exist across the medical NGOs sector. In *Local Justice*, Jon Elster (1992) identifies the distributive criteria and mechanisms, including lotteries, queuing, need, effort, merit, efficiency or some combination of these, which govern the distribution of justice in practice. Similar criteria are also used by NGO actors to decide whether or not an asylum seeker will be helped, or at least, to define the highest priority. Here we will present three different procedures and their justifications: one is mainly based on the medical gaze. In contrast, the second is based on faith. In between is Comede's procedure which associates moral consideration with its medical criteria.

A PURELY MEDICAL GAZE

The first model of allocation is based on the clinical apprehension of asylum seekers. The activity of a centre located in the second French metropolis, Lyon, for example, corresponds to this model. During a 2002 meeting, gathering three associations to discuss medical certificates in the asylum process, Dr Martin presented the activity of his centre:

> Our centre does not give medical care to asylum seekers. A forensic expert founded it twenty years ago. At the beginning, the centre was designed to solve medical disputes and to be a space for ethical debate. Over the last years, it has been faced with increasing requests from asylum seekers for a medical certificate. At the present time, all the appointments are booked for the next two months. So, we choose to provide medical certificates only for the asylum seekers rejected by OFPRA and going to appeal to Court. . . . We see people for one hour and a half on average. . . . Our practice is as close as possible to forensic expertise. We review some of the key events, kinds of torture endured and their dates. We register what the patient is complaining about and the psychological aspects. We pay attention to post traumatic stress disorder. We make a global exam and report it. We measure and describe scars. We mention if it is compatible or not with the allegation. . . . Finally, we conclude briefly about the compatibility of the whole elements.

In this centre, every asylum seeker should be provided with a detailed medical certificate, and they try to treat them on an equal basis by introducing the principle of queuing (the first arrived is the first examined). However, facing a huge demand, another criterion has been introduced based on need: medical certificates will be delivered to asylum seekers at the appeal stage, because it is their last chance, and so any document could be crucial. In this model, every clinical fact should be mentioned, and their consistency with the patient's account assessed.

Medical practitioners who refer to this model are the most often supporting the strict application of the UN-backed Istanbul Protocol for the documentation of torture, even if lack of time impedes them in practice from doing so. Any kind of sign of violence (e.g. shrapnel, shard) which could be identified by advanced technologies (such as medical imaging) should be examined, reported, evaluated and related to the patient's story. To identify and bring to light the harms experienced by asylum seekers, clinicians tends to favour the kind of 'mechanical objectivity' which Lorraine Daston (1995) described for scientists in the nineteenth century. Mechanical objectivity battles to suppress 'the universal human propensity to judge' or 'interpret' when collecting observation. In this model, it doesn't matter how a piece of information reported in the medical certificate could be misused by agents in charge of granting refugee status (e.g. pointing that some scars are not consistent with the patient's story, or consistent with other causes, may be interpreted by the agent as a lack of evidence). Every clinical fact, such as a 'tiny scar' or a pathology without any link to the asylum case, are mentioned. Sometimes, doctors who follow this model are just unaware that some decision-makers in charge of granting refugee status, over- or misinterpret their conclusions. Doctors do not necessarily follow an unshakeable belief in a division of labour between a medical profession in charge of a detailed clinical examination and reporting on the patient's body, and a judicial system in charge of evaluation and final decision about the asylum case, as if medical discourse was obvious, transparent and its conditions of reception neutral. Such a view prevailing in the social world (Dumoulin 2007) was seldom promoted in centres exclusively dedicated to expertise. During the meeting mentioned above, Dr Martin easily took another perspective, once he was warned that mentioning the patient's seropositivity could harm his asylum case. More specifically, he moved to the second model of local justice, which is promoted in the Comede Guidebook.

A CLINICAL GAZE TEMPERED WITH POLITICAL AND MORAL CONSIDERATIONS

In the different versions of the Comede Guidebook, three pages are dedicated to medical expertise in the French asylum procedure. Designed for social and healthcare providers, the Guidebook recommends 'a preliminary assessment of the request' and warns doctors against requests that do not directly come from patients, but from a third person – e.g. a solicitor, a judge or a social worker (Comede 2003: 173).[3] Here we see the figure of the doctor who is aware of power relations in which they are caught up. Since the late 1960s, criticism about medical power (Illich 1966) and social control exerted on patients has had feedback effects on the medical field. For doctors caring for people on the fringes of society a healthcare provider working for a selective or punitive administration has become increasingly objectionable. More often than not, patients made the request for medical certificates on their own, as they feared their application for asylum would be rejected without one. During the medical consultations observed as part of this research, all requests were made by patients themselves, even if a third person had influenced them. As Gerard Noiriel has noted (Noiriel 1999: 312), in state-led identification procedures, 'it is the individual who calls on requirements which powerful political institutions inflict on him'. Aware of the phenomenon, the authors of the Guidebook highlight the risks of potential distress caused by a refusal to provide a medical certificate when a patient has made the request his own (Comede 2003: 173). The Guidebook also states that the veracity of patients' allegations was not a relevant criterion in distinguishing whether patients deserve a certificate or not. A document from the archive of Comede, reads 'Medical practitioners do not have to give an opinion on veracity of patients' story, which is the role of institutions in charge of granting refugee status'.[4] For the Guidebook, clinical facts make the difference. Trauma, whether physical or psychic, is the criterion to grant a medical certificate.[5] This principle of allocation plays a part in the credibility that Comede has gained inside the institutions in charge of granting refugee status.

Nevertheless, clinical considerations may be tempered by ethical and political considerations. In Comede's archive, I found a note written in 1999, which set the following rule (included afterwards in the Guidebook):

> Medical practitioners should answer the patient's request provided time and communication enable it, and on condition that medical expertise will not harm the patient. . . . e.g. providing a patient with a medical certificate which mentions seropositivity may cause damage to the patient, since his request can be mistaken with a request for regularization on medical and humanitarian grounds.

Here, there are two ways to interpret 'harm'. What is at stake is either the psychological risk of the patient's retraumatisation if a certificate is produced without enough time and consideration, or the 'administrative' risk of rejection if the medical certificate is written without taking into account the perceptions of the decision-maker in charge of granting refugee status.

So one reason to refuse to produce a certificate or not is 'therapeutic' risk. Since the 1990s, research has been conducted on anxiety created by an ever more restrictive asylum policy, pointing to the risks of retraumatisation of asylum seekers (Silove et al. 1993; Watters 2000). The 'first, do not harm' principle is placed under strain, as the time for submitting an asylum request – and so too for obtaining a medical certificate – has been reduced. For some medical practitioners, an inquisitive mode of expertise, aiming to extract some facts about traumatic events in order to assess compatibility with physical and psychological evidence, is a far cry from the rehabilitation process, which is often a slow and tortuous progression in the labyrinth of the psychic reality.

In October 2002, during a staff meeting about trauma in Comede, the problem of medical certification was promptly tackled. One GP underlined the importance of silence and the painful expression of stories during the medical expert consultation. Another added: 'We feel intrusive. We have to know the details and it's very hard to elicit them. We are nearly acting like a perpetrator, even if you feel you can help. They don't want to tell their story in detail.' A similar concern had already been raised in the first reflection paper produced by the medical NGOs. In 1992, we could read: 'In his haste, the doctor takes the risk of reproducing a "police" interrogation that reactivates the victim's suffering.' (Didier 1992).

A second reason for declining a certificate is a political one. Comede's doctors are of the opinion that they have to anticipate how their products will be used, and give maximum opportunities to their patients to obtain refugee status. As a result, they set rules that enable doctors to refuse to provide patients with a medical certificate which could be harmful for their asylum case. Such 'harmful' certificates could, for example, be considered as 'poor' by a judge, as Dr Laurence anticipated in the scene described at the start of this chapter.[6] Mere clinical analysis of the case is in tension with a political judgement based on several years' experience of the institutions in charge of granting refugee status, and with doctors' concern about the administrative situation – and thus the living conditions affecting health – of a patient. As Nicolas Dodier (1993: 44) underlined, medical experts not only examine cases, they also establish connections between cases. Here, in Jon Elster's (1992) terms, a criterion of efficiency is introduced in the process of allocating a medical certificate: looking to the future, rare resources are allocated as a priority to the one who will use it best.

The example about seropositivity, quoted in the note above, can be understood with regards to changes that occurred in the 1990s in the French administration of foreigners: the growing suspicion toward asylum seekers was concomitant with recognition of a (limited) right of residence for foreigners suffering from a serious disease (Fassin 2001b).[7] At the beginning of the 1980s, Comede's GPs drew up an exhaustive report about patients' health conditions (all diseases were recorded). But now, Comede's doctors have interiorised norms of judgement activated by judges: some judges may come to the opinion that 'migration was motivated by medical reasons' (Comede 2003: 172) when they read in a medical certificate that an asylum seeker suffers from a serious disease. An instruction was made by the GP coordinator at Comede not to mix genres of asylum and humanitarian reports. This instruction was grounded in a political stand: to resist the delegitimisation of asylum, when humanitarian protection turns out to be problematic.

Moral considerations are also mixed with political ones. During a staff meeting in 2004, the GP coordinator underlined that a medical certificate should not be delivered when the patient's scar is visible at first sight. He reminds the audience that it is appropriate to write a certificate when the patient has a scar on his belly, or his back, so that he does not have to expose it in front of the judges. Here, medical certificates are less granted to attest a degree of compatibility between scars and allegations, but to prevent the patient from having to expose himself, especially during public audience. This principle established by Comede sheds light on current socially sanctioned approaches to the assaulted and tortured body. Changes in an affective economy, grounded in the civilising process described by Norbert Elias (2000), not only make the sight of torture (Foucault 1995) unbearable, but they also stigmatise exhibition in public space of any intimate sign of violence. The current norm is to have the marks of violence exposed through the discourse of a medical professional, who reports his examination in the doctor's office where privacy is guaranteed. Moral considerations are thus entangled with political and medical ones.

What is the procedure for the allocation of medical certificates, once patients turn out to meet the criteria presented above? At the time of writing this chapter, Comede's staff set great value upon equal treatment, and have introduced the principle of queuing. Fifteen years previously, this was not the case. Priority was given to their regular clients, and a sharp debate occurred in order to reform this rule and 'set every client on an equal footing', as the GP coordinator put it during an interview.

DESERVING PATIENT

In some medical centres, an opposite model of allocating certificates prevailed. Medical certificates were not delivered on the basis of clinical signs, but on the basis of the doctor's belief in the asylum seeker's story. In an NGO specialised in care for victims of torture, the director explained to me that he only provided his regular clients with a medical certificate and only if 'he was convinced of the veracity of their speech':

> We cannot attest torture on the basis of scars. Somebody who was dragged in a cell, who had his knees burnt and somebody who fell from his bicycle in the street, it will be the same scars. So it is impossible to attest to these scars … except for people who have marks from an iron. Then, even clumsy, even an ironer, could not have marks like that … So, to write a medical certificate, we have to be convinced that there is a real pain, etc. Otherwise, we say no to people, without any problem. … We usually deliver certificates in the long run.
>
> (Interview with the director of a medical centre
> for the victims of torture, Paris, 2002)

In this vein, we can quote the conclusion of a certificate delivered by another GP at the same NGO, which I read at Comede, when a patient went there for some advice: 'I'm intimately convinced about his experience of ill-treatment and suffering.' Basing their opinion on the patient's 'experience', these doctors put their intimate conviction forward in a manner very similar to the agents in charge of granting refugee status. As the latter make their judgement on the basis of investigation and hearing, the former base their opinion on the patient–doctor relationship built up during several consultations. Empathy is valued, and the GP does not attempt to shift from empathetic proximity to seemingly objective distance. In contrast to the two previous models, this model of justice is one exclusively based on a 'clinical gaze on the story', refusing, with a few exceptions, forensic techniques and any judgement about consistency between scars and account. GPs who adopt this point of view often claim skills for psychotherapy, sometimes due to their long experience with refugees, but without training in this field.

The history of Comede shows how an organisation can slide from one model to another. In 1991, patients received differential treatment according to the doctor's assessment of their story. Some patients were provided with a typed and more detailed medical certificate, others a more concise handwritten report (less valued by the institutions in charge of granting refugee status). Lack of time and the overload of the secretary were invoked to explain unequal treatment received by asylum seekers. But a note from the archived files underlined 'among criteria to provide a handwritten certificate', 'disbelief of the doctor toward

his patient's account' and the fact that 'most of the handwritten certificates are delivered not to say no to patients'.[8] Entangled with use
of forensic techniques, judgements about credibility were also important. Comede put an end to this differential treatment during the 1990s,
coming to the conclusion that it was not their role to assess the patient's
account, which was a very risky exercise, considering the lack of solid
grounds upon which to base their judgement. This example shows how
individuals, and even groups, can move from one model in the context
of the practical, political and moral about their consequences.

'TIRED OF FIGHTING ... ' BEYOND THE PRINCIPLES

Beyond models, the scenes described above invite us to question how
individuals might move away from their guiding principles during face-
to-face interactions. At the time of writing, there is a broad consensus
among Comede's staff on the rules established to allocate medical certificates to asylum seekers. GPs seldom break the rules despite the lack of
monitoring.[9] Nevertheless, during my fieldwork, a few 'transgressions'
occurred. A note, dated 2001, found in Comede's archive demonstrates
the relatively frequent occurrence of such transgressions, warning staff
that: 'without clinical facts supporting the account of the patient, the
certificate is nothing but medical'. In January 2004, in an informal conversation with Dr Laurence, she talked to me about the nature of medical expertise. She shared her regrets about the end of a time when
they wrote more detailed medical certificates, but also insisted on how
hard and time-consuming this was. Afterwards, she started to criticise
the kind of medical certificates provided by two GPs, both recently
recruited: 'They give them too easily'. She was blaming the first GP for
providing a patient with a medical certificate about back pains, and the
second one for giving his agreement to write a certificate for a patient
on the basis of his allegation alone, without any examination. In relation to back pains, the issued certificate was only based on the patient's
claim of suffering, without any clinical signs. Providing a medical certificate for a patient with back pains is simply reproducing their verbal
account.[10] The second GP she blamed agreed to provide a certificate to
a patient who said he was tortured (nails pulled out, testicles beaten).
One month later, I was in Dr Laurence's office when she saw this particular patient. He was from Sri Lanka, 50 years old, and did not speak
either French or English. She examined the patient and noticed there
were no marks on his nails. Willing to fill the medical report with

clinical facts, 'to have something coherent', she had ordered a scan of his testicles. While we were waiting for the translator, she explained that the previous time, the doctor had let things get on top of him: 'Nothing surprising, with ten cases per half-a-day's work, it's a production line!' He agreed without examining the patient, but the latter 'had just a tiny scar on his hand, that's all'.

How can one explain that doctor's move away from the institution's set of criteria, providing certificates when they should not? How can one understand that 'things get on top of one'? One possible answer to the question is given by Dr Laurence: ten cases per half-a-day's work is a high work rate for consultations during which different types of questions are dealt with, often not without time-consuming communication difficulties: health problems, access to social security, recalling of past experience, complaining about living conditions in France, anxiety about administrative case issues. For new doctors, time is necessary to learn about the large range of topics involved in the health of refugees. Furthermore, during face-to-face interactions, doctors find it difficult to turn down the request of a patient who has invested his hopes in a medical certificate. Some of the documents archived as far back as in 1990 mention how difficult it was to refuse a patient's request and underlined all the know-how necessary to explain why this has been done, so that patients do not consider themselves victims of injustice.[11] More recently, during an interview, Dr Abu Jalah still remembers that, 13 years ago, at the beginning of her work in Comede, she 'backed down' and provided an asylum seeker 'begging her' with a medical certificate about one scar related to 'what happened in prison'. Yet, she was more convinced that it was a scar due to varicella or something dermatological, rather than due to ill-treatment. Not to feel overburdened, she quickly wrote a medical certificate where her doubt filtered through. It was easier than 'arguing during half an hour and trying to convince him that it was useless'. In so doing, she departed from her usual caution. As Everett C. Hughes (1996: 85) remarked, such tensions characterise service jobs, which on a daily and routine basis deal with problems which are vital and urgent for their clients.

There were other deviations from the norm at Comede. At Comede, a rule specifies that GPs should not certify the psychic sequelae of violence which were claimed by the patient during the first visit. Instead, the GP should refer the patient for therapy with a psychologist. If the patient is reluctant to do so, GPs may follow the psychological state of the patient. Comede had decided to exempt psychologists from the role of medical experts. However, psychologists can nonetheless add elements to the file of their patient. GPs are told to certify only psychological elements if the patient has consulted with them on a regular basis. During first examination, contrary to what can be observed in other countries, none of the scales available to evaluate post traumatic syndromes are used (Newman et al. 1996). No systematic investigation is conducted to find what, in other countries, constitutes an objective, albeit psychological, trace of violence. Despite the rule, I observed several doctors introducing considerations about the patient's mental condition, even if they were seeing him for the first time. Every time, it was with a patient who had important physical effects of violence. According to the GP coordinator, psychological symptoms should be mentioned in the section of the certificate headed 'Claim of the patient'. However, I often observed psychological symptoms written alongside clinical facts reported after examination. Compassion experienced during face-to-face interactions might explain this lower attention to clinical standards. Furthermore, to mention the patient's mental health condition even without diagnosing it, might be a way for the doctor to take their patient's speech into consideration, to report back the suffering that asylum seekers face every day, which seems to stand in stark contrast to the large number of asylum applications refused by the French state.

Thus, at a local level, NGOs not only produce their model of expertise, but during face-to-face encounters they also move away from the very procedures of local justice they have previously established. Three protocols of local justice in the French NGO sector in France have been set out above: a 'pure' clinical gaze and the use of forensic techniques; a restrained use of forensic techniques based on a 'first, do not harm' principle extended to the political field; and a contempt for forensic techniques where narrative insight prevails. Subsequently, what is at stake for doctors, and especially for new recruited members, is how to stand their ground and negotiate through these different sets of principles. For asylum seekers, the various protocols established by NGOs represent a new set of rules to learn in the complex asylum process. Ultimately though, the attempt made by the medical NGO sector to invent forms of local justice, or the least unjust order they can promote, cannot overcome the French management of asylum based on dissuasion and repression.

What prevails in France, and more broadly in the European Union, is an unbalanced logic of compassion and repression (Fassin 2005), or more precisely compassion and selection. Successive governments have formally reaffirmed asylum right in the face of rising xenophobia. They have also set out minimum standards for reception conditions for asylum applicants and supported the NGOs sector in providing care and shelter for them. French governments have also consolidated regulations designed to promote basic procedural guarantees for asylum applicants. According to the liberal principles of equal opportunity (Rawls 1971), civil society organisations are financially supported by the state in order to provide claimants with social, linguistic and legal assistance. But the implementation of these regulations faces barrier caused by fiscal restraint and an increasingly restrictive immigration policy, where a large part of the French population considers foreigners as a potential threat (national security, job opportunities for nationals, welfare system and/or a specific conception of national cultural identity). Thus, the left hand of the state finances health centres – but with not enough means to assure equal and full access to them – while the right hand uses expert testimony 'to separate the wheat from the chaff' – in an informal manner – without any considerations for the variety of protocols that are followed by NGOs. As in other fields, such as monitoring and supporting the unemployed, the same professionals are charged with the duty of reconciling contradictory demands: promoting equal opportunities with rare resources involves classifying, prioritising and selecting; providing a personalised and humanised form of assistance while meeting the requirements of a more restrictive fast-track process.

Here, if most of the professionals pursue their activity despite their worry about the arbitrariness of the system and the potentially counter-therapeutic effects of its technologies, it is because of the tragic consequences that their defection could have on their patients (e.g. increase the risk of rejection and deportation). This ethical dimension is undoubtedly an important part of what sustains this model of regulation. This model of regulation is thus based on the 'twin movement of autonomisation and responsabilisation' (Rose 1999: 170) which affects citizens in liberal democratic societies. This is in the name of the responsibility for individuals forced into exile for their safety that the solidarity practices continue, even if the logic of immigration and asylum policies are undermining the scope for the many asylum seekers who remain rejected by physical and bureaucratic hurdles.

NOTES

1 First, the value granted to physical marks diminishes the Geneva Convention principle of 'fear of being persecuted', which, by definition, has no physical translation. Second, with certificates, more credit is granted to the expert's word than to that of the victim. The experts deprive refugees of their voice, of their truth. Finally, therapeutic aspects are often overshadowed by medicolegal ones and recounting violence may produce retraumatisation, especially when hurried by a fast-track procedure.

2 Comede, 'Éléments sur la question des certificats après la journée d'équipe du 6.10.1990, le CA du 18. 10. 1990 et le staff médical du 22.10.1990', 18 October 1990, archive, p. 11.

3 During an interview conducted in 2002, the medical staff coordinator explained to me how reluctant he was to deliver a certificate when it was not an initiative from his patient: 'when a solicitor uses a patient in order to have a thicker file, a priori, I will be less welcoming than when the patient comes spontaneously'.

4 Comede, 'Mise à jour des propositions. Principes de la certification médico-psychologique destinée à la demande d'asile', archive, late 1999.

5 GPs are not supposed to evaluate this psychic trauma, but to rely on an account written by a psychologist or a psychiatrist following the patient.

6 At the end of the consultation, the debriefing by Dr Laurence was 'I have nothing to tell. He was beaten in the street; he was beaten with a stick. From the OFPRA point of view, it is the kind of bad attestation ... a tiny scar for someone beaten up ... even if I would not have it measured (the scar)'. However, Dr Laurence, during an interview explained to me that there 'very tiny scars can hide terrifying stories'. But here, because she took into account conditions of reception of her medical certificate, she wished she had not accepted to provide the patient with a certificate about a tiny scar. She had worked in Comede for ten years and anticipated the judgement of the OFPRA's agent: this kind of certificate would discredit allegations of being brutally assaulted because they may think that more marks would remain.

7 According to the 1998 Law, an applicant must be suffering from a serious medical condition for which no adequate treatment is accessible in the country of origin, which would entail a real risk to his life or physical well-being or a real risk of inhuman or degrading treatment owing to the lack of adequate treatment. The permit granted is revised every year. To limit this right, a recent reform (2011) put the word 'available' instead of 'accessible'.

8 Comede, 'Remarques – analyse des données. Certificats de mars – avril 1991', internal records, Kremlin-Bicêtre, 4 September 1991, p. 2.

9 From time to time, a monitoring group is created to assess the medical certificates provided in order to improve standards, but never on a regular basis to supervise the doctors' daily practices.

10 It would be different if it was part of an overall clinical picture which included other clinical facts.

11 Comede, 'Si le Comede décide de ne plus faire de certificat, conséquences pour le patient', no date. Late 1990 considering a reference to a journal article.

REFERENCES

Anker, D. E. 1990. 'Determining Asylum Claims in the United States. Summary Report of an Empirical Study of the Adjudication of Asylum Claims before the Immigration Court', *International Journal of Refugee Law* 2: 252–264

Barsky, R. F. 2000. *Arguing and Justifying: assessing the Convention Refugees' Choice of Moment, Motive and Host Country*. Aldershot: Ashgate

Berlin Institute for Comparative Social Research 2006. *Traumatized Refugees in the EU: Analysis of Institutional Developments, Identification of Protection Systems, Best Practices and Recommendations*. Report about the Expert Roundtables. Berlin

Blériot, I. 2003. *Devenir Réfugié: entre Légalité et Pitié*. DEA d'anthropologie, EHESS

Calabresi, G. and Bobbitt, P. 1978. *Tragic Choices*. New York Norton. (Didier, 1992)

Comede 2003. *Guide du Comede 2003. Manuel Pratique de Prise en Charge Médico-Psycho-sociale des Demandeurs D'asile et des Étrangers en Séjour Précaire*. Kremlin-Bicêtre

Coutin, S. B. 1998. 'From Refugees to Immigrants: The Legalization Strategies of Salvadoran Immigrants and Activists', *International Migration Review* 32: 901–925

d'Halluin, E. 2008. *Les Épreuves de L'asile. De la Politique du Soupçon à la Reconnaissance des Réfugiés*. Thèse pour le Doctorat de Sociologie, Ecole des Hautes Etudes en Sciences Sociales (EHESS)

Daston, L. 1995. 'The Moral Economy of Science', *Osiris* 10: 2–24

Didier, E. 1992. Torture et Mythe de la Preuve. *Plein Droit*, 18–19, 64–69

Dodier, N. 1993. *L'expertise Médicale. Essai de Sociologie sur L'exercice du Jugement*. Paris: Métailié

Dumoulin, L. 2007. *L'expert dans la Justice de la Genèse d'une Figure à ses Usages*. Paris: Economica

Elias, N. 2000. *The Civilizing process*. Oxford: Blackwell

Elster, J. 1992. 'L'éthique des Choix Médicaux', in Elster, J. and Herpin, N. (eds.). Paris: Actes Sud

Ewijk, M. V. and Grifhorst, P. 1998. 'Controlling and Disciplining the Foreign Body: A Case Study of TB Treatment among Asylum Seekers in the Netherlands', in Koser, K. and Lutz, H. (eds.), *The New Migration in Europe*. London: Mac Millan Press

Fassin, D. 2005. 'Compassion and Repression: The moral Economy of Immigration Policies in France', *Cultural Anthropology* 20: 362–387

2001a. 'Charité Bien Ordonnée. Principes de Justice et Pratiques de Jugement dans L'attribution des Aides D'urgence', *Revue Française de Sociologie* 42: 437–475

2001b. 'Quand le Corps Fait la Loi. La Raison Humanitaire dans les Procédures de Régularisation des Étrangers', *Sciences Sociales et Santé* 19: 5–34

Fassin, D. and d'Halluin, E. 2005. 'The Truth in the Body: Medical Certificates as ultimate Evidence for Asylum-Seekers', *American Anthropologist* 107: 597–608

Fassin, D. and Kobelinsky, C. 2012. 'Comment on Juge L'asile', *Revue Française de Sociologie* 53: 657–688

Felstiner, W. L. F. and Sarat, A. 1991. 'Enactments of Power: Negotiating Reality and Responsibility in Lawyer–Client Interactions', *Cornell L. Rev.* 77: 1447

Fox, R. C. and Swazey, J. P. 1974. *The Courage to Fail: A Social View of Organ Transplants and Dialysis.* Chicago: University of Chicago Press

Foucault, M. 1995. *Discipline and punish: The birth of the prison.* New York: Vintage books

Franguiadakis, S., Jaillardon, E. and Belkis, D. 2004. *En Quête D'asile. Aide Associative et Accès au(x) Droit(s).* Paris: L. G. D. J.

Gilboy J. A. 1991. 'Deciding Who Gets In: Decisionmaking by Immigration Inspectors', *Law & Society Review* 25: 571–599

Good, A. 2006. *Anthropology and Expertise in the Asylum Courts.* Abingdon: Routledge-Cavendish

Harvey, C. J. 2000. 'Dissident Voices: Refugees, Human Rights and Asylum in Europe', *Social and Legal Studies* 9: 367–396

Hughes, E. C. 1956. 'Social Role and the Division of Labor', *The Midwest Sociologist* 18: 3–7

1996. *Le Regard Sociologique: Essais Choisis.* Paris: Ecole des Hautes Études en Sciences Sociales

Illich, I. 1966. *Medical Nemesis.* New York: Pantheon Books

Israel, L. 2001. 'Usages Militants dans L'arène Judiciaire: le Cause Lawyering', *Droit et Société* 49: 793–824

Kälin, W. 1986. 'Troubled Communication: Cross-Cultural Misunderstandings in the Asylum-Hearing', *International Migration Review* 20: 230–241

Legoux, L. 1995. *La crise de L'asile Politique en France.* Paris: Centre Français sur la Population et le Développement (CFPD)

Malkki, L. H. 1996. 'Speechless Emissaries: Refugees, Humanitarianism and Dehistoricization', *Cultural Anthropology* 11: 377–404

Marek, A. 2001. Le GISTI ou L'expertise Militante: Une Analyse des Répertoires D'action de L'association. Mémoire de DEA, IEP de Paris

139

Massé, J.-P. 1996. *L'exception Indochinoise. Le Dispositif D'accueil des Réfugiés Politiques en France, 1973–1991*. Doctorat de Sociologie Historique, Ecole des Hautes Études en Sciences Sociales

Newman, E., Kaloupek, D. G. and Keane, T. M. 1996. Assessment of PTSD in Clinical and Research Settings. In B. A. van der Kolk, B. A. McFarlane and L. Weisæth (eds.), *Traumatic Stress: The Effects of Overwhelming Experience on Mind, Body* (pp. 242–275). New York: Guilford Press

Noiriel, G. 1999. *Réfugiés et Sans-papiers. La République Face au Droit D'asile (XIXe-XXe siècle)* Paris: Calmann-Levy

Ogien, A. 1999. 'Situation de Décision: Une Analyse des Pratiques D'attribution D'argent Public', *Droit et Société* 42/43: 365–391

Rawls, J. 1971. *A Theory of Justice*. Cambridge: Harvard University Press

Rose, N. S. 1999. *Powers of Freedom: Reframing Political Thought*. Cambridge: Cambridge University Press

Rousseau, C., Crépeau, F., Foxen, P. and Houle, F. 2002. 'The Complexity of Determining Refugeehood: a Multidisciplinary Analysis of the Decision-making Process of the Canadian Immigration and Refugee Board', *Journal of refugee studies* 15: 43–70

Silove, D., McIntoch, P. and Becker, R. 1993. 'Risk of Retraumatisation of Asylum-Seekers in Australia', *Australian New Zelande Journal of Psychiatry* 27: 606–612

Watters, C. 2000. 'Emerging Paradigms in the Mental Health of Refugees', *Social Science and Medicine* 52: 1709–1718

CONTENTIOUS ROOMMATES? SPATIAL CONSTRUCTIONS OF THE THERAPEUTIC-EVIDENTIAL SPECTRUM IN MEDICOLEGAL WORK

Gethin Rees

Medical practitioners who are involved in the post-rape assault inter-vention, commonly known as forensic medical examiners (FMEs), forensic nurse examiners (FNEs) or sexual assault nurse examiners (SANEs), find themselves in the peculiar position of being required to meet the normative standards of both medicine and the law. The person they are treating is a patient and so the forensic practitioner is required to tend to their therapeutic needs, for instance treating any injuries, providing emergency contraception (and protection against sexually transmitted infections) and ensuring that the survivor has arrange-ments made for follow-up appointments with trauma counsellors, etc. However, at the same time, the question of whether the person is in fact the survivor of rape is still in doubt, that is, the legal decision of whether a criminal offence has taken place has yet to be made. As a result, the forensic practitioner is also expected to collect evidence from the body of the person they are investigating, all the while remembering to main-tain a critical distance and an air of scepticism about the account that the complainant is providing.

In the past, such role-conflict (i.e. between the therapeutic and the evidential) has been considered responsible for abhorrent treatment of victims during the forensic medical examination, with forensic practi-tioners choosing to emphasise the legal/evidential aspects of their role over the medical/therapeutic (Kelly et al. 1996, 1998; Savage et al. 1997). At the heart of this tension in forensic medical work lies the relationship between the recognition of harm and the allocation of rem-edy; clearly, both medical and legal institutions (and by extension their practitioners) are involved in these practices. For instance, the veracity of an alleged complaint of a criminal act is made via the decisions of police officers, prosecutors and eventually judges (assuming a case gets to court), and then, if the harm has been recognised, a punishment will be pronounced which, it is hoped, will serve as justice for the victim. Similarly, healthcare practitioners conduct physical examinations in order to diagnose whether the patient is harmed and, if so, the cause of the harm, and with the diagnosis completed they are then able to provide a therapy which will remedy that disorder. However, separating out the two processes of recognition of harm and allocation of remedy does not adequately portray the ways that medical, legal or medicolegal practitioners operate; rather, the recognition and amelioration processes are necessarily intertwined. For instance, as this chapter demonstrates (as do others in this volume), forensic medical practitioners do not separate medical/therapeutic/remedial processes from legal/evidential/recognition ones, but rather perform evidence gathering at the same time as they treat the complainant. To put it another way, recognition and remedy practices occur simultaneously. In this way, the post-rape intervention is truly forensic, in Mulla's (2011) use of the term, that is, by being medical and legal, therapeutic and evidential, and recognising and resolving harm simultaneously. In this chapter, I will outline the ways that medicolegal practitioners perform their duties in this forensic manner by focusing upon their use of the spaces of forensic medicine.

Social geographers and others interested in the spatial element of social life have highlighted how space and place are not blank stages upon which actors perform, but rather sites of negotiation, the meaning of which various actors attempt to stabilise at the expense of others (Massey 1994). For example, studies of medical spaces have demonstrated that there is no single determining relationship between the architecture of a hospital and the ways that it is used. Prior (1988) made clear that contemporary medical knowledge has a strong influence on the design of a hospital, and provides those working within the building with cues about performance; however, others have demonstrated that these medical meanings can themselves be challenged and contested (Fox 1997). Medicolegal spaces should not be considered purely as a backdrop to work, therefore, but rather as a focus of investigation in order to ascertain how forensic practitioners manage their medical and legal requirements. In a similar vein, Halford and Leonard (2003), in their investigation of the ways that space and place construct gendered nursing identities, suggest that the analyst should examine how actors inhabit and use space in order to get a sense of both the meanings that come to be stabilised over certain spaces and the way that those meanings reflect back upon the actors and their identities. The use of medicolegal spaces can therefore tell us a great deal about the ways practitioners perform their work, and, moreover, the emphasis that they place on therapeutic and/or evidential aspects. This focus on space draws attention to interprofessional conflicts over the stabilisation of meaning and the ways that forensic practitioners attempt to challenge or renegotiate the meanings of spaces, oftentimes in opposition to powerful actors or organisations involved in the criminal justice system's rape intervention. A study of medicolegal spaces can therefore illuminate the challenges and negotiations necessary to perform forensic work. To this end, in this chapter I will investigate the ways that sexual assault nurse examiners (SANEs) in Ontario, Canada, and forensic nurse examiners (FNEs) in England and Wales utilise the space of the specialist centres developed for them to perform their work.

METHODS

The data cited in this chapter derives from a broader study analysing the role and work of forensic nurses in different jurisdictions. Semi-structured interviews were conducted with FNEs presently employed in England and Wales (as well as a small number of physicians involved in the nurses' training, known as forensic medical examiners or FMEs). Seven respondents (including two FMEs) were eventually accessed via the United Kingdom Association of Forensic Nurses across five centres. Canada was chosen as it has a sufficiently similar legal setting to provide a 'most similar' (Pakes 2009) comparison with England and Wales, and Canadian legislation is often cited in debates on sexual offence law (Redmayne 2003; Temkin 2003). Ontario was specifically chosen because the Ontario Network of Sexual Assault/Domestic Violence Treatment Centres (hereafter 'Network') was known to be interested in research in this area, and had been the focus of various studies in the past. Eight nurses were accessed for interviews via the Network, from three hospitals across Ontario. These hospitals were randomly selected from the 33 centres that treat adult sexual assault survivors. Ethical approval was provided by a university's research ethics committee and the three Ontario hospitals. Interviews lasted between one and two hours, were digitally recorded and transcribed verbatim.

Once transcribed, framework analysis (Ritchie and Lewis 2004) was performed, whereby the data was reviewed and indexed into core and subsidiary themes. The development of these matrices enabled comparison between respondents and, crucially, across nations, enabling the comparative aspect of the project. In addition to the interview data, I will also make reference to official documents concerned with the development of specialist forensic medical centres. In the following section I will provide a brief history of the development of these specialist centres and thus a context for the findings of the chapter.

THE RISE OF SPECIALIST SPACES FOR SEXUAL OFFENCE EXAMINATIONS

The responses of a number of states (including England and Wales and Canada) to complaints of rape came under heavy criticism in the 1970s. Key among these criticisms were the institutionalised disbelief of police officers and the manner in which the forensic medical examination was carried out. With regard to the latter, critics noted the long delays between the reporting of the sexual assault and the arrival of the police doctor (during which time the complainant was prohibited from eating, drinking or relieving themselves for fear of losing forensic evidence), *his* (nearly all police doctors were male) unsympathetic, sometimes antagonistic attitude, the location of the medical examination (oftentimes in police stations, providing very little privacy), and the ad hoc way in which it was carried out, due to a lack of formalised training for sexual assault examiners (Chambers and Millar 1983; Du Mont and Parnis 2002; Temkin 2005). Governments, police and the professional organisations representing physicians in both Ontario and the UK did take these criticisms seriously. One strategy employed in both areas was the introduction of specialist sexual assault examination kits, which included guidance documents, reporting forms and standardised artefacts in order to provide guidance to physicians regarding which questions to ask and what information to collect, thereby attempting to limit the noted evidential omissions (McLay 1984; Du Mont and Parnis 2000, 2001; Parnis and Du Mont 2002, 2006).

While advocating these kits, the Ontario Provincial Secretariat for the Justice Consultation Group was also promoting the development of specialist hospital-based centres in order to provide 24-hour support for survivors of sexual assault and the collection of forensic evidence. The first of these was opened in 1984, funded by the Ontario Ministry of Health. Since then another 32 centres have opened, also funded by the Ministry. In 1993, the Network was formed in order to oversee and standardise the work of the various centres (Du Mont and Parnis 2002). Each centre employs a manager, at least one full-time SANE and a number of on-call SANEs. The centres provide a range of options to clients: medical examination, medical treatment (including contraception and prophylaxis against sexually transmitted infections), reporting to the police (if the client has yet to report), collection of trace material (via the standardised sexual assault evidence kit), and follow-up referrals with social workers and SANEs. The Network has a strong client empowerment agenda and places a significant emphasis on the training of nurses in order to perform examinations in a non-judgemental manner.

In comparison, the UK has been somewhat slower in developing specialist centres. While both the Association of Forensic Physicians and the Home Office initially advocated specialist examination suites (McLay 1984; Temkin 1996), resulting in the London Metropolitan Police opening eight victim examination suites and the Greater Manchester Police helping to set up the first sexual assault referral centre (SARC) in 1986, other specialist centres within English and Welsh constabularies were not commonplace until the 2000s, with examinations often performed in GP surgeries until then. In fact, it was only after the findings of a joint inspection in 2002 by Her Majesty's Crown Prosecution Service Inspectorate and Her Majesty's Inspectorate of Constabulary that specialist SARCs were considered best practice.[1]

The promotion of SARCs started as a result of a broader 'rediscovery of the [crime] victim' (Davies et al. 2010: 77) by the Labour government of the late 1990s/2000s. While the criminal justice system of England and Wales has traditionally focused upon perpetrators, during this period attention turned to victims and witnesses, as the police, prosecutors and government ministers became more aware of the criminal justice system's reliance upon the latter. However, the difficulties in reporting certain types of crime, for instance rape and sexual assault, are well documented, as are the distrusting and negative reactions that victims of such crimes receive when they engage with the police (Temkin 2005; Hoyle and Zedner 2007; Davies et al. 2010). In an effort to improve cooperation between the public and the police, the government announced a set of service rights that victims of crime could expect from the police. These included providing better information to the victim, if possible by the identification of a named liaison officer, and referral to Victim Support. Against this background, SARCs, 'one-stop shops' (jointly funded by the police, the National Health Service, the Department of Health and other interested local parties) where the survivors of rape and sexual assault can receive medical treatment and counselling, and report to the police (if they have yet to do so) and where forensic evidence can be collected, not only provide better care for survivors of rape but also increase the number of victims that choose to report (and the quality of evidence collected if the client does indeed decide to report). The interrelation between improved care and reporting of crime/evidence collection was evidenced in an Association of Chief Police Officers (ACPO) working paper:

> The above...give an overview of the different concepts that currently fall into the definition of a SARC. As can be seen the priority is not what the centre looks like or where it is situated but that it provides a multi-agency strategy for enhanced victim care and *as a result* aids any subsequent police investigation.
>
> (ACPO Rape Working Group 2005: 6 emphasis added)

This quotation exemplifies the way in which an improvement in the treatment of the survivor, for example by use of a SARC, is seen to improve evidence-gathering, and therefore that it is not necessarily the case that evidence-gathering and therapy can be easily juxtaposed. However, as mentioned above, it is only through the ways that a space is inhabited and used that we can gain a sense of the meanings that are stabilised within that space. In the following sections I will explore the ways that the specialist centres are used by the nurses who work within them, and how they actively construct the space, their work and themselves in terms of their medicolegal responsibilities.

SANES' CONSTRUCTION OF THE MEDICO-LEGAL SPACE

As mentioned above, all sexual assault and domestic violence treatment centres are based within hospital buildings; however, that is where the similarity between them ends. Some centres are sealed-off units where clients,[2] once they have been medically cleared by emergency room (ER) staff,[3] are based for the remainder of their stay. In other centres, the space is used as an administrative hub, and forensic medical examinations take place in an examination space in the ER. The remainder of centres fit somewhere between the two; for example, in some centres part of the SANE examination takes place in the ER and then the client is taken to a room that is retained by the centre. Although there are differences in the places where examinations take place, there are important similarities in the ways in which they construct the spaces within the hospital.

The chaotic emergency room

Although each client is required to be medically cleared within the ER before they can be seen by a SANE, all SANEs that I interviewed considered the ER to be a chaotic area that is detrimental to the wellbeing of the client. SANEs understood part of their role as moving the client away from the ER as soon as possible. Gail,[4] for instance, a SANE working in a hospital in a relatively rural part of Ontario, noted that

> In actual fact the head-to-toe assessment is done in the emergency room, and again it's a very cursory...I say it's a cursory examination because about 90%, 95% are coming in with a complaint of sexual assault have very few injuries, right, so we need to get them out of that chaotic area and into an area that's a little warmer and fuzzier where we can deal with why they are here.
>
> (Gail, Artonville)[5]

The perceived chaos of the ER was a result of the noise and general commotion pertaining to the kind of healthcare work that takes place in that location. One example highlighted by Beth (who worked at the same hospital as Gail) was the difficulty she found in actually locating the client and her equipment in the ER given the size and high level of activity prevalent. These factors, she suggested, actually made it difficult for her to get to the client within the timeframe advocated by the Ontario programme.

> OK, so we arrive in the room and usually the question I ask before I even leave the phone is where are they [client] going to be, because they can be in several different areas in Emerg and you set off walking like a chicken with it's head cut off, so I try and get a heads up of where they could possibly be, who do I talk to when I get there because there are so many different staff. Um, so once I get there I get my keys, go into my office, or the office and we have a cart that's all set up that has everything you

could possibly need from soup to nuts that we just wheel around instead of having to go to the office five million times.

(Beth, Artonville)

In order to try to conform with the Ontario programme's client-sensitive practices within the chaotic space of the ER, Beth uses a cart with all the equipment that she will need, so she can at least devote all of her focus to the client during the intervention and not have to return to other rooms to collect items, thereby reducing the time that the client will have to spend in that area. Another strategy to limit the amount of trauma for the client was finding a quiet room.

> But if someone was to come in our first thing would be to sit down with them alone and we try to find a spot, Emergency is very, very busy, and with renovations going on, space is rather limited, but we can usually find a quiet spot either a room, or a family room, or wherever we can just to sit down and talk to them, introduce ourselves and try and build up a bit of a rapport with them fairly quickly, these people don't want to be spending seven or eight hours here while we spend three hours building our rapport, so usually what I will say to them is, I will introduce myself, who I am, tell them what our programme is, and something like 'I understand that you've had a really difficult time tonight.', or something along those lines it depends on the person, 'can you tell me a little bit about it?'.
>
> (Anne, Artonville)

The practice of asking questions about the assault in a quiet room away from the ER couch where the client has been medically cleared constitutes an attempt to distance the interaction with the SANE from the chaos of the ER, and aids the development of a rapport between the SANE and the client. Once the SANE in Artonville has discovered some of the details of the assault, she will then take the client through to another room in order to conduct the examination. I will turn to the preparation of that room shortly; first, I will discuss the specialist examination rooms based within other centres.

'Warmer and fuzzier' examination suites

The SANEs I spoke to that worked in centres with specialist examination suites were highly enthusiastic about these locations, and, as has already been pointed out, aimed to relocate clients to the suites as quickly as possible. For instance, Diane, who had previously worked in a range of nursing specialties before turning to SANE work, was most complimentary about the design of the suite in Belleton:

> We have a very nice space here, as you may have noticed, it's very different from the hospital, when they have been here in Emergency for a few hours, or sometimes they've been in another Emergency, they've been transferred here, they are often traumatised, in shock, um, so it's very lovely here, as soon as you walk through the door, it's just a total different feeling, very peaceful, it's very supportive for women.
>
> (Diane, Belleton)[6]

The space is designed to look different to that of the rest of the hospital. As I have discussed in the ER section, the rest of the hospital is constructed by SANEs as threatening or chaotic for the client, something the SANE has to protect the client from, as Fran, a SANE at a busy, urban hospital suggested:

> So I prepare them again ... we're heading on to a ward, there'll be people sleeping, we're located at the end of a corridor and it's a long walk, so this person is tired, they may have their shirt ripped, bra strap showing, cops and that's what I'm doing again, to prepare them for, we try and keep them out of sight by taking the back elevator.
>
> (Fran, Corboro)

Although hospitals are generally considered therapeutic and restful spaces, SANEs are mindful of the threats and difficulties for their clients in all non-specialist suite parts of the hospital. The client may be tired or in shock after their assault and might struggle with the long walk from the ER to the suite; likewise, they may also be in a state of disarray, which could cause undue embarrassment for the client. As a result, SANEs who have access to specialist suites aim to get the clients there as swiftly as possible, as they consider the space of the suite to be a safe haven for female victims of sexual assault, and provide them with the opportunity to begin recuperating from their traumatic experience.

The forensic aspect of SANE examination spaces

Thus far I have focused on how SANEs construct examination suites as safe spaces in opposition to the rest of the hospital; however, I have yet to focus on the evidential aspects of the forensic examination. In Artonville, SANEs, after they have initially met with the client, move to an examination room within the ER. This is not one kept specifically for SANE examinations, and so the nurse has to prepare the room before the client enters. In the event that trace material will be collected for forensic scientific analysis, the room has to be thoroughly cleaned in order to avoid contamination of the samples.

> [W]hat I will do next is I'm going to go to the exam room and I'm going to clean it, um, I'll clean it with whatever disinfectant the hospital is using at that time, I'll clean the exam table and make sure there's a clean sheet on it, I'll clean any surface for my equipment, so usually I have a table and I try to lay everything out on that. I may, depending on the room, I may have to use the counter around the sink, and so I will clean that as well, or I may have a little stand that I might use; whatever I'm going to use, I'll clean.

> (Anne, Artonville)

As the room is not used solely for the examination of sexual assault clients, it must be cleaned in order to make it medicolegal. Anne's cleaning, combined with her following of the official sexual assault examination kit's protocol,[7] means that the trace material that she collects from the body of the client is considered uncontaminated, credible and fit to be used by others (forensic scientists for instance) in the criminal justice system.

Given the importance of cleanliness to the credibility of the evidence within criminal justice contexts, it is of interest that no mention was made of cleaning in Belleton and Corboro. The specialist centres' rooms would, of course, be cleaned under the routine hospital protocols, and SANEs use Sexual Assault Evidence Kits which contain equipment that are kept sterile, but as far as the room is concerned there is no specific cleaning plan. While in some centres the offices of the SANEs are separate to the examination room, in others they are used as the office for the permanent member(s) of staff, and other people walk in and out of these rooms for follow-up meetings. Access is somewhat limited to the examination rooms during examinations, but not for reasons of cleanliness; SANEs control access in an attempt to empower the client.

The chief aim of the SANE examination under the Network's protocol is the provision of a number of options to the client, who then determines the way that the examination will continue. Even if the client has already reported and arrives at the hospital accompanied by the police, the SANE will take her into the examination/quiet room on her own in order to provide the options. A senior SANE, who was involved with the management of her fellow nurses and as such used the examination suite as her own office, said the following about the negotiation of space with the police:

> when you have a client, it's all about not being judgemental and it's all about putting them in control, so when a client comes in here, um some of the issues I find to is that if there is police involvement, the police want me to do a kit, and they want me to make her, and sometimes there's a suggestion if they don't do a kit "I'm not sure this is really an assault" that kind of thing, so it is very important that the nurse knows that it is not about the police, it's not about the nurse, it's about the young woman, or young man. Once they get in here they get to choose what they do and don't do … we always see them first, which is, occasionally the situation where they [police] try and get them first, but we always try and get them here first because we can give them the freedom. So that for me is another part of our job too, giving her the control to decide what she wants to do, if she doesn't want to do a kit, that's her prerogative, and usually what I will say to them [client] is, don't worry that the police brought you, don't worry, you know what happened
>
> Interviewer: So you keep the police out there [another room]?
>
> Yeah, and we always see them first, which is, occasionally the situation where they [police] try and get them [client] first, but we always try and get them [client] here first because we can give them the freedom.
>
> (Emma, Belleton)

Explicit within Emma's comments are the conflicts over meanings of spaces discussed earlier. Accompanying police officers attempt to impose their evidence-gathering meaning on the centre. However, the SANE, being the embodiment of the Network's client empowerment agenda, wishes to stabilise her meaning for the space as a place in which the survivor has freedom to choose her medical and legal trajectories. By prohibiting the police from entering that space, and 'always try[ing] to get the [client] here first', the medical meaning of the space wins out; the client has the chance to decide whether or not to have forensic evidence collected. Similarly, nurses in other centres used additional rooms as a means to control access to the examination suite; in particular, Hannah, who tended to specialise in child clients, noted the ways that she used different rooms in order to empower the child:

> [A]lso there's a small room next door and that's where I drop off the police, depending on the age of the person, if they are with their parents, I might bring them back in there, and then say "do you want your parents here" and sometimes if they are particularly younger they want their parents there for the HIV pep discussion, maybe not for the other

stuff but for the HIV pep or other drugs, and sometimes if I've got a thir-teen year old girl, she's not sure if she wants to take those drugs or not, um so she needs to talk about, so I'll bring mom back in, if it's okay with her, if she doesn't want mom in, then she's, they're not there for all of it, but oftentimes the younger girls want mom there for that part, and then, otherwise everyone is in next door.

(Hannah, Corboro)

Hannah is empowering the client to identify whom she wants in the examination space, regardless of procedural rules concerning age, in order for the client to feel comfortable during the examination. As a result, the importance of client choice and its associated therapeutic discourse is emphasised within the workspace.

I do not wish to conclude here, however, that SANEs' practices nec-essarily subordinate the legal; it is after all the case that, if the client chooses to pursue a criminal case, the suites become evidence-gathering places in addition to therapeutic ones. As another SANE made clear, it is within the examination suite that the serious recording of medico-legal evidence is done:

I'm keeping it very loose and very, and um and you get more information once you're upstairs [in the examination suite] and going through the kit...I'm Lucy Goosey downstairs [in the ER], get more formal when we're up here, any pain, any bleeding.

(Fran, Corboro)

Once the SANE has offered the options, if the client chooses to have trace material collected, the nurses' practices demonstrate an acute awareness of the importance of the legal evidence-collection require-ments. For example, if a sexual assault examination kit is opened, the nurses know that they cannot leave it unattended, as they need to be able to vouch for the integrity of that evidence.

So then I do the, if they [client] decide to do it, then I do the bloodwork, and I will include, and I need to talk about the sexual assault kit as well, if they have decided to do it, because I don't want to do this twice, so if they are going to do the sexual assault kit I want to do all the bloodwork once, I do both at the same time, because there is one tube for the forensic kit, and then it's important to get the bloodwork down to the lab, so we have a 'Statlab', a rapid lab, so we can get the results back quickly, and, that's a piece of the, if you open up the kit, to get the grey-top tube, that's you have to keep that because it's the chain of evidence, so that's the start-time, so you have to keep the kit with you to take it down to the Statlab thing, so usually there are some extra grey-top, so usually I try to use an extra grey-top and I just put that in the kit. But sometimes there isn't so you're walking down the hall with the kit.

(Diane, Belleton)

Once the kit is opened, the meaning of the hospital space becomes both therapeutic and evidence-gathering, and SANEs are very aware of the importance of the chain of custody of their collected trace material. While the Network's overriding ethos is the empowerment of the client, once the client makes the decision to have evidence collected and a kit is opened, the nurses' practices and the meanings of the space become equally evidential and therapeutic.

FNES' CONSTRUCTION OF THE MEDICOLEGAL SPACE

As they are rather novel as medicolegal practitioners, FNEs only work within sexual assault referral centres (which, as was pointed out earlier, are considered best practice). SARCs are generally housed in self-contained buildings on hospital premises, but not within the hospital building itself.[8] They are known as 'one-stop shops', where survivors of sexual assault can refer themselves (or be accompanied by the police if they have already reported) for medical care, including contraception, a forensic examination and counselling, and the option of reporting to the police (if they have yet to do so). There are two key reasons for the separation of the SARC from the remainder of the hospital: security and privacy for both the clients and the staff; and the importance of cleanliness and limiting the potential for contamination. Advice from ACPO as well as the Department of Health (DH) and the Home Office (HO) emphasises that the SARC should be accessible 24 hours a day for both police and self-referrals, that the spaces should be kept secure (via the use of key code locks to ensure that only those who need the service have legitimate reason to be there or work there have access), and that the privacy of the client using the service should be constantly maintained (ACPO Rape Working Group 2005, DH/HO/ACPO 2009). A separate building helps maintain clients' privacy by providing them with immediate access to the services they need rather than requiring them to walk through other wards.

Further to the security and privacy aspect, SARCs' separate buildings also help to maintain their cleanliness. The 2009 joint Department of Health, Home Office and ACPO report provided a list of ten 'Minimum Elements' for a SARC, of which number five was that a SARC should be within a '[d]edicated forensically approved premises and a facility with decontamination protocols following each examination to ensure high quality forensic integrity and a robust chain of evidence.' (DH/HO/ACPO 2009: 18)

This quotation stresses the importance that the three governing bodies place upon the integrity of trace material collection and the potential harm that unclean or contaminated samples could cause to a future criminal investigation. To this end, the developers of each SARC are required to liaise with other interested parties in order to produce a decontamination protocol, and FNEs are made acutely aware of the necessity to clean and decontaminate the examination rooms. In some centres this is done both before and after they are used:

> I mean, to be honest, our decontamination, um, either, say it's either myself or [another nurse] we do the same thing, so at the time we do, we'll go upstairs, we'll change into theatre scrubs, hat and mask, we go upstairs, we make up the bucket of Actechlore, we will clean the unit down. Now bearing in mind that it gets cleaned after every case, and there is a record of decontamination which will stand up in court because the decontamination protocol was set up between the police lab and the infection control health board, um, so that's all done.
>
> (Ellie, Gorchester)

Whereas in others, the examination suite is cleaned following each client: 'We've obviously got, here, we've got a suite that's specifically, it's been cleaned after the last case, so it's ready to go basically, so again in order to save some time so I can get in and see the complainant as soon as I can.' (Alice, Dorland). SARCs where the examination room is cleaned after a case, and not before, also have routine decontamination at specific times; the doors in these centres come equipped with clipboards attached, stating who the last person to enter the room was, when they did so, and when it was last cleaned, in order to maintain a record of the chain of custody.

A corollary of the strict decontamination ethos is the aesthetics of the SARC. After visiting five SARCs, it was clear that sterile rooms with identical blue plastic wipe-clean seating were routine. My sense of the room as sterile and sparse was supported and justified by Ellie who worked in a large urban SARC that was attached to a hospital: 'There's a small, almost like sitting room area, it's very sparse and it's sparse for a reason, because we can't have any cross-contamination.' (Ellie, Gorchester) Diane, in her statement about Belleton, noted that the space was highly feminine and designed in a manner to demarcate the space from that of the rest of the hospital. This is not the case with the SARC, where the necessity to limit the potential for contamination results in sparse, homogenised, wipe-clean spaces in order to maintain the integrity of the collected trace material.

Clearly, SARC design has a far stronger emphasis on evidence-gathering than its Ontario counterpart, and to an extent the FNEs working within SARCs have assimilated that evidence-gathering focus, ensuring the cleanliness of the spaces and themselves via the use of surgical gowns and other protective coverings. However, as with SANEs, it would be too straightforward to say that FNEs emphasise the legal at the expense of the medical; looking at their practices and use of space, we find that FNEs make sure clients are comfortable with the people who are in the room during the examination. Chloe, for instance, a more experienced FNE, explained a case where she was able to use the space to empower a complainant:

> Absolutely, I did have a case, she was actually a porn star, and she had mum in and mum was an elderly mother, um so I had a word "would you like your mum to pop out?" possibly mum didn't know what she did, so we've got a special family room, so we just sat mum in there.
>
> (Chloe, Fourwaters)

As with Ontario, the practice of letting the client decide who is in the room at the time of the examination empowers them and is considered to be a therapeutic practice. However, FNEs do not have as much control as SANEs in terms of barring the police from the examination room in the case of a police referral, especially if the complainant has not changed their clothes since the time of the attack.

> [I]n cases where we did need the clothing of course, we took them into the medical room and the complainant would be behind the curtain and I'd warn them that the police officer would come in because it was going to be the police officer's evidence really, um, so the police officer would come in behind the curtain, in a discreet way, and the complainant would hand out each item of clothing for the evidence bag. And then the police officer was responsible for bagging and labelling that clothing.
>
> (Alice, Dorland)

In order to collect clothing, the police officer is invited into the examination suite, and handed the clothing by the client themselves through a curtain. The police officer then stays in the forensically clean room to label the evidence, so that contamination is limited and thereby the chain of custody is protected. In such cases, therefore, the client does not have the opportunity to choose whether they wish the police officer to be present during the examination, as it is considered necessary in order to protect the credibility of the evidence. However, once the examination is complete and the clothing bags and other trace material have been collected and stored in a refrigerator, the police officer will be requested to leave the room.

> Once all that forensic part is done, we ask the police officer to leave the room so we can have, um, a just a completely clinical interaction which is all about STIs, HIV post-exposure prophylactic and follow-up care, because that does not need to be, that's not part of the forensic examination, so that's done in private.
>
> (Deborah, Gorchester)

This quotation from Deborah reveals much about the meanings of space for forensic nurses working in SARCs. As I have made clear, there is a strong evidential discourse running throughout the design, development and use of the SARC space. Deborah is attempting to challenge, or at least interrupt, this evidential discourse (at least for a time) by removing the police officer from the room. This alters the space (in Deborah's words), into a 'completely clinical' one. Of course, this is not completely the case; as was evidenced in the ACPO guidance document cited earlier, greater care for survivors of sexual assault, such as access to follow-up counselling and sexually transmitted infection prophylaxis, in fact serves to increase reporting of sexual violence. As such, the therapeutic is actually a means to generate the evidential. Nevertheless, a representation of the space as medical for the post-examination period serves to ensure that the meaning of that place cannot be wholly reduced to evidence-gathering.

THE MEANING OF MEDICOLEGAL SPACES AND THE FORENSIC SPECTRUM

Traditionally the medical intervention following a report of rape was represented as placing the forensic practitioner under some form of role-conflict between the objective evidence collector (maintaining a critical – often cynical – distance from the complainant being examined) and the subjective therapeutic healer. Practitioners had to decide which one of those roles to take on, and perform their work accordingly, often to the detriment of the survivor (Kelly et al. 1996, 1998; Savage et al. 1997). While to a certain extent the dichotomy of objective evidence versus subjective care still exists in the meanings of the spaces in which forensic nurses continue to operate (for instance, the Ontario networks' spaces were seen to be soft, feminine and without an explicitly forensic cleaning protocol, whereas the SARC buildings were sterile), the nurses performing the examinations do not make these stark distinctions; rather, they construct the spaces that they work in as both therapeutic and evidential. For instance, SANEs clean ER examination rooms and maintain the chain of custody by carrying the sexual assault evidence kit around the hospital, while FNEs remove the police from the examination room in order to discuss medication and follow-up care. Such practices necessarily enable both aspects to be performed at the same time – what Mulla (2011) labels the 'forensic' mode.

Labelling medicolegal work as 'forensic' does not necessarily homogenise the work performed by forensic nurses; clearly there are still significant differences between SANEs and FNEs. Rather than understanding the forensic mode as some kind of monolithic category, as therapeutic and evidential have been used in the past, it should be considered a spectrum upon which practitioners position themselves, their work and their place through space and time. SANE centres, for instance, would be located very close to the therapeutic end of the forensic spectrum up until the point that the client agrees to report the crime to the police; at this point, the work and the space move further along the spectrum, towards evidence-gathering. Likewise, FNE work and space are predominantly evidential until the end of the examination, when they move closer to the therapeutic end. At no point is the work ever wholly medical or legal, evidential or therapeutic, but always somewhere in between.

It is clear that this increased compassionate approach to clients is altering the way that evidence is collected, not only by forensic practitioners but also by the police. Specialist police officers for rape and sexual assault investigations are now expected to allow the complainant to ask open questions during interviews, rather than closed, detailed questions (McMillan and Thomas 2009). As with the more therapeutic approach to forensic medicine, it is clear from such practices that the push to generate the best quality of evidence no longer involves criminal justice personnel (including forensic medical practitioners) performing from a distanced objective perspective; rather, they adopt a more empathetic standpoint. However, this is not to be understood as an abandonment of the evidence-gathering agenda; on the contrary, as evidenced by the reports from the joint organisations involved with the post-rape intervention in England and Wales, the belief is that more support for victims is likely to improve the quality and quantity of evidence retrieved from victims and witnesses. It appears, therefore, that the shift to a therapeutic-evidential spectrum evidenced within forensic medicine is part of a larger criminal justice project, itself partly motivated by a greater desire not to further harm the victims of crime, but also by this endeavour to improve the quantity and quality of evidence generated.

While police and prosecutors are increasingly dependent upon forensic medical professionals to provide high standards of care in order to produce good quality evidence, it does not follow that criminal justice is subservient to medicine. The law continues to set the parameters of what counts as credible evidence, and SANEs and FNEs are still required to follow its precepts while at the same time performing best-quality care. Medicine and law are co-dependent, and forensic medics must not embody one role alone (therapeutic or evidential) as physicians have done in the past; instead, they must draw from both medical and legal registers. FNEs' and SANEs' use of space evidences the familiarity that these practitioners have with both medicine and the law, and the sophistication with which they can move between them.

NOTES

1 As a result, it became policy that a SARC would be introduced in each constabulary in England and Wales by 2011.

2 'Client' is the respondent term for a person being examined. Throughout this paper I will use this word interchangeably with survivor.

3 Medical clearance involves the evaluation of each client before they are seen by SANEs to ensure that they meet the 'well women' criteria. The 'well women' criteria include: being conscious; not suspected of having overdosed; not pregnant; not suicidal and not suffering from any life-threatening injuries that require emergency treatment.

4 All names are pseudonyms.

5 All locations are pseudonyms.

6 It is illuminating that Diane highlights the femininity of the space; later on in the interview she stated, 'with men, we don't have men up here, we have to do all the work in Emergency, so it's a bit of a different protocol.' (Diane, Belleton) Clearly male survivors are not privileged to the same considerations as their female counterparts, and this is alarming given SANEs' construction of the ER as a chaotic place.

7 See Du Mont and Parnis (2000, 2001) and Parnis and Du Mont (2002, 2006) for discussions of the Sexual Assault Examination Kit in Ontario.

8 The exceptions to this rule are the Rape Examination Advice Counselling Help (REACH) centres in Northumbria and Derbyshire where houses are renovated and turned into SARCs. REACH centres were not visited during the fieldwork.

REFERENCES

Association of Chief Police Officers Rape Working Group 2005. *Sexual Assault Referral Centres (SARCs)*: 'Getting Started' Guide Accessed June 2010 at www.caada.org.uk/practitioner_resources/sarcs-getting-started.pdf

Chambers, G. A. and Millar, A. 1983. *Investigating Sexual Assault* Edinburgh: The Stationery Office

Davies, M., Croall, H. and Tyrer, J. 2010. *Criminal Justice* Harlow: Pearson Education

Department of Health, Home Office, Association of Chief Police Officers 2009. *Revised National Service Guide: A Resource for Developing Sexual Assault Referral Centres*. Accessed December 2010 at ww2.reading.gov.uk/documents/community-living/community-safety/ResourceforDeveloping SexualAssaultReferralCentres.pdf

Du Mont, J. and Parnis, D. 2002. *An Overview of the Sexual Assault Care and Treatment Centres of Toronto* Toronto: World Health Organisation

2001. 'Constructing Bodily Evidence Through Sexual Assault Evidence Kits', *Griffith Law Review* 10: 63–76

2000. 'Sexual Assault and Legal Resolution: Querying the Medical Collection of Forensic Evidence', *Medicine and Law* 19: 779–92

Fox, N. J. 1997. 'Space, Sterility and Surgery: Circuits of hygiene in the operating theatre', *Social Science and Medicine* 45: 649–57

Halford, S. and Leonard, P. 2003. 'Space and Place in the Construction and Performance of Gendered Nursing Identities', *Journal of Advanced Nursing* 42: 201–8

Hoyle, C. and Zedner, L. 2007. 'Victims, Victimization and Criminal Justice' in Maguire, M., Morgan, R. and Reiner, R. (eds.), *The Oxford Handbook of Criminology*. Oxford: Oxford University Press

Kelly, K., Moon, G., Savage, S. P. and Bradshaw, Y. 1996. 'Ethics and the Police Surgeon: Compromise or Conflict', *Social Science and Medicine* 42: 1569–1575

Kelly, K., Moon, G., Bradshaw, Y. and Savage, S. P. 1998. 'Insult to Injury? The Medical Investigation of Rape in England and Wales', *Journal of Social Welfare and Family Law* 20: 409–420

McLay, W. D. S. 1984. *The New Police Surgeon: Rape*. Northampton: Association of Police Surgeons

McMillan, L. and Thomas, M. 2009. 'Police Interviews of Rape Victims: Tensions and contradictions', in Horvath, M. and Brown, J. (eds.), *Rape: Challenging Contemporary Thinking*. Cullompton: Willan Publishing

Massey, D. 1994. *Space, Place and Gender*. Cambridge: Polity Press

Mulla, S. 2011. 'Facing Victims: Forensics, Visual Technologies, and Sexual Assault Examination', *Medical Anthropology* 30: 271–94

Pakes, F. 2009. *Comparative Criminal Justice*. Cullompton: Willan Publishing

Parnis, D. and Du Mont, J. 2006. 'Symbolic Power and the Institutional Response to Rape: Uncovering the Cultural Dynamics of a Forensic Technology', *The Canadian Review of Sociology and Anthropology* 43: 73–93

2002. 'Examining the Standardized Application of Rape Kits: An exploratory study of post-sexual assault professional practices', *Health Care for Women International* 23: 846–53

Prior, L. 1988. 'The Architecture of the Hospital: A study of the spatial organization and medical knowledge', *The British Journal of Sociology* 39: 86–113

Redmayne, M. 2003. 'Myths, Relationships and Coincidences: The new problems of sexual history', *International Journal of Evidence and Proof* 7: 75–100

Ritchie, J. and Lewis, J. 2004. *Qualitative Research Practice: A guide for social science students and researchers*. London: Sage

Savage, S. P., Moon, G., Kelly, K. and Bradshaw, Y. 1997. 'Divided Loyalties? – The Police Surgeon and Criminal Justice', *Policing and Society* 7: 79–98

Temkin, J. 2005. *Rape and the Legal Process*. Oxford: Oxford University Press

2003. 'Sexual History Evidence – Beware the Backlash', *Criminal Law Review*: 217–43

1996. 'Doctors, Rape and Criminal Justice', *Howard Journal of Criminal Justice* 35: 1–20

PART TWO

UNDERSTANDING AND ALLOCATING REMEDY

CHAPTER SEVEN

THE JURIDICAL HOSPITAL: CLAIMING THE RIGHT TO PHARMACEUTICALS IN BRAZILIAN COURTS

João Biehl

THE JUDICIALISATION OF HEALTH

A retired bus driver, Edgar Lemos lives in a lower-middle-class neighbourhood of Porto Alegre, the capital of the southern Brazilian state of Rio Grande do Sul. Dealing with significant motor difficulties, Edgar had to wait for more than a year for a specialised neurological appointment at a nearby public hospital. He was finally diagnosed with hereditary cerebral ataxia in November of 2008. The neurologist prescribed the drug Somazina, which is not included on any governmental drug formulary.

Raised in a destitute family, Edgar had worked since the age of eight. He was proud of the gated brick and mortar house he had built himself on the top of a hill. Edgar's ataxia affected not only his mobility but also his sense of dignity and worth, as it made him more dependent on the care of his wife and two adult daughters. Religion had become an important source of emotional sustenance and a complement to his pharmaceutical treatment. While Edgar felt that Somazina was helping to halt the degeneration of his motor abilities, he was also taking a variety of other drugs, from statins to anti-hypertensives and anti-anxiolytics, to soothe additional symptoms.

I want to express my deepest gratitude to Joseph J. Amon, Mariana P. Socal and Adriana Petryna for all their creative insights and wonderful help with this research project. I have also had the distinct pleasure of working with a superb group of postdoctoral fellows and graduate and undergraduate students over the past few years. I want to thank Ramah McKay, Peter Locke, Amy Moran-Thomas, Alexander Wamboldt, Igor Rubinov, Alex Gertner, Joshua Franklin, Jeferson Barbosa, Raphael Frankfurter and Naomi Zucker, whose help has been particularly important. The Ford Foundation and Princeton's Health Grand Challenges Initiative and the Woodrow Wilson School of Public and International Affairs generously supported the research. A first version of the chapter appeared in *American Ethnologist* 2013, 40(3).

During a conversation over his dining room table in August 2011, Edgar opened a box containing the five medicines that make up his regimen. As he held each one in turn, he said, 'This one I don't judicialise, this one I don't judicialise ... I only judicialise this medicine because I went into debt paying for it.' A monthly supply of Somazina costs about 200 dollars.

After paying for the drug out of pocket for several months, Edgar had to take out a bank loan. Unable to keep up the house expenses and bank interests, he had 'no other alternative but to judicialise'. He learned about the Public Defender's Office (Defensoria Pública) from other patients also waiting for specialists' referrals at the public health post and filed a lawsuit to compel the state to pay for his medication. The Porto Alegre district judge issued a court injunction on his behalf and Edgar received the medicine for several months, but then "the delivery stopped." He filed a new claim and won another injunction for three additional months of treatment. As state attorneys were appealing the judge's decision, Edgar nervously anticipated having to renew the lawsuit again.

A former union organiser, Edgar had a sense that aspects of racism and socio-economic inequality seemed to be improving with the rise to power of the Workers' Party (PT or *Partido dos Trabalhadores* – see Anderson 2011). As for why he was not judicialising the other drugs he was taking, Edgar reasoned, 'I know that the state cannot give everything to everyone. I have to do my part and pay for whatever I can.'

Across Brazil, patients like Edgar are seeking, and sometimes realising, access to healthcare through the courts, a phenomenon that has been termed the *judicialisation of health* (Biehl et al. 2009; Ferraz 2009; Marques and Dallari 2007). Though patients are suing the government for everything from baby formula to complex surgeries, a large portion of lawsuits are for access to prescribed drugs (Scheffer et al. 2005).

In this chapter, I explore how right-to-health litigation has become (in the wake of a successful universal AIDS treatment policy) an alternative route for Brazilians to access healthcare, now understood as access to pharmaceuticals that are either on governmental drug formularies or are only available through the market. Throughout, I show how the relations between individual bodies, political subjectivities, medical technologies and state institutions are compellingly rearranged along this judicialised front. Poor people are not waiting for medical technologies to trickle down; they are leveraging public legal assistance and a receptive judiciary to hold the state accountable to its mandate and to their medical needs, now. The chapter's ethnographic vignettes pave a path towards a relatively unexplored frontier of medical, legal and political anthropology, that zone where technology, medicine and law intersect in unexpected and deeply personal ways, and where our notions about how medicalisation and biopolitics operate from the bottom up must be rethought.

FROM THE RIGHT TO HEALTH TO THE RIGHT TO PHARMACEUTICALS

The 1988 Brazilian Constitution declared health as the 'right of all persons and the duty of the State' and the creation of the country's Unified Health System (SUS) extended health coverage to all citizens. Judicialisation stems from an expansive definition of the meaning of the right to health and also, in part, from the passage of a landmark law in 1996 establishing free universal access to antiretroviral (ARV) therapies for HIV-infected individuals (Berkman et al. 2005; Biehl 2007a; Galvão 2002). Ministry of Health policies and a 2000 ruling by the Supreme Court further advanced the right to medicines as part of the constitutional right to health (Supremo Tribunal Federal 2000).

SUS provides health services and medicines free of cost (Porto et al. 2011). As part of a broader process of decentralisation and in an effort to improve the administration of SUS, the federal Ministry of Health divided responsibilities for pharmaceutical distribution among three levels of government (Ministério da Saúde 2010). Federal, state and municipal tiers of government are responsible for purchasing and distributing medicines according to specific drug formularies. The federal Health Ministry continues to finance high-cost medicines called *specialised medicines* which are dispensed by state health secretariats. Municipal governments are responsible for purchasing low-cost *essential medicines* which are dispensed at local public pharmacies (Souza 2002). State governments finance and distribute *special medicines* that their state residents require but that do not appear on either of the other two formularies (Ministério da Saúde 2001). In addition, the federal Health Ministry funds strategic programmes for the control of certain infectious diseases such as HIV/AIDS, tuberculosis and leprosy, as well as rare disorders such as Gauchers disease (Ministério da Saúde n. d.).

Despite these laws, policies and judicial rulings, the experience of patients in realising access to medicines has been uneven. Today, about 200 000 Brazilians take ARV drugs paid for by the government. At the same time, many citizens go to local public pharmacies only to find that essential medicines are out of stock and that the newer medicines they seek are not included in official formularies (Mendis et al. 2007). Decentralisation delegated responsibility but did not ensure sustainable funding and technical capacity at local levels. Regional and municipal governments have not been able to adequately budget and administer the growing complexity of medical needs and technological and infrastructural demands within an already complex health system.

With a population of about 200 million people and an economy on the rise, Brazil has one of the fastest growing pharmaceutical markets in the world, with an estimated total value of more than US $25 billion in 2012 according to a business association (SINDUSFARMA 2012). Public and private doctors increasingly prescribe and patients demand new medicines, some of uncertain benefit. Newer medicines, however, are often only available through private purchase. Unable to pay out of pocket (as in the case of Edgar) or to find low-cost generics at public pharmacies, patients are increasingly suing the government to obtain what they need. People often use the expression *entrar na justiça*, "to enter the judiciary" or, literally, "to enter justice", to refer to their lawsuits.

PARA-INFRASTRUCTURES AND POLITICAL EXPERIMENTATION

For the past few years, I have been coordinating a multisited ethnographic study of right-to-health litigation in the southern Brazilian state of Rio Grande do Sul, which has the highest number of such lawsuits in the country.[1] Implementing collaborative evidence-making practices, our research team moved across domestic, clinical, judicial and administrative domains, to track the interconnection of sites and the interplay of scales that the judicialisation of health calls upon and calls into question. Some of the core queries that guided our investigation included: Is the judicial system an effective venue for implementing socio-economic rights? Which social fields and practices of citizenship and governance are crystallised in these struggles over pharmaceutical access and administrative accountability? How is it possible to gauge the market's influence on the medical demands and practices as well as on the public institutions of the world's seventh largest economy?

While examining the tense negotiations of the constitutional right to health in daily life, I often had a sense of social roles and political positions out of place: the judiciary as a sort of pharmacy, the public defender as a physician, the physician as an activist, the patient association as a legal counsel and the patient citizen becoming the consumer, among other translocations and displacements. I found Michel Foucault's tentative reflections on biopolitics and neoliberalism (Foucault 2008) helpful, as I tried to understand the form and reach of these novel medico-socio-legal realities, in particular what he describes as the frugality of government in contexts where market exchange determines value. But these realities also contravened Foucault's reflections as they underscored the importance of the juridical subject to late liberal political economies.

In his 1978–1979 Lectures at the Collège de France, Foucault argued that we can adequately analyse biopolitics only when we understand the economic reason within governmental reason, suggesting that the market shapes and even determines governmental logics. In Foucault's words: 'the market constitutes a site of veridiction-falsification for governmental practice. Consequently, the market determines that good government is no longer simply government that functions according to justice' (2008: 32).

The ways and means of right-to-health litigation in Brazil reveal an intense experiential-political-economic field. Here the penetration of market principles in healthcare delivery is unexpectedly aligned with the juridical subject of rights. The rational choice-making economic subject (necessarily a consumer of technoscience) is also the subject of legal rights. The right to life is claimed in between the clinic, the court and the marketplace. What do these processes of judicialisation mean for how anthropologists approach the study of politics and engage with ongoing debates, inside and outside the academy, about the relationship of health to human rights and social justice? How are the interpenetrating domains of health, therapeutic markets and the law emerging as implicit and explicit sites for claiming political rights and confronting political failures?

Jonathan Spencer has written about anthropology's difficulties in 'drawing bounds round "the political"' (2007: 29; see Biehl and McKay 2012). While classic political anthropology limited politics to formal and functional analyses (a 'politics without values'), the anthropology of politics that emerged in the 1980s and 1990s as a necessary and invigorating corrective (as exemplified by Subaltern Studies) 'deliberately exclud[ed] the state from the domain of authentic politics' (Spencer 2007: 23). In the intervening decades, the anthropology of politics has moved to include a consideration of the state and the development (Ferguson 1994; Sharma and Gupta 2006) of transnational politics and neoliberalism (Comaroff and Comaroff 2011; Englund 2006; Petryna 2002; Ong 2006), and of the affective domains and subjective experiences of political life (Povinelli 2011; Biehl et al. 2005). And while much recent anthropology has productively applied Foucault's concept of biopolitics to a variety of contexts (Fassin 2007; Nguyen 2010; Ong and Collier 2005; Rabinow and Rose 2006; Rajan 2006), we are only beginning to capture the fluidity and fragility of biopolitical processes and their entanglement with the market as a testing ground for techniques of governance and self-fashioning (Edmonds 2010).

Clearly anthropologists have stayed attuned to politics – even as the substance of what is considered 'political' has varied with disciplinary conversations – be it in the inequalities of the field, as activists, or in their theoretical concerns with postcolonial disorders, structural violence, social suffering and biopolitics, for example (Comaroff and Comaroff 2011; Chatterjee 2004; Das 2007; Good et al. 2008; Farmer 2003; Hansen and Stepputat 2001; Holston 2009; Kelly 2009; Merry 2006; Riles 2000; Scheper-Hughes 1992; Tate 2007). Most compellingly, anthropologists have begun to examine the politics involved in the formation of 'para-infrastructures' such as humanitarian interventions and therapeutic policies (Biehl and McKay 2012:1210 – see also Biehl 2007a; Fassin and Pandolfi 2010; McKay 2012; Ticktin 2011).

While Stephen Collier (2011) has explored how Soviet urban infrastructures reveal political and economic rationalities and negotiations over the form of the (post) social state, other anthropologists such as Nikhil Anand (2012) and Hannah Appel (2012) have shown how infrastructures (such as water networks and oil enclaves) form critical sites of engagement and negotiation for corporations, states and their subjects (or citizens) in everyday life. However, with the term 'para-infrastructure', I mean to call attention to, and account for, the interstitial domain of political experimentation that becomes visible in people's case-by-case attempts to 'enter justice' in Brazil. There is no predetermined strategy of control in the judicial para-infrastructure.

Norms are constantly in flux and numerous parties – state and market institutions as well as experts, legal representatives, and citizens – can manipulate levers of access. While laying claims to life, facing off and disputing over responsibility, evidence and cost-benefits, these various parties bide their time and become empirically present and permeable at once.

Although precarious, para-infrastructures such as the judicialisation of health significantly inform the ways of living that people take up in the context of ailing or inadequate public institutions as well as the scope and reach of governance in real time. Attention to such 'intermediary power formations' as I considered them elsewhere (Biehl 2007a: 94) and to the growing 'judicialisation of politics' (Comaroff and Comaroff 2006) presents new ethnographic quandaries. They compel us to engage and think through the ambiguous political subjectivities and social formations that crystallise amid the blurring of distinctions between populations, market segments, political movements and con-stituencies, and collective objects of intervention or disregard (Biehl and Petryna 2011; Schuch 2012).

Moving across various scales of anthropological analysis this article brings into view lives and living forged across exceedingly complex and often contradictory institutions. The experiences and vignettes from lawyers, patients and families, doctors, advocates, policy-makers and judges presented here do not and cannot perfectly cohere. I try to describe the entanglements of the judicialisation of health with-out claiming that it is seamless. Instead, I urge readers to consider how this new political phenomenon compels sick persons, laws, experts, offi-cials and commodities to shuttle between the home, the hospital, pub-lic offices and the courtroom, remaking those spaces and themselves. As ethnographic descriptions and people's stories move in and out of this larger narrative of the pharmaceuticalisation and judicialisation of health, I mean to leave the reader with a sense of how present-day insti-tutions and social fields dance, and how ethnographic writing situated at their intersections must also keep in step.

Ethnographic realities can help us to refine, complicate and even dislodge totalising assumptions about neoliberal structural adjustments and market-driven societies. In the Brazilian judicialisation of health, we do not see a top-down biopolitical model of governance in which population wellbeing is the object of knowledge and control but, rather, a struggle over the utility and purpose of government by multiple pri-vate and public stakeholders. At stake here are the ways in which government (qua drug regulator, purchaser and distributor) facilitates a more direct relationship, in the form of technology access, of atomised and ambiguous political subjects of rights and interests to the biomedical market.

Surprisingly, the decentralisation of state authority has created the space for a return of the juridical subject, but in an altered form. Not fully subject to the state or the market, these new political subjects negotiate the constraints and possibilities of a technological society using jurisprudence. They work through available legal mechanisms and instantiate new sociopolitical domains to engage and adjudicate their demands, making abstract human rights concrete. These various developments, in turn, end up consolidating the judiciary as a critical site of politics – and of political economy.

THE DISEASED CITIZEN, AND JUSTICE IN THE ABSENCE OF ADEQUATE PUBLIC POLICY

'Welcome to the juridical hospital', said Paula Pinto de Souza, the lawyer in charge of right-to-health litigation at the Public Defender's Office (*Defensoria Pública*) in Porto Alegre, during our first encounter in August 2009. This is where the poor get free legal assistance and where the majority of the lawsuits requesting medicines from the state originate. Souza did not mince her words in describing what she thought the state's biopolitics had become: 'When there are no defined public policies, or when they exist but are not executed, or when policies are not in touch with new maladies and medical advancements...what do we have? We have a diseased citizen.'

When people finally access public institutions, all their vulnerabilities are exposed and they have become quite sick, Souza continued: 'We are beyond preventive medicine here and the concept of health as physical, mental and social wellbeing is no more. When this infirmed person comes to me, the cure is most likely no longer possible. Her right to health has been profoundly injured by public power.'

While previous laws had exempted the poor from legal fees, the 1988 Constitution emphasised the autonomy of the judiciary from government and stipulated that 'the State shall provide integral and free juridical assistance to those who prove to lack resources' (Constituição Federal do Brasil). In its normative dispositions, the Constitution also stipulated the creation of Public Defender Offices to give poor people access to the judiciary.

In Rio Grande do Sul, the Public Defender's Office was established as early as 1991. Yet throughout the 1990s, due to political manoeuvres and lack of human and material resources, the Office had limited outreach and impact (Souza 2011). In the 2000s, however, with growing financial and administrative independence, the Office thrived and consolidated itself as a political institution to be reckoned with. There are now some 400 attorneys offering services throughout the state and in 2010 alone, the Public Defender's Office attended to about 450 000 cases, a considerable growth from 225 000 cases in 2006.

Souza speaks of her work in the Office as an attempt to ameliorate human suffering and to restore to the person his/her rights. For the public defender this means indicting local politics: 'The Constitution guarantees access to the judiciary and we bring concrete cases of injury to the judge. The person comes here sick and wronged by the failure of public policies. This is the medicine that I practice here: to help people survive with dignity. Even if the medication might not bring them life, the claim is also for their dignity.'

The judiciary, in her view, can acknowledge the person's medical emergency and call on 'the state writ large (federal, regional, municipal) to take on its responsibility to provide the prescribed treatment'. Souza is adamant that 'it is not the role of the judiciary to make public policies'. Yet without judicialisation, she reasons, state politics would remain populist and only electorally minded, failing to uphold constitutionally mandated responsibilities: 'The government lacks political will to make public policies work. There is no concern with the human being, but a lot of concern with publicity. Forget about infrastructure. When it is election time, *then* medicines get disbursed, drug formularies updated.'

In the past five years, right-to-health litigation, particularly over access to medicines, has become a subject of contentious debate throughout Brazil, and has attracted international attention (Azevedo 2007; 'An injection of reality' 2011). In a 2008 conference on 'Accessing Medicines via Courts', Dr Osmar Terra, then Rio Grande do Sul's Health Secretary, affirmed the state's commitment to address the issue of pharmaceutical dispensation in SUS 'in a manner that is more comprehensive, more just, and that benefits a growing number of people'. But instead of speaking of specific policies the government might champion, Terra highlighted the Secretariat's 'partnership' with the General Attorney's Office in addressing 'frontier issues in knowledge and technology' that are increasingly 'at the centre of public services'.

In his comments, Terra reduced the complex reality of right-to-health litigation to instances of demand for select and largely ineffective medical technologies recently brought to the market. 'We try to guarantee the availability of medicines. But it is extraordinarily perverse that we have to guarantee the most expensive medicines, which have no effect whatsoever. The laboratories use patients to increase profits.'

The Health Secretary mentioned the lack of accumulated knowledge of the efficacy and safety of drugs and asked whether 'a medical professional has the right to prescribe whatever he wants, independent of protocols and scientific proof'. Several times, he emphasised 'public disinformation', 'the draining of public health funds' and the 'inequality' that the demand for new medical technologies by a selective population has inaugurated; 'We are talking about public money here.'

In this official's rendering, there seems to be a clear line between good and bad science, need and interest, unconscionable for-profit medicine and responsible public health officials. And while medical professionals provide market-driven means of checking unwarranted patient claims to treatment, Terra proudly announced that the state's General Attorney's Office has created its own taskforce of medical consultants to verify or disqualify claims for treatment access and efficacy.

With the judicialisation of the right to health, courts have become battlefields of veridication-falsification and a politics of one-case-at-a-time medical rescues. But at a deeper level, I want to suggest, this process also makes the judiciary a site in which the state's biopolitical disregard (i.e. the ability 'to "let" die')[2] – in collusion with the market – is exposed for public critique.

THE PHARMACEUTICALISATION OF HEALTH

While the justiciability of the right to health is of increasing interest internationally (Gauri and Brinks 2008; Yamin and Gloppen 2011), the volume of individual right-to-health lawsuits in Brazil stands out. In 2009, 5536 cases appealing high court rulings related to the right to health reached the Superior Court of Justice and about half of these cases (n = 2583) were for access to medicines. In the same year, the Federal Supreme Court heard 806 cases related to the right to health, 142 of which were for access to medicines (Sarlet 2010). Many of the non-medicinal cases concerned access to things such as medical devices, prostheses and special foods, as well as the availability of hospital beds and specialised facilities for paediatric or drug dependence treatment.

In 2009, the federal Health Ministry spent US $47.8 million on court-attained drugs, a significant increase from the US $20.4 million spent in 2008 and US $4.2 million spent in 2007. By comparison, in 2003 federal expenditure on court-attained drugs was US $58 800 (Collucci 2009). In the past decade, Brazilian states have also seen the numbers of lawsuits and costs for court-attained drugs rise dramatically, particularly in the south-eastern and southern regions of Brazil (Biehl et al. 2012; Marques and Dallari 2007; Messeder et al. 2005). There are currently more than 240 000 health-related lawsuits under review in state and federal courts in Brazil. Almost half of all lawsuits (about 113 000) have been filed in the state of Rio Grande do Sul ('Saúde conquistada na Justiça' 2010).

HIV/AIDS activists were among the first to successfully equate the constitutional right to health to access to medicines, and the rights-based demand for treatment has now 'migrated' to other diseases and groups. As I documented in the book *Will to Live: AIDS Therapies and the Politics of Survival* (Biehl 2007a), an incremental change in the concept of public health has also been taking place. In terms of both delivery and demand, public health is now understood less as prevention and primary care and more as access to medicines and community-outsourced care; that is, public health has become increasingly *pharmaceuticalised* and *privatised*.

Today, a variety of actors – industry advocates, public health and private practice physicians, medical researchers and patient associations – have vested interests in making high-technology medicine accessible to all. In the process, the country is becoming a profitable platform of global medicine. It is estimated that almost 50% of the adult population (about 60 million people) uses pharmaceuticals on a daily basis. This is where the state comes into picture: pharmaceutical access.

In 2008, during a conversation about unequal drug pricing worldwide, a pharmaceutical executive suggested that his company was adapting to the human rights and social justice frameworks that had successfully politicised access to treatments and healthcare in the recent past. Referring, for example, to the ongoing struggle over continued access to state-of-the-art antiretroviral drugs in Brazil, he said rather bluntly that his company had co-opted the activist role. To make government act properly, he suggested, 'You don't need the activists, just buy our drugs and you will save money.'

The fact is that government-purchased medicines make up a formidable market in Brazil (Gertner 2010). The Health Ministry spent more than US $2.5 billion on the acquisition of drugs in 2007, accounting for 10.7% of its total expenditures that year, and twice as much as in 2002 (Vieira 2009). However, new drugs are often available only for private purchase. Furthermore, we know that drug prices in Brazil are, overall, 1.9 times higher than in Sweden and 13.1 times greater than the mean bulk unit price of the same drugs cited by the International Drug Price Indicator Guide.

Let me pause to unpack what I mean by describing the judicialisation of the right to health as part of a broader pharmaceuticalisation of care and of public health. First, the concept of pharmaceuticalisation builds on and revises the related notion of 'medicalisation', understood as a modern form of social control that obscures the political, economic and social determinants of health by approaching disease and treatment in exclusively biomedical terms (Conrad 2007; Scheper-Hughes 1992). Scholars have traced the public health, policy and treatment consequences of the medicalisation of a range of complicated social problems, from hunger and malnutrition to substance abuse and depression. In particular, critics note that the phenomenon has led to an overemphasis on access to healthcare (especially medicines) in health policy at the expense of equally needed improvements in financial and food security, education, housing and environmental conditions (Lantz et al. 2007). Medicalisation, it is argued, strains healthcare systems, national economies and household finances alike. Sociologist Peter Conrad and colleagues (Conrad et al. 2010) have gone so far as to estimate that in 2005, the pervasive medicalisation of social conditions cost the US $77 billion – 3.9% of total domestic spending on healthcare.

Increasing reliance on pharmaceuticals in treatment has gone hand in hand with the growing dominance of biomedical epistemology. In 1999, US spending on prescription drugs reached $100 billion, more than double the figure just ten years earlier.[3] A 2010 report produced by the Centers for Disease Control and Prevention notes that Americans' use of pharmaceuticals increased significantly between 1998 and 2008. The increase is especially noteworthy in the anti-depressant class: between 1998 and 1994, just 1.8% of Americans polled reported use of anti-depressants in the past month; from 2005 to 2008, that number jumped to 8.9%. With the advent of so-called 'second generation' anti-depressants, the number of disabled mentally ill in the USA – that is, citizens receiving monthly Social Security Disability Insurance payments – has more than doubled, from 1.25 million people in 1987 (the year the FDA approved Prozac) to 3.97 million in 2007 (Whitaker 2010).

The concept of pharmaceuticalisation, however, stands for something more complex than an increase in the quantity of medications that societies consume (Biehl 2007b). In the past decade, medical anthropologists have critiqued the medicalisation paradigm for being overly deterministic (Lock 2003); while the culture of biomedicine is undeniably powerful, people do not simply become the diagnostic categories applied to them – they inhabit them to greater or lesser degrees, refuse them or redefine and deploy them to unanticipated ends (Biehl 2005; Petryna et al. 2006; Han 2012). Likewise, both policy debates and patient struggles surrounding access to pharmaceuticals are part of broader transformations in public health (Biehl 2007a; Ecks 2008; Reynolds Whyte et al. 2013). Understanding pharmaceuticalisation requires moving beyond the unidirectional construction of patient subjectivity by medical diagnostics and treatments to account for the entanglement of multiple social forces and markets, the chemical concreteness and circulation of pharmaceuticals and illnesses, and the role of patients' agency and desires.

I also want to highlight that contemporary processes of pharmaceuticalisation have historical antecedents in international health policies and interventions. While health development programmes once focused primarily on large-scale public health measures (e.g. sanitation, availability of clean water, hygiene), in recent decades, global health organisations have increasingly focused on access to pharmaceuticals as an indicator of healthcare development.

This trend is crystallised in the WHO's Essential Medicines List, first proposed in 1975 and then codified in a published list revised every two years (Greene 2010). According to historian Jeremy Greene, while the idea that public health should be rooted in essential medicines 'has taken on somewhat of a moral universality ... and commonsensical status', creating such a taxonomy of fundamental drugs has revealed ambiguities and raised difficult questions (Greene 2011: 28). Access to new medical technologies and treatment strategies is increasingly thought of as a human right, like shelter, education and clean water – but how are 'essential' medications selected? Can effective, but new and experimental, treatments be considered 'essential'?

As the HIV/AIDS epidemic increased in severity in the early 1990s, the WHO did not identify any ARVs as essential medicines because of their high price and how recently they had been developed. The disease, however, claimed a larger and larger portion of total deaths in developing countries, and activists forcefully challenged the absence of ARVs from the Essential Medicines List (Greene 2011: 23). While the WHO now considers some antiretrovirals essential, the HIV/AIDS epidemic continues to provoke the difficult question of whether access to treatments that *extend* lives – but do not ultimately *save* them – should be considered a human right. This question over which things are 'truly indispensable' to health and living, and who is legally and financially responsible to make these things available, is central to how the characters of this chapter both invoke and critique biopolitics: from Edgar's comment in the beginning of the chapter that 'I know that the state cannot give everything to everyone' to the state official's deployment of evidence-based medicine to both rationalise care delivery and authenticate misrecognition and disregard.

The fact is that, in Brazil, pharmaceuticals have become key elements in the state's arsenal of action. As AIDS activism migrated into state institutions, and the state played an increasingly activist role in the international politics of drug pricing, AIDS became, in many ways, the 'country's disease' (Biehl 2007a). In May 2007, for example, Brazil broke the patent of an AIDS drug (Efavirenz, produced by Merck) for the first time – a step recently taken by Thailand – and authorised the import of a generic version from India. Activists worldwide hailed this sovereign decision as a landmark in struggles over the sustainability of countrywide treatment rollouts.

Yet, while new pharmaceutical markets have opened, and ARVs have been made universally available (in the case of AIDS, the state is actually present through the dispensation of certain medicines which carry high political stakes), it is up to individuals and makeshift communities to take on the local roles of medical and political institutions as they learn to interact with and in expert domains. These individuals and groups use survival strategies that require extraordinary effort and self-transformation and, increasingly, undergo juridical initiation as they become formal subjects of rights *and* engage the ritual travails of the courts (Biehl and Petryna 2011). In the process, the question of what is frugal and essential to health and wellbeing – what one can do without and what one needs to live with – is ever more tangled and contested.

THE RETURN OF THE JURIDICAL SUBJECT

Despite the growing scale and costs associated with lawsuits for access to medicines in Brazil, and amid polarised debate about the phenomenon, there has been scant information concerning the content of lawsuits and the characteristics of patient-litigants as well as the legal strategies and rationales deployed by the various stakeholders. States' data collection systems remain tenuous at best, and concerted efforts to gather comprehensive data on lawsuits for access to medicines are only in their beginning stages.

Research into right-to-health litigation has also been constrained by small samples, limited geographic coverage and the few variables examined (Messeder et al. 2005; Pepe et al. 2010; Da Silva and Terrazas 2008; Vieira and Zucchi 2007; Borges and Ugá 2010). Most studies tend to corroborate the arguments of public health administrators that the judiciary is overstepping its role, and that judicialisation generates enormous administrative and fiscal burdens, distorts pharmaceutical policies, widens inequalities in healthcare access and encourages irrational drug use within the public healthcare system.

To better understand the scale of right-to-health lawsuits in the state of Rio Grande do Sul, our research team first examined electronic registries of health-related lawsuits in the Health Secretariat (Biehl et al. 2012). We found that the number of new lawsuits grew more than tenfold, from 1126 new cases in 2002 to 17 025 new cases in 2009. Medicines comprised the majority of these judicial claims, making up 70% of cases in 2008 and 2009.

As a second step, we created a database of medicinal lawsuits against the state Rio Grande do Sul. Our data collection team worked in the Solicitor General's Office, which is responsible for defending the state. From September 2008 to June 2009, we analysed 1080 lawsuits being reviewed by state prosecutors.[4]

Edgar's case (presented upfront) was not among these lawsuits, but as I share some of our results you will see that his travails are not an exception. Among the plaintiffs who reported their employment status, more than half were retired and about one fifth were unemployed. Among those who reported income, over half earned less than the monthly national minimum wage (about US $300) and relied on the free legal services of public defenders.

Past research has suggested that right-to-treatment litigation is, for the most part, a practice of the financially better off (Chieffi and Barata 2009; Vieira and Zucchi 2007) and that low-income patients tend to sue for low-cost medicines, while higher-income patients tend to sue for very expensive medicines (Da Silva and Terrazas 2008: 12). In contrast, our results suggest that *patients who procure medicines through the courts are mostly poor individuals who are not working and who depend on the public system for both healthcare and legal representation.*

Roughly two-thirds of the medicines requested were already on governmental drug formularies. About a quarter of lawsuits were exclusively for access to specialised high-cost medicines, though low-cost essential medicines were frequently requested alongside them. Off-formulary medicines requested by plaintiffs were also often low-cost, and many had been available in the market for a long time. This suggests that government pharmaceutical programmes are failing to fulfil their role of expanding access and rationalising use (DECIT 2006; Guimarães 2004).

Moreover, judges at district and higher court levels almost universally grant access to all medicines requested, recognising that their provision is consistent with Brazil's constitutional right to health. For example, in almost all cases, district judges granted plaintiffs an immediate injunction for access to medicines. In cases where the initial ruling was in favour of the provision of medicines, the state's higher court most often upheld the decision.

This staggering number of lawsuits is generating significant legal and administrative costs. In 2008, the state, which has a population of about 11 million people, spent $30.2 million on court-mandated drugs. This expense represents 22% of the total amount spent by the state on medicines that year (Biehl et al. 2009).

While decentralisation tried to establish clear responsibility at specific administrative levels – municipal, state and federal – our analysis found that plaintiffs tend to hold the regional state responsible for medicines, regardless of the designated responsible party, and that judges rarely disagree. State attorneys frequently argue that the state is not responsible for the provision of certain services. Judges, however, cite the principle of 'unity' between levels of government to assert broad shared responsibility in guaranteeing the right to health. Lawsuits become the site of a reluctant and undisciplined cooperation. In this way, the judicialisation of the right to health momentarily instantiates the state as the singular governmental entity responsible for the provision of social rights.

THE JURIDICAL HOSPITAL

Patients in our sample of 1080 lawsuits were, for the most part, chronically ill. Almost half of patients (48%) reported cardiovascular disease, diabetes, disorders of the lipid metabolism and pulmonary diseases. Some 16% of the patients reported neurologic and psychiatric conditions. Patient-plaintiffs in our sample had various co-morbidities and procured multiple drugs for their treatments. On average, they reported 1.5 diagnoses and requested 2.8 drugs. Among the 25 most requested drugs, 23 were medicines to treat chronic diseases and only seven were not in official drug formularies. However, we also found patients with a single disease who demanded one high-cost treatment.

Patients with chronic hepatitis C, for example, made up a significant number of cases. These patients typically demanded ribavirin and peginterferon alfa, both of which are on the federal government's exceptional medicines formulary. The high frequency of requests for drugs to treat chronic hepatitis C in our sample stands in sharp juxtaposition to the rare request – one single case – for medicines for HIV/AIDS. Both pathologies have a similar prevalence in the south of Brazil and both treatments are distributed by governmental programmes at no cost.

What are some of the possible reasons for this sharp contrast? It may reflect variations in the efficiency of governmental pharmaceutical distribution programmes. While the strategic medicines programme which distributes HIV/AIDS drugs is centrally managed and funded by the federal Health Ministry, with a single acquisition process for the entire country, the exceptional medicines programme is decentralised: it is managed by states, which are federally reimbursed. The latter programme depends on administrative cooperation among federal and state government and is vulnerable to the vagaries of regional health policy and management.

The contrast may also result from the specific eligibility criteria and, in some cases, from the detailed treatment protocols through which exceptional and special medicines must be accessed in the public healthcare system. When patients fall outside of eligibility requirements and protocols, they may use lawsuits to access treatment. In addition, patients who were granted requests may use lawsuits to expedite treatment delivery or to guarantee provision of medicines when the government fails to provide them.

Lawsuits may be a mechanism with which to challenge treatment protocols that limit access based on cost-effectiveness and epidemiologically derived risk–benefit considerations. Our results show that, rather than accepting these protocols, judges give broad deference to individual circumstances and physicians' prescriptions – deference that may undercut efforts to rationalise pharmaceutical use (as the Health Secretariat cited earlier in the chapter would have it). As in the case of one patient named Nelson Silva, the judiciary seems to offer citizens that are once diseased and politically injured the possibility of articulating a time-sensitive legal effort to make the state act biopolitically so as to guarantee the possibility of survival.

Head down, Nelson Silva walked into the Public Defender's Office in August 2010 accompanied by his wife Sandra, who did most of the talking. At first, attorney Paula Pinto de Souza and I mistook Sandra for the patient, but it soon became evident that the 'we' she referred to in our conversation was a kind of domestic advocacy group. 'We cannot interrupt the treatment one more time', said Sandra. He had retired as a steel factory worker and she was still a kindergarten teacher. They resided in the nearby city of Esteio and had two adult children. Sandra begged the public defender to 'treat us', for 'we know that people who come here people get the medicine they need'.

Nelson had chronic hepatitis C and he was greatly benefitting from the 48 weeks treatment regimen of ribavirin and peginterferon alfa. His doctor said that he needed 24 extra weeks of treatment, but the state's medical expert denied the request and 'my doctor told me to come here', Nelson said. 'It's just a matter of the judge releasing the treatment.'

'Our first treatment', Sandra continued, 'was in 2001 with regular interferon.' Nelson added that 'but after a while the state pharmacy did not have interferon, so I had to interrupt the treatment.' In 2005, he fell ill and a doctor at Conceição Hospital prescribed ribavirin and peginterferon alfa. The Health Secretariat denied Nelson's treatment request alleging that this would be 're-treatment' which was not allowed by the medical protocol in place. 'Then we had to file a lawsuit for him to get it,' Sandra stated. In 2009, he was eligible for re-treatment and now needed the medicines for 24 additional weeks.

'The doctor gave me the meds for two weeks,' Nelson continued, 'but I am afraid that the legal procedure will take too long and that by the time I get the meds, if I get them, I will have to stop treatment for it failed once again. I need it fast.' Nelson was desperate to adhere to the treatment. For him and so many other patient-plaintiffs facing a fatal condition, judicialisation is a temporal lever. 'We don't want to stop everything we started,' lamented Sandra. In line with the philosophy of 'I will not let the citizen die,' Souza gave them a road map of all they had to do, and the documents they had to bring so that she could open the lawsuit the following day. Here, the court system – so often thought of as a place where claims go to die a quiet, bureaucratic slow-motion death – winds up being a surprising milieu of catalysis for the uncertainty and time-sensitivity of the body and its possibilities of repair and, ultimately, of survival. 'Afterwards,' Souza told Nelson, 'you open a lawsuit against the state for medical injury.'

OPEN-SOURCE ANARCHY

According to legal scholar David Fidler (2008), developments in health jurisprudence 'have produced open-source anarchy and a more elastic relationship between power and ideas in global politics' (2008: 410). In such an elastic relationship, 'changes in material capabilities of state and non-state actors, and changes in the world of ideas, have more impact on each other than in the closed, state-centric system that prevailed during the Cold War' (2008: 410). Fidler recognises a 'deeper importance for law in public health endeavours within and between countries' (2008: 394; see also Fidler 2007).

Anthropologists John and Jean Comaroff have been attending to such a 'judicialisation of politics' in post-apartheid South Africa, and how it has impacted social mobilisation, particularly in the field of HIV/AIDS. Class struggles, they argue, 'seem to have metamorphosed into class actions. Citizens, subjects, governments, and corporations litigate against one another, often at the intersection of tort law, human rights law, and the criminal law, in an ever mutating kaleidoscope of coalitions and cleavages' (2006: 26).

The judicialisation of right-to-health litigation speaks to a productive 'open-source anarchy' at both macro and micro levels in Brazil as well. Political scientist Luis Werneck Vianna (1999) would say that it is only one part of a broader pattern of the judicialisation of politics in the country. For him, judicialisation does not necessarily reflect judicial activism. Rather, it can be understood as a lever for multiple minority actors (from political parties to public defenders to civil society groups) to constitutionally challenge the political majority's efforts to determine the fundamental norms and objectives of government. In attending to these concrete and dynamic processes, the complex way in which the judiciary actively participates in everyday politicking in a large country with a young constitution comes to the foreground (Fonseca and Schuch 2009). The question is thus not who – the judiciary or the executive – is right in the debate over judicialisation, but how to integrate their actions in order to best serve individuals and collectives while making democratic institutions more robust (Vianna and Burgos 2005).

The fact is that in this new chapter of the Brazilian history of citizenship and the right to health, the judiciary has become a powerful arbiter and purveyor of care and medical technology access. Interviews we conducted with judges, attorneys and health officials revealed divergent and conflicting views on the litigation pathway. Policy-makers and administrators contend that the judiciary is overstepping its role and that judicialisation skews budgets and increases inequalities in healthcare access. Some acknowledge, however, that legal pressure has improved the distribution of some medicines.

Many local judges working on right-to-health cases feel they are responding to state failures to provide needed medicines and that these waves of lawsuits are a milestone in the democratisation of a culture of rights. For these judges, the poor Brazilians who are working through modes of legally arbitrated justice in order to access healthcare are not only fighting against legalised privileges and legitimated inequalities, as in James Holston's chronicle of 'insurgent citizenship' practices (Holston 2009) in Brazil's urban spaces; widespread litigation is rather seen as the expression of a distinct, equalising legal system and of a novel rights-conscious society. Whether such a democratisation of socio-economic rights can be attained through individual claims and in courts, however, is contested. The fact is that judges employ idiosyncratic rationales and create their own standards in adjudicating right-to-health cases. They tend to rule in terms of 'risk of death' and 'right to life', and base their rulings for the most part on constitutional interpretations and personal experiences – having specific tragic cases in mind.

The judiciary recognizes that the judicialization of health has the potential to attend to social inequality and to affirm citizens' rights.

Like Souza at the Public Defender's office, Judge Eugenio Terra finds that lawsuits are largely filed by poor and desperate patients seeking treatments that should be available in the public system. He is in charge of all health-related cases in Porto Alegre.

'I am doing social justice, one by one,' Terra told me in an interview in August 2010. 'When I am issuing an injunction for cancer treatment provision, I am also indicting services that have not kept up with people's needs.' It did not escape Alencar that the high number of right-to-health lawsuits in southern Brazil, might well speak of 'a distinct political culture' fostered by numerous administrations of the Worker's Party both in the capital and at the state level in the past two decades (PT regained state power in 2011).

Rather than accepting one-size-fits-all medical protocols, judges give broad deference to individual circumstances and physicians' prescriptions, a practice that may appear to undercut state efforts to rationalise pharmaceutical use. State high court judges like Denise Cezar are also holding pharmaceutical companies accountable, particularly to patients participating in clinical trials. As she puts it, 'We struggle for jurisprudence. We are challenged to create the right and to enable the person of rights.'

Dr Marga Tessler, President of the Southern Brazilian Federal Court, says that the judiciary is not activist but rather 'active' by challenging state politics in the name of the constitution. She suggests, however, that some limits have to be placed on what the state can actually provide for its citizens given pressing infrastructural needs and the accelerated development and circulation of medical technologies.

CASE BY CASE

Even as judges recognise the constitutionality of individual lawsuits and grant requested medicines in the overwhelming majority of cases, the judiciary has repeatedly avoided directly mandating changes in policy or issuing decisions that would broadly affect the public health system. In 2007, Minister Ellen Gracie, then Chief Justice of the Federal Supreme Court, overturned a lower court's decision that would include sex reassignment surgery in the list of procedures freely provided by the public healthcare system. Minister Gracie stated that cases for access to such treatment should be decided 'case by case, in a concrete manner, and not in an abstract or generic manner' (Supremo Tribunal Federal 2007).

In April 2009, the Brazilian Supreme Court held a rare public hearing to examine the pressing challenges posed by right-to-health litigation.[5] Public health officials, lawyers, physicians, activists and academics testified before the court, providing varied viewpoints and recommendations on how to respond to the enormous judicial demand for medical goods. As an immediate outcome, there was a long-overdue updating of governmental drug formularies. The Brazilian National Council of Justice also issued a set of recommendations for local judges, asking them to more systematically attend to scientific evidence and to strive for 'more efficiency' when ruling over health-related cases.[6]

If access to AIDS therapies was the litmus test of the right to health in the 1990s, now it is access to genetic therapies that plays this role. Twelve year old Alexandre Lima de Moura suffers from an inherited metabolic disorder called mucopolysaccharidosis (MPS). Every week the fourth grader travels with his mother Cleonice to Hospital de Clínicas in Porto Alegre, where he receives enzyme replacement therapy, a treatment that costs about $200 000 per year. Because of his age, Alexandre was not allowed to enrol in a clinical trial taking place at the hospital. Without 'the right to be researched', as the mother of another MPS patient put it, Alexandre became a patient-litigant.

With the legal support of a well-organised MPS patient association in São Paulo (partially funded by the drug manufacturer), the family won a court injunction forcing the federal government to begin providing the therapy. Like all parents of MPS children we spoke to, Cleonice suggested that not obtaining this treatment would be unconscionable and tantamount to killing her child. She knew that the federal attorneys would appeal and was ready for the struggle: 'Besides entering the judiciary, we also entered the media.' Cleonice has taken Alexandre's cause to all possible media outlets and is also using his condition to educate neighbours, local medical personal and officials about the meaning of, in her words, 'citizenship' and a 'normal life'. *Ela é uma mãe boa* – 'she is a good mother' – says Alexandre, who is thriving in school and seems to be responding positively to the treatment.

One of the latest right-to-health landmark cases involves a request for a high-cost medicine for a genetic disease. This treatment was not recommended by the Ministry of Health's therapeutic guidelines and was not publicly available. In March 2010, the court rejected the argument that the state was not responsible and decided in favour of the provision of the treatment. In his ruling, Justice Gilmar Mendes stated that once the disease was medically confirmed and treatment was indicated, 'the Ministry of Health's guidelines can be questioned'. Moreover, 'the state has to provide resources, not only to support and fund the provision of universal care for its citizens, but also has to provide variable resources to attend to the needs of each individual citizen' (Supremo Tribunal Federal 2010).

The role of market forces in judicialization—a mix of clinical trials and marketing strategies that target physicians' prescriptions and fuel patient demand and of industry lobbying to have new treatments included in governmental drug formularies while facing limited regulatory oversight—must not be overlooked (Petryna 2009). Ample evidence shows how the monopoly of medico-scientific information by the laboratories and pharmaceutical marketing strongly informs physicians' prescriptive habits and patients' demands (Lakoff 2006). Additional qualitative studies are in order – they could help us chart how judicialisation has become part of a pharmaceutical business plan in Brazil, supporting patient associations and lawsuits for access to high-cost medicines specifically to open or enlarge markets (Diniz et al. 2012).

There is a heated debate in Brazilian courts on the positive duty that the constitutional right to health imposes on the state, and the extent to which the courts must enforce this right. But the country lacks a substantial public debate about the meaning of the right to health in the light of medical advancements and financing, between what is possible and feasible and what is frugal and essential. As a 'right to pharmaceuticals' is consolidated in Brazil, the various branches of government have yet to develop a systematic approach to tackling drug value and financing and the responsibilities of private health insurance plans to cover drug costs (which they currently do not). Moreover, how can access to new medical technologies be reconciled with systems that foster the equitable inclusion of people into preventive as well as basic and sustained care initiatives? Is there a way to balance individuals' urgent demands for healthcare, often in the form of medicines, with the long-term programmatic aspect of healthcare management and reform? Attention is also needed on broader aspects of the right to health, such as education, water, sanitation, vector control, air pollution and violence prevention. These complementary rights, which can be understood as social determinants of health, are critical to addressing the health needs of both the chronically ill and co-morbid individuals in our database, and the Brazilian population more generally.

Meanwhile, hard to pin down patient-citizen-consumers draw from human rights language and jurisprudence and make governments work them as they negotiate medical inclusion and the vagaries of the market and survival. The judicialisation of health has indeed become a para-infrastructure in which various public and private health actors and sectors come into contact, face off and enact limited 'one by one' missions.

PATIENT-CITIZEN-CONSUMER

How is the subject of rights constituted in the face of the late liberal political economies? There is no pre-given biopolitical population to which Edgar, Nelson, Alexandre and thousands of other atomised subjects of rights belong to in Brazil today. Yet, in their private efforts to become such subjects, they have to rely on social relations and temporary collectivities that crop up at the intersection of patient/family demand, state institutions, therapeutic markets and law.

Seen from the perspective of these medical subjects – undesirable according to actual care delivery policies, budgets and state public relation efforts – biopolitics is an insecure enterprise, indeed, more a symptom of the limits of government than a marker of its presence and control. The ethnographic realities presented throughout this chapter also suggest that the subject of rights and the economic subject may actually be included or excluded according to shared or similar logics, practices, technologies and knowledges, and that inclusion in terms of rights may be a key means by which one becomes part of a market segment.

If for Foucault 'the question of the frugality of government is indeed the question of liberalism' (Foucault 2008: 29), then in Brazil's late liberal moment, one could argue, the biopolitical question is not necessarily about the 'futility' of the rehabilitation of diseased and underserved poor subjects (Biehl 2005), but about the expansion of frugal government in the form of pharmaceutical access in lieu of infrastructural reform. Thus, in this contemporary republic of interests we see the consolidation of an 'inclusionary state activism without statism' (Glauco and Martin 2010) coupled with extraordinary market expansion and the vanishing of 'civil society' as a viable transactional reality.

'Judicialisation today is a relation of individual consumption,' stated Miriam Ventura, a legal and public health scholar, during a 2010 interview in Rio de Janeiro. Ventura was the first lawyer in the country to successfully file treatment access lawsuits on behalf of HIV patients. The judicial activism of the 1990s used individual lawsuits to lay broad claim to collective rights, she argued: 'Individually, but always in search of a collective demand for the solution to the problem.'

Ventura is critical of right-to-health litigation being now an end in itself: 'It is necessary, and an important guarantee, but it is not sufficient to create any health policy.' While HIV/AIDS judicial activism created 'a strong subject of rights...so that those people could be recognised as citizens,' the contemporary judicialisation is no longer one of social mobilisation, she lamented. Even for patient associations, 'the judiciary is not treated as a political instrument, it is merely instrumental.'

For Ventura, the political subject of judicialisation is very much subject to the market and to consumer ideology, including the judiciary itself: 'When you enter with a class action, and there are ever fewer, judges normally are more cautious; they do not give a speedy decision, because they recognise that it will have an impact. Now, on the other hand, if you enter three hundred individual actions, a thousand individual actions, they will grant those thousand individual requests.' With Brazil's economic boom, the citizen is visible through participation in the market, she argues, but demands based on the right to health are ultimately limited to those who can be articulated as access to consumption: 'We have a very strong demand and there is a low politicisation of citizenship.'

In her critique, Ventura assumes a certain kind of political subject, one who recognises and represents him- or herself as such, and she regrets the dying out of the civil society paradigm for politics. But is there another possibility of citizenship in Brazil today which can navigate between a state that presents itself as activist and socially protective (beyond the minimum neoliberal state) *and* emerging therapeutic markets?

I have written elsewhere about *ambiguous political subjects*, in light of the country's pioneer policy of universal HIV/AIDS treatment access as it was actualised in urban poor contexts: 'Their political subjectivity is articulated through pastoral means, disciplinary practices of self-care, and monitored pharmaceutical treatment' (Biehl 2007a: 324–325).

For Paula Pinto de Souza and her patient-citizens at the Public Defender's Office, politics is not a sphere, but a lack, a technology and a process all at once. In Brazil today, medical commodities work in tandem with other ways of claiming citizenship, and desperate and creative interactions occasion novel public sites in which rights and health are privatised alongside the emergence of novel political subjectivities.

In the face of this, the public defender puts up a fight. Souza's pragmatic critique of the state brings attention to the symbiotic relationship between a hybrid government of social protection and market expansion *and* the ways that public institutions, in their frugality or futility, acquiesce to the social and biological death of those too ill or too poor to live in the new economy. Yet as abandoned and injured as they are by various levels of actual government, some people still understand themselves as the subjects of present rights, and they try to access care via the judiciary. People refuse to be stratified out of existence.

Souza's humanism and in-your-face politics produces a pathway to improving patients' situations. Against institutional realities that undermine health, control and effectiveness, public defenders utilise medical and legal modes of veridiction and the framework of constitutional rights and human dignity to sustain their work and demand that the state act biopolitically.

Chronically ill and poor people find their way into the judiciary reluctantly, tinkering with available human and material resources. They are neither governable nor disruptive of the system. This minimum biopolitical belonging is part and parcel of the immanent field that people invent to live in, and by, as they navigate the vagaries of market inclusion and survival in wounded cities.

CONCLUSION

This chapter focused upon novel forms of social becoming in the interface of law and medicine to show how politics matters differently to a growing number of low- and middle-income sick Brazilians. People's life chances and health outcomes are over-determined by the kinds of marketised/juridical subjects they are able to become through appeals to the judiciary, government and research and health industries driven by profit and the construction of new therapeutic market segments. As ethnographers we must attend to the forms of statecraft (national and regional) and jurisprudence as well as to the kinds of medico-scientific literacies and political subjectivities that are built into this para-infrastructure of rights and interests that the judicialisation of health has occasioned. We must consider both the possibilities opened up and the exclusionary dynamics at work in the judicialisation front evident throughout Brazil and in other emergent powers. Thus, from the perspective of judicialisation, health in the time of global health is a painstaking work-in-progress by monadic juridical subjects in relation to therapeutic markets, ailing public health infrastructures, and improvised medical collectives.

It is paradoxically by revealing the fragility of biopolitical interventions, showing how they are constantly entangled with and shaped by other (often economic) imperatives, that the stories of these patient-litigants point to the temporal dimensions of medical technologies and to their power to remake subjectivities and social worlds as they open up new spaces for claim-making, contestation and ethical problematisation. It is at the intersection of the therapeutic imperative, the biotechnical embrace and the reason of the market that the intensity of survival becomes visible and the political battle over what is frugal and vital is played out.

NOTES

1 This chapter derives from a 2008–2012 multi-disciplinary investigation of the judicialisation of the right to health in southern Brazil (See http://joaobiehl.net/global-health-research/right-to-health-litigation/). Funded by the Ford Foundation and by Princeton University's Health Grand Challenges Initiative, the project sought to characterize this patient-plaintiff population, to identify their medical needs and legal strategies and to apprehend the expanding role of the judiciary in remediating the limitations and failures of public health management. The study was carried out in collaboration with Adriana Petryna, Joseph J. Amon, Mariana P. Socal, Ingo W. Sarlet, Laura B. Jardim, Paulo D. Picon, Ida Vanessa D. Schwartz, Paula Vargas, Claudia W. Fonseca, Torben Eskerod, and it involved:
   i. A database of lawsuits for access to medicines in the state of Rio Grande do Sul;
   ii. An observatory of the evolving right-to-health jurisprudence in Brazil;
   iii. Interviews with key institutional actors (judges, public counsels, lawyers, physicians, policymakers);
   iv. Ethnographic research with patients and families filing lawsuits for treatment access;
   v. A visual documentary of the people involved in right-to-health litigation.
2 See the Foucaultian definition of biopolitics as 'to make live and let die' (Foucault 2003: 241).
3 See www.cdc.gov/nchs/nhanes.htm
4 See www.princeton.edu/grandchallenges/health/research-highlights/aids/Database-project.pdf

5 See www.stf.jus.br/portal/cms/verTexto.asp?servico=processoAudienciaPub
   licaSaude
6 See www.cnj.jus.br/index.php?option=com_content&view=article&id=
   10547:recomendacao-no-31-de-30-de-marco-de-2010&catid=60:recomen
   das-do-conselho&Itemid=515)

REFERENCES

Anand, N. 2012. 'Municipal Disconnect: On Abject Water and Its Urban Infrastructures', *Ethnography* 13: 487–509

Anderson, P. 2011. 'Lula's Brazil', *London Review of Books* 33(7): 3–12

'An Injection of Reality' 2011. *The Economist* (Editorial, July 30). Available online at www.economist.com/node/21524879

Appel, H. 2012. 'Walls and White Elephants: Oil Extraction, Responsibility, and Infrastructural Violence in Equatorial Guinea', *Ethnography* 13: 439–465

Azevedo, S. 2007. 'Remédios nos Tribunais', *Revista Época,* December 12. Available online at revistaepoca.globo.com/Revista/Epoca/0,,EDG80696-8055-501,00-REMEDIOS+NOS+TRIBUNAIS.html

Berkman, A., Garcia, J. Munoz-Laboy, M. Paiva, V. and Parker, R. 2005. 'A Critical Analysis of the Brazilian Response to HIV/AIDS: Lessons Learned for Controlling and Mitigating the Epidemic in Developing Countries.' *American Journal of Public Health* 95: 1162–1172

Biehl, J. 2007a. *Will to Live: AIDS Therapies and the Politics of Survival.* Princeton, NJ: Princeton University Press

    2007b. 'Pharmaceuticalization: AIDS Treatment and Global Health Politics.' *Anthropological Quarterly* 80(4): 1083–1126

    2005. *Vita: Life in a Zone of Social Abandonment.* Berkeley: University of California Press

Biehl, J., Amon, J. J., Socal, M. P. and Petryna, A. 2012. 'Between the Court and the Clinic: Lawsuits for Medicines and the Right to Health in Brazil', *Health and Human Rights* 14(1):1–17

Biehl, J., Good, B. and Kleinman, A. (eds.) 2005. *Subjectivity: Ethnographic Investigations.* Berkeley, CA: University of California Press

Biehl, J. and McKay, R. 2012. 'Ethnography as Political Critique', *Anthropological Quarterly* 85 (4): 1211–1230

Biehl, J. and Petryna, A. 2011. 'Bodies of Rights and Therapeutic Markets', *Social Research* 78(2):359–386

Biehl, J., Petryna, A., Gertner, A., Amon, J. J. and Picon, P. D. 2009. 'Judicialisation of the right to health in Brazil', *The Lancet* 373: 2182–2184

Borges, D. C. L. and Ugá, M. A. D. 2010. 'Conflitos e Impasses da Judicialização na Obtenção de Medicamentos: as Decisões de 1a Instância nas Ações

Individuais Contra o Estado do Rio de Janeiro, Brasil, em 2005.' *Cadernos de Saúde Pública* 26(1): 59–69

Chatterjee, P. 2004. *The Politics of the Governed: Reflections on Popular Politics in Most of the World*. New York: Columbia University Press

Chieffi, A. L. and Barata, R. B. 2009. 'Judicialização da Política Pública de Assistência Farmacêutica e Eqüidade', *Cadernos de Saúde Pública* 25(8): 1839–1849

Collucci, C. 2009. 'Triplicam as Ações Judiciais para Obter Medicamentos.' *Folha de São Paulo*, September 9. www1.folha.uol.com.br/fsp/saude/sd0901200901.htm

Comaroff, J. and Comaroff, J. 2011. *Theory from the South, or, How Euro-America is Evolving Toward Africa*. Boulder, CO: Paradigm Publishers

2006. 'Law and Disorder in the Postcolony: An Introduction', in Comaroff, J. and Comaroff, J. (eds.), *Law and Disorder in the Postcolony*. Chicago: University of Chicago Press

Collier, S. 2011. *Post-Soviet Social: Neoliberalism, Social Modernity, Biopolitics*. Princeton: Princeton University Press

Conrad, P. 2007. *The Medicalization of Society: On the Transformation of Human Conditions into Treatable Disorders*. Baltimore: Johns Hopkins University Press

Conrad, P., Mackie, T. and Mehrotra, A. 2010. 'Estimating the Costs of Medicalization', *Social Science & Medicine* 70(12): 1943–1947

Constituição Federal do Brasil 1988. dtr2004.saude.gov.br/susdeaz/legislacao/arquivo/01_Constituicao.pdf

Das, V. 2007. *Life and Words: Violence and the Descent into the Ordinary*. Berkeley: University of California Press

Da Silva, V. A. and Terrazas, F. V. 2008. 'Claiming the Right to Health in Brazilian Courts: the Exclusion of the Already Excluded', *Law and Social Inquiry*, forthcoming. ssrn.com/abstract=1133620

Davis, J. E. 2009. 'Medicalization, Social Control, and the Relief of Suffering', in Cockerman, W. C. (ed.) *The New Blackwell Companion to Medical Sociology*. Oxford: Wiley-Blackwell

DECIT (Departamento de Ciência e Tecnologia, Secretaria de Ciência e Tecnologia e Insumos Estratégicos do Ministério da Saúde) 2006. 'Avaliação de Tecnologias em Saúde: Institucionalização das Ações no Ministério da Saúde', *Revista de Saúde Pública* 40(4): 743–747

Diniz, D., Medeiros, M. and Schwartz, I. V. D. 2012. 'Consequences of the Judicialization of Health Policies: The Cost of Medicines for Mucopolysaccharidosis', *Cad. Saúde Pública* 28(3): 479–489

Ecks, S. 2008. 'Global Pharmaceutical Markets and Corporate Citizenship: The Case of Novartis' Anti-cancer Drug Glivec.' *BioSocieties* 3: 165–181

Edmonds, A. 2010. *Pretty Modern: Beauty, Sex, and Plastic Surgery in Brazil*. Durham, NC: Duke University Press

Englund, H. 2006. *Prisoners of Freedom: Human Rights and the African Poor.* Berkeley, CA: University of California Press

Farmer, P. 2003. *Pathologies of Power: Health, Human Rights and the New War on the Poor.* Berkeley: University of California Press

Fassin, D. 2007. *When Bodies Remember: Experiences and Politics of AIDS in South Africa.* Berkeley, CA: University of California Press

Fassin, D. and Pandolfi, M. 2010. *Contemporary States of Emergency: The Politics of Military and Humanitarian Interventions.* New York: Zone Books

Ferguson, J. 1994. *The Anti-Politics Machine: 'Development,' Depoliticization, and Bureaucratic Power in Lesotho.* Minneapolis: University of Minnesota Press

Ferraz, O. L. M. 2009. 'The Right to Health in the Courts of Brazil: Worsening Health Inequities.' *Health and Human Rights, an International Journal* 11(2): 33–45

Fidler, D. 2008. 'Global Health Jurisprudence: A Time of Reckoning.' *Georgetown Law Journal* 96(2): 393–412

2007. 'Architecture amidst Anarchy: Global Health's Quest for Governance', *Global Health Governance* 1(1): 1–17

Fonseca, C. and Schuch, P. (eds.) 2009. *Políticas de Proteção à Infância: Um Olhar Antropológico.* Porto Alegre: Editora da UFRGS

Foucault, M. 2008. *The Birth of Biopolitics: Lectures at the Collège de France, 1978–1979.* New York: Palgrave Macmillan

2003. *Society Must Be Defended: Lectures at the Collège de France, 1975–1976.* New York: Picador

Galvão, J. 2002. 'Access to Antiretroviral Drugs in Brazil', *The Lancet* 360(9348): 1862–1865

Gauri, V. and Brinks, D. M. (eds.) 2008. *Courting Social Justice: Judicial Enforcement of Social and Economic Rights in the Developing World.* Cambridge, UK: Cambridge University Press

Gertner, A. 2010. 'Science of Uncertainty: Making Cases for Drug Incorporation in Brazil', *Anthropological Quarterly* 83(1): 97–122

Glauco, A. and Martin, S. M. 2010. 'Beyond Developmentalism and Market Fundamentalism in Brazil: Inclusionary State Activism without Statism' law.wisc.edu/gls/documents/paper_arbix.pdf

Good, M.-J. D., Hyde, S. T., Pinto, S. and Good, B. J. (eds.) 2008. *Postcolonial Disorders.* Berkeley: University of California Press

Greene, J. A. 2011. 'Making Medicines Essential: the Emergent Centrality of Pharmaceuticals in Global Health.' *BioSocieties* 6(1): 10–33

2010. 'When Did Medicines Become Essential?' *Bulletin of the World Health Organization* 88: 483

Guimarães, R. 2004. 'Bases para uma Política Nacional de Ciência, Tecnologia e Inovação em Saúde', *Ciência & Saúde Coletiva* 9(2): 375–387

Han, C. 2012. *Life in Debt: Times of Care and Violence in Neoliberal Chile*. Berkeley, CA: University of California Press

Hansen, T. B. and Stepputat, F. 2001. *States of Imagination: Ethnographic Explorations of the Postcolonial State*. Durham: Duke University Press

Hogerzeil, H. V., Samson, M., Casanovas, J. V. and Rahmani-Ocora, L. 2006. 'Is Access to Essential Medicines as Part of the Fulfillment of the Right to Health Enforceable through the Courts?' *The Lancet* 368(9532): 305–311

Holston, J. 2009. *Insurgent Citizenship: Disjunctions of Democracy and Modernity in Brazil*. Princeton: Princeton University Press

Kelly, T. 2009. *Law, Violence and Sovereignty among West Bank Palestinians*. Cambridge: Cambridge University Press

Lakoff, A. 2006. *Pharmaceutical Reason: Knowledge and Value in Global Psychiatry*. Cambridge: Cambridge University Press

Lantz, P. M., Lichtenstein, R. L. and Pollack, H. A. 2007. 'Health Policy Approaches to Population Health: The Limits of Medicalization', *Health Affairs* 26(5): 1253–1257

Lock, M. 2003. 'Medicalization and the Naturalization of Social Control', in Ember, C. R. and Ember, M. (eds.), *Encyclopedia of Medical Anthropology Vol.1: Health and Illness in the World's Cultures*. New York: Springer Publishing Company

Marques, S. B. and Dallari, S. G. 2007. 'Garantia do Direito Social à Assistência Farmacêutica no Estado de São Paulo', *Revista de Saúde Pública* 41(1): 101–7

Mendis, S., Fukino, K., Cameron, A., Laing, R., Filipe, A., Khatib, O., Leowski, J. and Ewene, M. 2007. 'The Availability and Affordability of Selected Essential Medicines for Chronic Diseases in Six Low- and Middle-income Countries', *Bulletin of the World Health Organization* 85(4): 279–288

Merry, S. E. 2006. *Human Rights and Gender Violence: Translating International Law into Local Justice*. Chicago Series in Law and Society. Chicago: University of Chicago Press

Messeder, A. M., Osorio-de-Castro, C. G. S. and Luiza, V. L. 2005. 'Mandados Judiciais como Ferramenta para Garantia do Acesso a Medicamentos no Setor Público: A Experiência do Estado do Rio de Janeiro, Brasil', *Cadernos de Saúde Pública* 21(2): 525–534

McKay, R. 2012. 'Afterlives: Humanitarian Histories and Critical Subjects in Mozambique', *Cultural Anthropology* 27(2):286–309

Ministério da Saúde 2010. *Da Excepcionalidade às Linhas de Cuidado: O Componente Especializado da Assistência Farmacêutica*, Série B, Textos Básicos de Saúde. Brasília, DF: Ministério da Saúde

2009. *Boletín Epidemiológico AIDS & DST*, ano VI N°01. Brasília, DF: Ministério da Saúde

2001. *Política Nacional de Medicamentos*, Série C. Projetos, Programas e Relatórios, n. 25. Brasília, DF: Ministério da Saúde

n. d. 'Programas Estratégicos.' portal.saude.gov.br/portal/saude/visualizar_texto .cfm?idtxt=25311

Nguyen, V.-K. 2010. *The Republic of Therapy: Triage and Sovereignty in West Africa's Time of AIDS*. Durham, NC: Duke University Press

Ong, A. 2006. *Neoliberalism as Exception: Mutations in Citizenship and Sovereignty*. Durham, NC: Duke University Press

Ong, A. and Collier, S. 2005. *Global Assemblages: Technology, Politics and Ethics as Anthropological Problems*. Boston: Wiley-Blackwell

Paim, J., Almeida, C., Bahia, L. and Macinko, J. 2010. 'The Brazilian Health System: History, Advances and Challenges', *The Lancet* 26(3): 461–471

Pepe, V. L. M., Ventura, M., Sant'ana, J. M. B., Figueiredo, T. A., de Souza, V. R., Simas, L. and Osorio-de-Castro, C. G. S. 2010. 'Caracterização de Demandas Judiciais de Fornecimento de Medicamentos 'Essenciais' no Estado do Rio de Janeiro, Brasil', *Cadernos de Saúde Pública* 26(3): 461–471

Petryna, A. 2009. *When Experiments Travel: Clinical Trials and the Global Search for Human Subjects*. Princeton, NJ: Princeton University Press

2002. *Life Exposed: Biological Citizens after Chernobyl*. Princeton: Princeton University Press

Petryna, A., Lakoff, A. and Kleinman, A. (eds.) 2006. *Global pharmaceuticals: ethics, markets, practices*. Durham, NC: Duke University Press

Porto, S. M., Ugá, M. A. D. and Moreira, R. S. 2011. 'Uma Análise da Utilização de Serviços de Saúde por Sistema de Financiamento: Brasil 1998–2008', *Ciência & Saúde Coletiva* 16(9): 3795–3806

Povinelli, E. 2011. *Economies of Abandonment: Social Belonging and Endurance in Late Liberalism*. Durham, NC: Duke University Press

Rabinow P. and Rose, N. 2006. 'Biopower today.' *Biosocieties* 1(2): 195–217

Rajan, K. S. 2006. *Biocapital: The Constitution of Postgenomic Life*. Durham, NC: Duke University Press

Reynolds Whyte, S., Whyte, M., Meinert, L. and Twebaze, J. 2013. 'Therapeutic Client-ship: Belonging in Uganda's Mosaic of AIDS Projects', in Biehl, J. and Petryna, A. (eds.), *When People Come First: Critical Studies in Global Health*. Princeton, NJ: Princeton University Press

Riles, A. 2000. *The Network Inside Out*. Ann Arbor: University of Michigan Press

Sarlet, I. W. 2010. 'Access to Medicines and the Judiciary: Some Remarks in the Light of the Brazilian Experience.' Paper presented at the conference 'The Judiciary and the Right to Health: an International Conference,' Princeton University, Princeton, NJ, 25–26 March

Saúde conquistada na Justiça' 2012. *Zero Hora*, 29 August

Scheffer, M., Salazar, A. L. and Grou, K B. 2005. *O Remédio via Justiça: um Estudo Sobre o Acesso a Novos Medicamentos e Exames em HIV/Aids no Brasil por Meio de Ações Judiciais*. Brasília, DF: Ministério da Saúde

Scheper-Hughes, N. 1992. *Death Without Weeping: The Violence of Everyday Life in Brazil*. Berkeley: University of California Press

Schuch, P. 2012. 'Justiça, Cultura e Subjetividade: Tecnologias Jurídicas e a Formação de Novas Sensibilidades Sociais no Brasil', *Scripta Nova* vol. XVI, n. 395 (15)

Sharma, A. and Gupta, A. 2006. *The Anthropology of the State: A Reader*. Malden, MA: Blackwell Publishers

Sindicato da Indústria de Produtos Farmacêuticos no Estado de São Paulo (SINDUSFARMA) 2012. Indicadores Econômicos: Vendas em Dólares (US$). Available at www.sindusfarmacomunica.org.br/indicadores-eco nomicos (accessed 21April 21 2013)

Souza, F. L. M. de 2011. *A Defensoria Pública e o Acesso à Justiça Penal*. Porto Alegre: Nuria Fabris

Souza, R. R. De 2002. 'O Programa de Medicamentos Excepcionais', in Picon, P. D. and Beltrame, A. (eds.), *Protocolos Clínicos e Diretrizes Terapêuticas – Medicamentos Excepcionais*. Brasília, DF: Ministério da Saúde

Spencer, J. 2007. *Anthropology, Politics and the State: Democracy and Violence in South Asia* Cambridge: Cambridge University Press

Supremo Tribunal Federal 2010. Acórdão. STA/175 AgR/CE- Suspensão de Tutela Antecipada. Ministro Gilmar Mendes. April 30

2007. Despacho. STA/185. Agravo Regimental na Suspensão de Tutela Antecipada. Ministra Ellen Gracie. December 14

2000. Acórdão. RE 271286 AgR/RS. Agravo Regimental no Recurso Extraordinário. Relator: Celso de Mello. *Diário da Justiça Eletrônico*. November 24

Tate, W. 2007. *Counting the Dead: The Culture and Politics of Human Rights Activism in Colombia*. Berkeley: University of California Press

Ticktin, M. I. 2011. *Casualties of Care: Immigration and the Politics of Humanitarianism in France*. Berkeley: University of California Press

Vianna, L. W. 1999. *A Judicialização da Política e das Relações Sociais no Brasil*. Rio de Janeiro, RJ: Revan

Vianna, L. W. and Burgos, M. B. 2005. 'Entre Princípios e Regras: Cinco Estudos de Caso de Ação Cível Público.' *Dados* 48(4): 777–843

Vieira, F. S. 2009. 'Ministry of Health's spending on drugs: program trends from 2002 to 2007', *Revista de Saúde Pública* 43(4): 674–681

Vieira, F. S. and Zucchi, P. 2007. 'Distorções Causadas Pelas Ações Judiciais à Política de Medicamentos no Brasil', *Revista de Saúde Pública* 41(2): 1–8

Whitaker, R. 2010. *Anatomy of an Epidemic: Magic Bullets, Psychiatric Drugs, and the Astonishing Rise of Mental Illness in America*. New York: Crown Publishers

Yamin, A. E., and Gloppen, S. eds. 2011. *Litigating Health Rights: Can Courts Bring More Justice to Health?* Cambridge, MA: Harvard University Press

Yamin, A. E. and Parra-Vera, O. 2010. 'Judicial Protection of the Right to Health in Colombia: From Social Demands to Individual Claims to Public Debates.' *Hastings International and Comparative Law Review* 33(2): 101–130

CHAPTER EIGHT

COURTS AND THE CONTROL OF TB: QUARANTINE, TRAVEL AND THE QUESTION OF ADHERENCE

Ian Harper

My work in tuberculosis control – both initially as practitioner and latterly as an anthropologist – has long been concerned with the implications of categorising those suffering with this awful condition in particular ways (Harper 2005, 2006, 2010). Ian Hacking was certainly correct when he declared 'semantics intrigues the logician, but the dynamics of classification is where the action is' (Hacking 1999: 124). Access to treatment in complex bureaucratic contexts where those placed into certain classificatory categories receive certain treatments, equally denies others. In Nepal, I have looked at how the definition of 'new smear positive patient', for example, in the context of the WHO Direct Observation of Treatment, Short-course (DOTS) strategy allowed many patients into the public treatment system, but denied others (Harper 2005, 2006). It is frequently a matter of life and death. The categories being used for recording and reporting, those used in defining programmatic success, are complicit with what Biehl (2005) has called 'technologies of invisibility'.

More recently I explored the implications of the category 'default' – an outcome indicator that TB programmes report against for those entered into treatment – and the implications of this for issues of 'compliance' (Harper 2010). On the one hand, the rise in concern over

I thank Professor Leslie London for inviting me to present a version of this paper in Cape Town; to Joost Fontein and Jo Veary for the invitation to participate in the British Academy funded workshop 'The (Un)healthy Body in Southern Africa: multi-disciplinary approaches to corporeal dimensions of health' at the Wits Reproductive Health and HIV Institute, Johannesburg, South Africa; and to Laura Winterton for further feedback on the paper itself.

drug-resistant forms of tuberculosis (DRTB), and on the other, the push towards 'patient centred' and rights based approaches has created a central discursive tension in international attempts to control the disease and its spread. Legal and public health considerations have played out along utilitarian and deontological grounds, playing off the public's right to health against the rights of the individual. An appendix in a policy document produced by the WHO in 2008 as an 'emergency update' to their 'guidelines for the management of drug-resistant tuberculosis', focuses on 'legislation, human rights and patients' rights' (WHO 2008a). This document stated that any compulsive measures introduced around resistant forms of tuberculosis should only be provided under law. It left the article rather weakly suggesting that the law is one arena where these issues will be defined and decided, and that these new regulatory futures are indeterminate and emergent.

In this chapter I tentatively delve into this domain. What are the relationships between the law and medicine as applied to the control of tuberculosis? To do this, firstly, I look at the broadly discursive, and the problem around movement of people as a problem for the control of tuberculosis. Focusing on the case of an individual with DRTB in the USA who travelled to Europe, we shall look at the specific regulatory and legal issues that arose around this and how they fed into the rise of international concern (as reflected through the WHO) with issues of flying and the spread of the disease. Secondly, I review the rise of legal issues in the USA during the epidemic of tuberculosis in New York from the early 1990s, and how this led to a hardening of public health concern inscribed in law around the practice of incarceration. Finally, I compare this with the legal and public health issues around the attempted confinement in South Africa of those infected with XDRTB (see below). The limits of this relationship between law and medicine are teased out, particularly in light of a lack of focus on broader public health issues in relation to poverty and inequality.

MOVEMENT AND TB

A major concern for both national governments and global institutions is that increasingly mobile bodies also facilitate the movement of infectious diseases such as tuberculosis. With TB, the WHO has represented the movement of people – with trade, in airplanes, as refugees and the displaced – as one of the major factors contributing to the ever more dangerous global epidemic (WHO 2000a). This has been the case from the start of rejuvenation of attempts to deal with the disease when, in 1993, the WHO reconstituted the tuberculosis problem as a 'global emergency', declaring that its control needed to be coordinated across countries and continents (WHO 1994). Increasing economic interdependence and co-dependency mean that cooperation is more and more important for control (Small 1999), as these 'airborne killers' are traversing the globe in ever shorter periods of time (WHO 2000b). I have elsewhere charted a number of examples of discourses of globality, and how the interconnectedness of infectious diseases and TB have been represented – as problems for US security, and thus for global security – of how epidemiology and the object of its gaze, the tubercle bacillus, or 'statistic-tuberculosis' is put to work within political orders (Harper 2005). Advocating the rise of tuberculosis as a security issue for the USA and other powerful nations has raised its global political profile. In particular, it was this discourse that facilitated the entry of the bacillus (in addition to the malaria parasite and HIV virus) into the G8 negotiations in Japan in 2001, and the subsequent formation of the Global Fund.[1]

Although a more thorough historical excavation of epidemiology journals would be necessary, my sense is that the signifier 'foreign born', an epidemiological category, was on the rise through this period as well.[2] It is reified, for example, in a range of published medical and public health literature examining the population dynamics of tuberculosis.[3] Once articulated around this category, it becomes possible to state that higher levels of tuberculosis are found in immigrant populations. Two predominant political concerns emerge from these data within the public health literature: first, the value of increased screening of immigrants as a public health tool,[4] and second, questions around how these 'foreign born' access health services. Nicholas King has reviewed the problems that arise from this reification of difference and borders in thinking about tuberculosis – drawing on a number of case studies and publications – and how this category leads all too easily to the blame of immigration for the rise of tuberculosis in low-burden countries (King 2003). He is surely right to assert that this simplifies our understanding of the huge complexities of tuberculosis and its spread, not least hiding questions of race and income levels, questions of access to services, and being blind to the social consequences of such categorisations (ibid: 51).

There is a long genealogy to these issues. Historically, international migration has been associated with the transport of disease, and regardless of the available medical and epidemiological evidence, metaphors of plague and infection have circulated and been used to marginalise and keep out migrants in host countries (a summary can be found in Harper and Raman 2008). As Ho has pointed out in her research looking at tuberculosis and Chinese immigrants in the USA, for example, 'designating immigrants [to the USA] as importers of tuberculosis appears to be a natural tendency in the maintenance of cultural boundaries' (Ho 2003: 454). This 'geography of blame' (Farmer 1992) tends to identify the individual and their nation of origin as the source of the problem, and discriminatory public health measures flow all too easily from this discursive constitution of the issue. Effaced from these representations – as Farmer (2003) demonstrates for Haitian refugees, and Ho (2003) for Chinese immigrants – are the very conditions of their holding and migration which are all too ideal for the development of tuberculosis. As King suggests, most immigrants don't transport the disease, but develop it once they have arrived (King 2003). Nonetheless this 'structural violence' (Farmer 1998) all too easily becomes transcribed onto readily naturalised stereotypes of infecting foreign bodies.

Movement thus remains a central and significant issue for the control of TB. The WHO has constituted the problem of tuberculosis, its spread and control as an issue that affects all of us, and one that all nations must address, as they declared the problem of tuberculosis a global emergency. Migration is one aspect of this problem, but so is the act of flying. It is to this that I now turn.

TB AND FLYING

On 12 May 2007 the Atlanta lawyer, Andrew Speaker, flew from the USA to Rome. He then travelled back to the USA via Prague and Canada and into a media and public health storm of some ferocity. It transpired that he had multidrug-resistant tuberculosis (MDRTB). He was, briefly, the focus of attention in the US media – mostly confused and alarmist – and blogs. He was pummelled on the Law Blog, for example, under the title 'Law Blog Lawyer of the Day: Andrew Speaker...Not!' where his recklessness was attacked, and his ethical values as a lawyer questioned, many calling for his disbarment (reviewing this, I was surprised at the venom of some of the statements, many made in total ignorance of the medical and public health issues at stake).

To summarise, he had been diagnosed with (non-infectious) tuberculosis in March 2007, and put on standard treatment, but susceptibility testing of pulmonary isolates revealed later that he had MDRTB.[5] At a meeting with his private physician he was told not to travel. However, he did so, bringing his flight forward and thus missing an advisory letter from the county health department concerning his MDRTB. After he had gone, just to complicate things further, the CDC – who checked the isolates – suggested that he had XDRTB (TB resistant to four drugs, as opposed to the two required for the MDRTB diagnosis).[6] The CDC tracked him to Rome and informed him not to take commercial flights, and submit himself to hospital. While he indicated to them that he would stay put, he later flew to Prague, then Montreal. As the CDC were unable to track him down, the US Transportation Security Administration issued an order to prevent him from boarding any US flights: a no-fly list that was made to keep terrorists out, created in the wake of 9/11 (Mariner et al. 2009). The CDC notified the Italian Ministry of Health. In addition, the US Department of Health and Human Services (DHHS) contacted the WHO and informed them that they might have 'a public health emergency of international concern under the International Health Regulations' (Fidler et al. 2007: 617). Eventually, after Speaker got back to the USA, the CDC issued him with a provisional federal quarantine order, the first issued since 1963. Finally, he ended up in the National Jewish Medical Centre, where he was treated and his diagnosis downgraded to MDRTB again. The incident stimulated considerable legal and political activity: Congressional hearings,[7] tort litigation against Speaker brought by the Montreal passengers, and in 2009 Speaker suing the CDC for violating his individual rights (later dismissed by a District Court Judge).[8]

The legal debates this stimulated have mainly been published in Law Journals, including the *Journal of Biosecurity, Biosafety and Biodefense Law*; *Drexel Law Review*; *Journal of Law, Medicine and Ethics*, although there has been other commentary as well. As Fidler et al. suggest, this event is likely to go down in the history of public health as 'an incredible set of facts and sequence of events' with broad implications for ethics, the law and governance in public health (2007: 626). These authors highlight how there is a need to update laws on isolation and quarantine in an age of bioterrorism; that the federal government should update its regulations on quarantine so the federal response can be stronger in the future; that public health officials should be confronted with the need for greater compulsion; and that laws need to be crafted that can deal with the increased threats of the future. At the same time, these authors suggest, the incident points to the need for greater individual responsibility towards the consequences of their behaviour. To other commentators, however, it points to just the opposite. For Mariner et al. it is indicative of how, post 9/11, the combined focus on national security and heightened attention towards individual responsibility has skewed public health policy. It results in the expansion of surveillance and increased control over individual behaviour and it increases the power to confine those who are ill (2011). As Lakoff (2010) has suggested, from the perspective of those working in global health security, his case was read as whether we are prepared for the biological terror attack to come; although for those working in humanitarian biomedicine, it raised awareness about tuberculosis in public consciousness and also pointed to the failings of the public health system more generally. For the historian, David S. Barnes, in the wake of the rise of discourses around SARS and other scare stories of infectious diseases, it points to the power of 'patient zero' narratives, of which Speaker's is one in a long list of distinguished predecessors, including 'Typhoid Mary' (Barnes 2010). He argues that the tropes are familiar, staging transgression, calamity and punishment and – following Wald (2008) – notes that these are deeply rooted in American culture.

For the WHO, it stimulated a new edition of their guidelines *Tuberculosis and Air Travel, Guidelines for Prevention and Control*, first published in 1998, following concerns of transmission among passengers and crew on long-haul flights. This was updated in 2006, but was based on limited evidence (7 contagious passengers and 2600 potentially exposed in flight). A second edition was published in 2008 with the emergence of XDRTB and 'several incidents...involving air travel and potential transmission of TB' (WHO, 2008b: v). This time it also incorporated the 2007 International Health Regulations (IHR), which the preface argues, present a legal frame to better coordinate international responses to 'public health emergencies'. As the summary acknowledges, the document was produced in the light of the revised IHR, which entered 'into force' in June 2007. The document lists algorithms for how to deal with suspected cases and their contacts, and deals with technical issues of transmission in planes.

The section in the air travel document on legal and regulatory issues states that the IHR are legally binding:[9] 'to prevent, protect against, control and provide a public health response to the international spread of disease in ways that are commensurate with and restricted to public health risks, and which avoid unnecessary interference with international travel and trade'. In relation to the IHR, these activities include: the reporting and notification to the WHO; verification from the country in whose territory the event occurred; collaboration in assessing the potential for international spread; providing technical assistance and assessing existing control measures; exchanging information (via the 'secure WHO IHR Event Information web site') and that confidentiality can be overridden if serious disease is already spreading across international borders;[10] and contact investigation. Confidentiality is a key concern, and there are restrictions under Article 45, as to how to manage this.[11]

Thus flying remains an issue around the control of TB. Despite the limited evidence as a cause of spreading the disease, it has become embedded in increasingly complex webs of international and national regulatory processes. In the next section I turn to a series of issues that emerged in New York in the early 1990s. These had significant ramifications for the legal domain as pertaining to TB, particularly with regards to incarceration as a means to prevent the spread of the disease.

WHAT HAPPENED IN NEW YORK IN THE EARLY 1990s?

As has been argued, the capacity to identify the source of an outbreak has significant implications. The logic of this line of thought leads all too comfortably into suggesting that incarceration and detention are part of the solution to control the spread of the disease. In New York in the early 1990s, forcible containment became part of the renewed TB control programme, in the wake of increased concern with MDRTB. As is now well documented, New York experienced a significant rise in its rates of tuberculosis in the late 1980s and, with it, a significant rise in the numbers of those suffering with MDRTB. As a consequence, an old health code was revitalised, and on an island in the East River a secure hospital wing was opened and designed to hold patients until they were cured or 'expired' (Draus 2004: 40). This shift was first articulated in a 72-page report, *The Tuberculosis Revival: Individual Rights and Societal Obligations in a Time of AIDS*, published by the United Hospital Fund of New York in 1992. It outlined the 'Ethical, legal and public policy issues in screening, treatment, and the protection of those in congregate facilities'. The preface suggests that the multidisciplinary team involved was not able to reach consensus on all issues, particularly around 'the call for universal mandatory directly observed therapy'.[12]

The issues addressed included: mandatory HIV screening in TB programmes; protecting those with HIV from TB infection and restrictive employment practices; public health policies to ensure identification of those with the disease and the provision of treatment until cure. A section on 'guiding ethical principles and constitutional standards' (p.13) draws on the classic bioethical pillars of respect for persons, the harm principle, beneficence and justice, but in addition constitutional issues:

> The US Supreme Court has held that the government has the inherent power to protect the public health and that, in exercising its power, government may impose restrictions on individual liberty. This power is limited, however, by judicial rulings that were initially developed from litigation involving mental patients. In that context the Court has held that, in exercising its authority, government must respect the due process rights of those whose freedoms may be limited and that the limitations imposed must represent the least restrictive alternative necessary to achieve public health goals. Although the doctrine of the least restrictive alternative is a broad and important standard it does not provide a basis for resolving all the conflicts that may emerge in the shaping of policy – any more so than the previously described ethical principles. In particular instances it will still be necessary to determine whether marginal increments to the protection of the public health justify measures that are incrementally more restrictive.
>
> (p.13)

One recommendation was that 'State and city health agencies must develop a new law that requires treatment until cure and commits the state to creating and implementing appropriate policies and financing programs that will enhance and assure patient compliance.' In effect, this was to ensure the public health responsibility to assure treatment *until cure* (with this italicised in the original document). The definition of cure here includes the completion of treatment, and proof that they are non-infectious once treatment is over. In effect, this shift in authority would allow for the 'non-compliant' to be isolated under court order. The wording of the DOT component proved most controversial, particularly whether it should be required of all patients after discharge from hospital.[13] It was resisted on grounds that it was felt by some to be an imposition and infringement of individual liberties – and argued that this be determined only at juridical hearing. Recommendation (14) then sets out that those who are non-compliant should have rapid judicial and administrative hearings, focused on the protection of individual rights: 'Although short term emergency powers should be granted to a public health officer or a physician in the face of an immediate public health threat, adequate due process protection for the patient can be assured only by mandating a judicial hearing or a hearing before an independent administrative tribunal at which the patient is represented by counsel.' In addition Recommendation (15), drawn from principles developed in the realm of psychiatric patients and confinement, states that even under conditions of the loss of liberty, individuals still have the right to refuse treatment. S/he must be represented by a lawyer and 'only after finding that the individual lacks capacity' can a judge compel treatment.[14]

The series of public health and legal events that followed this in New York have been carefully charted by Coker (2000). After this committee's recommendations were related two problems remained: a lack of facilities, and the need to strengthen the legal framework to withstand the court challenges that would follow the increased authority of the public health component. A multidisciplinary working group was formed: they took a utilitarian stance, but limiting the compulsory DOT component. With considerable increased resources, four areas were focused on: 1) infection control in hospitals; 2) screening and prevention; 3) improved treatment completion rates; and 4) 'non-compliant patients'. As Coker argued, most physicians felt that the threat of detention was a necessary requisite for successful DOT. The changes focused on giving the commissioner greater powers when they deemed it necessary to protect public health, and the removal and detention of individuals when there is 'substantial likelihood' of transmission; and 'where there is substantial likelihood, based on a person's past or present behaviour, that he or she cannot be relied upon to participate in and/or to complete an appropriate prescribed course of medication' (Coker 2000: 104). The response to this from the New York City Tuberculosis Working Group (advocates for those living with HIV and in poverty) was that it was inappropriate to talk of detention without first addressing the issues of the absence of housing, health-care and services for substance abuse. Drawing on the Americans with Disabilities Act (ADA), an argument between what was *speculative* and *actual* in terms of risk was developed, and that 'actual' should be proven. The second argument drawing on the constitution and ADA was that detention should be the last resort, after other efforts, like the building of decent support services.[15] A public hearing was held, positions articulated and the Department of Health responded. They did not reply to the broader social issues, but made a response based on 'herd protection', that is, that 'the aggregate risks arising from many individuals failing to comply with treatment meant that any individual who could not or would not comply with appropriate treatment should be detained until he or she no longer posed a public health threat, however small that threat was' (ibid: 109). The CDC articulated the federal response some six months later, suggesting that all states should start with DOT, then DOT with a court order, and finally detention, and that this was to apply to non-infectious patients as well.

In conclusion to this section, we see that the rise of the threat of TB in New York in the early 1990s led to a hardening of public health principles in law, to assist in the problem of the recalcitrant patient. A key component of the struggle to control TB in the USA has been the focus on this. As the lawyer Tim Westmoreland comments in the forward to Coker's book, it is easier to respond with coercive, focused interventions than deal with the underlying issues of homelessness, HIV/AIDS, drug abuse and poverty. I turn, to finish, with South Africa and their response to the XDRTB crisis.

XDRTB AND SEGREGATION: THE SOUTH AFRICAN EXAMPLE

Although XDRTB has now been reported on from all areas of the world, South Africa was the country where the issue was first articulated. In particular, a now widely cited piece published in the Lancet highlighted this in a rural area in KwaZulu Natal (Gandhi et al. 2006). They reported that of 53 patients with XDRTB, 52 died. The question of involuntary detention was raised early in the response, and a questioning of the WHO, whose focus on individual responsibility is perhaps too 'permissive' (Singh et al. 2007). In a series of letters in PLoS Medicine, in reply to this article, the following positions advocating and resisting the idea became clear: one UK-based doctor suggested that there are those whose memory of isolation for TB in South Africa could be used to advocate for the idea of the sanatoria's re-entrenchment. After all, he argued, it was only 25 years ago that they were discarded. A group of Yale-based medical practitioners find it ironic that isolation and confinement is being suggested when many of those affected are being turned away from under-resourced institutions which provide second line TB treatment. They quote the New York City Tuberculosis Working Group who concluded that it was 'unethical, illegal, and bad public health policy to detain "non-compliant" persons before making concerted efforts to address the numerous systemic deficiencies…'. Médecins Sans Frontières (MSF – Doctors Without Borders, the humanitarian medical aid group) was also concerned with the overwhelming attention to confinement and detention that the article generated, and how blaming patients displaces energy and resources from other issues (improvements in general TB control, infection control, under-diagnosis in those infected with HIV, protection of health staff, greater access to diagnostic and treatment capabilities). The same general concerns that emerged in New York, resurface in the discussions internationally about the issue in South Africa.[16]

It has been South Africa's policy to hospitalise those diagnosed with XDRTB until they are no longer infectious. In 2007, a patient was shot and a guard stabbed at Sizwe hospital in Edenvale. Confined to the hospital, the patients were reported as being unhappy with their treatments and wanted to leave the hospital.[17] In the same year, at the San Jose Pearson TB Hospital, patients cut through the fences and ran away, and hospitals have sought court orders to compel the return of those who have 'run away'.[18] While the High Court granted Gauteng Health Department an urgent injunction granting it the ability to confine patients with MDR/XDRTB to Sizwe hospital, it also stated that they should be provided with State-paid lawyers to protect their rights.[19] The Bill of Rights in South Africa has two arguments: on the one hand, section 12, for 'everyone's right to bodily integrity', and section 36 which can limit this from the perspective of public health; 'provided the limitations are "reasonable and justifiable in an open and democratic society"' (ibid). In addition, the legal issues also pertain to a range of legislation around health practitioners, in particular the Compensation of Occupational Injuries Act; Employment Equity Act; Labour Relations Act; Basic Conditions of Employment Act, all of which obligate employers to provide safe measures for health workers.[20] What was lacking, concludes this presentation on 'M/XDR-TB and the Law: South African Context' tracked down to the WHO website and archived for 2007, is test cases in the South African courts to see what is acceptable within the context of individual rights and public health.[21]

I shall finish this section with the concerns raised by the South African Medical Research Council. They stated that it was public anxiety that had resulted in the increase of coercive measures to prevent the spread of XDR-TB.[22] The council was concerned with the possibility of the huge stigma associated with the condition, combined with coercive measures that could drive the problem underground. In addition this piece cites the Treatment Action Campaign (a TB/HIV rights based group) as stating that incarceration is a bad idea for the following reasons: most DR infections occur in hospitals; the scale with which it would have to be done means that it will not make any difference; it causes alarm and people will not want to be screened as a result; and locking up people who have not committed a crime can result in riots, as happened in Sizwe. One of the key issues is that infection control in institutions needs to be strengthened, the article states. As a piece in the South African Medical Journal suggests, many of the hospitals dealing with XDRTB in South Africa require structural modification to deal with the infection control, and to improve isolation issues, in addition to the need for broader social interventions around poverty.[23] As such this resonates with London's call for a greater focus on improving the broader issues of health system's functioning, combined with further investment in drug research and development, and to not solely focus on confinement (London 2008).

CONCLUSION

Since 1993, when the WHO declared the problem of tuberculosis as a 'global emergency', their policy and guidelines for the control of TB have broadened considerably. As resources, focus on programmatic matters in countries and research have proliferated, so it seems has the complexity of the issue and the suggested solutions. The current STOP TB strategy, introduced by the WHO in 2006, acknowledged this and suggested that countries broaden their focus to include TB/HIV; MDRTB and the needs of the poor; broader health systems strengthening; patient centeredness and community involvement; and research. Since then, the emergence of the International Health Regulations, the development of XDRTB and the high profile cases of the likes of Andrew Speaker, among others, has further complicated the picture. In both the USA and South Africa this has had effects. Both countries have seen a shift to more draconian responses in the name of the public's health, but at the expense of a broader conception of public health itself. The specificities of how these have played out in each country, and the influence of the WHO and International agendas, are quite different. Different political histories, differing relations between utilitarian and deontological ideas as inscribed in law, and differing capacities of the state to implement legal changes. Attention to these cases and their specificities may teach us much of the capacity of public health agendas to assist in the treatment of those with increasingly hard-to-treat TB. The law may well, more and more, define how those with DRTB are treated, as individuals and countries become enmeshed in increasingly complex legal webs. And yet the limits of the law here are starkly realised: in the USA we see the boundaries of both individual and public rights once applied to attempts to prevent the spread of infection in an era of increasing security concern. In South Africa, the limits of legislating against the spread of infection are simply unrealisable because of the scale of the problem. Both these scenarios point to the need to deal with the spread of DRTB beyond a move to the legal attempts to regulate the movements of individuals, and as such points to the limits of such an interplay between the law and medicine.

NOTES

1 A more complete picture would include the influence of the economist Jeffery Sachs and his work that rearticulated infectious diseases, in particular malaria, as the cause of poverty; and the emergence of the Millennium Development Goals, which were heavily criticised for their focus on health indicators, in particular disease targets.

2 New scientific and technological capacity have also converged to redefine how the epidemic is understood. The new field of 'molecular epidemiology', which emerged in the early 1990s, allows for the more accurate pinpointing of sources of infection. Gene fingerprinting technologies allow the identification of strains of bacteria, and whether cases come from the same strain. Restriction fragment-length polymorphism (RFLP) allows relations to be detected, objectively so to speak, where previously they had been hidden. The first application of this to tuberculosis was with the publication in *The New England Journal of Medicine* in 1992. Using the RFLP to profile the isolates of the causative organism mycobacterium tuberculosis from a number of infected patients, this method was able to reveal who had been the source of an outbreak in a San Francisco hospital (Barnes 2010). Further examples followed. As Barnes has suggested, the ability to articulate who the index case (or patient zero) is when there are a cluster of cases, has shifted the debate over how to control the disease. Even without this new technology, 'patient zeros' were still articulated as the sources of infection: in New York in 1990 this was a homeless heroin addict, and a woman on a flight from Honolulu to Baltimore via Chicago and back (ibid).

3 See for example Kunimoto et al. 2004; Salihu and Spittle 1999; Jump et al. 2004; Nelson et al. 2004.

4 See for example LoBue and Moser 2004; Coker 2003; Coker et al. 2004.

5 This account is summarised mainly from Fidler et al. 2007, but the facts of the case are available in a number of publications.

6 This was just after the WHO had released a statement announcing the problem of XDRTB, following an outbreak in South Africa, and the issues around this difficult-to-treat form had been highlighted in the media and press.

7 The details of this can be found in: Swendiman K & N Jones 2008. CRS Report for Congress: Extensively Drug-Resistant Tuberculosis (XDR-TB): Emerging Public Health Threats and Quarantine and Isolation. Order Code RL34144.

8 See the *Atlanta Journal-Constitution*. www.ajc.com/health/judge-dis misses-andrew-speaker-211263.html

9 Appendix 2 of the IHR lists reservations and other communications and includes for the USA: 'The United States understands that the provisions of the Regulations do not create judicially enforceable private rights'.

10 In accordance with Article 11.2 of the IHR, that articulates in what circumstances this is possible: if, for example, 'the event is determined to constitute a public health emergency of international concern' (defined by Article 12), and confirmed by the WHO, and if the State lacks the capacity to carry out the necessary measures among others.

11 These new IHR have shifted the focus on stopping the spread of infectious diseases at borders, onto the idea of responding to the spread of infections at source (Dry 2010). This, argues Dry, has involved a shift from spatial to temporal dynamics, as speed is of the essence within the networks of surveillance and rapid responding. She gives the discussion around the outbreak of Extensive Drug Resistant Tuberculosis in South Africa as an example: The WHO set up a Global Task Force on XDRTB to decide whether this event should be constituted as a 'public health emergency of international concern' (or PHEIC, in Article 6.1 of the 2005 IHR). The decision, which hinged on whether the event was 'acute' or 'acute-on-chronic', decided that it did not pose an immediate threat for international spread.

12 The team was chaired by David Rothman, a medical historian based at Columbia University. Although it is beyond the scope of this paper, Tom Frieden, who was central to the New York response to dealing with the outbreak, moved to the WHO and was an ardent advocate of DOT as central to their revitalised TB programme, once the disease had been declared a global emergency.

13 With the adoption of this principle by the WHO in 1993, this has remained the most controversial aspect of TB treatment and has generated a great deal of debate and subsequent research, including three in-depth reviews of the evidence base for its efficacy (see Harper 2010 for a summary of these).

14 Appendix C of the document is a case study, and questions generated around 'The recalcitrant patient'. It has 81 associated questions that should be thought through (general, technical, screening, informed consent, mandatory prophylaxis, HIV screening, safety and mandatory treatment and long-term care).

15 Yet as Coker also points out, legal scholars have argued as to the antidiscrimination mandate of the ADA (Coker 2000: 113 ff).

16 Lessons learned from the New York case are being applied as part of the international response by the CDC and others in their assistance to South Africa in dealing with the issue: www.scribd.com/doc/24551505/ Www-cdc-gov-Tb-Xdrtb-Update-htm-Hwn4i3hs

17 http://mg.co.za/article/2007–10–30-two-hurt-in-joburg-hospital-rampage

18 www.nytimes.com/2008/03/25/world/africa/25safrica.html

19 www.samj.org.za/index.php/samj/article/viewFile/533/330

20 www.who.int/tb/events/archive/icmeeting_oct07/03_duse.pdf

21 www.who.int/tb/events/archive/icmeeting_oct07/03_duse.pdf

22 Why quarantine may backfire. www.health24.com/Medical/Tuberculosis/ Quarantine/Why-quarantine-may-backfire-20120721

23 See: www.samj.org.za/index.php/samj/article/viewFile/533/330

REFERENCES

Barnes, D. 2010. 'Targeting Patient Zero', in Condreau, F. and Warboys, M. (eds.), *Tuberculosis Then and Now: Perspectives on the History of an Infectious Disease*. Montreal & Kingston, London, Ithaca: McGill-Queen's University Press

Biehl, J. 2005. 'Technologies of Invisibility: Politics of Life and Social Inequalities', in Inda, J. (ed.), *Anthropologies of Modernity: Foucault, Governmentality, and Life Politics*. Oxford: Blackwell Publishing Ltd

Coker, R. 2003. *Migration, Public Health, and Compulsory Screening for TB and HIV*. London: ippr (Institute for Public Policy Research)

2000. *From Chaos to Coercion: Detention and the Control of Tuberculosis*. New York: St. Martin's Press

Draus, P. 2004. *Consumed in the City*. Philadelphia: Temple University Press

Dry, S. 2010. 'New Rules for Health? Epidemics and the New International Health Regulations', in Dry, S. and Leach, M. (eds.), *Epidemics: Science, Governance and Social Justice*. London: Earthscan

Farmer, P. 2003. *Pathologies of Power: Health, Human Rights and the New War on the Poor*, Berkeley, Los Angeles and London: University of California Press

1998. 'On Suffering and Structural Violence: A View from Below', in Kleinman, A, Das, V and Lock, M (eds.), *Social Suffering*. Delhi: Oxford University Press

1992. *AIDS and Accusation: Haiti and the Geography of Blame*. Berkeley, Los Angeles and London: University of California Press

Fidler, D., Gostin, L. and Markel, H. 2007. 'Through the Quarantine Looking Glass: Drug-Resistant Tuberculosis and Public Health Governance, Law, and Ethics', *Journal of Law, Medicine and Ethics* Winter: 616–628

Gandhi, N. R., Moll, A., Sturm, A. W., Pawinski, R., Govender, T., Lalloo, U., Zeller, K., Andrews, J. and Friedland, G. 2006. 'Extensively Drug-resistant

Tuberculosis as a Cause of Death in Patients co-infected with Tuberculosis and HIV in a Rural Area of South Africa', Lancet 368:1575–1580

Hacking, I. 1999. *The Social Construction of What?* Harvard University Press

Harper, I. 2010. Extreme Condition, Extreme Measures? Compliance, Drug Resistance and the Control of Tuberculosis. *Anthropology & Medicine*, 17(2): 201–214

2006. 'Anthropology, DOTS and Understanding Tuberculosis Control in Nepal' *J. Biosoc. Sci.* 38: 57–67

2005. 'Interconnected and Interinfected: DOTS and the Stabilisation of the Tuberculosis Control Programme in Nepal', in Mosse, D. and Lewis, D. (eds.), *The Aid Effect: Giving and Governing in International Development*, London: Pluto

Harper, I. and Raman, P. 2008. 'Less than Human? Diaspora, Disease and the Question of Citizenship',*International Migration* 46(5): 3–26

Ho, M.-J. 2003. 'Migratory Journeys and Tuberculosis Risk', *Medical Anthropology Quarterly* 17(4): 442–458

Jump, S. M., Sauver, J. L., Weaver, A. L., Bagniewski, S. M., Wilson, J. W., Huskins, W. C., Aksamit, T. R., Brutinel, W. M., Scalcini, M. C., Sia, I. G., Correa, A. G., McCoy, K. and Boyce, T. G. 2004. 'Incidence of tuberculosis in Olmsted County, Minnesota, 1990–2001', *Mayo Clin Proc* 79(9):1110–2

King, N. 2003. 'Immigration, Race, and Geographies of Difference in the Tuberculosis Pandemic', in Gandy, M and Zumla, A (eds.), *Return of the White Plague: Global Poverty and the New Tuberculosis*. London: Verso Press

Kunimoto, D., Sutherland, K., Wooldrage, K., Fanning, A., Chui, L., Manfreda, J. and Long, R. 2004. 'Transmission Characteristics of Tuberculosis in the Foreign-born and the Canadian-born Populations of Alberta, Canada', *Int J Tuberc Lung Dis.* 8(10):1213–20

Lakoff, A. 2010. *Epidemic Intelligence and the Technopolitics of Global Health.* Paper prepared for the Berkeley Workshop on Environmental Politics. www.globetrotter.berkeley.edu/bwep/colloquium/papers/lakoff_BWEP.pdf

LoBue, P. A. and Moser, K. S. 2004. 'Screening of immigrants and refugees for pulmonary tuberculosis in San Diego County, California', *Chest* 126(6): 1724–5

London, L. 2008. 'Confinement in the Management of Drug-resistant TB: The Unsavoury Prospect of Balancing Individual Human Rights and the Public Good', *South African Journal of Bioethics and Law* 1(1): 11–19

Mariner, W. K., Annas, G. J., Parmet and W. E. 2009. '*Pandemic Preparedness: A return of the Rule of Law*', *Drexel Law Review* 1(2): 341–382

Singh, J. A., Upshur, R. and Padayatchi, N. 2007. 'XDR-TB in South Africa: No Time for Denial or Complacency', *PLoS Med* 4(1): e50 doi:10.1371/journal.pmed.0040050

Small, P. 1999. 'Tuberculosis in the 21st Century: DOTS and SPOTS', *International Journal of Tuberculosis and Lung Disease* 3(11): 949–955

Wald, P. 2008. *Contagious: Cultures, Carriers, and the Outbreak Narrative*. Duke University Press

WHO 1994. *TB: A Global Emergency – WHO Report on the TB Epidemic* available online at whqlibdoc.who.int/hq/1994/WHO_TB_94.177.pdf?ua=1

　2008a. *Guidelines for the Programmatic Management of Drug-resistant Tuberculosis*. Available online at: WHO/HTM/TB/2008.402

　2008b. *Tuberculosis and Air Travel: Guidelines for Prevention and Control: Third Edition*. Available online at: WHO/HTM/TB/2008.399

DYING TO GO TO COURT: DEMANDING A LEGAL REMEDY TO END-OF-LIFE UNCERTAINTY

Naomi Richards

Voluntary euthanasia, or the 'right-to-die', as it is currently termed, is one of the most visible and divisive bioethical issues to be routinely debated in medically advanced countries. Central to the issue is the conflict between the rights of individuals to determine their own lives and, by extension, the ending of that life, and the duty of the state to protect the lives of its most vulnerable citizens. For some, the medical hastening of death by way of a deliberate intervention is the next step in a trend which has seen technological advances in medicine turn death into something which can now be orchestrated, negotiated and timed (turning off a ventilator, deciding not to treat, etc.). For others, this is a step too far and must be resisted at all costs. As attempts to legalise and institutionalise the practice of euthanasia have increased over the last century, it is no longer considered a private matter between doctor and patient but rather has become a matter of public concern where the language of rights now dominates. In the UK, the primary focus for this dramatic conflict of rights is the courtroom. Legal redress is sought, as individuals living with serious progressive illness lose confidence in the medical profession to sufficiently ease their suffering as their body deteriorates and their capacities lessen. Not only is the law valued for the potential remedy it provides, but a favourable judgement also offers some formal validation of a particular ethical position. In recent years, the courts have become the most productive (and provocative) forum for shifting the terms of the debate and applying pressure on British lawmakers.

This chapter focuses on a high-profile legal challenge which was mounted in the UK in 2008 and was finally determined by judges in the country's supreme court in 2010. The case involved a woman named Debbie Purdy and her husband Omar Puente. Debbie had been living with multiple sclerosis, an incurable and degenerative disease, since 1995. The couple wanted to challenge the possible application of the criminal law in cases where individuals have asked their relatives to aid them in travelling abroad to a jurisdiction where they may lawfully be helped to die. Since 2002, a number of Britons have travelled to Switzerland, where right-to-die organisations can legally assist in their suicide in accordance with a unique provision in Article 115 of the country's penal code allowing anyone to assist in a suicide for altruistic reasons. In the UK, the Suicide Act 1961,[1] explicitly states that it is illegal to encourage or assist the suicide or attempted suicide of another person and that the offence is punishable by up to 14 years in prison. Debbie's was an appeal to the judicial process to help her clarify the risks to her husband of a future decision to end her life abroad. In lieu of a medical remedy for her disease, Debbie sought out a legal remedy in terms of knowledge about the likelihood of her husband being prosecuted, should she ask him to accompany her to Switzerland at some unspecified future time.

The principal outcome of the case has been the publication, in 2010, of a policy statement which, for the first time, puts into written and public form reasons why the decision might be taken not to prosecute a person for helping another to take their own life. This chapter discusses the development of this new policy document, and the moral reckoning which determined its final form. Although the chapter focuses on the specifics of Debbie's case and its outcome, it also extrapolates from those specifics to comment on the broader cultural context in which assisted suicide is undoubtedly gaining social acceptance. The central focus of the chapter is the way in which the law was used instrumentally by campaigners to bring about a policy which has changed the way assisting someone to die is regulated. As other chapters in this volume relate, the technicalities of the law might on the face of it appear quite alienating for ordinary citizens who are seeking redress for a perceived injustice. However, in the case put forward here, it was the technicalities of the law which were debated and wrangled over in lieu of any political or medical consensus about the moral or ethical rightness of assisting people in their suicide. It was these technicalities which were used as an instrument to extract a significant concession from the Director of Public Prosecutions (DPP), forcing him to devise a new policy document. Some may view this as an example of the law overstepping its boundaries, changing policy where it should rightly be left up to those democratically elected to do so. Others argue that the law is simply too blunt an instrument to tackle the delicate ethical dilemmas which arise around end-of-life decisions. However, in this case, the law was *productive*. It produced an outcome which, on the face of it, may appear only as yet another regulatory instrument, but concealed within that is what is perceived as a validation of the demands of right-to-die campaigners, and the opening up of further opportunities for applying legal as well as political pressure on politicians to change the law in a more definitive way.

This chapter is based on data gained from anthropological research conducted from 2007 to 2009, as Debbie Purdy's case journeyed through the British courts. The overall aim of the research was to trace and contextualise the values, beliefs and convictions of both sides in the right-to-die debate. The research conducted was multisited and involved following the 'chains, paths, threads, conjunctions, locations' (Marcus, 1998: 90) where the terms of the debate were decided. I interviewed Debbie Purdy at length early in 2008 before her application for Judicial Review was heard and before media attention turned her into a recognisable public figure. I was present at her Court of Appeal hearing in February 2009 and interviewed her again over the phone afterwards. I also spent a week working for her lawyer collating information collected through questionnaires sent to the relatives of people who had died at Dignitas. I formally interviewed the Human Rights Officer of the campaigning organisation Dignity in Dying which supported her case and had other informal contact with the Chief Executive, the Head of Legal Strategy and Policy and the Director of Campaigns and Communications at two AGMs and various public events and conferences. In addition, the larger research project led me to interview a wide array of campaigners lobbying both for and against legalised assistance to die, along with other people who were planning to travel to Switzerland for help to die. This knowledge informs my approach and helps me to ground the outcome of the case in the wider political context.

DEBBIE PURDY'S PREDICAMENT

> If I could write the future, we would clarify the law as it stands, change the law in the next couple of years, and in the meantime someone would find a cure for primary-progressive MS.
>
> (Debbie Purdy writing in her 2010 autobiography: 280).

Debbie Purdy was diagnosed with primary progressive multiple sclerosis (MS) in 1995, when she was just 32, although it is likely that she was experiencing the symptoms of the disease for years before that. MS is the most common disabling neurological disease affecting young adults. It affects about 100 000 people in the UK.[2] Symptoms include, among others: loss of sensitivity and muscle weakness/spasms leading to mobility difficulties; problems with coordination and balance; fatigue and acute and chronic pain; and difficulties with speech and swallowing. Debbie has a progressive form of the disease and there is no known cure or remedy. Shortly after diagnosis she asked her doctor what she could expect and he replied: 'the only thing I can tell you is that it's not going to get any better. And that's pretty much it' (Purdy 2010: 36). However, Debbie is not 'dying'. She has lived with her disease for a long time now, and although her symptoms steadily increase, she may live with it for many years to come. In fact, people with MS have a life expectancy which is only five to ten years lower than that of the unaffected population (Compston and Coles 2008). Even if her life were to be considerably foreshortened, it is not this which she fears so much as the prospect of future 'unbearable'[3] suffering which may cause her to feel that her life is no longer worth living. It is at this point that Debbie would like the option of hastening her own death. Ideally, she would like to be assisted to die in the UK with the help of a doctor. However, in lieu of a change in the law which would allow this to happen, the most likely place for her to want to hasten her own death would be Zurich, Switzerland, with the help of the organisation, Dignitas.

Dignitas, founded in 1998, is one of three Swiss organisations which help foreign nationals to die. However, Dignitas is the only one to have repeatedly made tabloid headlines in the UK, the majority of which have portrayed its activities in a very negative light (cf. Hall 2009; Weathers 2011). The organisation operates strictly within Swiss law, which states that people who assist in a suicide can only be prosecuted if they are motivated by self-interest. As such, the fees which Dignitas charge people only cover its operating costs and no profit is made. A retired doctor initially meets and assesses the individual wishing to die and, if they are satisfied that the various conditions are met, they then write the lethal prescription. The prescription is then collected by a Dignitas volunteer who prepares the drug and gives it to the individual to self-administer. The death 'event' itself is therefore de-medicalised, and I will return to this concept later in the chapter. When cases of Britons being assisted to die at Dignitas have been reported in the British press, it is often referred to as a 'clinic'. However, the setting is intentionally non-clinical and there is no medical professional present when the lethal liquid is taken. On the day of Debbie Purdy's appeal hearing in February 2009, Dignitas released the information that 100 Britons had died there since 2002. In January 2012, this figure had increased to 182 Britons (Beckford 2012).

The context in which Debbie's case arose is one where notions of the 'good death' are slowly changing. Cross-culturally, the 'good death' has been identified as one where there is some degree of control over the arbitrariness of physiological deterioration (Bloch and Parry 1999: 12) and where death comes at the end of a long and successful life, at home and without violence or pain (Seale and van der Geest 2004: 885). While these attributes continue to hold in the UK, the point of cleavage has become whether the good death must be a natural death or whether it can be artificially procured. Palliative care philosophy, which occupies the mainstream in terms of an ideal-type model of end of life care, has much in common with right-to-die philosophy in that both seek to personalise and individualise dying and both emphasise that choice and control should reside with the dying person herself (Walter 1994). However, where the two movements differ is that palliative care philosophy takes the position that it seeks neither to hasten nor to postpone death (Maddocks 1996). Right-to-die philosophy, on the other hand, takes the view that for some, natural death can cause such a profound loss of control over the physical boundaries of the body, as Lawton (2000: 7) documents in her ethnography 'The Dying Process', that they can experience a diminishment of self. It is in such situations, advocates argue, that only by artificially hastening a person's death can social and biological death be realigned, and a person's suffering be brought to an end. It is an uncontrolled natural death which Debbie Purdy fears awaits her, and it is this which inspired her to take up her legal challenge to make viable her option of an artificially induced death abroad.

When I interviewed Debbie, she told me that she characterises herself as a 'loud-mouthed, obnoxious' pro-choice activist: 'I'm not the type of person to just drift into the background'. She sat on the board of Dignity in Dying, the UK's main organisation campaigning for the legalisation of assisted dying,[4] for a number of years before stepping down in 2007 to begin her legal challenge. For some time she has worked as a 'simulated patient' for a medical school, a project that aims to educate doctors about how to engage appropriately with disabled patients. She thinks that disabled people should have the same access to services as everyone else, but she also thinks that disabled people should be allowed to decide what they want for themselves, even if that deviates from what is expected of them. She doesn't support the paternalism she encounters in the disability rights movement and resents being called 'vulnerable'. As she told me: 'If you are going to argue for disabled rights, then you have to argue for their right to decide what they want. It's easy to say you support free speech with someone who is agreeing with you.' By this rationale, Debbie Purdy feels strongly that disabled people should be able to choose an assisted death, without needing to be 'protected from ourselves'. This is why she launched her case with the help of Dignity in Dying which arranged her legal representation and her media appearances.

Assisted suicide first entered Debbie's consciousness through the media coverage of Dianne Pretty's legal case six years earlier. In 2001, Dianne petitioned the courts to allow her husband to help her commit suicide with legal immunity (meaning he would not be charged for committing a crime after her death). It was never specified how or where her suicide would take place. Dianne was living with motor neurone disease and was paralysed from the neck down, making it very difficult for her to take her own life. Dianne took her case to the House of Lords and then to the European Court of Human Rights, where it was finally dismissed. When Dianne heard that she had lost her case, she declared that 'the law has taken away my human rights'. This comment highlights the way in which the language of human rights is often used rhetorically to register disapproval of state law. Its appeal rests in maintaining a critical distance from the law, and its ability therefore to stretch the boundaries and limits of the law (Douzinas 2000: 344). Dianne's case was the first to frame requests for help to die as a 'human right' in an attempt to do just that: stretch the limit of the law and give a desire for a certain type of death transcendent value (Douzinas 2000: 367).

Dianne's case, like Debbie's, was supported by Dignity in Dying (at that time called the Voluntary Euthanasia Society) and marked a new phase in the campaigning strategy of the organisation. The impetus now appears to be to highlight the suffering of specific individuals with whom the public can identify, in order to promote its cause. These individuals become 'spectacles of suffering' so that 'whether or not anyone speaks to his or her suffering, an observer is likely to understand and acknowledge that suffering is taking place' (Williams 2007: 137). At the same time, the courts have been viewed instrumentally as a potentially more expedient route to success when compared to the more cumbersome, parliamentary process. It was Dianne Pretty's high profile appeal that raised public awareness of assisted dying in Britain and paved the way for Debbie Purdy subsequently to bring her own legal challenge.

Debbie's case was this. If, at an unspecified future date, she feels compelled to travel to Switzerland for an assisted suicide because her MS has advanced to a stage where she no longer feels her life is worth living and she determines of her own accord that she is suffering 'unbearably', she may need to ask her husband, Omar Puente, to accompany her and assist her with the journey. If he were to agree, there is a possibility that he would be prosecuted under Section 2(1) of the 1961 Suicide Act which makes it illegal to encourage or assist in the suicide or attempted suicide of another person.[5] Debbie was not seeking immunity for Omar, as in the Pretty case where Dianne sought immunity for her husband. Rather, Debbie was asking for the DPP, at whose discretion a criminal case against Omar would be brought, to clarify exactly what counts as 'assistance' and what factors he would be likely to take into account when deciding whether or not to prosecute him. Her lawyers claimed that Article 8[6] – the right to respect for private and family life – of the European Convention on Human Rights was engaged in Debbie's decision to want to take her own life, and that the state was only entitled to interfere with this right 'such as in accordance with the law' (ECHR, Article 8(2)). In order that individuals like Debbie and Omar know in advance what is 'in accordance with the law', it was argued by her team that there needed to be a clear statement of policy outlining the factors tending for and against a prosecution. Debbie said that if she was not 100% certain that Omar would not be prosecuted after her death, then she would not allow him to accompany her. As she told me: 'I've got to be certain that my decision will not hurt him.' Her argument was that in lieu of a clear prosecutorial policy she would be forced to travel to Switzerland and die earlier than she wanted to while she still had the physical capacity to travel alone. For this reason, Debbie always framed her claim not as a 'right-to-die' but as a 'right-to-live longer'. This sentiment is similarly reflected in the title of her autobiography: *It's not because I want to die.*

What was intriguing about Debbie's case was that although it was *her* campaigning efforts that brought the legal challenge in the first instance and it was *her* future death decision which was the focus, it was her husband's potential actions that were the subject of the legal dispute. This actually mirrors Dianne Pretty's case in which it was Dianne's husband, Brian, whose potential actions were being judged. Debbie's husband Omar is the one who risks prosecution for helping her to make the journey to Switzerland. However, he has said in many interviews with the press that he will go with her regardless of the risks. It is Debbie who refuses this offer out of a desire to protect him. They are trying to determine the freedom of their future selves. Yet the criminal law operates retrospectively and is not anticipatory. It responds to what has already happened and the discretion to prosecute cannot be exercised in advance. It is not designed to offer certainty in the face of future events which have yet to take place. This is the limit to the remedy the law can provide.

Debbie and Omar are mutually implicated in her death decision. Right-to-die rhetoric would have us believe that demands for help to die are purely a matter of individual choice and a desire for individual control. Advocates argue that such demands are made by individuals who want to determine the end to their own lives through their own subjective assessment of whether they are suffering 'unbearably'. As Debbie told me: 'I don't want to be in other people's control. I don't want to be at their whim. I want to have complete control and autonomy about what I do and how I do it.'

This focus on the individual as the locus of decision-making is indicative of a more general reliance on individual autonomy as the cornerstone of medical law and ethics (Mason and Laurie 2006: 6). At its most pared down, autonomy relies on 'negative liberty' or freedom from interference, as famously described by Isaiah Berlin (2006 [1958]). O'Neill (2002: 29) describes autonomy as a 'capacity' or 'trait' which individuals have and which they manifest by acting independently. John Stewart Mill (2006[1859]) influentially extended the idea beyond independent action to include the enabling of self-expression or the flourishing of individuality. For some philosophers, this extension too closely aligns the concept with liberal individualism which champions the fulfilment of the unimpeded individual, while ignoring the impact of that fulfilment on the broader community. After all, the social dimension of life requires that individual autonomy be qualified by the legitimate interests and expectations of others (Mason and Laurie 2006: 5–7). This is what is known as the communitarian approach to ethics.

In the UK, it was the case of *Re C (adult: refusal of medical treatment)[1994]* that established the legal precedent granting patients the right to refuse treatment, including life-sustaining treatment,[7] on the grounds of self-determination with regard to a person's own body. The legal consequences of unauthorised invasion of that bodily integrity include civil actions for damages and criminal liability for assault (Mason and Laurie 2006: 349). The right was made unequivocally enforceable with the case of Ms B *(adult: refusal of medical treatment)[2002].*[8] However, where the law is seen to value individual autonomy over and above the obligations we owe to those around us, there are concerns that an exaggerated absoluteness and hyper-individualism can take hold (Glendon 1991: x–xi) which neglects people's unavoidable dependency on others and the fact that an individual's decision has consequences for other people. As Butler writes: 'Although we struggle for rights over our own bodies, the very bodies over which we struggle are not quite ever our own' (Butler 2004: 26).

In demanding a human right to have her private life respected, Debbie's decision depends on her husband and his support. She cannot act alone. Despite the fact that it is Debbie who has pursued the case, in reality it is *he* who will feel the effects of the law should he be prosecuted for helping her. What becomes clear from reading Debbie's autobiography (2010) is that Omar was always a reluctant passenger in her campaign. She writes of his 'hurt look' when she talked to journalists about the prospect of taking her own life and recalls his response when she first asked him if he would come with her to Dignitas: 'Of course I would come, Debbie. I don't even have to think about it. But for now can we not talk about it? Can we just get on with enjoying our lives together?' (Purdy 2010: 232). Omar is intimately involved in Debbie's decisions. He must anticipate her death, not because he chooses to, but because Debbie is a determined campaigner who has decided to prepare for her death in a very public way. When she says 'I've got to be certain that my decision will not hurt him', it is clear that she conceives of her death decision as hers alone to make, and yet she refuses to criminally implicate Omar, indicating the limits to her autonomy. As Strathern highlights, 'To an age that thinks of itself as individualistic, the revelation of relationship can come as something of a surprise. The person as an individual turns out to be the person as a relative' (Strathern 2005: 10).

In the public spectacle which surrounded Debbie's case in its passage through the courts, Omar featured heavily in the extensive press coverage. Her autobiography is presented as something of a love story, and pictures of the two of them together grace both the front and back covers. The strength of their relationship was a fact which implicitly strengthened their case in the court as well as in the eyes of the public, a point I will expand on later.

Another crucial factor in Debbie and Omar's case, which was often overlooked in its reporting, was the many hypothetical circumstances at stake. *If* she finds herself 'suffering unbearably' at some point in the future, she *might* want to have an assisted death at Dignitas. Perhaps she is anticipating the worst, but she wants to be prepared anyway. As she told me:

> I don't want to make the decision now. Until you are in an unbearable situation you don't *really* know what is unbearable. When I was twenty-one, I thought being in a wheelchair would be the most terrible thing that could happen – that I'd kill myself if that ever happened. It's not that bad. You learn to cope in a different way, you learn to see yourself in a different way. You are not prevented from being you.

Debbie does not yet know what degree of bodily deterioration and loss of function she can tolerate while still finding life worthwhile. She does not know which capacities and activities will, in her eyes, represent the essential components of an acceptable life and indeed there is no certainty that she will ever have to confront these questions. As Lawton's (2000: 7) ethnographic work shows, in a British cultural context, in order for selfhood to be realised and maintained, certain specific bodily capacities and attributes *must* be possessed, namely the bodily ability to act as the agent of one's embodied actions and intentions. People who lack this ability can fall out of the category of personhood and experience a 'diminishment of self'. In some respects, Debbie's appeal to the law to provide a remedy for her uncertainty stems from her lack of trust in her doctor's ability to prevent or ameliorate just such a diminishment of self. As philosopher Onora O'Neill (2002: 17) emphasises, while an increase in patient autonomy (often consumer choice by another name) has challenged the asymmetrical relations of knowledge and power which historically defined the doctor–patient relationship, transforming the patient from a grateful supplicant into a wary consumer, it has also resulted in a loss of trust. This has been exacerbated, O'Neill argues, by a culture of blame and accusation which is widespread both in the media and in the literature of campaigning organisations. A loss of trust in professionals, when combined with a pervasive rights rhetoric, results in a culture in which, according to O'Neill (2002: 10), 'incoherent demands' like a 'right to health' can gain political traction. Given that no human action can secure health for all, she argues that there can be no obligation to meet that demand. Many who oppose a 'right to die' might similarly argue that it is an 'incoherent demand' because there can be no obligation for doctors to bring about the kind of death the individual chooses. As Mason and Laurie (2006: 7) stress, the doctor, as the administrator of the lethal drugs, is also himself a moral agent and might be affected by the task. As already established, Debbie's rights claims stem not only from a loss of trust in her doctors, but also from a sense in which she may suffer in a way which is beyond the scope of medicine to remedy. Because there is no cure for her bodily deterioration, doctors cannot give her confidence in her future. By seeking a 'right' to die, she is appealing to the law to provide that certainty and to offer the implicit recognition that there are certain types of illnesses that can result in certain types of suffering and diminishment of self, which medicine cannot ameliorate.

The unpredictability of the progressive symptoms of her disease was causing Debbie ontological insecurity (Giddens 1990; Richards and Rotter 2013). As Toombs (1995: 20) points out, for people with progressive disability, time may be disturbed in that the future, rather than the present, assumes overriding significance. Yet the future also becomes inherently problematic because of its unknown aspect. There is a lot of uncertainty in Debbie's approach to her future, but she wants the law to help her keep her options open. One gets a sense of her uneasy relationship with her future when she writes in her autobiography: 'I want to know where I stand, so I don't have to decide now about what may happen in the future' (2010: 280).

The desire for ontological security is also evident in Debbie's recounting of her life story for the media and the subsequent publication of her autobiography. These can be theorised as a way of trying to establish narrative control over the events of her life. The construction of such narratives creates the 'necessary illusions' by which people imagine that their actions and words make a difference in determining the shape of their lives (Jackson 2002: 14). In Debbie's own words, her legal battle has given, and continues to give, her life purpose, now that she has become a recognisable public figure who is called upon to comment on other right-to-die cases that make the headlines. The 'clarity' she wanted to bring to the law has actually brought clarity to her own biographical narrative, particularly her biography-in-illness, at a time when the progression of her MS was depriving her of bodily and ontological security. Her high-profile litigation and the media spectacle which surrounded it has also given her dying (when it eventually happens) an extraordinary aesthetic. It could be argued that it is in the media that Debbie's protracted dying has been recognised in its specificity, not in the court with its focus on the 'technocratic rationalities of law' (Riles 2000: 59) and where the specificities of each case must be downplayed in order to give precedence to general principles of law (Good 2008: S50–51). It is the media which challenges the so-called public absence of death (Walter et al. 1995) by granting extensive coverage to extraordinary deaths such as Debbie's.

THE JUDGEMENT

Debbie Purdy and Omar Puente's request for clarification from the DPP was refused at the Judicial Review in June 2008 and at the Appeal hearing (which I observed) in February 2009. However, in July 2009, five Law Lords in the House of Lords, the highest court in the UK,[9] ruled unanimously in the couple's favour and ordered the DPP to produce a crime-specific policy identifying the factors he was likely to take into account in deciding whether or not to consent to prosecuting a suicide assistor. Debbie and Omar appeared jubilant outside the House of Lords on the day of the verdict. Standing alongside their lawyers and the Chief Executive of Dignity in Dying, Debbie and Omar smiled and kissed each other affectionately for the assembled press photographers. The legal ruling was the leading story on every TV news channel, and the couple appeared on the front cover of every newspaper in the country. Headlines focused on Debbie's point, which I cited earlier, that she was not demanding a 'right-to-die' so much as a 'right-to-live-longer': 'This has given me my life back';[10] 'I feel like I have my life back' – Right-to-die victory for Purdy;[11] and 'We've got our lives back' – Debbie Purdy Triumphant'.[12] The five Law Lords determined, in the end, that the law needed to give citizens clarity, and that, in this instance, clarity was unjustifiably lacking. Their sympathies clearly rested with Debbie and Omar: 'It cannot be doubted that a sensible and clear policy document would be of great legal and practical value, as well as being...of some moral and emotional comfort to Ms Purdy and others in a similar tragic situation' (Lord Neuberger para 101).

The recognition shown here for the law's role in giving 'moral and emotional comfort' seems to contradict the usual association of the law with dispassionate, objective rationality. Nussbaum (2004: 5, 54) argues that while some would like to regard the law as entirely separate from emotions, in reality it ubiquitously takes account of people's emotional states, and the judge's (or jury's) compassion is constantly solicited. In statements such as this, the judges formally acknowledged Debbie's suffering and recognised the law's role in offering her some certainty over the legality or otherwise of possible future actions.

Following the Law Lords' final decision, in September 2009, the DPP produced his 'interim guidance',[13] accompanied by a call for public participation in a 12-week consultation exercise. In the interim guidance, the DPP stated that factors against a prosecution included: the 'victim had a clear, settled, and informed wish to commit suicide'; the 'victim had: a terminal illness; a severe and incurable physical disability; or a severe degenerative physical condition'; and the person suspected of assisting in the suicide was a 'spouse, partner, or a close personal friend' who was 'wholly motivated by compassion'. He made no reference to assistance being received from a medical professional.

Nearly 5000 responses were received from the public and the DPP's final 'Policy for Prosecutors in Respect of Cases of Encouraging or Assisting Suicide' was published in February 2010. Issues raised by respondents in the public consultation resulted in a fundamental shift of emphasis from the interim policy. Most significantly, all mention of the physical condition of the person being assisted to die was removed. The relationship between the assistor and the person being assisted was also removed. An important added factor which tended in favour of prosecution was whether the assistor was a medical doctor, nurse or other healthcare provider. These changes are all significant in terms of how they relate more broadly to some of the central conflicts within the assisted suicide debate. Before I move to discuss these conflicts, it should be noted that the existence of a policy of this nature is seen as moving the UK a step closer to effectively decriminalising a non-medicalised form of assisted suicide. It removes the risk of prosecution, albeit within carefully defined parameters, for those assisting loved ones to die both at Dignitas *and* in the UK. Figures released 18 months after the publication of the policy showed that 30 suspected assistors had not been prosecuted (O'Dowd 2011). However, the policy has not quelled the concerns or intense lobbying efforts of either proponents or opponents of assisted suicide. While proponents continue to fight for a formal legal right to a medically hastened death, the most recent manifestation of which is Lord Faulkner's *Assisted Dying Bill* 2014–2015, opponents continue to demand that the lives of those with a terminal illness or a severe, degenerative or, incurable physical disability are protected.

THE POLICY – ASSISTED SUICIDE DE-MEDICALISED AND DECRIMINALISED?

The removal from the policy document of any mention of the physical condition of the person who had taken or attempted to take their own life was a significant victory for those who oppose a change in the law on assisted dying. Their concern centred on the idea that positing a physical condition as a 'reasonable' motive for a person wanting to take their own life effectively sent a powerful symbolic statement that life with such a physical disability, whether terminal or severe and incurable, is of a lower quality. By identifying a certain category of person in this way, it is argued that an implicit judgement is made about whole groups of people who are living with severe and incurable illness and disability. As Asch (2001: 302) writes, the cultural emphasis on self-sufficiency leads people to doubt that anyone who cannot execute 'normal' life tasks like eating, walking or managing personal hygiene could enjoy life as much as someone who performs these tasks without assistance.

This is what the Italian philosopher Agamben (1998) called 'bare life': a human life that is left exposed to death when it becomes separated from its normal political status and the protection of the law. Lock's (2002) analysis of organ transplantation in Japan and the USA drew attention to the way in which the law creates certain categories of persons in order to facilitate certain outcomes; in her example, the category of the 'brain dead' in order to facilitate the harvesting of organs. To stipulate in a policy document certain categories of ill or disabled persons who would 1) be more likely to *want* to commit suicide and 2) whose assistors would be less likely to be held criminally accountable, would not just facilitate an outcome of leniency to people in Omar's situation but would also, according to opponents' arguments, send a strong message that certain categories of persons were less worthy of protection

227

by the state. This would likely exacerbate the fears of those currently living with severe illness and disability who had no desire whatsoever to hasten their own death.

An alternative view is that certain physical conditions, specifically terminal or degenerative diseases, can result in bodily and existential suffering, the experience and continuation of which some people can feel is 'unbearable' to them. To be officially diagnosed with a known illness which has severe symptoms is recognised by the majority of people (if social attitudes polling is accurate) as being a reason someone might want to hasten their death. Haussman's (2004) discourse analysis of press coverage of assisted dying found that illness was nearly always seen as a decisive factor in justifying a sympathetic response to assisting someone's suicide: 'Whereas this sympathy cannot be openly expressed by stating categorically that "serious illness is enough to justify the killing of people", it can be argued that this same sentiment is expressed more subtly by making extensive reference to the poor health of the patient' (Haussman 2004: 215).

Indeed, a medical diagnosis is a fundamental requirement made of those wishing to die at Dignitas. This is because it is seen to legitimise someone's request to die. However, there is an important qualifier which those advocating for a right-to-die say undermines opponents' arguments that whole categories of persons are assumed to be living 'potentially worthless lives' (Greasley 2010: 324). This qualifier is that the medical diagnosis and the statement that a person is 'suffering unbearably' are necessary but not sufficient conditions for warranting help to die. What is of overriding concern is that a 'considered and persistent request'[14] is made by individuals themselves. To those who support a change of the law, the need for a voluntary request demonstrates that to legalise hastened death would not result in whole categories of persons being implicitly judged, but would instead show respect for the autonomy of someone who, by their own subjective determination, had judged their own suffering to be 'unbearable'.

Here we return to the thorny issue of autonomy. As already described in this chapter, the inter-subjective aspect of people's end-of-life decisions is often obscured by right-to-die rhetoric and its focus on individual autonomy. Debbie may see her death decision as hers alone to make, but how she experiences her suffering on a daily basis is dependent on the care and support she receives from Omar. Biggs (1998) has interrogated this inter-subjective/inter-corporeal aspect from a feminist perspective. She argues that it is no surprise that the loudest voices demanding legal reform belong to women like Dianne and Debbie. She relates this to the gendered nature of care in society as a whole (Young and Cullen 1996), and the fact that women's perceptions and tolerances of their own illnesses and infirmities are inescapably coloured by their role as carer. Many women feel concerned at the prospect of becoming the cared-for rather than the carer, and this makes them feel particularly vulnerable (Biggs 1998: 294). Similarly, Arber et al. (2008) found that older women were twice as likely as older men to refuse life-prolonging medical technologies, which they attributed to women's greater life course involvement in caring and empathising with the wishes and concerns of others.

It is such inter-subjective evaluative judgements which made the DPP's job of producing a codified response very difficult. In trying to write a policy document which was not encumbered by the rhetoric of either 'side' in the debate, the DPP decided, on balance, to omit all reference to the physical condition of the person taking their own life. He tried to depoliticise the policy-making process while the campaigners tried to use it as a forum for political action. As a result of his attempts to defuse tensions and limit the scope of his policy, the DPP now has a document that emphasises the compassionate motivation of the assistor, but makes no mention of the motivation of the person who wants to take their own life. Some have argued that 'this makes the basis upon which the assistor is expected to feel compassion rather unfathomable' (Biggs 2011: 86).

The second 'factor' which appeared in the DPP's interim guidance and disappeared in the final policy was that of the relationship between the person taking their own life and the person helping them. Being a spouse, partner or a close friend of the person requesting help was not included as a mitigating factor in the final version of the policy, due to the fact that some relatives might be manipulative. However, while the DPP may have been persuaded that this was not a relevant factor, the media coverage of Debbie and Omar's case suggests that it was deemed to be relevant by journalists and by the wider public. Their relationship also seemed to be of significance to the judges in the Court of Appeal who described Omar's potential assistance with her suicide as a 'final act of devotion' and 'the culmination of a lifelong loving relationship' motivated by 'raw compassion and devoted love' (Para 7, 10). In the final House of Lords ruling, their relationship continued to be viewed as significant: 'the difficult and tragic cases where a loving relative assists a person' (Lord Neuberger, para 97). And later: 'the offender will often be a relatively reluctant participator, and will often be motivated solely by love and/or sympathy' (Lord Neuberger, para 102).

The involvement of relatives or 'compassionate friends' in techniques of hastening death is a form of de-medicalised assisted suicide. For many commentators, modern death became over-medicalised in the twentieth century. Illich (1977) was possibly the most scathing critic, declaring the medical profession to be a 'disabling profession' destroying our will to self-care. Howarth and Leaman (2001: 411) refer to de-medicalisation as 'the point at which the medicalisation of social life is turned back, or reversed.' For Ost (2010), the involvement of relatives in assisted suicides might result in a better death than were it to be a wholly medicalised procedure. Ost gives the following reasons for this: that a less medicalised and less clinical procedure would produce 'a less tense affair'; that it might reassure the person concerned that their relatives approve of their decision; and that they will benefit from the emotional support that their relatives provide (2010: 507). It is clear from her reasoning that Ost, like Lord Neuberger, assumes the involvement of a beneficent spouse or relative, which the DPP decided was not an assumption which was likely to reassure the public or properly safeguard 'vulnerable' individuals. As one lawyer I interviewed said, 'There is often a misconception that families actually like each other.'

The third factor which was not part of the DPP's interim guidance but featured in the final policy and which tended in favour of prosecution was if the assistor was 'acting in his or her capacity as a medical doctor, nurse, or other healthcare professional'. Again, this points to the 'de-medicalised' notion of assistance to which the policy relates. Medicalised forms of assisted dying inspire three predominant fears among those who oppose any change in the law. The first of these fears relates to what is generally known as the 'slippery slope' (or what philosophers term 'consequentialist' arguments), which is the idea that once the *principle* of intentional killing has been revoked, there can be no future principled opposition to an extension of the law to incorporate other categories of persons who may reasonably be entitled to enlist help to die. The second fear is that hidden pressures will come to be applied to elderly, frail or otherwise 'vulnerable' people who may be made to feel a 'burden' by others, particularly their relatives, and so avail themselves of the law to satisfy others. Thirdly, there is a fear that legalising medical assistance to die would result in an irreversible change in the medical profession's ethics and code of practice. For all of these reasons, there continues to be vociferous opposition from a number of parties (not all religious) to a medicalised form of assisted death. The majority of British doctors, for example, do not support assisted suicide, opposition being particularly strong among palliative medicine specialists (Seale 2009). The DPP's inclusion of a list of healthcare professionals in his 'reasons in favour of prosecution' shows his desire to differentiate a version of non-medicalised assistance with suicide, which encompasses those travelling to Dignitas from medically assisted suicide which remains illegal. In 2014, the new DPP amended the policy yet again. This time it was to clarify that healthcare professionals would only face a greater chance than others of being prosecuted if it was shown they had a duty of professional care to the 'victim', rather than the fact of their professional identity per se. For example, family carers who happen to be healthcare professionals but who want to assist a loved one to die are not exposed to greater risk of prosecution, neither are retired British doctors who write medical reports for people applying to die with Swiss right-to-die organisations.

The central paradox of the assisted suicide debate is that while, on the one hand, advocates reject the professionalisation and overmedicalisation of dying and advocate giving 'choice' to patients about how and when they want to die, on the other hand, they are demanding a medicalised form of assisted suicide whereby it is doctors who would decide who qualifies under any act of parliament and doctors who would supervise the process. A palliative care physician told me that campaigners' insistence on an entitlement or 'right' to a hastened death assumes that this 'translates into some kind of obligation for other people to do it...which is bizarre!' Certainly there are some pro-campaigners who would like to follow the Swiss model and take the procedure out of the hands of doctors entirely. However, the more mainstream pro-lobbyists would prefer to retain the involvement of the medical profession. One of the most obvious reasons for this is that they are the main gatekeepers of the medications which are required (Lewis 2007: 130). Another reason, I would argue, is that doctors' involvement imbues that decision or that act with greater legitimacy than receiving help from a relative, friend or Dignitas volunteer. Assisted dying campaigners like Debbie Purdy seem caught up in both rejecting professional determination over their lives and wanting the legitimacy that an official medical diagnosis or legal judgement brings. Professionals have a special position in the political economy and however society may try to rationalise their services, professional ideology is suffused with a 'transcendent value' (Friedson 2001: 122) that people want conferred upon their decisions. The question is whether giving doctors the power to decide on someone's 'bare life' (Agamben 1998) is actually in the interests of society as a whole, or whether it dangerously concentrates power in the hands of one profession.

CONCLUSION

The ultimate conclusion to the case study I have presented here will be Debbie's death. Whether she dies an 'artificial' death with the help of Dignitas, or a 'natural' death with or without the help of the pain-easing medications offered by palliative care professionals, her death undoubtedly will gain international media coverage and will be scrutinised by all of those who are invested in the debate for evidence of its 'goodness' or 'badness'. The more immediate outcome of her case which has significance beyond the life of one individual has been the publication of a policy document which for the first time gives the reasons why a person might not be prosecuted for assisting in someone's suicide. The existence of this policy marks a controversial shift in the social sanction of deliberate death in the UK. While it seems fair to assume that most people, regardless of whether they support assisted dying or not, would not want to see Debbie's husband Omar prosecuted for helping her to travel to Dignitas, there is still a concern, particularly among those who resist a change in the law, that the policy goes some way towards creating exceptions to the prohibition on killing. Those who, like Dianne Pretty and (possibly, at some future time) Debbie Purdy, might want to be classified as 'exceptions' to that prohibition, argue that the law is not protecting them but rather abandoning them to the vagaries of their diseases and to the suffering those diseases cause. For Dianne, it was as if she was being 'made to live' (Foucault 2003: 241) by a state which had taken away her human rights. The law had failed to provide a remedy for her suffering. Defenders of the status quo, however, argue that if the state were to enable these women and other people with similarly incurable illnesses to die with the help of a doctor it would create a dangerous exception to the prohibition on killing and thereby expose people to being designated what Agamben terms 'bare life' or 'life which ceases to have any juridical value and can, therefore, be killed without the commission of homicide' (Agamben 1998: 139). While the DPP's policy does not apply to so-called 'mercy killings', where the would-be helper actually takes the person's life, this provision is barely enough to stem the rising fears of an opposition concerned about the unintended or unforeseen effects of creating such a legal exception.

In the common law system, once an exception is made, that exception establishes a precedent, which can then ground the logic to establish further exceptions: 'the ends of one analytical practice become the means of the next' (Riles 2004: 783). This can be considered the legal 'slippery slope' which so concerns those campaigning against a change in the law. Two successive legal challenges have since been brought in order to apply further pressure on the law and exploit the exceptions exposed by Debbie Purdy's successful appeal: that of Tony Nicklinson[15] and a subsequent appeal brought by his widow, Jane Nicklinson, and two others, Paul Lamb and a man named only as 'Martin' (Richards 2014).[16] Effectively, Debbie's lawyers and the campaigners who instructed them used the law instrumentally to force the development of a key policy document which the British parliamentary system had not seen fit to create. The charge laid against this type of activism is that assisted dying is in danger of being legalised 'by the back door',[17] and that the judiciary is overstepping its role.

The ruling in Debbie Purdy's case provided some remedy for the uncertainty about Omar's possible treatment by the state following his (potential) journey to Switzerland and, according to Debbie, has extended her life in that she no longer feels the need to travel to Switzerland before she is ready or before her suffering has become 'unbearable'. However, the existence of the policy has not totally removed uncertainty about Omar's possible prosecution or provided a remedy for the uncertainty about how Debbie's disease will progress. Neither the court nor medical science can cure her disease, predict her future suffering or determine how long she will live. While the lawyers in the courtroom spent only a short amount of time outlining the bare facts of Debbie and Omar's dilemma before moving to debate the general points of law arising from the case, the media obliged the couple with air time and column inches in order to tell the specifics of their story. Debbie's autobiography, published presumably on the strength of her legal victory, gives her further opportunity to provide a detailed account of her life, including her life-in-illness and her fears about the future. Debbie was then a public figure, an ordinary person whose death planning or death-in-waiting has made for an extraordinary spectacle. Disputing Aries's view that modern death 'no longer makes a sign' (Aries 1985: 266), Walter et al. (1995: 593) have argued that the mass media is where death makes its sign, and does so in a more public and accessible way than the medical discourses of death. The instrumental use of both the law and the media in Debbie's case gave a platform to those trying to apply pressure on the government to change the law on assisted dying. Her legal victory and the opinions of the judges validated her account of her suffering, while the official written policy made public an 'implicit legitimisation' of her option to go to Dignitas (Greasley 2010: 325). Debbie's successful legal case has provided further impetus to the pro-campaigners to bring more test cases to the courts and has helped them to apply political pressure on the lawmakers in London. As long as people continue to opt for the services of Dignitas, and these journeys are reported in the media, the public will be reminded that there are certain types of suffering which lie beyond the scope of the medical profession to ameliorate.

POSTSCRIPT

In December 2014, it was widely reported in the British media that Debbie Purdy had died as a result of refusing food and fluid at a hospice in the north of England. In a 'final article' published in *The Independent on Sunday* in January 2015, reportedly penned by Debbie herself before her death, she describes how life since 2012 had become 'unbearable' to her, following a worsening in her MS. She wrote that both she and Omar were concerned, despite the CPS policy, that Omar might still be prosecuted if he helped her to travel to Switzerland, due to the fact that 'Omar is black'. She therefore determined to end her own life without assistance, by refusing food and fluid.

NOTES

1 Amended in 2009 by the Coroners and Justice Act
2 Simon Gillespie, Chief Executive of the Multiple Sclerosis Society, in evidence to the Commission on Assisted Dying 23 March 2011, available online at www.commissiononassisteddying.co.uk/wp-content/uploads/2011/04/Simon-Gillespie-Transcript.pdf
3 This term is from the Dutch *Termination of Life on Request and Assisted Suicide (Review Procedures) Act 2002* and was also used in the UK's *Assisted Dying for the Terminally Ill Bill.*
4 It is useful to mention terminological distinctions here. Dignity in Dying draws a distinction between 'assisted dying', defined as assisting a terminally ill, mentally competent adult to shorten the dying process at their

request, and 'assisted suicide', where the person asking for help is chronically, but not terminally ill (Wootton 2010). While this terminological distinction is not widely adhered to by those in the right-to-die movement, I regard it as a useful distinction to make and so have conformed to this terminology throughout the chapter.

5 Section 2(1) of the Suicide Act was amended by the Coroners and Justice Act 2009. The language was updated from 'aid, abet, counsel or procure the suicide of another' to 'encourage or assist', but the criminal offence remains the same.

6 Article 8: 1) Everyone has the right to respect for his private and family life, his home and his correspondence. 2) There shall be no interference by a public authority with the exercise of this right except such as is in accordance with the law and is necessary in a democratic society in the interests of national security, public safety or the economic well-being of the country, for the prevention of disorder or crime, for the protection of health or morals, or for the protection of the rights and freedoms of others.

7 The case involved a 68 year old man with paranoid schizophrenia who had developed gangrene in a foot while serving a prison term. Despite being told he had only a 15% chance of survival if his lower leg was not amputated, the man refused the operation saying he preferred to die with two feet than to live with one. The hospital questioned his capacity to exercise his autonomy in this matter, but the court held that although his general capacity to make decisions was impaired by his schizophrenia, he understood the 'nature, purpose and effects' of the treatment being refused and so was within his rights (Mason and Laurie 2006: 375).

8 Ms B was paralysed from the neck down and her life was sustained only by a ventilator. She requested that the ventilator keeping her alive be switched off. The dilemma for the doctors was whether she had legal capacity to make such a decision. After conflicting psychiatric reports about her mental capacity, her case went to court and the judge presiding attended Ms B's bedside to hear her story and assess her mental capacity in person. Ms B was found competent to make the decision and the ventilator was switched off. As a symbolic gesture, notional damages of £100 were awarded in recognition of the technical assault that the health carers had committed by continuing to treat Ms B against her wishes (Mason and Laurie 2006: 377).

9 It has now been superseded by the Supreme Court.

10 *The Daily Mail*, 31 July 2009.

11 *The Guardian*, 31 July 2009.

12 *The Independent*, 31 July 2009.

13 www.cps.gov.uk/consultations/as_policy.html

14 This was the phrase used in the House of Lords *Assisted Dying for the Terminally Ill Bill*.

15 In 2012, Tony Nicklinson, who was paralysed from the neck down and unable to speak following a stroke, sought a declaration from the courts that it would not be unlawful, on the grounds of necessity, for a doctor to assist in the termination of his life. Mr Nicklinson was represented by the same lawyers as Debbie Purdy, and, as in her case, they also appealed to

Article 8 of the ECHR (respect for private life). Mr Nicklinson lost his case and died of pneumonia six days later after refusing food and fluids.

16 In 2013, Jane Nicklinson (Tony Nicklinson's widow); Paul Lamb, who is paralysed from the neck down following a car accident; and a man named only as 'Martin', who has locked-in syndrome, appealed the decision of the High Court in *Re Nicklinson (on the application of) v Ministry Of Justice [2012]*.

17 Richard Hawkes, Chief Executive of Scope, in 'People who assist suicide will face test of motives, says DPP', *The Guardian*, 25 February 2010.

REFERENCES

Agamben, G. 1998. *Homo Sacer: Sovereign Power and Bare Life*. Stanford, California: Stanford University Press

Arber, A., Vandrevala, T., Daly T. and Hampson S. 2008. 'Understanding Gender Differences in Older People's Attitudes Towards Life-prolonging Medical Technologies', *Journal of Aging Studies* 22: 366–375

Aries, P. 1985. *Images of Man and Death*. Cambridge: Harvard University Press

Asch, A. 2001. 'Disability, Bioethics, and Human Rights', in Albrecht, G. L., Seelman, K. D. and Bury, M. (eds.), *The Handbook of Disability Studies*. London: Sage

Beckford M. 2012. '14% rise in British members of Dignitas', *Daily Telegraph*, 23 January 2012

Berlin, I. 2006 [1958]. 'Two Concepts of Liberty', in Goodin, R. and Pettit, P. (eds.) *Contemporary Political Philosophy: An Anthology (2nd Edition)*. Oxford: Blackwell Publishing

Biggs, H. 2011. 'Legitimate Compassion or Compassionate Legitimation? Reflections on the Policy for Prosecutors in Respect of Cases of Encouraging or Assisting Suicide', *Feminist Legal Studies* 19: 83–91

1998. 'I Don't Want to Be a Burden! A Feminist Reflects on Women's Experiences of Death and Dying', in Sheldon, S. and Thomson, M. (eds.), *Feminist Perspectives on Health Care Law*. London: Cavendish Publishing Ltd

Bloch, M. and Parry, J. 1999. 'Introduction'. In Bloch, M. and Parry, J. *Death and the Regeneration of Life*. Cambridge: Cambridge University Press

Butler, J. 2004. *Precarious Life: the Powers of Mourning and Violence*. New York: Verso

Compston, A. and Coles, A. 2008. 'Multiple Sclerosis', *Lancet* 372 (9648): 1502–17

Douzinas, C. 2000. *The End of Human Rights: Critical Legal Thought at the Turn of the Century*. London: Hart Publishing

Foucault, M. 2003. *Society Must Be Defended: Lectures at the College de France, 1975–76*. Trans. D. Macey. New York: Picador

Freidson, E. 2001. *Professionalism: The Third Logic*. Oxford: Polity Press

Giddens, A. 1990. *The Consequences of Modernity*. Stanford, C. A.: Stanford University Press

Glendon, M. 1991. *Rights Talk: The Impoverishment of Political Discourse*. New York; London: Free Press

Good, A. 2008. 'Cultural Evidence in Courts of Law', *Journal of the Royal Anthropological Institute* (N.S.), S47–S60

Greasley, K. 2010. 'R(Purdy) v DPP and the Case for Wilful Blindness', *Oxford Journal of Legal Studies*, 30(2): 301–2

Hall, A. 2009. 'Cashing in on Despair? Suicide Clinic Dignitas is a Profit Obsessed Killing Machine, Claims Ex-worker' 25 January 2009. Available at: www.dailymail.co.uk/news/article-1127413/Cashing-despair-Suicide-clinic-Dignitas-profit-obsessed-killing-machine-claims-ex-worker.html

Haussman, E. 2004. 'How Press Discourse Justifies Euthanasia', *Mortality* 9(3): 206–222

Howarth, G. and Leaman, O. 2001. *Encyclopaedia of Death and Dying*. London: Taylor Francis

Illich, I. 1977. *Limits to Medicine: Medical Nemesis; the Expropriation of Health*. Harmondsworth: Penguin

Jackson, M. 2002. *The politics of storytelling: Violence, Transgression, and Inter-subjectivity*. Copenhagen: Museum Tusculanum Press, University of Copenhagen

Lawton, J. 2000. *The Dying Process: Patients' Experiences of Palliative Care*. London: Routledge

Lewis, P. 2007. *Assisted Dying and Legal Change*. Oxford: Oxford University Press

Lock, M. 2002. *Twice Dead: Organ Transplantation and the Reinvention of Death*. London: University of California Press

Maddocks, I. 1996. 'Hope in Dying: Palliative Care and a Good Death', in Morgan, J. (ed.), *An Easeful Death? Perspectives on Death, Dying and Euthanasia*. Sydney: Federation Press

Marcus, G. 1998. *Ethnography Through Thick and Thin*. Princeton, NJ: Princeton University Press

Mason, J. K. and Laurie, G. T. 2006. *Mason and McCall Smith's Law and Medical Ethics 7th Edition*. Oxford: Oxford University Press

Mill, J. S. 2006[1859]. *On Liberty and the Subjection of Women*. Oxford: J. Currey

Nussbaum, M. 2004. *Hiding from Humanity: Disgust, Shame, and the Law*. Princeton, Oxford: Princeton University Press

O'Dowd, A. 2011. 'Prosecutors Have Taken no Action over Cases of Suspected Assisted Suicide since New Guidance was Issued', *British Medical Journal* 2011: 343

O'Neill, O. 2002. *Autonomy and Trust in Bioethics*. Cambridge: Cambridge University Press

Ost, S. 2010. 'The De-medicalisation of Assisted Dying: is a Less Medicalised Model the Way Forward?' *Medical Law Review*, 18, Winter: 497–540

Purdy, D. 2010. *It's Not Because I Want to Die*. London: Harper Collins

Richards, N. 2014. 'The Death of Right-to-die Campaigners', *Anthropology Today* 30(3):14–17

Richards, N. and Rotter, R. 2013. 'Desperately Seeking Certainty? The Case of Asylum Applicants and People Planning an Assisted Suicide in Switzerland', *Sociological Research Online* 18(4), 26

Riles, A. 2006. 'Anthropology, Human Rights, and Legal Knowledge: Culture in the Iron Cage.' *American Anthropologist* 108(1): 52–65

2004. 'Property as Knowledge: Means and Ends', *Journal of the Royal Anthropological Institute* 10(4): 775–795

Seale, C. 2009. 'Legalisation of Euthanasia or Physician-assisted Suicide: Survey of Doctors' Attitudes', *Palliative Medicine* 23(3): 205–212

Seale, C. and van der Geest, S. 2004. 'Good and Bad Death: Introduction', *Social Science and Medicine* 58(5): 883–885

Strathern, M. 2005. *Kinship, Law, and the Unexpected: Relatives are Always a Surprise*. Cambridge: Cambridge University Press

Toombs, S. K. 1995. 'The Lived Experience of Disability', *Human Studies* 18: 9–23

Walter, T. 1994. *The Revival of Death*. London: Routledge

Walter, T., Littlewood, J. and Pickering, M. 1995. 'Death in the Media: The Public Invigilation of Private Emotion', *Sociology* 29: 579–596

Williams, A. 2007. 'Human Rights and Law: Between Sufferance and Insufferability', *Law Quarterly Review* 122:132–157

Weathers, H. 2011. 'Dignified? It Was Like an Execution Chamber': Verdict of Loving Daughter Who Took her Mother to Die at Dignitas'. *The Daily Mail*, 18 June 2011. Available at: www.dailymail.co.uk/femail/article-2004980/Euthanasia-Verdict-loving-daughter-took-mother-die-Dignitas.html

Wootton, S. 2010. 'Only Clearer Laws Can Bring Compassion to the Euthanasia Debate', *Letters to the Editor*, *The Independent*, 27 January 2010. Available at: www.independent.co.uk/voices/commentators/sarah-wootton-only-clearer-laws-can-bring-compassion-to-the-euthanasia-debate-1879-738.html

Young, M. and Cullen, L. 1996. *A Good Death. Conversations with East Londoners*. London: Routledge

CHAPTER TEN

REHABILITATION OF PAEDOPHILES AT THE INTERSECTION OF LAW AND THERAPY

John Borneman

Rehabilitation is the official goal of the German penal system. As stated in the Criminal Legal Code, amended on 16 March 1976, rehabilitation aims 'to enable prisoners to live in the future a life of social responsibility without illegalities; it should also serve to protect the general public from further criminal acts'. In pursuit of these ends, a 2002 federal law (which went into effect on 1 January 2003) mandates that individuals sentenced for sexual abuse to more than two years of imprisonment have not only a duty but also a right to *Behandlung*, therapy/treatment.[1] Consequently, key to the rehabilitation of such offenders has become therapy, which is seen as the primary means for *die Aufarbeitung der Tat*, reckoning with the act or deed.

Among those categorised as sexual criminals, child sex offenders encounter an additional demand in their rehabilitation. To reckon with the act means also to find a mode of relating to, and modifying, a set of assumptions about psychological predispositions and sexual identifications that construct them as 'paedophiles'. In Foucauldian terms, the act risks making the offenders into a distinct 'sexual species' (Foucault 1978: 43).

Definitions of paedophiles include a wide variety of intentions and behaviours, which vary considerably by time and place, as well as by the speech community to which any person belongs. As a working

This research was supported by NSF grant # 0921817, and approved by the Senatsverwaltung für Justiz in Berlin, Germany. I would also like to thank Michaela Stiepl, Jürgen Lemke, Achim Perner, Irene Berkel, Sigrid Richter-Unger and Christoph Wulf for much help and vibrant intellectual exchanges.

definition, I will follow popular use and construe a paedophile to be an individual with any sexual interest in children. In contemporary European legal systems, the criminalisation of paedophiles is generally restricted to people who have sexually engaged children or youth, in most cases up to the age of 18. In Germany, the legal age of consent (the right to 'sexual self-determination') is 14, but 16 for youths to have sex with an individual over 21.

This chapter addresses not *whether* therapy is successful in the rehabilitation of paedophiles but *how* it can be and often is successful. That therapy can be successful has already been established by many scientifically controlled and comparative studies in English- and Germanspeaking countries, a point I elaborate below. The question of how therapy is successful is more readily addressed by ethnographic means: on-site participant observation in the process of transformation and rehabilitation that therapy intends to effect. I will draw from ethnographic research that took place primarily between August 2008 and August 2009, with follow-up research for three months in 2010. I worked in two sites. One was a minimum security, open prison (*offene Strafvollzug*) where I had access to the archives of the Berlin Senatsverwaltung für Justiz, and also to individuals who evaluate the security risks of prisoners. The other was Berlin's largest centre for child-focused therapy, Kind im Zentrum (KiZ), which treats abused children but in addition specialises in group therapy for child sex offenders, using an eclectic mix of systematic techniques, some Anglo-American inspired. The centre currently divides offenders into five groups – youth offenders (under age 17), young adult offenders (ages 17 to mid/late 20s), adult 'paedosexuals', adult incest abusers and mentally handicapped abusers.[2] My fieldwork included attending one session weekly of youth offenders and of incest abusers, and two weekly of paedosexuals.[3]

For society, successful treatment of child sex offenders tends to be equated solely with reduction of the risk of relapse. For the offender, a fully successful reckoning means that his (over 95% of all such offenders in the West are men) risk of repetition will be assessed as negligible or null, and that he will be released from prison after serving two-thirds of his sentence. A less than successful reckoning means that he will not only serve his full sentence, but perhaps be confined to a psychiatric clinic or indefinitely detained, or, if and when released, placed by the judge in charge of his case under '*Führungsaufsicht*' – extended, often quasi-secret, and perhaps indefinite probation and surveillance.

Increasingly today in the West, the sexual abuse of children is considered less a cultural transgression of a taboo than a human rights violation, the most stigmatic and shameful of acts, the worst of all possible crimes. Increased valuation of children, and a recent legal acknowledgement of their right of self-determination (*Selbstbestimmungsrecht*), contributes to the stigma attached to the abuser. For the public at large, however, there is a phantasmatic quality – captured in the phrase 'soul murder' popularised by Leonard Shengold (1991) – to the two most prominent categories of child abuse: incest and paedophilia (Godelier 2004; Laplanche 1989:126). Discovery of the act often becomes an immediate national or global event, as interlinked media chains obsessively report such acts, exaggerating their social significance in front-page articles of newspapers and magazines or in lead stories for television news (Berkel 2006). Especially since the late 1970s, child sexual abuse has become a central security issue in northern Europe and North America, rivalled as a phantasm only by the threat of 'Islamic terrorism'.

Both as phantasm and in practice, to rehabilitate sex offenders of this type poses a supreme challenge: how to reconcile the hope of transformation with the widespread assumption that in their abuse paedophiles are expressing a relatively fixed sexual orientation or preference – a 'paedosexual' core. If their desires are immutable, the therapeutic goal cannot be a transformation of desire or motivation but must be limited to cognitive-behavioural change alone. Public pressure for longer sentences and for preventive detention or restrictions on the movement of paedophiles is, then, buttressed by this general scepticism about the possibility of fundamental change in the nature of the self.[4]

In this climate of lay and expert opinion, the demands on therapists and legal professionals are much greater and paradoxical in the treatment of paedophiles than for all other criminal types. Any positive assessment of therapy or imprisonment that claims the success necessary for rehabilitation must be balanced against the risk of recidivism. One incorrect assessment can severely damage the reputation, if not end the career, of a therapist or judge or prison warden.

The demands of therapy on the paedophile are also great. The stigma attached to this act leads to cultivated concealment, lying and self-deception, which in turn encourage perverse forms of internalisation of the stigma. In therapy, offenders must work through the shame often attached to these perverse forms in order to transform that shame into guilt. Such a transformation would enable an assumption of responsibility for the act – considered an integral step toward successful rehabilitation. But to be effective in the eyes of the law, treatment must go further and also assure the public of non-repetition of the crime after release, which is difficult to assume based on an assessment of behavioural therapy alone. The most definitive way to speak to the insecurity and fear produced by paedophiles is to attest to what Betty Joseph (1989) called a 'psychic change' in the self. To move toward a changed self in a new relation to the child as object of desire, therapists must gain access to the unconscious of the adult offender, where much of the knowledge necessary for a transformation is stored.

THE EVIDENCE

Research is conclusive in suggesting we revise several commonplace prejudices about sexual criminals: they do not share the same etiology, most do not suffer from fixed perversions and treatment of sex offenders does in fact reduce the likelihood of repetition of the crime. Despite inherent problems in measuring the effectiveness of therapy for sex offenders, studies uniformly confirm that, regardless of the form used, therapy decreases the likelihood of recidivism (Ward et al. 2008; Mandeville-Norden and Beech 2004; Matson 2002). Research conducted in the 1980s in the UK comparing the effects of therapy (restricted to 'cognitive-behavioural') versus mere supervision began to find lower recidivism rates for treated offenders in both institution-based and community-based programmes (Marshall et al. 1991). With additional relapse prevention treatment, recidivism rates declined to less than 5% over the four years of follow-up study (Marshall et al. 1992; Marshall et al. 1993). In an analysis of 79 treatment outcome studies, comprising almost 11 000 offenders convicted for many different forms of sexual offending, Alexander (1999) found that that treatment lowered recidivism across type of offence, with the exception of adult rapists. Moreover, offenders enrolled in relapse prevention programmes were 10% less likely to reoffend than their untreated counterparts. In a general assessment of studies in different countries, Günter (2005: 68, 76, 77) claims that therapeutic and educational interventions have been shown to reduce the recidivism rate of sex offenders generally by up to 50%. Overall, recidivism rates for treated offenders declined in the 1990s, to below 11% for all categories of offender, except for rapists and child molesters who had abused boys.

It is impossible to know from these statistical studies whether these reductions mean a renunciation of sex altogether, a renunciation of specific kinds of interaction considered sexual or a change in sexual object choice. In any event, this chapter addresses the stronger claim that therapy effected psychic changes in the self and reoriented the understanding and expression of sexuality. There are, of course, many other factors that matter, each requiring a different line of explanation, such as whether the offender is related to the child, ages of offender and child, emotional maturity of the child or youth, cognitive and emotional capacities and erotic-cultural dispositions towards children (Beech 1998).

Since the 1950s, in Germany, the incidence of crimes of sexual violence has remained relatively constant if not in some cases decreased, while the classificatory categories of sexual crimes have changed radically (Dünkel 2005). Likewise, in the course of the 20th century, the category of abuse itself in the West generally has shifted from physical to sexual abuse, and the concern for prepubescent children has expanded to include youths up to the age of 18. As Ian Hacking writes, 'many unrelated kinds of harms to children [have been lumped] under one unreflective but powerful emblem' (Hacking 1991: 284–6). In Germany, specifically, a wave of decriminalisation after 1969, specifically of female prostitution and homosexuality, was followed, in 1998, by a lengthening of minimum penalties and a new criminalisation of specific sex acts involving abuse of power or status, which brought child sexual abuse to the fore among sex crimes.[5]

INCARCERATION AND THERAPY

Incarceration, or its threat, is in the register of law, and in some sense antithetical to therapy. In prison, paedophiles become 'Sexualstraftätern', 'Verurteilten' and 'Gefangenen' (sex offenders, the sentenced, prisoners). In therapy, they are called 'Klienten'; no longer registered as 'patients' of therapists, they receive a service for which they have responsibilities. The clients in group therapy include not only those who come from prison, either released for the purposes of the therapy session alone or attending therapy on the way back from a day job before returning to prison. They also include men who either have already served their prison sentences or attend therapy before their scheduled trial as a way to build a case to avoid imprisonment. Although legal and therapeutic experts prefer not to use the term 'forced therapy', group treatment contains both strong incentives and a strong element of coercion.

Important to note here is that the experience or anticipation of incarceration factors into the success of therapy. It arises as an issue in nearly every therapy session, as men learn from each other what to expect in prison life and how to be proactive in negotiating penalisation with both the Ministry of Justice (e.g. lawyers, public prosecutors, judges), which deals with sentencing and the conditions of parole, and the Ministry of the Interior (*Bundesministerium des Innern*, responsible for security, e.g. prison officials, security personnel, police), which deals with imprisonment and the mechanics of indefinite detention and parole. These two ministries generally work together, but they also frequently conflict as to the balance between the 'civil rights' of the accused and the 'protection of society' (specifically an ambiguous preventive detention). With respect to paedophiles and sexual criminals generally, this conflict plays itself out around the assessment of risk.

When judges are asked to revisit a case for the purposes of early release or parole, or receive a request from a state prosecutor for preventive detention, they often ask for a letter from the therapists about the success of treatment, or they even telephone the therapist. The same interactions occur, though less frequently, with prison officials. All therapists are very careful to assure their clients of confidentiality, and hence reticent to reveal in letters or phone conversations much about the content of the therapy. Most of the letters that I read are short and merely factual (e.g., x completed so many hours of therapy, between these dates, attendance was ir/regular, prognosis good/non-committal).

Judges, in turn, complain about the brevity and lack of detail in the letters, or tend to dismiss them altogether. Most rely solely on outside psychological *Gutachten* (evaluations) to inform or justify their decisions. Such outside evaluators are not obligated to any notion of confidentiality, and therefore often quite willing to make dire predictions about the future behaviour and sexual interests of the offenders. There is a noticeable trend in the decisions of judges toward mandating the serving of a full sentence, or minimally two-thirds.

In discussions of the effects of incarceration, most men in therapy who have already completed their prison sentences do not report the prison experience as merely wasted time.[6] In fact, they often say that it afforded them the opportunity to think through their pasts – having very little else to do – and to assess perhaps for the first time their own persons, including who they have become for others. This introspection is quite different from Irving Goffman's dramaturgical model of 'impression management' (Goffman 1959). Instrumental goals of trying to curry the favour of, or ingratiate themselves to, prison officials or to intimidate or impress fellow prisoners are of course never totally absent. And because some legal and prison professionals are concerned only with good behaviour while in prison and a prognosis for abstinence upon release, the incentive for prisoners to present themselves as 'good' is strong. The narrowing of relevant 'data' to impression management is also supported by a trend in prisons to hire professionals who employ models of behavioural-cognitive therapy, including pharmacological treatment (called 'chemical castration'), and no longer ask about unconscious factors motivating the offence.

However, the offenders I observed were less concerned with how to express themselves to others in prison and manage their appearance than with how to confront their own dissociation between self-images and the behaviours and desires they associate with their newly ascribed label of paedophile. Under the intense coercive pressure of psychiatrists and psychologists within the prison, and of other officials, they were most often, as I shall elaborate below, labouring both to deny the stigma of paedophilia and to arrive at an image of themselves that is somewhat coherent or consistent in its self-understandings and rationalisations.

TWO CASE STUDIES OF THERAPY

To understand how therapy facilitates psychic change, I will now compare the cases of two men I observed over the course of a year in two different groups. I'll restrict myself to description of the most relevant facts concerning changes in intrapsychic and interpersonal relations.

Konrad

Konrad is a man in his late 30s, a recovering alcoholic recently released from the special section for sexual abusers of a maximum-security prison in Berlin. After serving a six year sentence for two counts of aggravated sexual abuse of a 14 year old boy, he was released on probation, under police supervision (*Führungsaufsicht*), with the stipulation that he remain in therapy and take medicine to suppress his sex drive.

For the first nine months at KiZ, Konrad behaved as if this group therapy was his first encounter with treatment, even though he had years of experience at the maximum security prison. He seemed unprepared, even irritated, by the questions. He suffered from depression and appeared distracted and uninterested, which I attribute both to the drugs – selective serotonin reuptake inhibitors (SSRI) to suppress his sex drive and Zoloft for depression – and to his resistance to the 'talking cure' and to what he might gain by self-reflection.

In his first attempt to explain his delict to other members of the group, he claimed to remember nothing about the crime, including the decision of the judge. When asked what he knows for sure, his response: 'That I did something twenty-four hours ago and not now. Years have passed.' Through the first ten weeks, Konrad conditioned his responses so as to give the 'right' answer. He did not seem to invest anything of himself in therapy. He responded to all questions with simple adages: What is your explanation? 'That I was neglected.' Why did you drink so heavily? 'Because I needed it.' What are you going to use therapy for? 'That this doesn't happen again.' (*Das sowas nicht mehr vorkommt.*) How are you going to deal with your romantic desire for children? 'Who knows what life will bring?' (*Wer weiß was das Leben bringt?*) Do you approach others for sex? 'No.' Why? 'Because I fear I will relapse.' (*Ich habe Angst daß ich rückständig werde.*)

Konrad's resistance to becoming aware of what he had done and who he had become was enormous. He had painfully learned not to know certain things about himself, and, while his story is tragic, he never appeared particularly sympathetic to others in the group. He seemed virtually incapable of introspection of any depth, and therefore unable to empathise – what Heinz Kohut (1975: 352) calls 'vicarious introspection' – with either his victims or the other clients in the group. The therapists appeared unable to find a language to enable him to become more conscious of his past and of those around him.

Through about six months of therapy, I had no basis from which to assess the truth of Konrad's story of what he had done. My focus, instead, was in accounting for his inability or refusal to remember his deeds. If it were due to inability, then he was containing somewhere in his unconscious the material that he had deeply repressed and made unavailable to himself; if it were due to stubborn refusal, then he was repressing nothing but was merely unwilling to incriminate himself in front of the group.

In the fourth session, after a quite confusing recapitulation of his recent history, the therapists appeared perplexed when he began confusing the crime for which he had served his rather lengthy sentence with a previous delict. The first delict was for the seduction of a 12 year old boy in a summer camping place. It was the early 1990s. The Wall separating east and west had come down, and Konrad used the summers to do what had been denied to him as a German Democratic Republic (GDR) citizen: to travel in West Germany. The boy, Konrad said, visited him in his tent to drink and smoke, because his parents did not allow him to, and they also left him sitting alone while they went from tent to tent drinking the whole night. One morning the boy told his mother that Konrad forced him into sex. She called the police and brought charges. For this, Konrad received three years probation. The therapists asked him about his feelings on the morning after this first offence. He said that because he was so drunk and stoned, 'On the next day I remembered nothing about what happened.'

Konrad also claimed to not know that he had abused the 14 year old boy in the second offence, the crime for which he served his lengthy prison sentence. After that arrest, he was so depressed that he twice attempted suicide. That boy had been a neighbour in Konrad's home village, who Konrad had met at a Dunkin' Donuts in Berlin, where young male prostitutes hang out. After a few weeks, the boy showed up at Konrad's apartment in the village, moved in and came and went as he pleased.

Two years later, he moved out, unprecipitated by a fight or incident, with no explanation. He simply disappeared and never came back. After another two years passed, the boy, now age 18, brought charges. Konrad said he had been in love with him, but that he did not know until the trial that the boy had worked as a prostitute while living with him, nor, apparently, was he aware that the boy did not feel any love. At the trial, the boy insisted he had had sex with Konrad only because he needed a place to stay. Konrad countered that he had understood the boy's cohabitation, continuous visits, mutual affection and willingness to put up with his drinking, as a sign of love.

Given the low self-esteem in which Konrad held himself, one goal of the therapists was to enable him to identify with himself as someone other than the worthless person he had come to be identified as. Perhaps if he empathised with himself, rather than wallow in self-pity, he could begin to feel empathy for his victims also. To do this, however, he had to work through his own history of abuse and self-abuse. He did this in a singsong, whiny voice: his parents both drank heavily and beat him frequently. In his early 20s, he had two loves in his life, which he says were mutual. Both men were in their late 20s at the time, and both died of AIDS. Konrad cared for them as they were dying. It was in this period of care and grief that he became addicted to alcohol, he said, although he had always drunk, though not the entire day.

As for why he was now interested sexually in underage boys, Konrad adamantly refused to elaborate what it was about a boy that he found attractive. In response to questions about 'type' – innocent, hairless, lively, stocky, pretty face – Konrad had a standard response: 'I don't know.'

Konrad seemed extremely closed to both therapists for the first nine months. When he consistently refused to elaborate anything, the male therapist became more confrontative and challenging. When that elicited no response, he moved on and gave more time to the other clients. Meanwhile, the female therapist would show sympathy, despite Konrad's apparent withdrawal, but her efforts also brought about little engagement – until a session about ten months into the therapy. Konrad was elaborating the story of the death of one his adult male lovers, when he explained that his motivation after the death was to find a partner who, he said, 'will not die before me'.

This utterance, positing a link between his sexual desire for adolescent boys and his anxiety about death and separation, marked a turning point in therapy. It is not that these words took away his pain of loss and fears of abandonment, but they offered the group empirical and conceptual access to an integral part of Konrad's experience and facilitated emotional transference between him and others in the group. For the first time, others began to express empathy for Konrad that was believable to him, which, in turn, made him more confident in reflecting on his past relationships, as he felt others were actually interested in his fate. The goal of the therapists was not to locate the origin of his fear of being left behind with the death of his two lovers. Most likely his anxiety of aloneness emerged from his relations with negligent parents, or out of belonging to a social underclass in the former GDR, or from a feeling of social exclusion based on an early discovery of homosexual desire. Rather, for the therapists the point was that the loss of two intimate partners overwhelmed his ego and he found himself in a space of deadness. Their access to a particular emotional experience of loneliness enabled Konrad to enter the chain of associations and contexts to which his anxiety of abandonment was linked.

It is highly questionable whether Konrad's fear of abandonment could have ever been alleviated through the anxiety-relieving, psychotropic drugs he was taking without also dealing with the history of this affect of deadness. What is even more doubtful is whether he might ever re-cathect to a different love object, an adult man, and displace his sexual attraction from those 'who will not die before me', without first dealing with his fears of abandonment.

After this utterance, Konrad began to tell the group about distinctions he had deeply hidden from himself. Lacking language or words or friends to contain or take the place of his pain, he had turned to intoxication to anaesthetise himself from feeling. His own indulgence in extremely self-destructive behaviour might be understood as an attempt to kill something within himself. It showed a disregard for his own self. His attachment to underage boys was both an attempt to anaesthetise himself against having to lose or separate from someone he loved and an experience of aliveness. To enable him to bear the thought of loss, he had to feel empathically understood before he could develop an ability to empathically understand and invest in the world of others. The therapists had to grasp the suffering behind Konrad's offence and demonstrably empathise with his pain before they could work on the conditions that might prevent a repetition of the offence.

Even into the eleventh month of therapy at the centre, Konrad insisted on the correctness of his interpretation of events leading to his imprisonment. He doubted the boy's perception of abuse, and he doubted that the relationship existed only because he 'bought the sex'. He contended that the boy, along with two of his friends who testified as material witnesses, made the charges up. Hence, when it came time to submit to the group a letter of apology to the victim, Konrad hedged on showing any true empathy for the boy. Some of the clients in the group, who otherwise remained emotionally distant from Konrad and critical of his general unwillingness to talk, sympathised with his version of the story, as it remained consistent and entirely plausible. Although Konrad was clearly using his age and stable residence to seduce the apparently destitute boy, the boy already had some sexual experience with men, working as a prostitute. He also came and went as he pleased. His decision to live with Konrad and have sex with him was most likely not the result of Konrad's coercion but of accidental social circumstances outside the control of either of them.

Driven by questions from the therapists, the group also discussed the plausibility of the boy's account, since the recognition of abuse frequently occurs years after the event, especially among children, and the charges were filed only two years after the sex had ended. Konrad had indeed taken advantage of the boy's lack of other options at the time. Yet, it was difficult for other members of the group to assume that a 14 year old boy was not yet '*mündig*', mature enough to consent, although they acknowledged Konrad had violated the legal age of consent. Konrad's lack of empathy for the victim of his particular act of abuse did not, however, prevent him from seeing the wrongness of child sexual abuse and neglect. Slowly, Konrad began to show a general capacity for empathy that before had seemed entirely non-existent.

In the final two months of Konrad's therapy, he underwent a transformation that surprised other members of the group, including a client who had before shared several years with him in group therapy in the maximum-security prison. Encouraged to comment on how Konrad reacted to therapy back then, this client said Konrad had always been '*bockig*' (stubborn) in his relations with the therapists; he had changed very little until the final month. The therapist in the prison had been extremely impatient with him. She had focused solely on the delict – no work on biographies or empathy – and countenanced no evasion, he said, techniques which were quite effective with himself but that did not lead to any introspection by Konrad.

The sudden changes in Konrad coincided with success in obtaining an apartment for himself (he had been living in a group home), and then securing employment in a social service agency offering advice to underclass men like himself. He began to cut and wash his hair before coming to therapy, and suddenly shaved regularly. He no longer complained about fights with his sister or father, or bureaucratic obstacles he encountered as an ex-prisoner, or the difficulties of subsistence by support through Harz IV, the 2004 governmental welfare reform that severely curtailed social benefits for the poor. He no longer always avoided eye contact with the other men or therapists, and often cracked jokes, showing a cynical and irreverent Berlin humour. He reported joy at having and decorating his own apartment, and at serving coffee and cake, and cola, to his father and sister. When they asked him to talk about himself now, the therapists had to stop him from going on. He was proud of being free of his alcohol addiction, and expressed pleasure at his work, even though it was menial labour with menial pay and barely kept him subsisting. He even began talking concretely about what specifically might interest him in young men over 18.

Reinhard

In 2007, Reinhard was sentenced to two years and three months on probation for the sexual abuse of a 12 year old girl. The judge then asked for a psychiatric evaluation, which concluded that Reinhard was severely depressed, 'dangerous, with a chronic paedosexual orientation', and suffered from a 'personality disorder'. Instead of endorsing the psychiatrist's recommendation to send Reinhard to the psychiatric ward of Berlin's maximum-security prison, he instead followed the recommendation of a therapist from KiZ, with whom he had prior contact on another case, to send him to group therapy for child sexual abusers.

From the beginning of his therapy at KiZ in September 2008, Reinhard differed from most other clients in that he was consistent and clear about what he had done to the girl, whom he calls Olga, and about why it was a transgression of a social norm and abusive. It happened only once, over a weekend, three years before he was sentenced by the court. At the time of the abuse, he was doing well. 'I knew that it was a punishable crime *immediately* after I did it,' he says. On the way home after the night of the abuse, he took pills to numb himself, after which he was committed to psychiatric treatment. The treatment there was for his depression alone. Only several years later did Reinhard's abuse on that night come to light, leading to his arrest and conviction.

Reinhard has become wary of all therapy. In the late 1980s, in East Germany, he had been mistreated by psychiatrists while serving a sentence in Bautzen, where most political prisoners were kept, for the crime of '*Republikflucht*', attempt to escape the GDR. Whenever this or some similar topic came up in therapy, Reinhard would become extremely still, psychically and physically withdrawing into himself, as if he needed every last ounce of energy to survive that particular moment of thought. Only after nine months of group therapy was Reinhard able to talk of this experience. And only in his last month of therapy at KiZ was he able to talk about what he had a few months before revealed in individual therapy, that he had been raped many times at Bautzen, while the guards looked on, after which they sent him to the psychiatric division of the prison.

He is now 51 years old and works as a specialist in care for the handicapped and elderly. At the start of his therapy, the therapists asked him what he wants from the group? 'I see myself as a ghost, a paedophile, unlike others, unlike you,' he says, and adds, 'I want to say, I am not the person that the psychiatrist said I am.'

Reinhard spent most of his childhood in an orphanage for boys, from the age of seven to twenty. His parents had separated when he was six months old, and sent him to a home for infants. At six years old, he came out to live with his father, and his stepmother, who beat him and forced him to work for her. After a year, they sent him to the orphanage. 'The boy's home was the best time for me,' he explains, 'everything was structured, everything secure, but I didn't learn anything there, I didn't learn how you live outside the home.'

He was introduced to the child Olga by a friend he had met on a retreat to recover from drug addiction. This friend, who is extremely shy, is very attracted to obese women, and Olga's mother is obese. Reinhard agreed to seduce Olga's mother for him, although he was not attracted to her. Suddenly, Reinhard found himself regularly visiting and caring for a single mother with two kids: Olga, age ten at the time, and her brother, age 14.

The mother's obesity was such that physical movement was difficult, so she rarely left the apartment, and did very little even within it. The kids took advantage of her immobility and ignored her.

'At first the mother slept on the sofa, and I in her bedroom,' Reinhard says. 'She wanted me to stay over every night, so I would make breakfast in the morning, and she didn't have to do anything. Sometimes, if she had a guest, or wanted to stay up and watch television, she would say, you can sleep with Olga. So it became habitual, when I came, I'd sleep with Olga.' Olga soon became attached to him, and turned jealous whenever he directed attention to anyone else. She sent him love letters, and wanted to be with him all the time. Reinhard began thinking of somehow raising her so she would be with him permanently. 'What did Olga offer me?' he asks.

> It went on a long time without any sensual contact. I would lay on my back, and she on my belly. I was not aroused, it felt good. It was nice, it was tenderness. After about nine months it developed into affectionate contact. She tried to feel under my T-shirt, I said no. I enjoyed this. I thought she was really neat. Olga paid attention to me. She paid more attention to me than my partner at the time. I suffered an emotional deficit, and Olga was always there. All was going well in my job; I was working 12 hours a day, more than I wanted to, taking care of 17 to 80 year old handicapped people. I enjoyed it. I am the type who must always

be working. I can't just lay on the beach. When Olga did something wrong, I wanted only to look away, for example, when she stole from me, cigarettes or money. I didn't scold her; I kept quiet, consciously. Olga is not my type; I have always dated women. But at another level I was thinking that the reciprocity will come.

Nothing happened for several years. In this interim, his relationship with his partner went sour. She took over all responsibilities in the home, leaving him feeling useless. She even spent an entire weekend helping him clean the apartment of Olga's mother, which was filthy, and then warned him that Olga wanted something from him, that he should be careful. His self-esteem plummeted, however, as his partner clamoured for more love than he felt capable of giving. He became depressed and started drinking and taking pills. Then he noticed he could stroke Olga in other places, on her genitals also. How was she? 'She was very still,' he says. 'I thought that it pleased her. Now I know that this wasn't true.'

Immediately after Reinhard came out of the psychiatric institution, two years after the evening of abuse and self-abuse, he went back to visit Olga. 'She stood there, and she was afraid! I knew what was up, that she had probably told her brother. I thought, "what should I do now?" I stayed. Then her brother came out with a friend to talk with me. We smoked together. Olga had told him that this man and that man had fondled her.' Her brother asked him what she had told him about her past, but he refused to betray her confidence. 'He would have believed me [whatever I said]. I knew, as I stood there, that she [Olga] was calling the police. They came after an hour, arrested me, put me in handcuffs.'

Reinhard met Olga once more, after the sentencing, and she told him that everything pleased her 'to that point. As a mature adult man,' he explains, 'my thoughts were distorted. I thought I always wanted only the best for such families, but I wormed my way in. I chose socially weak families, and today I avoid this old group of friends, and have built a new circle.'

Shortly before concluding therapy, Reinhard began employment in training as an instructor in care-giving, with a specialisation in the care for invalids. In his final summary of his progress in therapy, he responded to the therapist's request to, once more, explain why he abused Olga,

> It satisfied my lust, which I now have under control. I allowed my lust to drive me, I turned off my interior laws in a wave of lust. Perhaps in

thirty years sex with a fourteen year old will be normal, as homosexuality is today. But the nature of affection and the boundary between affection and abuse is difficult to draw. [Olga and I] shared this, and at that moment you don't think about the act as criminal.

THERAPEUTIC INTERVENTION

I have chosen two quite different cases of therapy of child sex offenders to illustrate some of the key features that make such an intervention efficacious. Success entails changing the way the offender thinks about himself, changing the way he thinks about and with others, as well as a reassessment of what he has done (the wrongful sexual acts) as part of a reorientation to acceptable intimacy within the confines of legality. Psychic change is less a matter of correcting what psychologists call 'cognitive distortion' than of addressing the inexplicable affect that offenders attach to their relations to children or youth. For both Konrad and Reinhard the affect was disturbing precisely because they had deluded themselves as to what they were doing and therefore had no critical perspective from which to understand their own motivations, much less those of the youths they abused. They initially resisted therapy, fearing not cognition per se but that thinking the deed would empty the unconscious, outside of which, ultimately, might stand little more than that symbolic albatross 'paedophile', or what those who land in prison are called: *Kinderficker*.

In talking of affect, I rely on a strict and narrow definition offered in a 1916 essay by Sandor Ferenczi that,

> only such things (or ideas) are symbols in the sense of psychoanalysis as are invested in consciousness with a logically inexplicable and unfounded affect, and of which it may be analytically established that they owe this affective over-emphasis to unconscious identification with another thing (or idea), to which the surplus of affect really belongs. . . . [Symbols are] only those [substitutions] in which one member of the equation is repressed into the unconscious.
>
> (Ferenczi 1952: 277–278)

Simply put, the unconscious might be conceived as a response to a surplus of affect, which by means of a repressive mechanism stores things or ideas. Problems with affect regulation have been shown to be greater in individuals who have not experienced secure attachments, a phenomenon commonly reported about sexual offenders generally. One goal of therapy is to develop the ability to regulate this affect, which depends on gaining a capacity to engage in imaginative mental activity that allows for the interpretation of one's own and others' behaviour as intentional (Fonagy and Target 1996; Fonagy et al. 2002).

Therapy at KiZ in the idiom of a 'talking cure' offers the possibility of a self-transformation through access to the unconscious, and therefore access to some degree of affect regulation. To be sure, my analysis here breaks from those of most of the KiZ therapists, who do not think of themselves as primarily concerned with unconscious activity. Nonetheless, the therapy for child offenders that I observed always tried to go beyond a narrow idea of reckoning with the deed, *die Aufarbeitung der Tat*. To 'treat' the offenders, therapists at KiZ did not rest at the goals of behavioural, drug or delict-focused treatments: an admission of the deed, an installing of impulse control or an agreement to renounce drives. In the most successful cases, clients arrived at an understanding of what their offensive acts stood for within their own very personal histories. Not merely a product of a specific kind of sex drive, the deeds are revealed to be symbolic substitutes in an infinite regress of prior, frequently ambiguous and fragmentary, experiences. Awareness of these substitutes enabled offenders to develop a sense of self more open to imagining and assessing alternatives for a life of 'responsibility without illegalities'.

In this, the treatment orientation of KiZ therapists advances the more recent proposals by forensic psychologists to replace the dominant risk-need-responsibility model (RNR) with what they call the good lives model (GLM), to provide 'individuals with the necessary internal and external conditions to pursue pro-social personal projects *that replace* previously offensive criminal behaviours' (italics added, Ward et al. 2007: 206; cf. Andrews et al. 2006; Ward and Gannon 2006). In pursuit of the goal of rehabilitation, then, treatment aims not only to avoid risk but also to enhance the readiness to change, and to increase the responsiveness of the offender to a potential psychic change. The particular open prison where I worked in fact placed as much responsibility on the offender as possible in a system of incarceration, calling itself a '*Selbsterstellmodel*' (self-administered model), which is congruent with the further refined self-regulation model (SRM) advocated by Ward et al. (2008).

This kind of treatment and incarceration must be modified for different individuals; it is unlikely to work for all child sex offenders. For some offenders, there may indeed be a singular drive behind the deed, in which case the task of the therapist would be to encourage the offender-client to externalise and make alienable a certain paedophilic desire, or paedophilic drive. For some, this drive may be internal to the self, and not only internal but submerged and unrecognisable as such, repressed and stored in the unconscious. For other men, there may be little repression as they are highly conscious of their desires and the means necessary to satisfy them while evading the law. But in the case studies presented here, which are not exceptional or outlier cases, it is difficult to infer that the person speaking is externalising paedophilic desire. This interpretation is in line with much contemporary psychoanalytic clinical practice, where, Peter Fonagy writes, 'Psychosexuality is...more frequently considered as disguising other, non-sexual self- and object-related conflicts than the other way around' (Fonagy 2006: 1).

When Konrad and Reinhard speak, they are not giving voice to a simple desire or motivational force that can be transformed according to Freud's initial formulation: 'Where id was, there ego shall be.' The 'drive' that most motivated Konrad – as he and the therapists came to understand his speaking self after over four years of intermittent therapy in prison and another ten months at KiZ – was not a 'sexual interest in children', not even a sexual interest in youths, although his passions seemed to lead him, much like a drive, to seek out adolescent boys in need of attention and help. Rather, in response to repeated questions about sexual type, Konrad frustratingly reiterated, 'I don't know'. At the time, the therapists and I inferred from Konrad's 'I', which insistently disavowed knowing itself, a resistance to introspection about his motivations. Instead, perhaps, we should have taken seriously his disavowal, for, as he himself later concluded, his behaviour was not primarily about finding an appropriate object for his sexual desire, but the repetition of a pattern, following the deaths of two lovers, to find a partner who 'will not die before me'.

The 'Konrad' that was speaking to the therapists toward the end of his sessions – less wary, more optimistic, joyful in small daily acts, ironic, eager to share experience – is one who had remained for years, it seems, perhaps also due to chemical castration, partially hidden to himself if not non-existent. During the time of his abuses, he had neglected his appearance and drank huge amounts, as if the fog of intoxication might camouflage the phenomenal emptiness of his everyday life. This neglect had much to do, I suspect, with his same-sex desire and the stigma attached to it as he grew up in East Germany. Later, his stubborn refusal to remember his offences expressed that side of his dissociated self necessary to protect an inner self, less from accusations of child abuse than from the affect attached to memories of neglect from childhood and fear of abandonment by his lovers and acquaintances. That is also why, perhaps, when he spoke to the group in therapy, he adopted an unusual singsong voice of fake optimism, as if his fear of disclosure could be allayed only by putting the words to music. It seems likely that the deadness of his own demeanour and lack of attachments to others – he claims to have had no friends minimally since the time of his first offence – mimicked his relatively recent experiences of death and loss. The therapists at KiZ listened closely, empathised, pried, attacked, argued, and threatened, but for a very long time they seemed at wit's end to get behind the voice he inhabited in the group that comically flattened all differences within his experience into silly adages and homilies, ostensibly for them.

When the self emerged that he had sought to hide, Konrad twice attempted suicide. That step would have been an annihilation of both his manifest self that appeared unkempt, stubborn, paedophilic and his latent, secret one. More disturbing for him, I suspect, was not the paedophile, who was fairly recent in origin, appearing in full gestalt only as an adult in his late 20s, but the self reeling from loss and death. In any event, Konrad did not appear particularly shameful about his sexual relationships with the underage youths he had picked up; he had lived with them publicly in his village, and in therapy addressed them openly, if consistently incoherent about what went on. Konrad's hidden self was the more fragile, the more interpersonally sensitive, the more fearful of abandonment, similar to what D. W. Winnicott (1965: 148) characterised as the True Self, which 'does nothing more than collect together the details of the experience of aliveness'. With the accusation of child sexual abuse, Konrad's search for aliveness in relation to boys was betrayed, relationships that he had regarded as loving and caring turned persecutory.

Law was an essential instrument in transforming Konrad's experience of love into persecution. Raised in the former East Germany in a poor and 'asocial' family, he had learned a strategy of survival that meant evading the law, in particular criminal law. GDR law, although authoritarian, also assured the advantages of a wide-net social welfare state (e.g. free healthcare, cheap subsistence goods and housing, regular-if under-employment) without requiring much in return. Konrad internalised both versions of law: the paranoid-authoritarian and the

257

minimally caring. Following his arrests and (after the second violation) imprisonment, he initially experienced the democratic *Bundesrepublic* law in the united Germany in the register of persecution alone.

Confronted with a state and social order that labelled him a paedophile – a label not widely bandied about in the former East but which became a major spectre evoked by the newly freed and sensationalist press after unification – he was imprisoned with other sexual criminals, among whom he had the most abject status. These circumstances led him to drive his longing for the 'experience of aliveness' deeper into his unconscious; his external shell – or what we might, following Winnicott (1965: 140–152), call False Self – was the only appearance available for others to see. Konrad then transferred this persecutory and non-reciprocal yet care-taking relationship with the law to the one he had with his therapists. This transference relation changed only several months before the end of therapy at KiZ.

Let me contrast Konrad's relation to therapy with that of Reinhard. Like Konrad, Reinhard also was sceptical of therapy, having experienced a long history of psychiatric abuse in prison in the former GDR, where the psychiatrists and psychologists allied with a purely punitive and persecutory law against him as someone convicted of 'political crime'. And like Konrad, we might say that Reinhard's True Self withered or was repressed in prison, becoming less visible in its 'spontaneity and internality' under the weight of demands for 'compliance and externality' (Winnicott 1965: 148). By True Self here, I do not mean, as Winnicott suggests, some original core anchored in the early maternal relation, but I refer only to some potentiality for authenticity inside interpersonal relations as he had experienced them. Reinhard remarks that relations with his neglectful father and abusive stepmother were counterbalanced by the very positive caring and secure environment of the orphanage where he largely grew up. He learned how to trust in a group environment, but that group care in turn had inadequately prepared him to deal with the vicissitudes and instability of interpersonal relations outside of institutions.

It was that strong internal voice of responsibility and care, not a paedophilic desire, which Konrad had developed in his collective childhood environment and which now made him relatively defenceless to the demands of others – in this case, to the demands of Olga's family. Growing up outside the family seemed to have made him particularly vulnerable to its appeal and the perverse aspects of its functioning. Whereas Konrad, having experienced a dysfunctional family since childhood, resisted these external demands, Reinhard found them confusing and allowed himself to be seduced. Hence Konrad developed a False Self – surly, sullen, uncommunicative – to defend himself from external demands and protect him from revealing his own True Self, while Reinhard did not have adequate resources to engage in this deception. Instead Reinhard repressed little. He even tried to inhabit the location of the paedophile, condemning himself as such before his arrest and suicide attempt. 'I see myself as a ghost, a paedophile, unlike others, unlike you', he says, and adds, 'I want to say, I am not the person that the psychiatrist said I am'. Here he has openly identified with the external ascription, and reconstructs a story of his desire for Olga along those lines. Yet his own sexual history reveals an entirely different person, a 'ghost', a more complex person ('not the person the psychiatrist said I am'), one with no pattern of abuse of any sort but with a primary sexual interest in adult women, specifically in women who allow him to assume responsibility for them.

What does Reinhard mean, then, in declaring himself a paedophile? It is not surprising that when he found himself in the presence of a pubescent, neglected, admiring young girl as she grew into womanhood, he would find her attractive and imagine the possibility of making this presence permanent, turning it into a family of his own making. Today that kind of desire is understood as perverse, although historically it has been quite common if not accepted. In acquiescing to the paedophile label, Reinhard was complying here with legal and therapeutic demands to acknowledge that he overstepped a 'boundary' that is 'difficult to draw', driven by a 'wave of lust' and a failure of his 'interior laws'. This expression of lust and the failure of interior laws was in tension with his True Self, which shows a responsive, caring man who is also, as he says, 'addicted to harmony'.

CONCLUSION

In this chapter, I have neglected several issues crucial to understanding the conditions of therapy that I observed and the conditions necessary for success in the rehabilitation of child sex offenders. First, I have omitted a discussion of the dynamic of group therapy, as well as of the work of transference and countertransference in my own relation to the group as observer, issues that deserve a lengthier discussion than I can provide here. Second, I have omitted incest abusers from consideration, though they are usually prosecuted under the same laws of sexual abuse and confined in the same prisons and share many of the same therapeutic issues as do paedophiles (Borneman 2012).

Perhaps the most important condition I have not discussed is the way the label paedophile glosses over distinctions between the various types of offenders and the diversity of their behaviours. To the extent that every man accused of the offence is legally classified as paedophile, and most frequently treated as a paedosexual in therapy, each offender must address the same set of projections from the outside world. But the experiences of offenders differ by the kinds of relations they have had with their victims, leading to widely varied degrees of internalisation of these ascriptions. Although all clinical evidence suggests that these relations are clearly more abusive for five year old children than for 18 year old youths, the law tends to treat these offences as similar in kind.

Law tries to resolve the problem of the asymmetrical experience by fixing an age of consent, generally 14 in Europe (and in Germany), in some countries up to 18. Trying to specify an age alone as the marker for 'sexual self-determination', or sexual maturity and agency, may establish legal clarity but it also creates therapeutic problems by representing all victims below a certain age as 'children'. The uniformity of this category is contradicted by the varied experiences of offender and victim alike. While law in its interest in uniform application excludes experience by relying on chronological age to define consent, therapy must take into account the experience of the offence, *die Tat*, in order to access both the victim's and the offender's self. But because therapy is the key to a legally and socially consequential rehabilitation, therapists are always under pressure to prioritise legal assumptions and categories that assume a homogeneity in victims and in the experience of the offence. Such assumptions often run counter to the lived experience of the men they treat and therefore are counterproductive for therapeutic efficacy.

The two case studies of offenders presented here fall into an intermediate category: the objects of 'ephebophilia', the psychological classification most often used to delineate a sexual interest in mid to late adolescents. These victims clearly had varied sexual interests, too, but, in their immaturity, those interests appeared ambivalent, confused and embedded in other needs of which they were unaware. Therefore, relations with adults were highly susceptible to manipulation and abuse. Social and legal norms now dictate that those interests, however defined and determined, be categorically protected from adult sexual desires. Therapists charged with rehabilitation must minimally bring the attitudes and interests of offenders in line with these norms.

Men who repeatedly seek out pre-pubertal children for sex are certainly more difficult to rehabilitate, and they may in fact be less treatable through therapy generally. The choice given them is either complete sexual renunciation or chemical castration, since at the moment we are at a loss on how to imagine and create a socially acceptable sexuality for them. There appears to be more ambiguity and variance in the abuse of post-pubertal children, however, and therefore more room for therapeutic efficacy. I hope to have demonstrated not only that the therapeutic intervention in these types of cases can be successful, a point made repeatedly by survey-based studies, but also *how* it is successful in rehabilitating offenders.

In demonstrating how therapy can be successful, then, I drew attention to the importance of psychic change for men under the stigma of social abjection and the threat of permanent incarceration. The self tied to the act of child sexual abuse may actually be a False Self, which hides or protects the self that must be made to appear in therapy. For therapy to be successful, I have specifically identified the potentiality for authenticity inside interpersonal relations and affect regulation as integral to treatment. Treatment models limited to controlling impulses, cognitive-behavioural correction of thinking errors about child sexuality, changing sexual object choice or committing to sexual abstinence are inadequate for such a task (Waldram 2010). The regulation of affects is hardly a developed science, but we do know that access to affects is a uniquely individual process, not group or type-specific, and crucial to begin the internal conversation that the offender must have to reckon with the act. The offender after successful therapy should not only assume responsibility for the act but also find, as Christopher Bollas (1987: 62) writes, 'a more generative way of holding...the self as an object of one's nurture'. Able to nurture his self, the rehabilitated offender might open himself up to empathy for, and life with, others.

NOTES

1 The sexual offence provisions pertain to those sentenced under §§174–183 StGB of the German Criminal Code.
2 Each therapy centre offers a slightly different treatment protocol. Perhaps most unusual in the Berlin landscape is the programme at the Berlin Charité, the Prevention Project Dunkelfeld, which offers voluntary counselling for

men who self-identify with 'paedophilia' or 'hebephilia' before committing any criminal offence.

3 In both institutions, I am obliged to strict protection of human subjects (Datenschutz), and hence have fabricated all the personal names and anonymised places, except for KiZ. The treatment of the specific men included in this paper is drawn from the 35 cases of men and boys, between the ages of 13 and 62, who participated in the therapy groups that I attended.

4 In a Wisconsin study, Zevitz and Farkas (2000) conclude that community notification programmes have had no effect in managing sex offenders and anti-therapeutic effects on their rehabilitation. They argue that a more effective strategy to reintegrate ex-offenders would be to provide stable housing and employment.

5 In Germany, criminological discourse today tends to classify the sexual abuse of children as a crime against sexual self-determination, rape as a crime of violence and pornography as an economic crime. In the 1970s and 1980s, prostitution and homosexuality were fully decriminalized, and are no longer important for criminological classification. Over the past several decades, the number of sexual crimes has remained constant while public reporting of them has increased manifold. Between 1960 and 1985, 'paedosexual crimes' declined, and have since remained relatively constant, with a very slight increase after 1987. While it is unclear what exact effect public sensitivity and awareness has on the commission of such criminal acts, increased sensitivity has surely led to more willingness to prosecute (Urbaniok 2005: 143–57).

6 For comparison, see Rhodes (2004) for an ethnographic account of the experience in a maximum security prison in the USA.

REFERENCES

Alexander, M. A. 1999. 'Sexual Offender Treatment Efficacy Revisited', *Sexual Abuse: A Journal of Research and Treatment* 19: 101–116

Andrews, D. A., Bonta, J. and Wormith, J. S. 2006. 'The Recent Past and Near Future of Risk and/or Need Assessment', *Crime & Delinquency* 52: 7–27

Beech, A. R. 1998. 'A Psychometric Typology of Child Abusers', *International Journal of Offender Therapy and Comparative Criminology* 42: 319–339

Berkel, I. 2006. *Missbrauch als Phantasma: Zur Krise der Genealogie.* Paderborn: Wilhelm Fink Verlag

Bollas, C. 1987. *The Shadow of the Object: Psychoanalysis of the Unthought Known.* New York: Columbia University Press

Borneman, J. 2012. 'Incest, the Child, and the Despotic Father', *Current Anthropology* 53 (2): 181–203

Dünkel, F. 2005. 'Reformen des Sexualstrafrecht und Entwicklungen der Sexualdelinquenz in Deutschland', in Schläfke, D., Häßler, F., Fegert, J. M. (eds.), *Forensische Begutachtung, Diagnostik und Therapie.* Stuttgart: Schattauer

Ferenczi, S. 1952 [1916]. 'The Ontogenesis of Symbols,' First Contributions to Pscho-Analysis. Ed. Ernest Jones, Hogarth Press; Karnac, London, 276–281

Fonagy, P. 2006. 'Psychosexuality and Psychoanalysis: an Overview', on Fonagy, P., Krause, R. and Leuzinger-Bohleber, M. (eds.), Identity, Gender and Sexuality 150 Years after Freud. London: International Psychoanalytical Association Controversies in Psychoanalysis Series

Fonagy, P., Gergely, G., Jurist, E. L. and Target, M. 2002. Affect Regulation, Mentalization and the Development of the Self. New York: Other Press

Fonagy, P. and Target, M. 1996. 'Playing With Reality: I. Theory Of Mind And The Normal Development of Psychic Reality' International Journal of Psycho-Analysis 77: 217–233

Foucault, M. 1978 [1976]. The History of Sexuality: An Introduction. NY: Pantheon Books

Godelier, M. 2004. Métamorphoses de la parenté. Paris: Fayard: Paris

Goffman, E. 1959. The Presentation of Self in Everyday Life. New York: Doubleday

Günter, M. 2005. 'Jugendliche und erwachsene Sexualstraftäter im Vergleich: Psychiatrische Charakteristika und späteres Rückfallrisiko', in Clauß, M., Karle, M., Günter, M., Barth, G. (eds.), Sexuelle Entwicklung – sexuelle Gewalt: Grundlagen forensischer Begutachtung von Kindern und Jugendlichen. Berlin: Pabst Science Publishers

Hacking, I. 1991. 'The Making and Molding of Child Abuse' Critical Inquiry 17 (2): 253–288

Joseph, B. 1989. Psychic Change and the Psychoanalytic Process. New York: Routledge

Kohut, H. 1975. 'The Psychoanalyst in the Community of Scholars', Annual of Psychoanalysis 3: 341–370

Laplanche, J. 1989. New Foundations for Psychoanalysis, transl. D. Macey. Oxford: Basil Blackwell

Mandeville-Norden, R. and Beech, A. 2004. 'Community-based Treatment of Sex Offenders', Journal of Sexual Aggression 10 (2): 193–214

Marshall, W. L., Eccles, A. and Barbaree, H. E. 1993. 'A Three-Tiered Approach to the Rehabilitation of Incarcerated Sex Offenders', Behavioral Sciences and the Law 11: 441–455

Marshall, W. L., Hudson, S. M. and Ward, T. 1992. 'Sexual Deviance', in Wilson, P. H. (ed.), Principles and Practice of Relapse Prevention, New York: Guilford Press

Marshall, W. L., Jones, R., Ward, T., Johnston, P. and Barbaree, H. E. 1991. 'Treatment Outcome with Sex Offenders', Clinical Psychology Review 11: 465–485

Matson, S. 2002. 'A Critical Management Tool', Corrections Today: 114–117

Rhodes, L. 2004. *Total Confinement: Madness and Reason in the Maximum Security Prison*. Berkeley: University of California Press

Shengold, L. 1991. *Soul Murder: The Effects of Child Abuse and Deprivation*. New York: Ballantine Books

Urbaniok, F. 2005. 'Validität von Risikokalkulationen bei Straftätern. Kritik an einer methodischen Grundannahme und zukunftige Perspektiven', in Schläfke, D., Häßler, F., Fegert, J. M. (eds.), *Sexualstraftaten: Forensische Begutachtung, Diagnostik und Therapie*. Stuttgart, Germany: Schattauer

Waldram, J. 2010. 'Moral Agency, Cognitive Distortion, and Narrative Strategy in the Rehabilitation of Sex Offenders', *Ethos* 38 (3): 251–274

Ward, T., Gannon, T. and Yates, P. 2008. 'The Treatment of Offenders: Current Practice and New Developments with an Emphasis on Sex Offenders', *International Review of Victimology* 15 (2): 179–204

Ward, T., Gannon, T. and Birgden, A. 2007. 'Human Rights and the Treatment of Sex Offenders', *Sex Abuse* 19 (3): 195–216

Ward, T. and Gannon, T. 2006. 'Rehabilitation, Etiology, and Self-regulation: The Good Lives Model of Sexual Offender Treatment', *Aggression and Violent Behavior* 11: 77–94

Winnicott, D. W. 1965. The Maturational Processes and the Facilitating Environment: Studies in the Theory of Emotional Development. Madison, CT: International Universities Press

Zevitz, R. and Farkas, M. A. 2000. 'Sex Offender Community Notification: Managing High Risk Criminals or Exacting Further Vengeance?' *Behavioral Sciences and the Law* 18: 375–391

CHAPTER ELEVEN

A REPUBLIC OF REMEDIES: PSYCHOSOCIAL INTERVENTIONS IN POST-CONFLICT GUATEMALA

Henrik Ronsbo

By the mid 1990s, Guatemala emerged from three decades of violent internal conflict. More than 400 indigenous villages had been burned down; as many as 200 000 civilians were killed or disappeared during the conflict; in their efforts to flee the atrocities as many as two million were living in internal displacement; and more than 500 000 had fled to exile in Mexico and the United States. Today the history of the Guatemalan genocide is well known. Numerous are the monographs in English (Carmack 1988; Manz 2004) and Spanish (Centro de Estudios Integrados de Desarrollo Comunal CEIDEC 2008; Falla 1978; Sanford 2009; Wilson 1995) that explore local and national histories and experiences generated by Guatemala's genocidal internal conflict.

In this chapter, rather than focusing on the experiences of conflict and genocide, we focus on understanding the remedies that have been provided for ameliorating the devastation, pain and loss. How did these remedies emerge? Who carried them forward? And how may we, from an anthropological perspective, understand their effects on the intended beneficiaries, members of indigenous communities, in this case those of the Ixhil Highlands?

This chapter has been produced through extensive and long-term collaboration with numerous people in the period 2005–2010. Research in and on the DIGNITY archive was undertaken in collaboration with Stine Finne Jakobsen. Data collection in Guatemala was undertaken together with Walter Paniagua, Bruce Osorio, Ana Laynez and from Equipo de Estudios Comunitarios y Acción Psicosocial as part of the Histories of Victimhood research project partly financed by the Danish Research Council for Social Sciences, and data from the project was analysed in collaboration with Solveig Jensen. I would like to acknowledge these multiple forms of collaboration.

From the mid 1990s onwards, there emerged in Guatemala an extensive network of organisations and programmes that provided assistance for survivors of the genocide. Advocacy-oriented NGOs tried to influence government programmes dealing with the psychosocial effects and history of the genocidal internal conflict. Alongside advocacy they also developed specific professionalised knowledge such as standards for the forensic exhumations of mass graves and identification of individuals in these, as well as standards for the psychosocial accompaniment of victims and surviving family members. In the same period numerous community-based victim associations started to emerge from rural communities, in particular in the indigenous areas of the country. Often these worked in collaboration with national political movements and parties active in municipal and national politics. At the San Carlos University a programme for the study of the relationship between social psychology and violence was opened, and so was a two-year diploma programme for school teachers and other professionals wanting to qualify for work in the mental health sector. The all-encompassing focus of these diverse activities was the long-term mental health consequences that the internal conflict had on the civilian population. In particular, focus was on the Maya-speaking groups of the Guatemalan Highlands, the population most affected by the internal armed conflict.

The severity and length of the conflict, together with the scope and size of the remedial interventions, makes Guatemala an exemplary case for exploring psychosocial remedies in post-conflict societies. As case, Guatemala represents the plethora of psychosocial interventions carried out in the Western Hemisphere during the 1990s and 2000s, targeting 40–60 million individuals in the countries of Argentina, Chile, Peru, Colombia and Guatemala. However, parallel to the emergence of this modality of interventions, its nature and character has become increasingly debated and questioned.

In anthropology there has, over the past decades, emerged two key arguments through which anthropologists understand psychosocial interventions. Drawing inspiration from Foucault's work on power/knowledge complexes in general and his critique of clinics in particular, one group of authors have argued that psychosocial work signals the emergence of new and globalised forms of psy-governance (Rose 1993), a novel realignment of security and development paradigms through which the borderlands of the neoliberal project are subsumed by a combination of psychological discipline and development oriented interventions (Duffield 2007; Pupavac 2002, 2004a, 2004b). Clinical forms of knowledge are being projected onto post-conflict societies, reshaping these in much the same ways as clinical psychiatry and mental health institutions reshaped mentalities in the latter half of the nineteenth century.

Following this line of argument, Fassin and Rechtman argue that the discourse of psychotraumatology based on a humanitarian notion of trauma has created an 'empire of trauma' supported by global NGOs such as Medicin sans Frontier (Fassin and Rechtman 2007). While we are sympathetic to the notion that the clinical construct of trauma can be understood as circumscribing not only a clinical but also a humanitarian project (Feldman and Ticktin 2010), we think that the idea of 'empire' conjures up notions of centralised governance and singular logics, which on the one hand overemphasises the efficacy of discourse while on the other hand blinds us to the complex networks through which knowledge is generated and shared.

Opposed to the Foucauldian line of argument, we find a group of anthropologists and historians (Hollander 1997; Sanford 2003; Zur 1998) who suggest that psychosocial work represents an efficacious therapeutic tradition, which has helped victims and survivors work through their pain, trauma and fear. They argue – in particular based on the Latin American experiences – that this work, cumulatively since the 1980s, by creating strategies of truth telling, healing and litigation, has changed the social and political course of Latin American countries, as they have embarked on processes of democratisation.

The opposing conclusions in these two bodies of literature indicate – we believe – the high stakes that are at play in this particular scholarly debate. In intervention terms, stakes are high because psychosocial remedies to civilians as well as combatants in post-conflict societies have become a standard component for the international donor community. In scholarly terms, stakes are high because the debate regarding these interventions touches on some of the key assumptions regarding the nature of power and subjectivity which have shaped social and cultural anthropological since the 1980s.

What is notable in the debate regarding the nature of psychosocial work is that, despite the different attributes ascribed to it – one argument seeing it as a manifestation of occidental power, the other as one of popular resistance – both interpretations stress its efficacy and impact and its ability to transform entire societies, Palestinian (Fassin and Rechtman 2007), ex-Yugoslavian (Pupavac 2002) or Guatemalan (Sanford 2003).

Our approach to the discussion of psychosocial remedies is somewhat different. In our work we try to understand psychosocial remedies as relations that translate and mould agency between different forms and scales of sociality. In particular, we focus in this chapter on the social spaces of the Guatemalan state, the international donor community in Guatemala, the indigenous communities in the Highlands and, last but not least, the different subjects and modes of identification within these that emerge around notions of guilt, debt, shame and suffering.

In this sense our project is akin to Bruno Latour's project of a sociology of associations, we 'follow the traces left behind by (actors') activity of forming and dismantling groups', in this case the associations emerging in the Guatemalan post-conflict assemblage. From this perspective 'action is not done under the full control of consciousness; actions should be felt as a node, knot, and a conglomerate of many surprising sets of agencies that have to be slowly disentangled' (Latour 2005: 44).

We understand this as a call to disentangle the assemblage of post-conflict Guatemala, by making its constituent actants visible and, while we do so, we explore the tensions and contestations, as these flow between the actants, and the registers of agency through which they relate. The corollary of this view is that we understand psychosocial remedies as elements of the post-conflict assemblage rather than merely as techniques. As elements in an assemblage, psychosocial remedies have expressivity and materiality, they territorialise and deterritorialise (Delanda 2006) and in this sense they provide the conditions of possibility for specific subjectivities to be imagined, gestured and voiced; this we explore in the final section of the chapter.

This view entails that we see the emergence of the psychosocial movement and the remedies it carried forward, neither as the teleological unfolding of a dispositif with global efficacy and reach, nor as an autonomous gesture of parrhesia, rather it should be understood as an emergent field in which donors, NGOs, therapists and their victims (imagined and real) at meetings and therapeutic encounters negotiated and weaved a bricolage of expressions and materiality that brought different actants together in contacts and contracts, concentrating and disseminating words and gestures in a world shaped by decades of violence, where it is less the inability to talk (Scarry 1985) than the ability to listen (Das 2007; Kelly 2012) that shapes the conditions under which remedies are seen as platforms for recognition.

Taking this point of departure we move through three sections in this chapter. First we follow the emergence of the psychosocial movement from the early 1970s to the ways in which it shapes a form of recognition in post-conflict Guatemala. We pay attention to how the notions of psychosocial damage and the provision of psychosocial remedies have developed. As we do so we explore the social life of the notion of trauma, forcing us to see beyond the view of psychosocial work as either caught within the 'empire of trauma' or alternatively representing 'love in the time of hate'.

In the second section of the chapter we then engage what we call the political economy of trauma in Guatemala. We provide an analysis of the context for psychosocial interventions in terms of the development of international aid to Guatemala and identify what we have chosen to call the 'post-conflict bubble'. We call it so because from 1996 to 2003 post-conflict aid rose dramatically, only to drop towards the end of the first decade of the new millennium. Does this indicate that attention to post-conflict remedies was a donor induced policy as Pupavac and others have argued?

Our final section works towards an answer to this question, arguing that if we understand remedies not as techniques but as relations, we are able to understand how community members in the Ixhil High-lands of Guatemala used the psychosocial interventions surrounding the national reparation programme to negotiate the forms of inclusion and recognition within the Guatemalan nation-state that were available within the post-conflict assemblage. Analysing narratives collected for a communal reparation claim, we suggest that community members voice their claim for recognition in a set of contradictory gestures in which the longstanding relationship of power characterised by patronage, is combined with claims made for the recognition of suffering within a framework of rights.

Throughout the chapter we therefore stress the broken and multi-local emergence of psychosocial thinking and practice. Psychosocial remedies did not emanate from a single authoritative source, neither donor nor activist-scholar, but from the entanglements of a multiplicity of rationalities (clinical, developmental, political) with indigenous forms of life. Such entanglements are socio-historical alloys or what Latour calls nodes. Understanding psychosocial practices as nodes enable us to understand that these practices are alloys of power and subjectivity moulded as particular subjunctive spaces in the relations and conflicts created between NGOs, therapists, donors, state institutions and survivors of the Guatemalan genocide, enabling the survivors to imagine and express their hopes for recognition in a future democratic Guatemala.

THE PSYCHOSOCIAL MOVEMENT

Psychosocial interventions represent a therapeutic and professional tradition based on the eclectic conjoining of social-psychology with different individual as well as group-based psychotherapeutic traditions. In some contexts psychosocial work is referred to as 'liberation psychology', stressing the impact of Jesuit scholar Martín-Baró's theoretical work on the social psychology of liberation and war, and the crucial role played by liberation theology emerging from the 1960s Catholic Church.

Throughout South and Central America its practitioners have been dedicated to alleviating the suffering of people and communities victimised by genocide, torture, disappearances and displacements that accompanied the political history of Latin America in the second half of the 20th century, work which continues into the current period.

Among the practitioners, there is an understanding of Latin American societies as characterised by a long history of exploitation (Cardoso and Faletto 1970; Galeano 1992), combined with racism, machismo and patriarchalism (Erazo 2007). Hence, psychosocial interventions work not specifically on the symptoms of post traumatic stress, but always try to understand these within the context of the broader material, social and political origins of harm, while it simultaneously gestures towards the development of psychological remedies that facilitate political, social and legal action, with positive psychic effects in individual as well as group dimensions (Anckermann et al. 2005). The key concepts in this transformation of the subject, from marginalisation to potential liberation, are those of 'silencio' (silence), 'dolores congelados' (frozen grief or pain), 'trauma psicosocial' (psychosocial trauma) and 'memoria social' (social memory). Silence is the condition created by frozen grief and fear, leading to psychosocial trauma, and the construction of social memory by a community is the potential remedy.[1]

To be frozen in emotional terms translates into political and legal arenas. The notion of frozen grief or pain is the state of harm that leads to silence, and which subsequently inhibits social transformation and individual and social healing. It is the work of memorialisation (memorialización) that opens up the individuals and communities, enabling them to express their grief and pain and thus move through the recuperation of their voice, to healing and empowerment (Ancker-mann et al. 2005). It is by intervening on social memory at the inter-section of the individual and the communal, that we find the remedy to the trauma left by the internal conflict.

In the remainder of this section we will explore the emergence of this particular view of the effects of the internal conflict – how did this very particular idea appear, and how did it translate into a specific view of remedies for the pain and suffering created by the Guatemalan conflict? The notion of frozen memory emerged in the late 1970s from therapeu-tic practice carried out in refugee camps and safe houses in Mexico and Honduras, in mental health clinics of the Sandinista state, and from the transnational networks between Latin American NGOs and col-laborating organisations in Europe and North America that worked on the development of rehabilitation therapies for refugees and torture sur-vivors.[2]

The origin of this community-oriented form of psychoanalysis lay in the split in the global psychoanalytical movement. In 1971 in the Southern Cone, notably Argentina, a minority of the members of the Argentinian Psycho-analytical Association active in what was known as the 'Plataforma' movement, broke with the association-based model of the remunerated individual psychoanalytical therapist, in order to start politically informed psychotherapy from public hospitals and com-munity clinics in working class neighbourhoods in Buenos Aires.[3] These experiences were transformative and as militarisation of the Argentinian left escalated, and repression increased, this group of polit-ically active psychoanalysts became involved in therapeutic work with survivors of disappearances, extra-judicial executions and torture.

Throughout this period, psychoanalysts in the Southern Cone were forced by political developments in the hemisphere to explore affects and emotions, grief, fear, terror and the feelings of the loss of friends and loved ones, as such material came forward through therapy. Of course, different therapists contributed with different approaches – individual, play-based, group-therapy etc. – but the outcome was a psychoanalyti-cally inspired psychotherapy focusing on the harm created by political violence to the inter- and intra-psychic realms of human existence.

A set of contingent factors led to the spread of this therapeutic tra-dition to Central America. Most important was the flight of a group of Argentinian psychoanalysts to Mexico during the 1970s, in particu-lar the senior analyst, Austrian-born and trained psychoanalyst Maria

Langer who, following Anschluss, fled Europe, ending up in Argentina. In Mexico during the mid 1970s, this group created a community centre for refugees from Argentina and the other Southern Cone countries. During the late 1970s they came into contact with the Sandinista movement and provided, among other things, short-term group therapy to Nicaraguan fighters while they rested in Mexico City from fighting in Nicaragua (Langer 1989: 213).

After the fall of the Somoza regime in late 1979 these initial encounters gave rise to the creation of the 'Internationalist Team of Mental Health Workers Mexico-Nicaragua' (*Equipo Internacionalista de Salud Mental México–Nicaragua*) which, during the 1980s, assisted the Sandinista government in the development of a Nicaraguan mental health system and the training of mental health workers, based on a psychodynamic approach (Martinez 1990).

Another tradition of psychology would, however, also come to play a role, this one having an equally complex genealogy. During the 1960s, the Catholic Church, in collaboration with military dictatorships under the Kennedy-backed Alliance for Progress,[4] had expanded its social work among the rural poor in Central America, creating church-based cooperatives, labour unions and peasant organisations as a means to halt the development of revolutionary organisations and to expand the Catholic Church's evangelisation campaigns in Central America. The cornerstone of this work was called the Christian Base Community. In these groups, the participants – often illiterate peasants – would study the Holy Scriptures, learning to read and write, while exploring the conditions and possibilities for changing their lives. Soon, however, the plan backfired, and the base communities became the cornerstone in ever-expanding popular movements, which by the mid 1970s had changed the political landscapes of the Central American republics.

The base communities affected large populations, in particular through the methods and teachings of Liberation Theology (Cabarrús 1983; Falla 1978; Manz 2004). In Guatemala, this ecclesiastical movement was particularly strong in the Quiché region of Western Guatemala, subsequently one of the regions experiencing among the most devastating acts of genocide in the early 1980s. Based on these experiences, Ignacio Martín-Baró[5] started developing what he saw as a Central American social psychology at the Jesuit university, Universidad de Centro America (UCA) in San Salvador publishing his key work 'Action and Ideology' in 1983 (Martín-Baró 2001 [1983]), a work which rapidly spread throughout Latin American university institutions (Ibáñez 2006).

Martín-Baró's theoretical approach was based on historical materialism and the Chicago School's attention to environment as a conditioner of human behaviour, and, by implication, he was deeply critical of prevalent forms of individualism in psychological theory and practice, not only in cognitivist and behaviourist traditions, but also in its psychoanalytical incarnation, as propagated by the Langer-group in Mexico.

From this encounter between Southern Cone psychoanalytical theory and practice, Liberation Theology and a Central American social psychology created under conditions of civil war, emerged an approach for working with the effects of genocide and violence that was to have wide-ranging effects throughout the region. Although Martín-Baró in a posthumous publication strongly opposed the usage of psychoanalytical therapies – group as well as individually based (Martín-Baró 1990: 82–83) – these two therapeutic traditions were merged with his own brand of liberation psychology (Martín-Baró 1986: 219–231) in a way that accommodated the insights produced by the Argentinian psychoanalysts working in Mexico and Nicaragua.

In particular, it was a cohort of psychologists who graduated from Martín-Baró's own institution, UCA, which came to shape the notion of harm that sustained the NGOs of post-conflict Guatemala. The basis for this was a very specific analysis of the entanglement of individual and social memory in the shaping of affects, behaviours and social relations following the wars of Central America and thereby also in the conceptualisation of the harm created and the remedies this harm called for.

FROM FROZEN GRIEF TO PSYCHOSOCIAL TRAUMA

The core concept – and this was the crucial innovation of Maria Langer – for understanding the multiple sequelae of genocidal warfare, disappearances and state violence is that of 'frozen grief'. Sigmund Freud argued that the healthy psyche copes with the separation of the self from the lost other through grief, an attachment which is resolved through the acceptance of loss. Langer argued, based on her clinical experience from Argentina, Mexico and Nicaragua, that a different situation pertained when there was no proof of death, as was the case in the large massacres and the practices of disappearances in Central America. Because of the absence of tangible proof, Langer argued, relatives engaged in the ongoing elaboration of fantasies about the continued survival and possible torture that the disappeared was living through. Although these fantasies are recognised as fantasies by the self, they find continued sustenance in the ways in which violence is displayed in public space.

The fantasy, that my loved one has survived, reached into the psychic structure of the individual and the group from the executed and tortured persons that were thrown alongside roads, moulding on the one hand an omnipresent feeling of terror, that 'this could be my Antonio' while on the other hand doubling itself in the denial of his death seen and felt as an act of resistance. Fantasies become double-binds which cause anxieties, and over time Langer argued, they result in the repression of fantasy life altogether – they become frozen grief. The alternatives, to either imagine the death of a loved one or to imagine their continued survival and torture, are both too painful and they both produce an omnipresent sense of guilt in the survivor. This was the dilemma that Maria Langer observed among refugees from South and Central America and for which she coined the term frozen grief, '*dolores congelados*'.

The affects and emotions identified with the notion of frozen grief build on Freud's work with melancholia (Freud 1914–16). However, three differences are worth mentioning: first, the inability to separate oneself from the lost object of desire (the disappeared family member) is not a property of the inter-psychic process, hence it is not a psychopathology, it is an effect of the economy of violence; second, the ability to sustain a mourning process is constrained due to the feelings of terror and fear that political violence generated within the population; third, these sensations of fear were sustained on purpose by the economy of violence and the circulation of anonymous dead bodies within the national security model applied by armies throughout Central American wars.

Hence, it is argued, the sense of terror and fear inhibits the sharing of experiences and the development of knowledge about the effects of torture and disappearances, and thus generates frozen grief, leading not only to individual afflictions but likewise to a freezing of social agency leading to the rise of what was called 'psychosocial trauma'.

REMEDIES FOR FROZEN GRIEF

Work on psychosocial trauma covers a wide variety of interventions and models. One could argue that it is precisely the malleability of the term that makes it so powerful and productive. Its ability to create connections, to the need for improvements in the legal system so as to remove fear and combat impunity, to ideas of a trauma wandering from the survivors to the generations that follow.

In the present analysis we have chosen to focus specifically on the term frozen grief, not because it is the only possible elaboration of the term psychosocial trauma, but because this particular notion constitutes the master-term behind most of the psychosocial work undertaken in Guatemala, although it is not always mentioned specifically. While the notion of 'frozen grief' was already circulated at the beginning of the Central American civil wars, it would take considerable time before the intervention models currently in use emerged among Central American NGOs. During the 1980s, the Internationalist Team in Nicaragua had already experimented with group sessions in the Centre for Psychosocial Attention in León (Sepúlveda 2011) and during the latter half of the decade similar work was carried out by Langer's group and others in Mexico City and Chiapas (Farías Campo and Miranda Redondo 1994; de la Aldea Guerrero, Elena, personal communication, November 2001) with Central American refugees.

During the same period, the Social Diocese of the Catholic Church in Quiché under the leadership of Bishop Gerardi,[6] started to develop a more specific psychosocial intervention model, through the work of psychologists who, for the most part, were trained in Martín-Baró's department of psychology in El Salvador. By the second half of the 1990s, the psychosocial intervention model for survivors of genocide, torture and disappearances, which incorporated therapeutic group work and psychotherapeutic interventions for particularly afflicted individuals, had become fully developed in theoretical terms.

Different organisations developed different intervention setups, some used the group-based psychosocial accompaniment together with legal processes, the majority developed the psychosocial interventions as an element of the exhumation of clandestine graves, and the Catholic Church used it in the devolution of its truth commission report to the communities who had participated, echoing the work of Christian Base communities with the Scriptures three decades earlier.[7]

Despite the different organisational setups, the objective of these interventions was to generate reflections among indigenous community members, which could lead to the reconstruction of individual affects and emotions, based on a reassessment of biographical and historical memory. This would lead to a reshaping of social memory in a dialectical relationship between personal memories as they emerged through group work and forms of communal action, in particular action linked to the quest for recognition of the genocide by the Guatemalan state.[8]

In this context, it is important to note that group work consisted not merely in oral session, a variety of relaxation, play and performance-oriented techniques are employed, enabling survivors to elaborate their memories and affects in a variety of non-verbal as well as verbal registers. The model suggests that by working on frozen memory through the socialisation of affects and emotions, together with community members, participants come to rework their frozen grief and build new agentive communities. It is important to note that while the concept of frozen grief in many ways resembles the more classic Freudian notions of mourning and melancholia, one crucial difference exist. While mourning is characterised by the loss of an object of desire and melancholia is characterised by the loss of the self, and they may both be pathological if the subject is unable to work through the displaced libidinal attachments (Freud 1914–16), frozen grief is generated by structures of terror beyond the psychic economy of the subject. It is this difference which is crucial for understanding the ways in which what hitherto had been conceived as individual psychological sequelae was reconstituted as thoroughly social experience created by war and conflict.

The socialisation of individual grief may take place in a variety of formats that all lead towards the production of personal healing and the re-creation of social memory. Only on rare occasions was individual psychotherapy used. Much more frequent was the usage of self-help groups facilitated by trained volunteers who were then supervised by professional psychologists. It should be noted that this was by far the most prevalent intervention model in Highland Guatemala during the late 1990s and 2000s. Through this system, communities were attended and surveyed, and individuals or families in special need of therapeutic interventions would then be referred to such offers. At the same time, it should be remembered that far from everyone accepted such offers – either as individuals or as communities. Throughout the Guatemalan Highlands there has been a strong resistance to the advance of the 'Republic of Remedies'. Evangelicals have worked systematically against the construction of memory separated from the 'sacred space' of the church, and 'costumbristas' (Maya traditionalists) have continuously tried to appropriate or 'vernacularise' memory projects, so as to support the recreation of traditional forms of male leadership within communities based on what is referred to as 'Cosmovision Maya'.

A different method, one which required far more input from professionals, consisted of group interventions facilitated by psychotherapists. In these, a variety of expressive formats were used, such as painting or word games, theatre or play, in which community members engage in collective acts of remembering massacres and other forms of political violence. One particular intervention model worked through the making of a model of the community, using dolls, toy houses, animals, furniture and utensils, thus recreating the community as participants remembered it before the events and losses they had suffered. The exercise takes several hours, depending on the number of participants and their ability to cooperate. With chalk powder, participants start marking the main streets of the community. Then the houses, shops, as well as churches, etc. are placed in the model. This work is shared, participants agreeing on the specific location in the community of houses, trees, gardens, etc. Then households would be fitted with animals, inhabitants and utensils, and while the adults work, children are running around between them, everybody engaged in the recreation of the model, playfully engaged in recreating a past, simultaneously dissociating from the painful memories linked to it. According to psychodynamic theory, the model enables the survivors to displace their affects onto the objects of the model. A temporary relief takes place, as the life of the dolls in the model displaces the memory of the lost family members.[9] A transition takes place as the participants subsequently are asked to place the perpetrators in the model. These are represented by plastic army dolls in the 1:32 scale, leaving little doubt about the nature of the perpetrator. The full return of the affects then takes place, as each participant is handed over the specific number of dolls. These dolls represent the deceased family members of the survivor. As the 'beneficiary/survivor' retells her story of loss, she places the dolls where she found her family members or where they were buried, depending on the particulars of the narrative. At this stage the return of affects is abrupt. Within a short period, the 'beneficiary/survivor' experience that the model, which hitherto had been a depository of affect, suddenly empties itself onto her. She steps into the world of the past, asked to speak in the present about it.

The nature of the performance is multilayered. It provides diagnostic information for the therapists about the distribution, nature and severity of trauma in a given community. It provides forensic evidence on the location of clandestine graves and it provides legal evidence for the subsequent prosecution of perpetrators. But all of it, is undertaken so as to facilitate the production, expression and circulation of affect and narratives thus enabling participants to share their pain, recognise that of the other and thus overcome the effects of frozen grief and fear.

It is this work that is referred to as on the one hand as '*sanación psicosocial*' and on the other '*trabajar la memoria social*', psychosocial healing and the production of social memory. This work, according to the psychosocial practitioners, liberates shored libidinal bindings, releases fear and shapes communal agency, and thus on the one hand challenges the militarised forms of authority prevalent in many communities of rural Guatemala, and on the other hand, facilitates the struggle against impunity enjoyed by the perpetrators of the Guatemalan genocide.

So far, we have outlined the multiple avenues through which psychosocial remedies became dominant in post-conflict Guatemala, and we have provided a description of the ways in which its practitioners conceive of their capacity to generate change. We have underlined the importance of regional intellectual networks and we have provided a more detailed description of one particular project format and the ways in which it was carried out. But it is clear that, as this movement started to gain momentum in the mid 1990s, it did so on a platform that was suddenly being reworked by massive donor funds flowing into Guatemala. What we argue is that remedies developed in Central America were entangled with global donor concerns from the mid 1990s onwards, and it is this development we explore in the following section, through the notion of the post-conflict assemblage.

THE POST-CONFLICT ASSEMBLAGE

Elsewhere we have argued (Ronsbo and Paniagua 2014) that we may understand Guatemala in the years following the internal conflict through the notion of a post-conflict assemblage. We use the notion of assemblage because the phenomenon we try to understand was a short-lived articulation of global donor flows starting to emerge during the

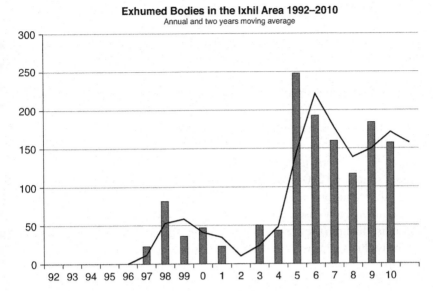

Exhumed Bodies in the Ixhil Area 1992–2010
Annual and two years moving average

Figure 11.1 Exhumed Bodies in the Ixhil Area 1992–2010

mid 1990s and disappearing towards the end of the first decade of the new millennium on the one hand, and on the other hand the Central American notions of remedies, rehabilitation and empowerment as these were brought together in the movement of social psychology. To study the emergence of an assemblage is in many ways difficult; it is a contradiction in terms. The notion of assemblage is theoretical, while its verification is ethnographic. One of the key areas in which we suggest that we are able to trace the emergence of this particular assemblage is in the number of bodies that are exhumed by the Guatemalan Federation of Forensic Anthropologists (FAFG) in the Ixhil Area (Figure 11.1). The phenomenon is closely associated with the emergence of post-conflict politics and sensibilities; it is material and expressive at the same time.

As we explore the quantity of exhumed bodies, they seem to show two separate phases in the Guatemalan post-conflict assemblage. The first phase is when the immediate effects of the Peace Accords make themselves felt, effects are small but noticeable, starting around 1996. This is the period when a variety of different Northern donors start to fund Guatemalan NGOs, of which FAFG is one. Later, following the turn of the millennium, we see a second, much larger rise in

279

exhumation activities, peaking in 2005 and then falling towards the end of the decade. This period corresponds to the phase when different donors align their activities, creating multilateral donor funds that work directly with the state entity PNR (*Programa Nacional de Resarcimientos*, the National Reparation Programme), in order to accelerate the national rehabilitation programme for survivors of the internal conflict, a mandatory programme according to the 1996 Peace Accords. The PNR was the national programme through which exhumation and rehabilitation work was being implemented. It organised a legal recognition of survivors (in particular, relatives of people who were killed), it paid a sum of 26 000 Guatemalan quetzales (4000 USD) per deceased, to be shared among relatives. It organised inhumations and other forms of events in a few cases, but most of the work, which we explore in more detail in the final section, consisted of the legal recognition of the death of individuals who were killed by the armed actors during the internal conflict.

A less tangible, but equally indicative way of exploring the emergence of the post-conflict assemblage is by exploring overseas development aid (ODA) to Guatemala (Figure 11.2). As we do so, a very similar picture seems to emerge. While ODA is complex to work with, due to the large amount of fiscal support to budgetary items (debt reduction, etc.), which is included in the general overviews of ODA, it is possible to single out post-conflict assistance by focusing on the key donors in post-conflict development aid and the type of aid (humanitarian aid and technical assistance) that reflects the types of programmes that have a specific post-conflict component.[10] As we do this, based on the World Bank data,[11] two pictures emerge.

One is the quite significant rise in foreign aid, a rise we may refer to as 'the post-conflict bubble', taking off around the time when the Peace Accords come into effect (1996), and fading out towards the end of the first decade of the millennium, mirroring the more specific development of exhumations.[12] The kinds of programmes supported by these funds span from justice and legal sector reform (changing from an inquisitorial to accusatorial legal process), police reform and support for a large network of civil society organisations engaged in expanding the rights and entitlement of the country's large Mayan population, with special focus on victims of the genocide.

Apart from the post-conflict bubble, we are able to discern a pattern in relation to humanitarian aid which is slightly different. In the first instance, we see that this type of aid *did* play a role at the end of the

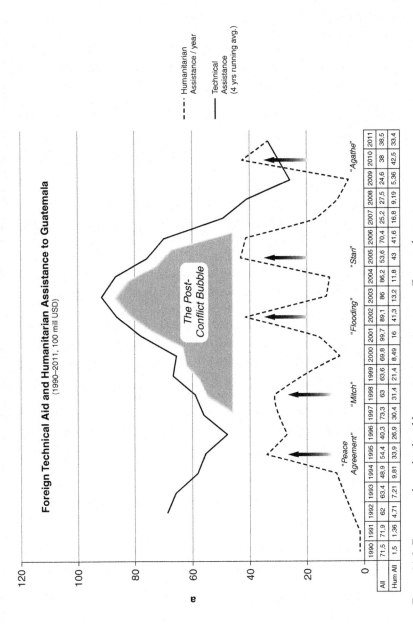

Figure 11.2 Foreign technical aid and humanitarian assistance to Guatemala

conflict – in particular, in assisting the return of refugees from Mexico during the middle of the 1990s. However, we also see that subsequent fluctuations in humanitarian aid reflect not the impact of war, but the multiple natural disasters which, with great regularity, hit the entire Isthmus, including of course, Guatemala.[13] The existence of a discernible post-conflict bubble and its contemporaneous reflection in the surge of exhumed bodies (Figure 11.1) is what leads us to argue that a specific post-conflict assemblage (Delanda 2006) existed, its constituent parts being both material and expressive. On the one hand, material, in the sense of exhumed skeletal remains, textiles, ID cards and DNA samples, and on the other hand, expressive, because through institutions such as NGOs and community-based organisations, international donors enabled the encoding and expression of what has become known as the 'Guatemalan genocide'.

Furthermore, from this perspective, we are able to appreciate that the Guatemalan post-conflict assemblage was – at least in temporal terms – an ephemeral conjoining of actants and territorialisations, expressive planes and material interbeddings which articulated different regionally developed therapeutic traditions with a specific set of donor priorities that emerged in the years following the end of the Cold War. The enthusiasm which surrounded the Guatemalan post-conflict interventions is understandable in the light of the relative success that neighbouring El Salvador had represented by the mid 1990s. From 1992 to 1996, El Salvador moved from a war-torn country occupied by two opposing armed groups, to a country with reformed state institutions, notably those of democratic representation, security and law enforcement institutions, and with a president elected democratically in a competition between the two opponents of the civil war. Donor commitment to the Guatemalan transition project can only be understood in this isthmian context.

However, work in Guatemala took place in a very different human geography, one shaped by small and often remote indigenous communities, unlike the case of El Salvador where a bi-party national structure hegemonised post-conflict memories, sentiments and politics. The post-conflict bubble in Guatemala, unlike that of El Salvador, was not shaped by a bi-party structure, but by a large professional NGO-state-donor network which took it upon itself to create the memory of internal-conflict in post-conflict Guatemala.[14]

This work culminated as the PNR implemented the reparation policy in the period from 2006 to 2010. While the programme had been included as an obligation of the Guatemalan state in the Peace Accords between the state and URNG (National Revolutionary Union of Guatemala) from 1996, it had acquired a political and institutional structure that steeped it in a perpetual struggle between the government and the NGO sector. However, by 2005 the government changed the governance structure, by taking over direct control of the entity, and it started implementation of economic reparation to survivors.

In the final section of the chapter we will explore how these divergent pressures and possibilities exerted by actants shaped the post-conflict assemblage, and how they were experienced and negotiated by indigenous community members in the Ixhil Highlands. Beyond doubt, most NGO employees felt that the state-run PNR was the opponent, and that indigenous communities were their natural allies in the work for a democratic and pluri-ethnic Guatemala. But, as we focus on the expressive registers, in particular linguistic ones, used by members of an indigenous community[15] working to be recognised by the PNR, we may begin to acquire a more nuanced understanding of the ways in which remedies, rule and recognition are entangled in the post-conflict assemblage.

While numerous communities had accommodated the militarised Guatemalan state early in the internal conflict, the particular community we focus on in the final section had been in hiding during most of the war, and it is therefore known as 'a community in resistance'. At the time of our fieldwork, members of the community had participated in various exhumations as well as psychosocial processes in the communities from which their families originated, and they were now (2008) organising a community-based reply to the work of getting PNR recognition of their individual victim status. Yet, despite this history of opposition to the Guatemalan state, the community, as we will see in the final section of the chapter, assumed a much more complex and often contradictory position vis-à-vis the PNR as an external patron, often leaving in doubt the nature of its relationship with the Guatemalan state.

'DO US THE FAVOUR TO RECOGNISE A LITTLE BIT THE WAY WE SUFFER'

In his work on narratives from survivors who had been through army re-education camps in the mid-1980s Guatemala, Wilson (1991) describes how memories of Guatemalan army officers were merged on the one hand with imagery of coffee plantation owners from the early 20th century known as '*patrones*', and on the other with mountain spirits originating in Mayan cosmology and religious practices. Similar syncretic imagery has also been described in Central Peruvian Highland (Ronsbo 2006). Here notions of patronage shaped by a century of work in mining and agro-industrial complexes merged with imagery of political authority generated by the post-conflict Fujimori state, shaping novel yet historically informed images and notions of authority at the margins of the post-conflict state (Das and Poole 2004; Ronsbo 2008).

As we explore the opening of a narrative told by Maria, a female member of the indigenous community of Santa Rosa, we can note similar elements. Maria understands her engagement with the PNR through moral ideas of patronage shaped by centuries of servitude and migrant labour in the Guatemalan Highlands, and PNR and the remedies it provide are engaged through many of the same expressive registers with which community members would engage a powerful agricultural patron. This observation has major implications for the ways in which we think about the Guatemalan post-conflict assemblage and the role played by remedial forms of intervention as these come to form the key arena of mediation between the Guatemalan state and indigenous communities.

What Maria, and the numerous other applicants we have interviewed in the Ixhil area, underlines is that to get recognition as a victim under the PNR programme requires the expenditure of substantial amounts of time and money. Days of travelling across the Highlands to one's parents' place of birth, acquiring documentation, crossing back to the municipality where family members were killed, waiting in lines at the Office of the Public Registry in both places, bribing clerks, paying for notarial work, paying for photocopies, all this referred to as '*trabajar la papelería*' (to work the papers). When our interlocutors employ the notion of 'working the papers', they do so because they – the 'beneficiaries' – have spent weeks of work and easily more than 100 quetzales per application.[16] We have argued previously (Ronsbo and Paniagua 2014) that applicants express their emotions and feelings about this process as if it was work, and evaluate the clerks and case managers they meet, in terms that are derived from notions of a patron, whose services and help on the one hand is needed, but on the other hand is recognised as both abusive and amoral.

Often – and this is hardly surprising – such reflections on the PNR emerge in individual conversations and interviews undertaken with applicants. But, more surprisingly, it also appears in the supplications. It seems that both critique and supplication are moulded by notions of patronage, though disjointed in terms of the linguistic strategies by which patronage as such is interpelated. In Santa Rosa, we collected narratives on the community's request for recognition from the PNR, in order to compile a document that could support the individual and collective applications for reparation.[17] Such collaborative work with the community entangled us in the multiple processes of recognition of victims, but it also gave rise to a specific insight into the application process, which would otherwise have remained hidden. The document we compiled for the PNR was in this sense a collaborative work, in which community authorities selected our interlocutors, who provided their life stories, while we transcribed and compiled the interviews which they subsequently submitted to the PNR. It was during this process that Maria was appointed to contribute her life story and it was for this reasons that we interviewed her.

Maria is a child of the conflict. In 1982, the army arrived in the community and in her narrative she recounts how soldiers went from house to house asking the community members to assemble at the church. In much detail, Maria recounts her father's dialogue with a soldier and the subsequent negotiations her parents engaged in before finally deciding to follow the soldier's order to assemble at the church rather than fleeing. At the church adult males were separated from the rest of the population, then executed and hastily buried. Following this, the rest of the community including Maria, her siblings and her mother fled to the dense forest that covers the mountains stretching towards the Mexican frontier. Here they lived as a community in resistance and by 1989 the community returned and settled in an isolated part of the Municipality of Chajul, where they still live.

Rather than engaging in this long narrative of Maria's, our analysis will centre on a small argumentative and meta-discursive remark (Briggs 1996) that Maria makes at the opening of the long narrative (Figure 11.3). The opening is significant because this is the only time during her narrative in which Maria elaborates on her personal intentions and motivations for engaging in the interview. It is a meta-discursive in the sense that Maria steps out of the narrative, acknowledging that the PNR rather than the interviewer is the intended recipient of her story and that narrating the story is part of a larger imaginary

Y hasta <u>ahorita</u> pues no	*and until <u>now</u>, right,*
nos reconocen así(x) así	*they don't recognize like*
como nosotros los	*that, like that how we*
huérfanos como las viudas	*the orphans, how the*
no lo conocen no lo	*widows they don't know*
reconocen pues (0.5) y	*they don't acknowledge,*
*por eso <u>ahorita</u> **ojala si***	*right, and that's why <u>now</u>*
*el gobierno que **ojala** nos*	***hopefully if** the*
hace (0.5) el favor de	*government **hopefully** do*
reconocer un <u>poco</u> así	*us the favour*
como sufrimos nosotros	*to recognize <u>a little bit</u>*
huérfanos	*the way we suffer, us*
	orphans

Figure 11.3 A small argumentative and meta-discursive remark made by Maria

transaction with the PNR. Furthermore, it is noticeable because of the variety of linguistic strategies Maria employs, as she negotiates the relation with the imaginary recipient of the narrative.

First, it is noticeable how Maria seeks to tone down her life story which is to follow, by using different forms of diminutive. The usage of diminutive is a strategy widely used in the maintenance of social relations imbued with power. The use of the diminutive postfix '-ito' (masculinum) or '-ita' (femininum) serves to tone down the overall strength of any claim, assertion or pledge. Most often its use is associated with adjectives, i.e. *'poquito'* (a little bit) or nouns, i.e. *'mamacita'* (little mother).

In Maria's case, however, the diminutive is used together with the temporal adverb (*ahora*) *'ahorita'* (literally little-now). Maria uses this term twice in her opening remark, and the effect is to down-tone the salience of the pledge for recognition that she is about to make. A similar effect is generated by the direct down-toning of the pledge for recognition that Maria voices as she states that the PNR may 'recognise the way we suffer, a little bit'.

PNR is a state entity, a potential patron that could provide both support and protection. By interpelating the agency through down-toning, Maria gestures towards the legitimate authority of the PNR and her dependence on their sovereign decision. But simultaneously, the use of down-toning gestures towards Maria's own position as an indigenous woman, engaged in the presentation of claims against a state that killed her father. Maria seems to acknowledge that her claim emanates from a position of less than full citizenship.

In short, as we identify the strategy of toning-down in Maria's opening remark, it is drawn to our attention that she orients herself in a field of force characterised by historically situated power differentials, which informs the ways in which she interpelates the post-conflict state. The language she adopts is derived from the moral order of the coffee-republic, and the state recognition of her suffering is couched in a language of her own status as insignificant and less than that of a citizen. But Maria's quest for recognition is not only shaped by the larger field of force in which rule and recognition acquire meaning and are shaped. Towards the end of her introductory remark, Maria makes a subtle, but important change in her linguistic strategy: suddenly she addresses the PNR in the subjunctive mode. 'Hopefully, if the government hopefully will do us the favour... [to recognise us]'.

By using the qualifier 'hopefully if', Maria displaces her claim from the indicative mood to the subjunctive mood (Turner 1987: 101–102; Bruner 1986), from the space of indexicality to the polysemic space of possibilities and hopes. In the indicative mood that we identified above, diminution served to modulate and down-tone Maria's gesture for recognition. But as she enters the subjunctive mood, Maria is displaced towards an entirely new temporality; as Maria moves away from the temporality of the indicative and the toned-down indexical representations of authority, and into the subjunctive mood with their dreams and wishes, she suddenly positions herself in a space of a future pluri-ethnic Guatemala in which indigenous women enjoy full rights.

As Maria moves between these linguistic strategies, she is constantly negotiating the nature of her claim vis-à-vis the PNR. On the one hand the nature of her claim is carried out in a world of real power differentials. But as Maria, consciously or not, voices her claim for recognition in an idiom which indexes centuries of patronage and labour control, she also states that claims are never universal, they are always also historical. On the other hand, as Maria places the object of her speech-acts, her imaginary interlocutor, the government, in a double of the adverb 'hopefully' she enters the subjunctive mood thereby transcending indexicality and representation.

In a certain way, it seems that Maria's two linguistic moves carefully map onto the two prevalent interpretive strategies that we outlined in the introduction to this chapter. On the one hand, in the world of the indicative, Maria seems to be subsumed by the 'empire of trauma' or what may alternatively be called dispostif of PNR psy-governance. On the other hand, the subjunctive mood into which Maria enters immediately after, seems to indicate that the PNR opens up a space of liberation, that recognition is the road to 'love in the time of hate', the title of one of the key volumes on psychosocial practice in Latin America.

However, what we would like to stress is the simultaneity of these two positions and the inherently schizoid nature that derives from Maria's simultaneous presence in both. It seems that recognition projects such as the PNR, and the different kinds of interventions they are based upon (i.e. exhumations, psychosocial interventions and legal aid), can only acquire actuality if 'beneficiaries' accept to enter a schizoid space in which they, on the one hand must navigate organisations, agencies and institutions (state and non-state) which they perceive and talk about as '*patrones*', while they simultaneously must embrace hope and enter a subjunctive mood in which recognition and inclusion in a pluri-cultural Guatemalan nation is imaginable. The schizoid position we thus point towards thus seems to correspond to a Batesonian double-bind under which 'beneficiaries' such as Maria are placed in two contradictory positions: 'dream about your recognition!', but simultaneously 'respect the authorities!'.

But is such a schizoid position not a negative one? Is it not just another twist of the psy-mode-of-governance? Not necessarily we would argue. In the schizoid position there lies a negation of the dogmatic image of thought (Deleuze 1994: 148) based on the notion of stable representations of reality manifest at the level of the subject and the cogito. Leaving this behind, the schizoid position is pregnant with the possibility of new modes of thinking and being. This way the schizoid is an implicit yet rarely talked about implication of post-conflict reparation, one that asks of the subject to be both liberated and subsumed at the same time.

REPUBLIC OF REMEDIES?

In this chapter we have been focusing on understanding what we call the republic of remedies, how it emerged in post-conflict Guatemala, and the kinds of effects it has generated. We have shown that psychosocial remedies became dominant in post-conflict Guatemala due to the presence of two very different groups, one being exiled Argentinian psychoanalysts active in Mexico and throughout the isthmus, the other the liberation psychologists linked to different branches of the Catholic Church in Central America. To reduce these genealogies to a global form of psy-governance or an empire of trauma can only take place if we forget about the regional intellectual networks and the ways in which these moulded the psychosocial remedies of post-conflict Guatemala. Simultaneously, we argued that these intellectual movements and their ability to grow and multiply was possible only because of a massive growth in overseas development aid to Guatemala in the years after the Peace Accords. Hence, the ways in which psy-chosocial remedies multiplied, territorialised and acquired a larger insti-tutional reality was always contradictory; it was always an alloy of rule and recognition, perceptible in the expansion of reparation strategies, simultaneously inclusion and exclusion.

We therefore see the republic of remedies neither as the teleolog-ical unfolding of a *dispositif* with global efficacy and reach, nor as an autonomous gesture of *parrhesia*; rather, as we have shown, it is a bricolage of materialities, human remains and donor funds that bring together, in contacts and contracts, different agencies concentrating and disseminating words and gestures in a world shaped by decades of violence. As we explored the words and gestures of 'beneficiaries' in this world, more specifically the words of Maria, we concluded that the post-conflict assemblage created neither subjection to the psy-empire nor liberation from the 'time of hate', but rather seemed to bring into the world a schizoid position where it seems pertinent to ask if our ethno-graphies are capable of accommodating the schizoid voices from the republics of remedies.

NOTES

1 The ways in which these concepts intersect, and the tensions between them, are shown nowhere more clearly than in the title of the report from the 'Historical Clarification Commission' functioning under the United Nations mandate, '*Guatemala, memoria del silencio*' (Guatemala: Memory of Silence). To have memory of silences and to share these is the strategy for the entire post-conflict project. Hence psychosocial truth telling and remembrance is an act of healing.

2 The number of essays from this period is truly amazing (Allodi and Berger 1981; Amnesty International 1981; Bonaparte 1984; Bleger 1986; Colectivo Chileno de Trabajo Psicosocial 1983; Cienfuegos and Mon-elli 1983; FASIC 1980; Herrera 1986; Kordon et al. 1983; Lira 1982; Lira and Weinstein 1986a; 1986b; Lira et al. 1985; Liwsy and Guar-ino 1983; Martínez and Maciel 1985; Martirena and Mandressi 1986; MSSM 1986; Pais and Schulpen 1986; Pichot et al. 1985; Pesutic 1985; 1986; Puebla et al. 1981; Reinoso 1986; Ruderman and Veraldi 1986;

Salamovich and Dominguez 1986; Various authors 1986). All of these are held in the archives of DIGNITY: Danish Institute against Torture, from 1985 to 2012 known as the Rehabilitatin and Research Centre for Torture Victims, Copenhagen.

3 See (Langer 1989) for a longer narrative of this process or radicalisation among Argentinian and Uruguayan psycho-analysts.

4 Alliance for Progress was announced by John F. Kennedy in 1963 as a democratisation and modernisation policy towards Latin America. It was strongly influenced by the recent success of left-wing guerrillas in Cuba and sought to provide a policy that furthered social reform in Latin America (Blasier 1976).

5 Ignacio Martín-Baró was one of the five Jesuits who were murdered together with the maid and the maid's daughter by the Salvadoran army on the campus of UCA on 16 November 1989.

6 Gerardi would later become the key force behind the Catholic Church's truth report, the REMHI project, for which he was killed two days after its publication.

7 The parallels between the two exists in the sense that in both cases, indigenous members of the Christian base communities used a text produced by the Church (the Scriptures in the 1960s and the Truth Report in the 2000s) as a basis for reflections on the nature of their everyday life and the conditions for liberation.

8 Let me underline that this is merely the intervention logic of the project. The extent to which this logic was reproduced by project activities is difficult to assess, even for those involved.

9 Carlos Paredes, personal communication, Ciudad Guatemala, December 2011.

10 Technical assistance includes assistance to NGOs and civil society, as well as support for capacity development in victim support programmes (i.e. development of the exhumation capacity). Humanitarian assistance includes the more well-known elements of support for service delivery etc. directed towards specific groups of victims and often supported by UN Agencies (UNHCR, UNDP, WFP, to mention the most relevant in the case of post-conflict assistance as well as MINUGUA, United Nations Mission to Guatemala) or large transnational donors such as the International Committee of the Red Cross in collaboration with local Red Cross committees.

11 Available at www.wb.org. The figures presented cover the following countries: USA, European Union, Sweden, Norway, Holland, Germany, Denmark, UK and Spain.

12 It is also worth noticing that the early 1990s saw a steady decline in foreign funds primarily from USAID. This reflects the increased pressure that the Clinton Administration put on the Guatemalan government to accept a Peace Agreement, even though the insurgency was defeated in military terms.

13 Our ability to single out these unrelated policy driven events validate the overall quality of the data analysed.

14 Just note the difference in terms. The Salvadoran conflict is referred to as the 'civil war', the Guatemalan as the 'internal conflict'. The difference is subtle but significant, and it provides important clues about the ways in which memories of violence and war are entextalised within particular national political communities and their foundational narratives.

15 Having first turned down our proposal to do research with them, community authorities contacted us one month later and asked us to return with the explicit purpose of collecting life stories that could be edited into a document which presented the community members as victims of the war, and hence qualified for reparation from the PNR. The process was successful and the applicants were all awarded the 25 000 quetzales by the PNR.

16 100 quetzales equals approximately 20 USD or the equivalent of 6–8 days' work as a labourer.

17 In two additional communities the application process was individualised, and our narratives only served to understand the effects of post-conflict interventions either from the PNR or in the form of psychosocial accompaniment for exhumations.

REFERENCES

Allodi, F. and Berger, P. 1981. *The Children of Refugee Families: a Follow-up and Rehabilitation Programme: Proposal*

Amnesty International 1981. *Labor de la Profesion Médica Contra la Torture, Muerte y Desaparision de Presos Políticos*

Anckermann, S., et al. 2005. 'Psycho-social Support to Large Numbers of Traumatized People in Post-conflict Societies: An Approach to Community Development in Guatemala', *Journal of Community and Social Psychology* 15: 136–152

Blasier, C. 1976. *Hovering giant: U.S. Responses to Revolutionary Change in Latin America*

Bleger, L. 1985. Presented at Seminario International *Consecuencias de la Represion en el Cono sur* 18–23 May 1986, Montevideo, Uruguay

Bonaparte, L. 1984. *Militares en la Argentina y su Método de Tortura Interminable* Copenhague

Briggs, C. L. 1996. *Disorderly Discourse: Narrative, Conflict, & Inequality*. 7th edition. New York: Oxford University Press

Bruner, J. S. 1986. *Actual Minds, Possible Worlds*. Cambridge, Mass: Harvard University Press

Cabarrús, C. R. 1983. *Génesis de una Revolución: Análisis del Surgimiento y Desarrollo de la Organización Campesina en El Salvador.1a ed Edition*. México, D. F: Centro de Investigaciones y Estudios Superiores en Antropología Social

Cardoso, F. H. and Faletto, E. 1970. *Dependencia y Desarrollo en América Latina Ensayo de Interpretación Sociológica.2. ed. Edition*. México: Siglo Veintiuno Editores

HENRIK RONSBO

Carmack, R. M. e. 1988. *Harvest of Violence. The Maya Indians and the Guatemalan Crisis.* Oklahoma: University of Oklahoma Press

Celectivo chileno de Trabajo Psicosocial 1983. *Lecturas de Psicologia y Politica.* Santiago, Chile: Colectivo Chileno de Trabajo Psicosocial

Centro de Estudios Integrados de Desarrollo Comunal CEIDEC 2008. *Guatemala: Polos de Desarrollo. El Caso de la Desestructuración de las Comunidades Indígenas Vol.II.* México: Centro de Estudios Integrados de Desarrollo Comunal CEIDEC

Cienfuegos and Monelli 1983. 'The Testimony of Political Repression as a Therapeutic Instrument', *American Journal of Orthopsychiatry* 53(1)

Das, V. 2007. *Life and Words: Violence and the Descent into the Ordinary.* Berkeley: University of California Press

Das, V. and Poole, D. 2004. 'State and Its Margins Comparative Etnographies', in Das, V. and Poole, D. (eds.), *Anthropology in the Margins of the State.* Oxford: James Currey Ltd

Delanda, M. 2006. *A New Philosophy of Society.* London, UK: Continuum

Deleuze, G. 1994. *Difference and Repetition.* London: Athlone Press

Duffield, M. R. 2007. *Development, Security and Unending War Governing the World of Peoples.* Cambridge: Polity

Erazo, J. 2007. *La Dinámica Psicosocial del Autoritarismo en Guatemala.* Guatemala: ECAP; Colección Psicología Social

Falla, R. 1978. *Quiché Rebelde Estudio de un Movimiento de Conversión Religiosa, Rebelde a las Creencias Tradicionales, en San Antonio Ilotenango, Quiché (1948–1970). v. 7 edition.* Guatemala: Editorial Universitaria de Guatemala

Farías Campo, P. J. and Miranda Redondo, R. 1994. *Perspectivas de Salud Mental y Psicosocial.* San Cristobal de las Casas, Chiapas, Federación Mundial de Salud Mental

FASIC 1980. 'A Social-psychological Study of 25 Returning Families' Seminar on mental Health and Latin American Exiles, London, U. K. Published in 'Mental health and Exile'

Fassin, D. and Rechtman, R. 2007. *L'empire du Traumatisme Enquête sur la Condition de Victime.* Paris: Flammarion

Feldman, I. and Ticktin, M. I. 2010. *In the Name of Humanity: The Government of Threat and Care.* Durham N. C.: Duke University Press

Freud, S. 1914–16. 'Mourning and Melancholia', in *The Standard Edition of the Complete Pychological Works of Sigmund Freud*, translated by James Strachey in colaboration with Anna Freud, Vol XVI

Galeano, E. H. 1992. *Las Venas Abiertas de América Latina.63. ed edition.* México: Siglo Veintiuno Editores

Herrera, S. 1986. 'Documentos de Trabajo de la Fundacion PIDEE' Presented at Seminario International *Consecuencias de la Represion en el Cono sur* 18–23 May 1986, Montevideo, Uruguay

Hollander, N. C. 1997. *Love in a Time of Hate: Liberation Psychology in Latin America.* New Brunswick, N.J.: Rutgers University Press

Ibáñez, L. d. l. C. 2006. 'La Psicología Social de Ignacio Martín-Baró o el Imperativo de la Crítica', in N. P. Peña, M. Gaborit, and J. M. Cruz Alas (eds.), *Psicología Social en la Posguerra: Teoría y Aplicaciones Desde El Salvador.* San Salvador, El Salvador: UCA Editores

Kelly, T. 2012. *This Side of Silence: Human Rights, Torture, and the Recognition of Cruelty.* Philadelphia: University of Pennsylvania Press

Kordon et al. 1983. *La Tortura en la Argentina.* Group of Mothers: Plaza de Mayo

Langer, M. 1989. *From Vienna to Managua; Journey of a Psychoanalyst.* London: Free Association Books

Latour, B. 2005. *Reassembling the Social: An Introduction to Actor-Network Theory.* Oxford: Oxford University Press

Lira, E. 1982. *Psicoterápia de un Detenido Politico Apolitico*

  et al. 1985. 'El Miedo: Un Enfoque Psicosocial', Presented at Seminario International *Consecuencias de la Represion en el Cono sur* 18–23 May 1986, Montevideo, Uruguay

Lira, E. and Weinstein 1986a. 'La Tortura: Un Trauma Psicologico Especifico. Conceptualizacion y Aspectos Psicodinamicos' Presented at Seminario International *Consecuencias de la Represion en el Cono sur* 18–23 May 1986, Montevideo, Uruguay

  1986b. 'Psicoterápia de la Tortura', Presented at Seminario International *Consecuencias de la Represion en el Cono sur* 18–23 May 1986, Montevideo, Uruguay

Liwsy and Guarino 1983. 'Efectos Secuelares en el Nino Sometido al Abandono Forzado, en los Niveles Juridico Social y Clinico Psicologico', *IV Simposio Nacional de Pediatria Social,* Buenos Aires

Manz, B. 2004. *Paradise in Ashes: A Guatemalan Journey of Courage, Terror, and Hope.* Berkeley: University of California Press

Martín-Baró, I. 2001. *Acción e Ideología.* San Salvador: UCA Editores

  1990. *Psicología Social de la Guerra.* San Salvador: UCA Editores

  1986. 'Hacia una Psicología de la Liberación', *Boletín de Psicología* 22: 219–231

Martínez and Maciel 1985. *Repercusiones de las Violaciones de DD.HH. en la Comunidad Infantil*

Martinez, I. M. 1990. 'Mental Health: The History of an Internationalist Cooperation with Nicaragua', *Families, Systems & Health* 8: 327–337

Martirena and Mandressi 1986. 'Organization of Psychological Help to Victims', Paper presented at Seminario International *Consecuencias de la Represion en el Cono sur* 18–23 May 1986, Montevideo, Uruguay

MSSM. 1986. 'Programa Psicoasistencial para Personas Afectadas por las Violaciones de los DD. HH en la Argentina', Paper presented at Seminario

International *Consecuencias de la represion en el cono sur* 18–23 May 1986, Montevideo, Uruguay

Pais and Schulpen 1986. 'Los Hijos de las Victimas', Paper presented at Seminario International *Consecuencias de la Represion en el Cono sur* 18–23 May 1986, Montevideo, Uruguay

Pesutic, S. 1986. 'Algunas Consideraciones Sobre la Tortura y la Responsabilidad de los Profesionales de la Salud', Paper presented at Seminario International *Consecuencias de la Represion en el Cono sur* 18–23 May 1986, Montevideo, Uruguay

1985. *Tortura y Psiquiatria; (I)responsibilidades*

Pichot, P., Berner, P., Wolf, R. and Thau, K. (eds.) 1985. *Psychiatry: The State of the Art, Volume 6, Drug Dependency and Alcholism, Forensic Psychiatry, Military Psychiatry.* New York: Plenum Press

Puebla et al. 1981. *La Tortura en Chile de Hoy. Experiencias Medicas*

Pupavac, V. 2004a. 'International Therapeutic Peace and Justice in Bosnia', *Social & Legal Studies* 13:377–401

2004b. 'War on the Couch, The Emotionology of the New International Security Paradigm', *European Journal of Social Theory* 7(2)149–170

2002. 'Pathologizing Populations and Colonizing Minds: International Psychosocial Programmees in Kosovo', *Alternatives* 27, 489–511

Reinoso, D. G. 1986. 'El Nino Bajo el Terror de Estado', Paper presented at Seminario International *Consecuencias de la Represion en el Cono sur* 18–23 May 1986, Montevideo, Uruguay

Ronsbo, H. 2008. 'Hybridity and Change: Gamonales, Montoneros and Young Politicos in South-Central Peru', *Bulletin of Latin American Research* 27:1

2006. 'Displacing Enigma and Shaping Communal Hegemony – Towards the Analysis of Violent Experience as Social Process *Dialectical Anthropology*, 30(1-2): 147–167

Ronsbo, H. and Paniagua, W. 2014. Between Recognition and Care: Victims, NGOs, and the State in the Guatemalan Postconflict Victimhood. pp. 124–143. In *Histories of Victimhood*. S. Jensen and H. Ronsbo (eds.) Philadelphia: University of Pennsylvania Press

Rose, N. 1993. 'Government, Authority and Expertise in Advanced Liberalism', *Economy and Society* 22(3): 283–299

Ruderman and Veraldi 1986. 'Programmeea de Prevencion y Asistencia en Salud Mental a Afectados por la Represion', Paper presented at Seminario International *Consecuencias de la Represion en el Cono sur* 18–23 May 1986, Montevideo, Uruguay

Salamovich and Dominguez 1986. 'Proceso Psicologico de Deexiliado. Una Respuesta Psicoterapeuta', Paper presented at Seminario International *Consecuencias de la Represion en el Cono sur* 18–23 May 1986, Montevideo, Uruguay

Sanford, V. 2009. *La Masacre de Panzós: Etnicidad, Tierra y Violencia en Guatemala.1a. ed Edition*. Guatemala: F&G Editores

2003. *Buried Secrets: Truth and Human Rights in Guatemala*. New York: Palgrave Macmillan

Scarry, E. 1985. *The Body in Pain: The Making and Unmaking of the World*. New York: Oxford University Press

Sepúlveda, L. 2011. *Marie Langer y los Grupos, en la Nicaragua Sandinista*

Turner,V. 1987. *The Anthropology of Performance*. New York City: PAJ Publications

Wilson, R. A. 1995. *Maya Resurgence in Guatemala: Q'eqchi' Experiences*. Norman: Oklahoma University Press

1991. 'Machine Guns and Mountain Spirits. The Cultural Effects of State Repression among the Q'eqchi of Guatemala', *Critique of Anthropology* 11:133–61

Zur, J. N. 1998. *Violent Memories: Mayan War Widows in Guatemala*. Boulder, Colo: Westview Press

INDEX

CAMBRIDGE STUDIES IN LAW AND SOCIETY

Books in the Series

Lost in China? Law, Culture and Society in Post-1997 Hong Kong
Carol A. G. Jones

Security Theology, Surveillance and the Politics of Fear
Nadera Shalhoub-Kevorkian

Opposing the Rule of Law:
How Myanmar's Courts Make Law and Order
Nick Cheesman

The Ironies of Colonial Governance:
Law, Custom and Justice in Colonial India
James Jaffe

The Clinic and the Court:
Law, Medicine and Anthropology
Ian Harper, Tobias Kelly and Akshay Khanna